P9-CRS-160

HIDEYUKI FURUHASHI

Volume 3 is out.

The story's moving along at its own pace with new characters and some real growth from our protagonist.

Feeling good about it!

BETTEN COURT

This series is serialized biweekly now, and it's almost got me at my wit's end.

Wait. No. Forget the "almost."

MY HERO ACADEMIA VIGILANTES

VOLUME 3
SHONEN JUMP Manga Edition

STORY: HIDEYUKI FURUHASHI
ART: BETTEN COURT
ORIGINAL CONCEPT: KOHEI HORIKOSHI

Translation & English Adaptation/Caleb Cook
Touch-Up Art & Lettering/John Hunt
Designer/Julian [JR] Robinson
Editor/Mike Montesa

VIGILANTE -BOKU NO HERO ACADEMIA ILLEGALS-
© 2016 by Hideyuki Furuhashi, Betten Court, Kohei Horikoshi
All rights reserved.
First published in Japan in 2016 by SHUEISHA Inc., Tokyo.
English translation rights arranged by SHUEISHA Inc.

The stories, characters and incidents mentioned in this publication
are entirely fictional.

No portion of this book may be reproduced or transmitted in
any form or by any means without written permission from
the copyright holders.

Printed in the U.S.A.

Published by VIZ Media, LLC
P.O. Box 77010
San Francisco, CA 94107

10 9 8 7 6 5 4 3 2 1
First printing, January 2019

viz.com

shonenjump.com

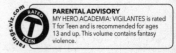

PARENTAL ADVISORY
MY HERO ACADEMIA: VIGILANTES is rated
T for Teen and is recommended for ages
13 and up. This volume contains fantasy
violence.

MY HERO ACADEMIA
VIGILANTES

3

Writer / Letterer
Hideyuki Furuhashi

Penciller / Colorist
Betten Court

Original Concept
Kohei Horikoshi

【professional】

noun | pro · fes · sion · al

: a person engaged in a specified activity as a main
occupation rather than as a pastime

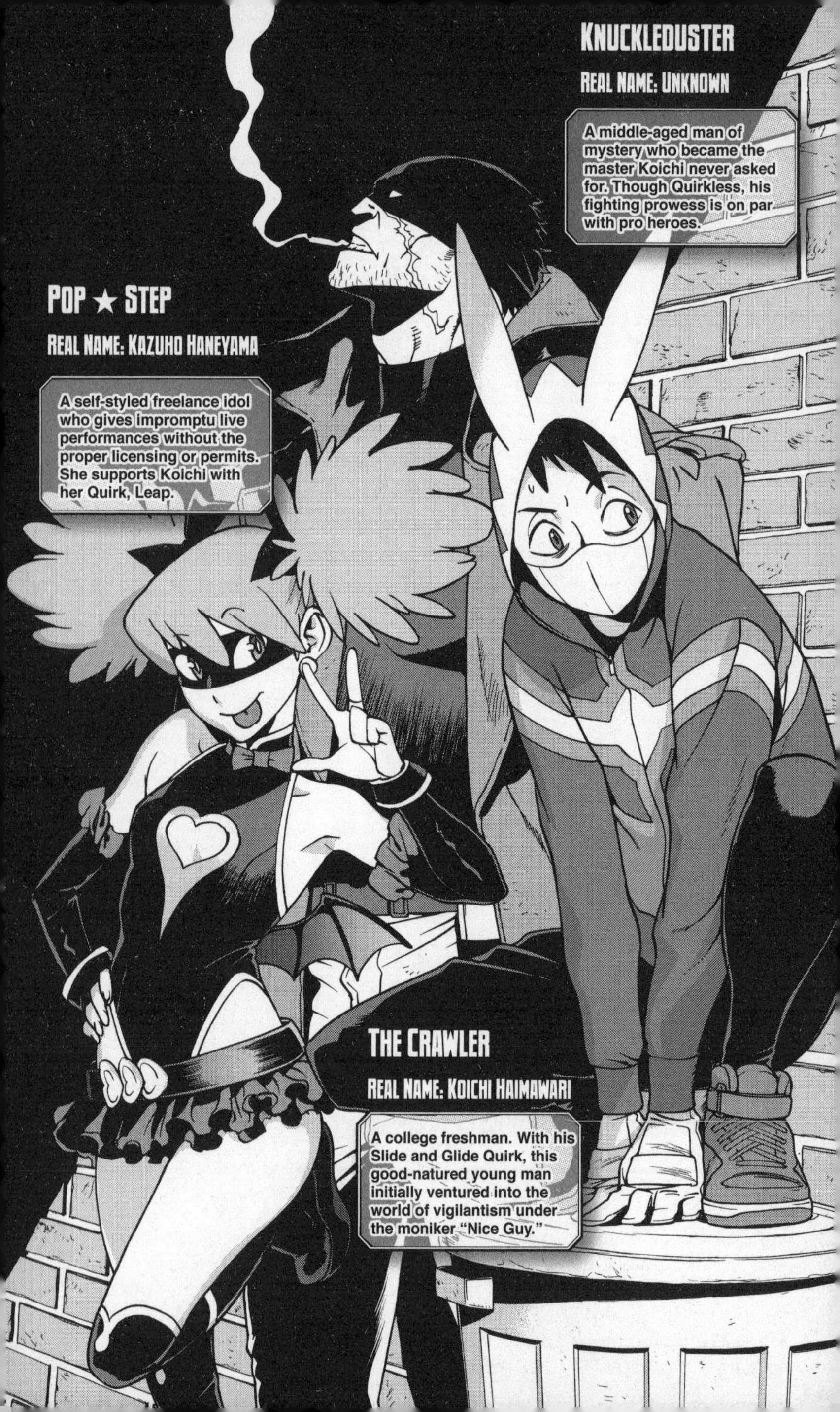

Knuckleduster
Real Name: Unknown
A middle-aged man of mystery who became the master Koichi never asked for. Though Quirkless, his fighting prowess is on par with pro heroes.
Pop ★ Step
Real Name: Kazuho Haneyama
A self-styled freelance idol who gives impromptu live performances without the proper licensing or permits. She supports Koichi with her Quirk, Leap.
The Crawler
Real Name: Koichi Haimawari
A college freshman. With his Slide and Glide Quirk, this good-natured young man initially ventured into the world of vigilantism under the moniker "Nice Guy."

CHARACTERS

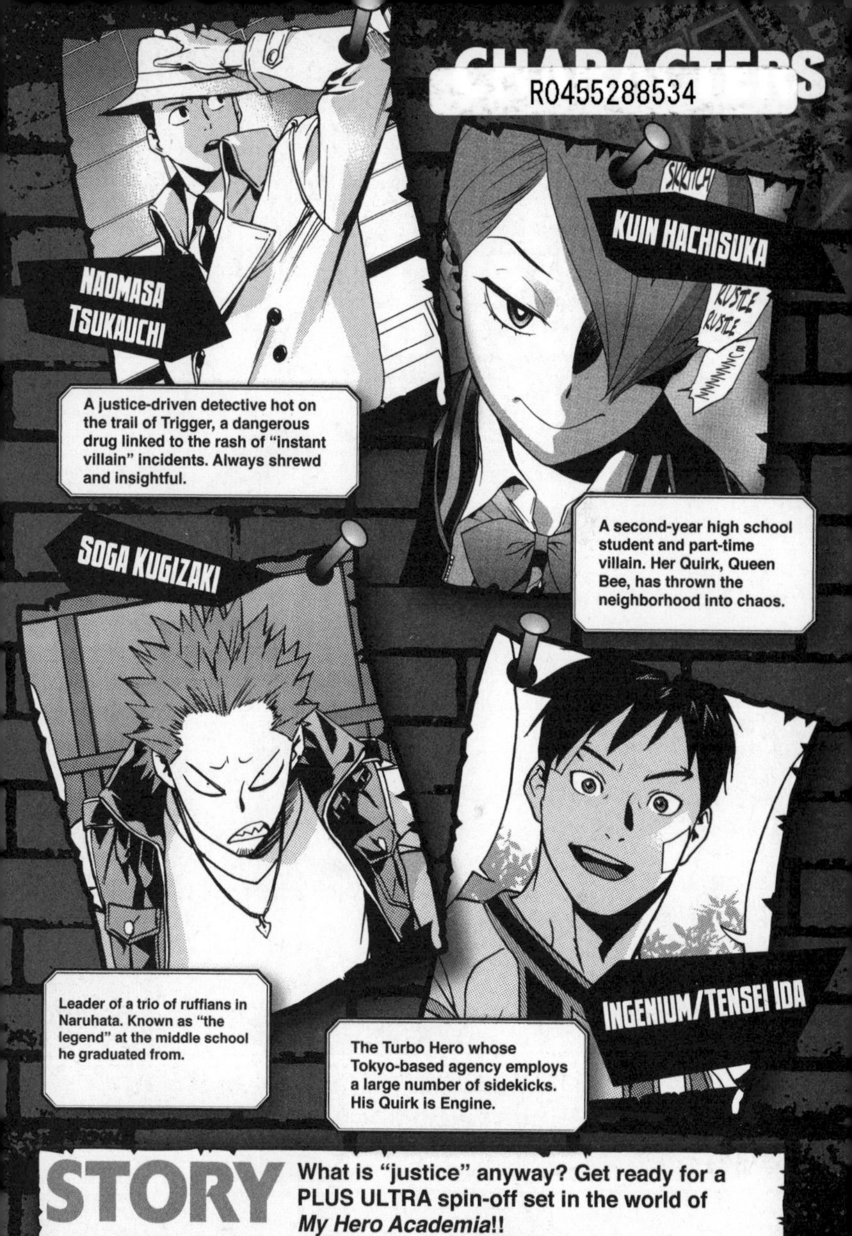
NAOMASA TSUKAUCHI
KUIN HACHISUKA
SKRITCH
RUSTLE RUSTLE
BZZNNNNNN
SOGA KUGIZAKI
INGENIUM/TENSEI IDA

A justice-driven detective hot on the trail of Trigger, a dangerous drug linked to the rash of "instant villain" incidents. Always shrewd and insightful.

A second-year high school student and part-time villain. Her Quirk, Queen Bee, has thrown the neighborhood into chaos.

Leader of a trio of ruffians in Naruhata. Known as "the legend" at the middle school he graduated from.

The Turbo Hero whose Tokyo-based agency employs a large number of sidekicks. His Quirk is Engine.

STORY

What is "justice" anyway? Get ready for a PLUS ULTRA spin-off set in the world of *My Hero Academia*!!

Heroes. The chosen ones who, with explicit government permission, use their natural talents, or Quirks, to aid society. However, not everyone can be chosen, and some take action of their own accord, becoming illegal heroes. What does justice mean to them? And can we really call them heroes? This story takes to the streets in order to follow the exploits of those known as *vigilantes.*

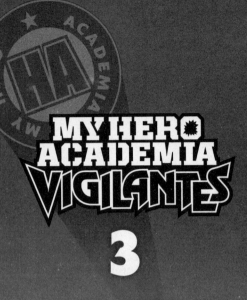

MY HERO ACADEMIA VIGILANTES

3

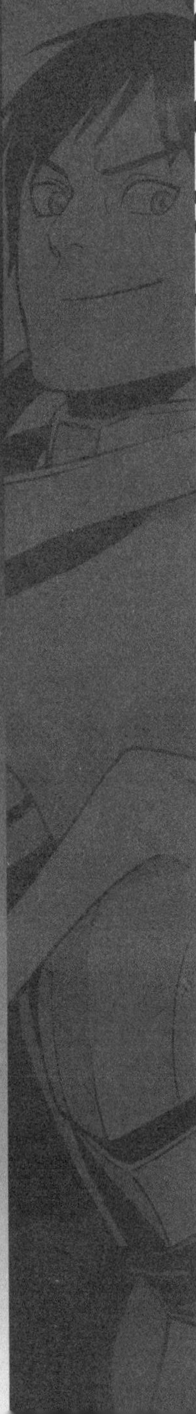

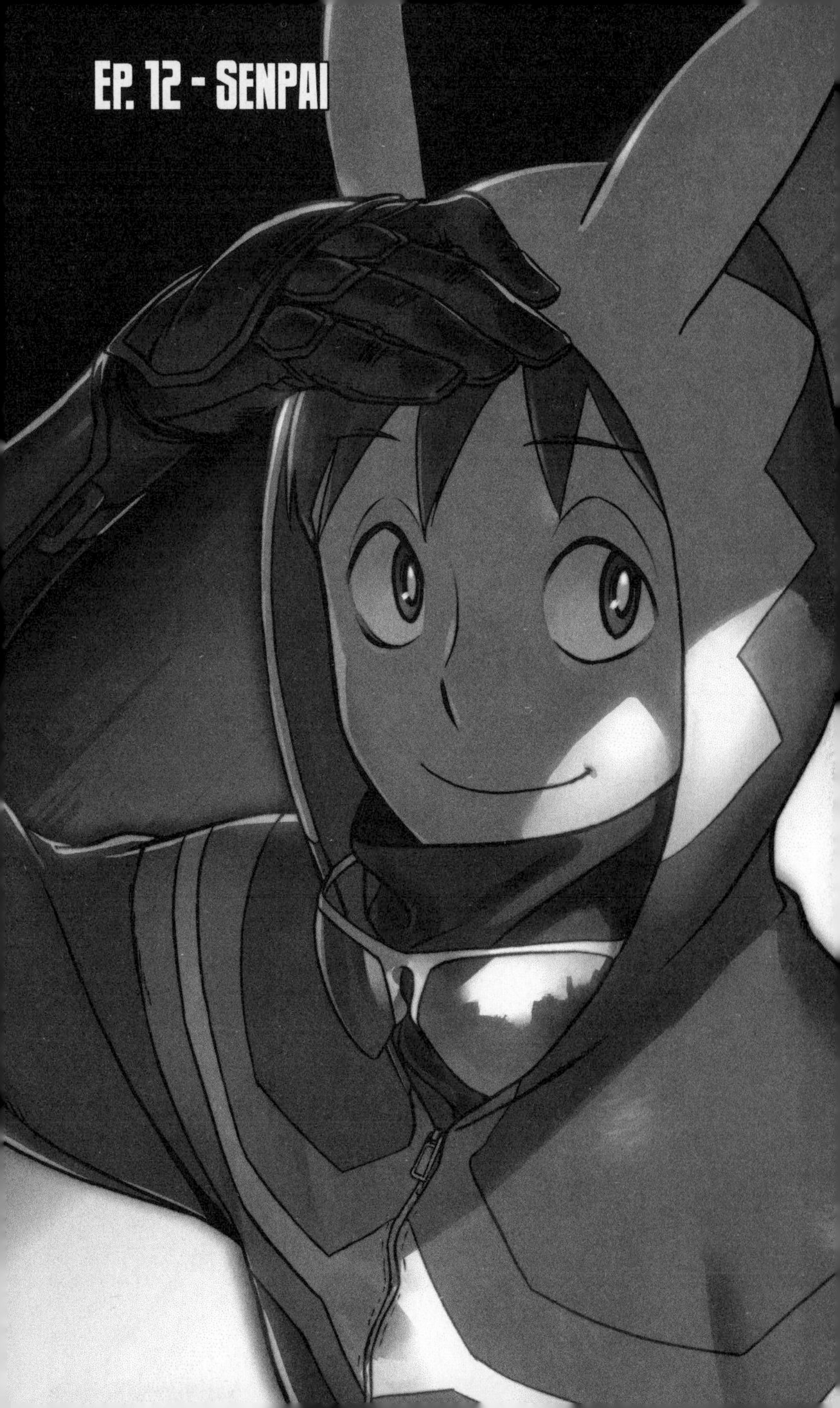
EP. 12 - SENPAI

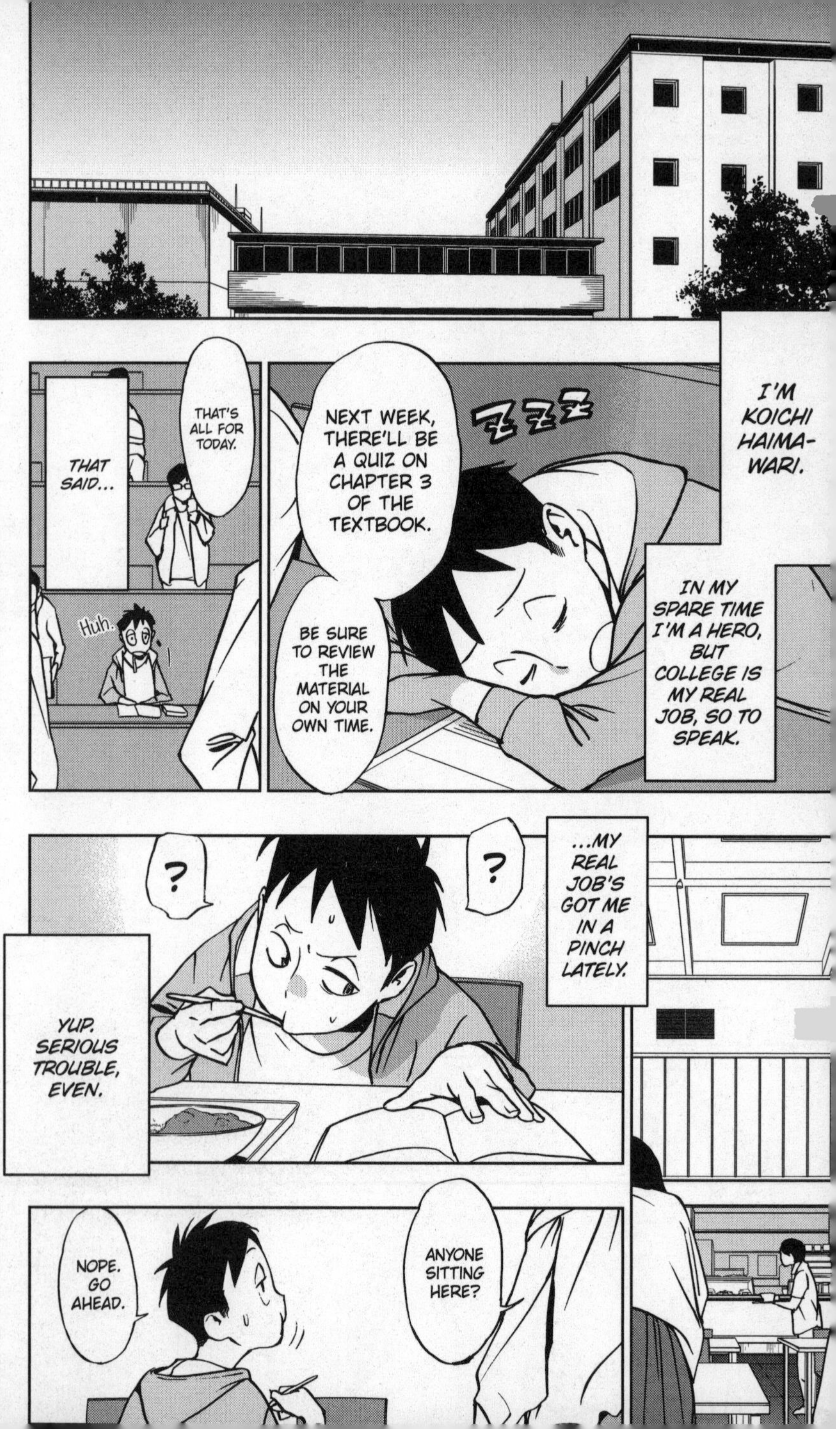
I'M KOICHI HAIMA-WARI.
IN MY SPARE TIME I'M A HERO, BUT COLLEGE IS MY REAL JOB, SO TO SPEAK.
NEXT WEEK, THERE'LL BE A QUIZ ON CHAPTER 3 OF THE TEXTBOOK.
BE SURE TO REVIEW THE MATERIAL ON YOUR OWN TIME.
THAT'S ALL FOR TODAY.
THAT SAID...
Huh.
...MY REAL JOB'S GOT ME IN A PINCH LATELY.
?
?
YUP. SERIOUS TROUBLE, EVEN.
ANYONE SITTING HERE?
NOPE. GO AHEAD.

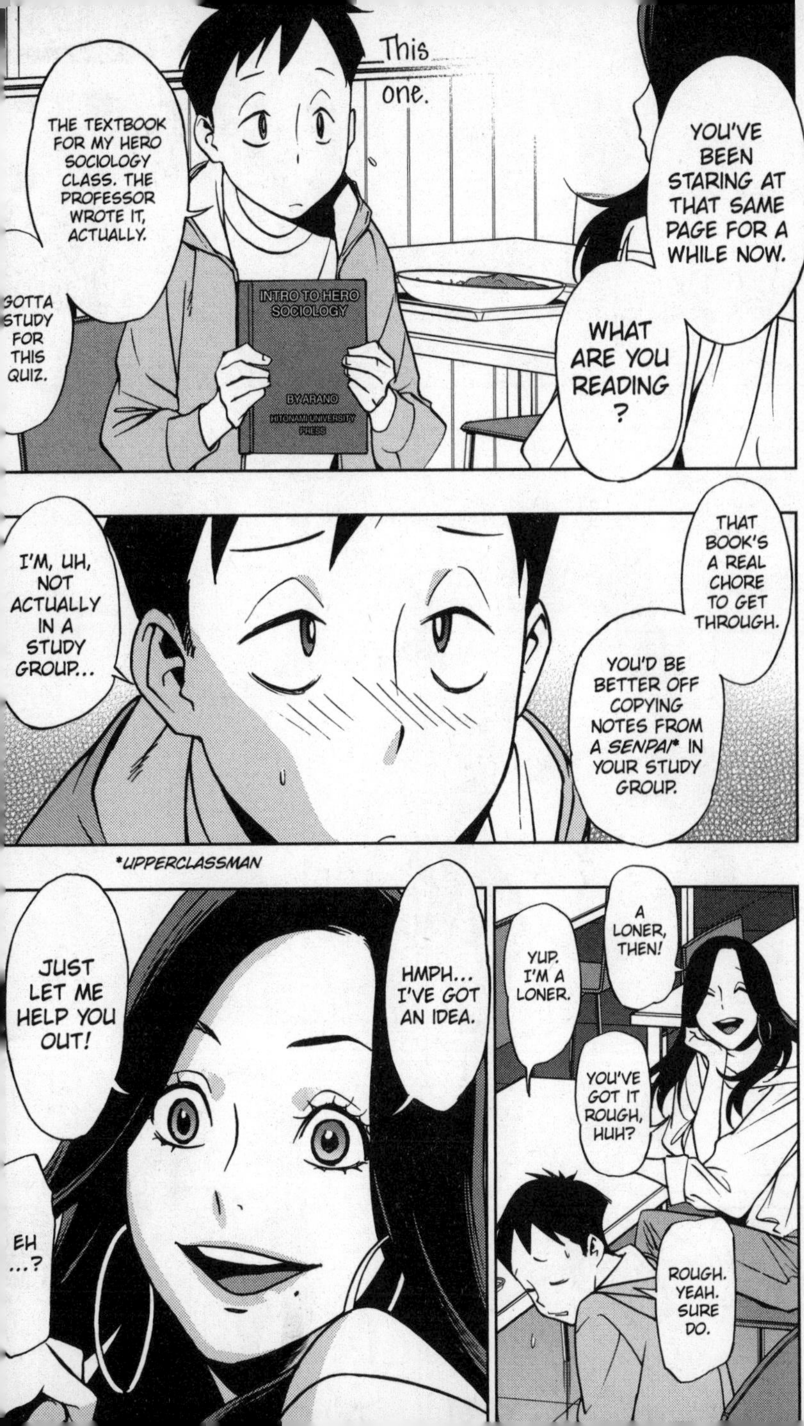
YOU'VE BEEN STARING AT THAT SAME PAGE FOR A WHILE NOW.
WHAT ARE YOU READING?
This one.
INTRO TO HERO SOCIOLOGY
BY ARANO
HITONAMI UNIVERSITY PRESS
THE TEXTBOOK FOR MY HERO SOCIOLOGY CLASS. THE PROFESSOR WROTE IT, ACTUALLY.
GOTTA STUDY FOR THIS QUIZ.
THAT BOOK'S A REAL CHORE TO GET THROUGH.
YOU'D BE BETTER OFF COPYING NOTES FROM A *SENPAI** IN YOUR STUDY GROUP.
I'M, UH, NOT ACTUALLY IN A STUDY GROUP...
*UPPERCLASSMAN
A LONER, THEN!
YUP. I'M A LONER.
YOU'VE GOT IT ROUGH, HUH?
ROUGH. YEAH. SURE DO.
HMPH... I'VE GOT AN IDEA.
JUST LET ME HELP YOU OUT!
EH...?

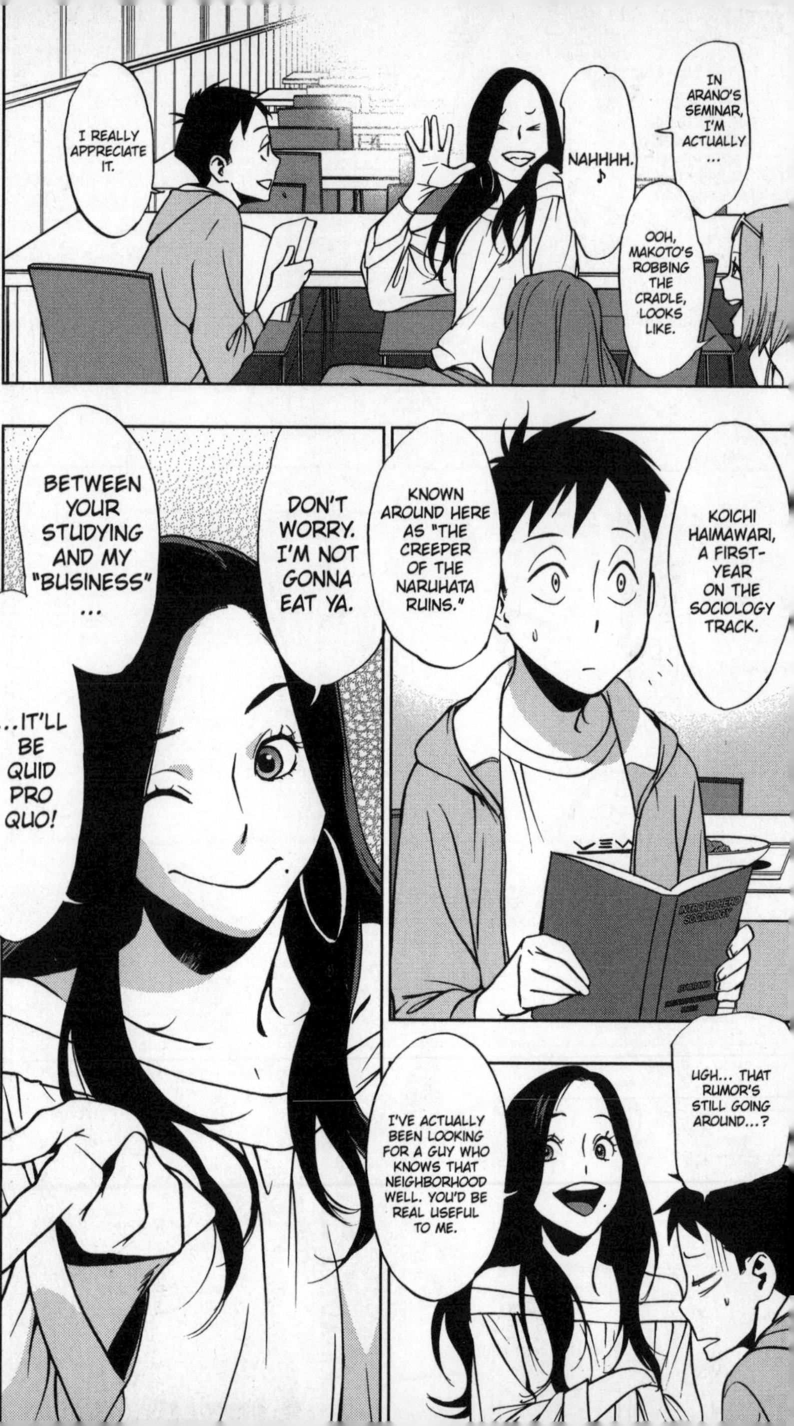
IN ARANO'S SEMINAR, I'M ACTUALLY ...
OOH, MAKOTO'S ROBBING THE CRADLE, LOOKS LIKE.
NAHHHH. ♪
I REALLY APPRECIATE IT.
KOICHI HAIMAWARI, A FIRST-YEAR ON THE SOCIOLOGY TRACK.
KNOWN AROUND HERE AS "THE CREEPER OF THE NARUHATA RUINS."
INTRO TO HERO SOCIOLOGY
UGH... THAT RUMOR'S STILL GOING AROUND...?
I'VE ACTUALLY BEEN LOOKING FOR A GUY WHO KNOWS THAT NEIGHBORHOOD WELL. YOU'D BE REAL USEFUL TO ME.
DON'T WORRY. I'M NOT GONNA EAT YA.
BETWEEN YOUR STUDYING AND MY "BUSINESS" ...
...IT'LL BE QUID PRO QUO!

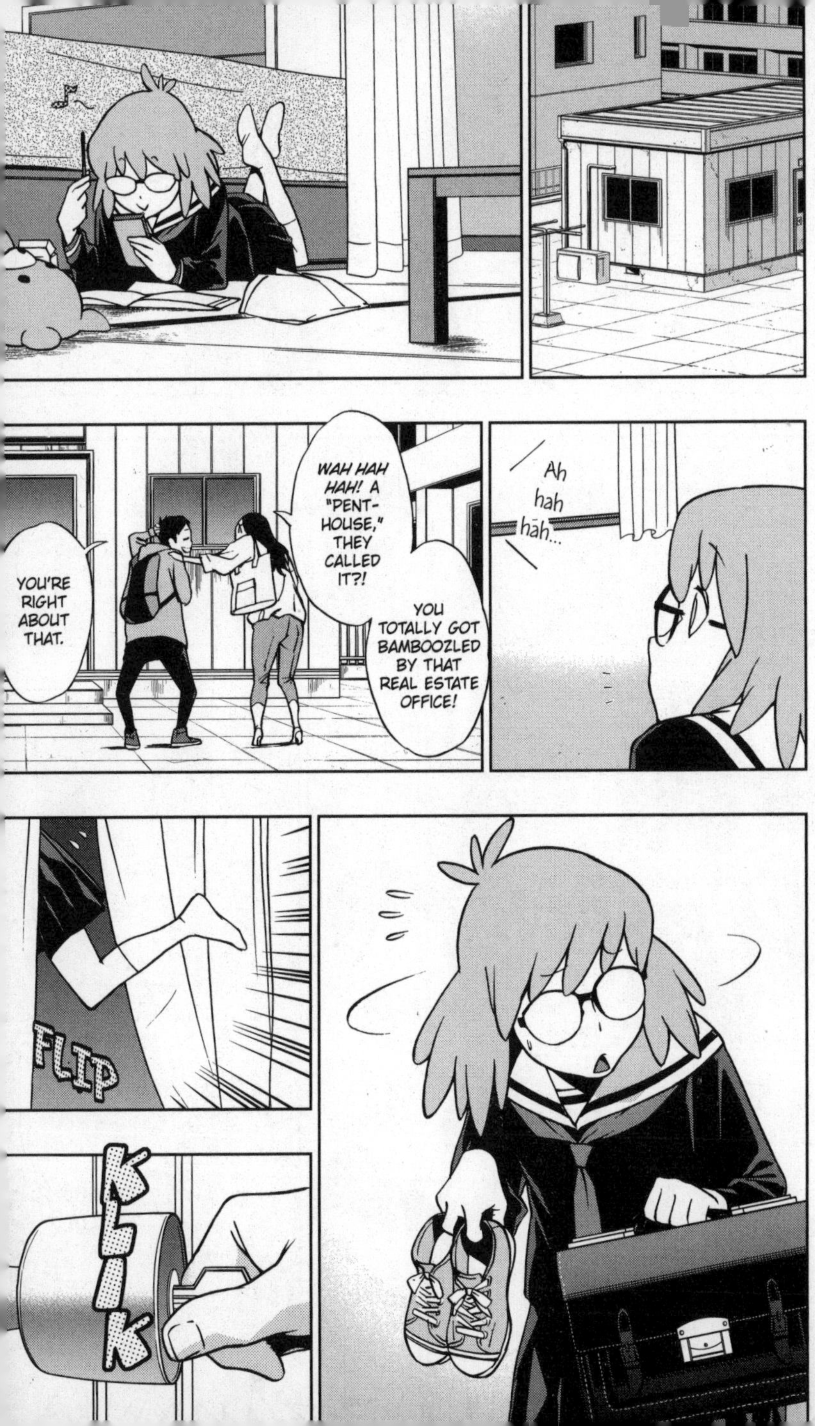
Ah hah hāh...
WAH HAH HAH! A "PENT-HOUSE," THEY CALLED IT?!
YOU TOTALLY GOT BAMBOOZLED BY THAT REAL ESTATE OFFICE!
YOU'RE RIGHT ABOUT THAT.
FLIP
KLIK

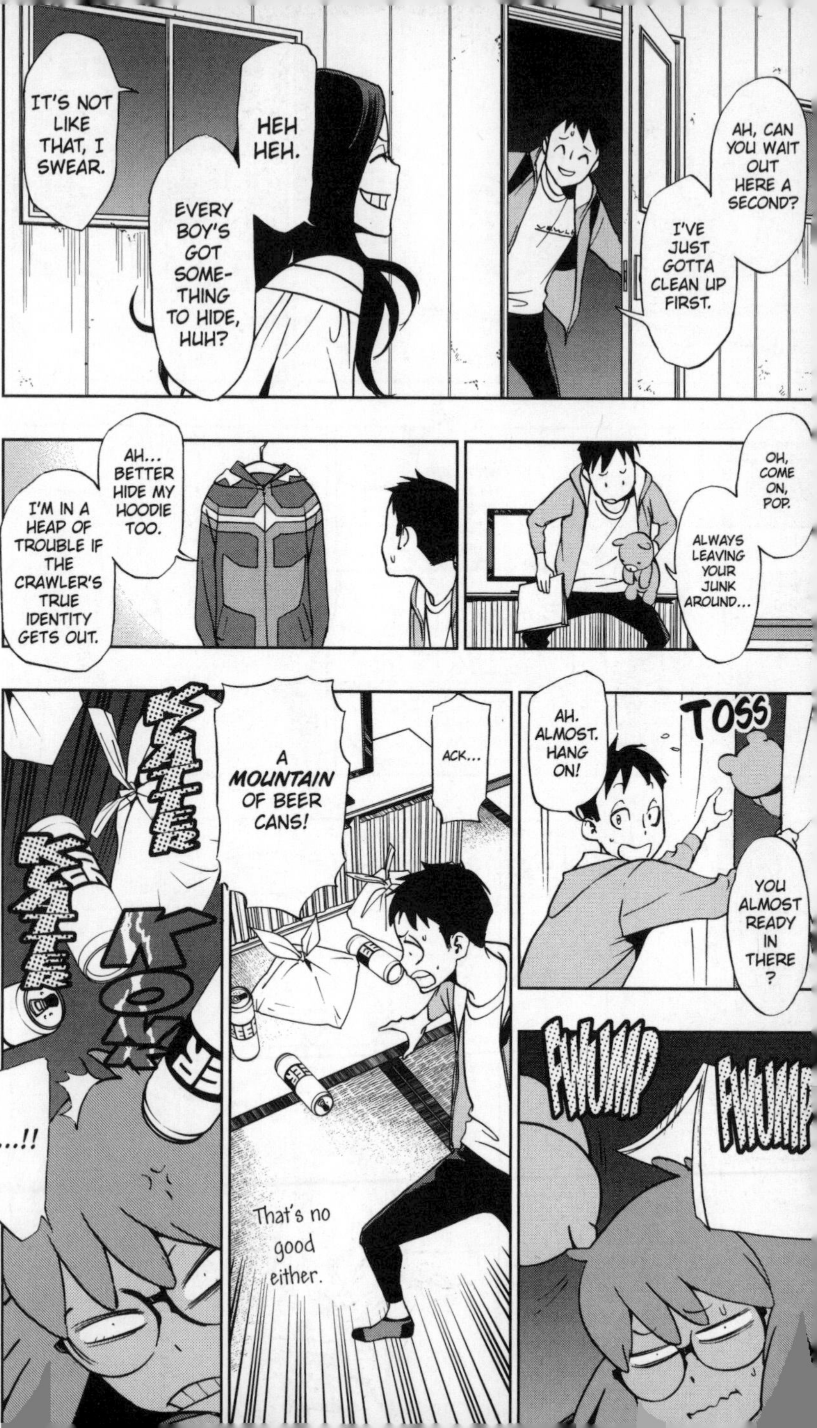
AH, CAN YOU WAIT OUT HERE A SECOND?
I'VE JUST GOTTA CLEAN UP FIRST.
HEH HEH.
EVERY BOY'S GOT SOMETHING TO HIDE, HUH?
IT'S NOT LIKE THAT, I SWEAR.
OH, COME ON, POP.
ALWAYS LEAVING YOUR JUNK AROUND...
AH... BETTER HIDE MY HOODIE TOO.
I'M IN A HEAP OF TROUBLE IF THE CRAWLER'S TRUE IDENTITY GETS OUT.
TOSS
AH. ALMOST. HANG ON!
YOU ALMOST READY IN THERE?
PWUMP
PWUMP
ACK...
A *MOUNTAIN* OF BEER CANS!
That's no good either.
...!!

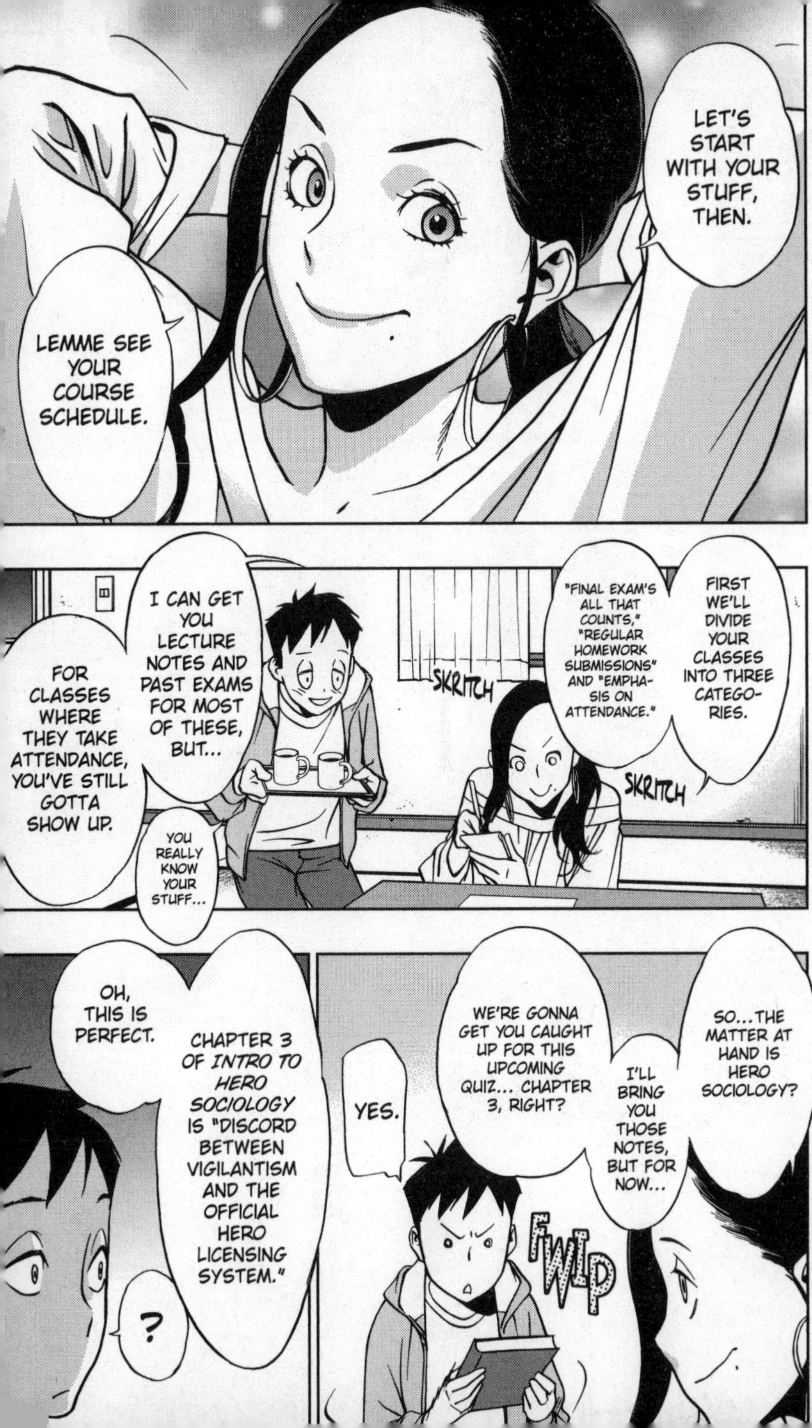
LET'S START WITH YOUR STUFF, THEN.
LEMME SEE YOUR COURSE SCHEDULE.
FIRST WE'LL DIVIDE YOUR CLASSES INTO THREE CATEGO-RIES.
"FINAL EXAM'S ALL THAT COUNTS," "REGULAR HOMEWORK SUBMISSIONS" AND "EMPHA-SIS ON ATTENDANCE."
SKRITCH
SKRITCH
I CAN GET YOU LECTURE NOTES AND PAST EXAMS FOR MOST OF THESE, BUT...
FOR CLASSES WHERE THEY TAKE ATTENDANCE, YOU'VE STILL GOTTA SHOW UP.
YOU REALLY KNOW YOUR STUFF...
SO...THE MATTER AT HAND IS HERO SOCIOLOGY?
I'LL BRING YOU THOSE NOTES, BUT FOR NOW...
WE'RE GONNA GET YOU CAUGHT UP FOR THIS UPCOMING QUIZ... CHAPTER 3, RIGHT?
YES.
FWIP
OH, THIS IS PERFECT.
CHAPTER 3 OF *INTRO TO HERO SOCIOLOGY* IS "DISCORD BETWEEN VIGILANTISM AND THE OFFICIAL HERO LICENSING SYSTEM."
?

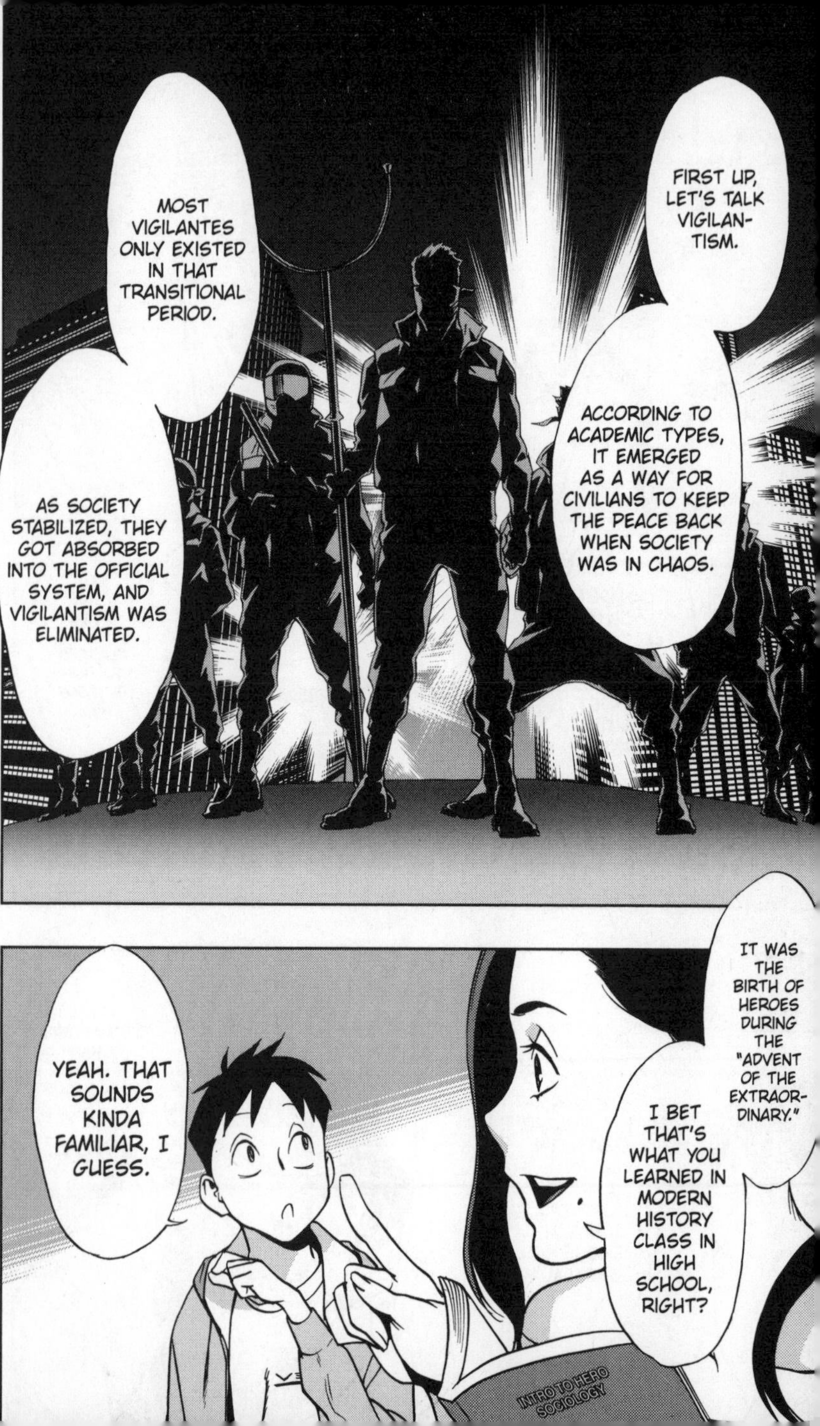
FIRST UP, LET'S TALK VIGILAN-TISM.
ACCORDING TO ACADEMIC TYPES, IT EMERGED AS A WAY FOR CIVILIANS TO KEEP THE PEACE BACK WHEN SOCIETY WAS IN CHAOS.
MOST VIGILANTES ONLY EXISTED IN THAT TRANSITIONAL PERIOD.
AS SOCIETY STABILIZED, THEY GOT ABSORBED INTO THE OFFICIAL SYSTEM, AND VIGILANTISM WAS ELIMINATED.
IT WAS THE BIRTH OF HEROES DURING THE "ADVENT OF THE EXTRAOR-DINARY."
I BET THAT'S WHAT YOU LEARNED IN MODERN HISTORY CLASS IN HIGH SCHOOL, RIGHT?
YEAH. THAT SOUNDS KINDA FAMILIAR, I GUESS.
INTRO TO HERO SOCIOLOGY

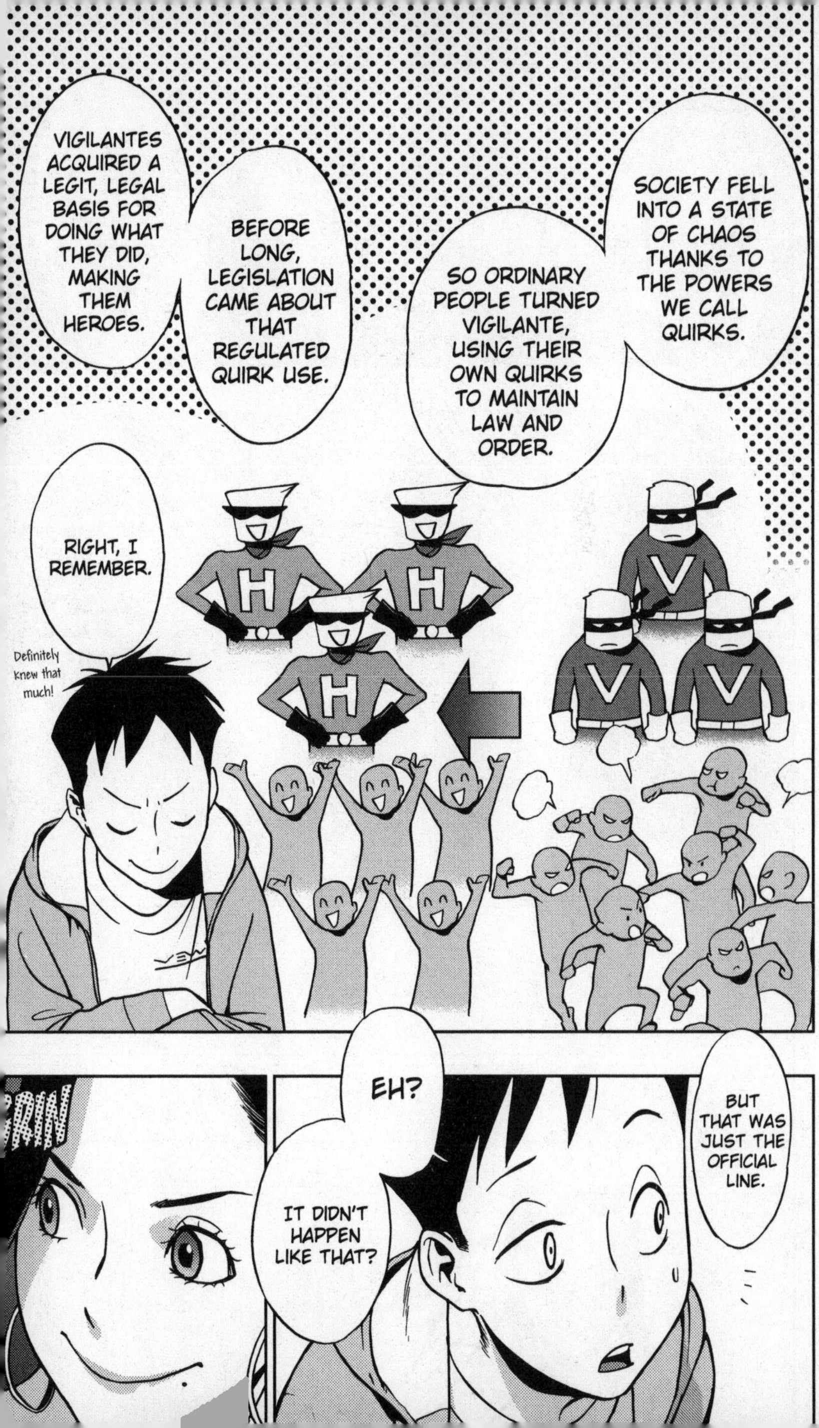
SOCIETY FELL INTO A STATE OF CHAOS THANKS TO THE POWERS WE CALL QUIRKS.
SO ORDINARY PEOPLE TURNED VIGILANTE, USING THEIR OWN QUIRKS TO MAINTAIN LAW AND ORDER.
BEFORE LONG, LEGISLATION CAME ABOUT THAT REGULATED QUIRK USE.
VIGILANTES ACQUIRED A LEGIT, LEGAL BASIS FOR DOING WHAT THEY DID, MAKING THEM HEROES.
RIGHT, I REMEMBER.
Definitely knew that much!
BUT THAT WAS JUST THE OFFICIAL LINE.
EH?
IT DIDN'T HAPPEN LIKE THAT?

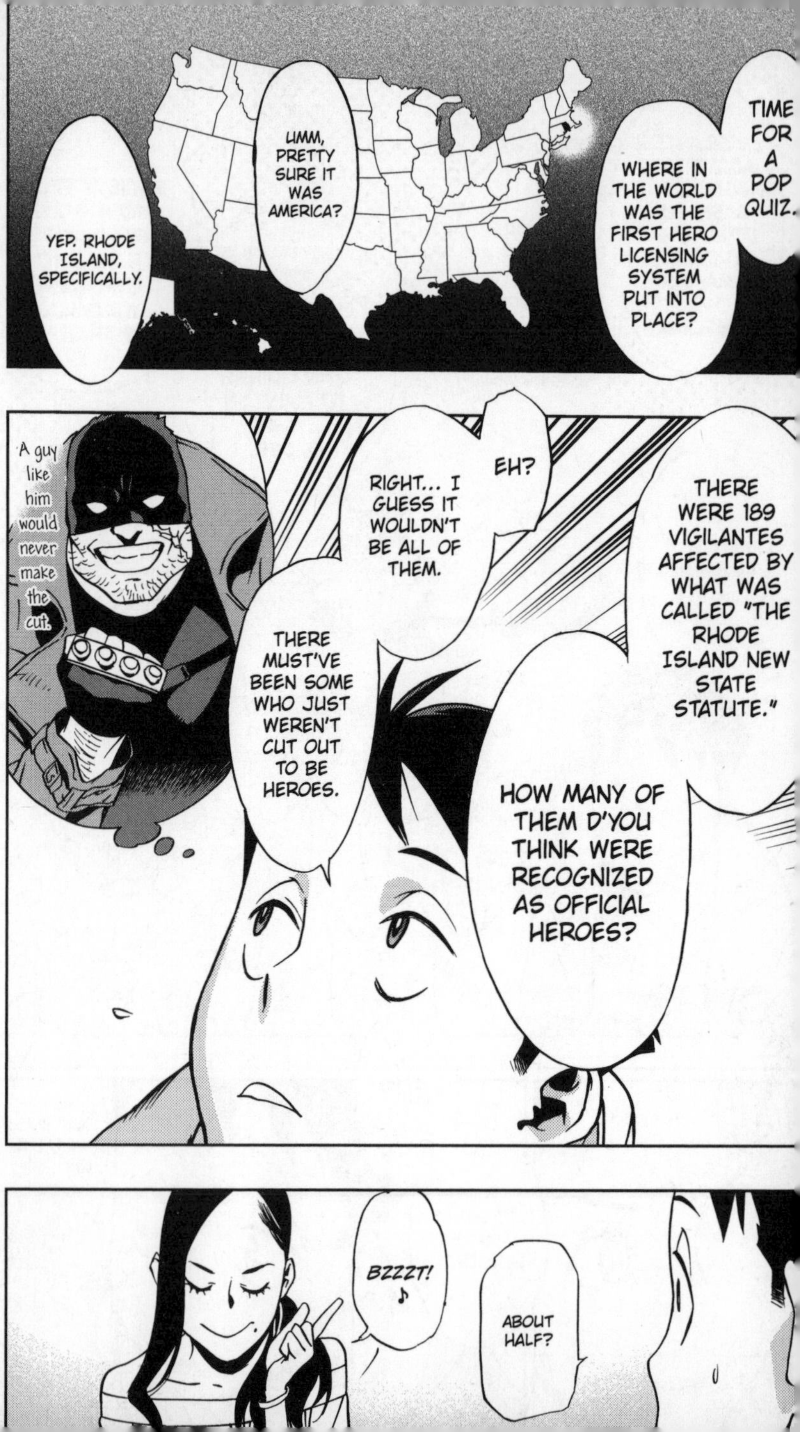
TIME FOR A POP QUIZ.
WHERE IN THE WORLD WAS THE FIRST HERO LICENSING SYSTEM PUT INTO PLACE?
UMM, PRETTY SURE IT WAS AMERICA?
YEP. RHODE ISLAND, SPECIFICALLY.
THERE WERE 189 VIGILANTES AFFECTED BY WHAT WAS CALLED "THE RHODE ISLAND NEW STATE STATUTE."
HOW MANY OF THEM D'YOU THINK WERE RECOGNIZED AS OFFICIAL HEROES?
EH?
RIGHT... I GUESS IT WOULDN'T BE ALL OF THEM.
THERE MUST'VE BEEN SOME WHO JUST WEREN'T CUT OUT TO BE HEROES.
A guy like him would never make the cut.
ABOUT HALF?
BZZZT! ♪

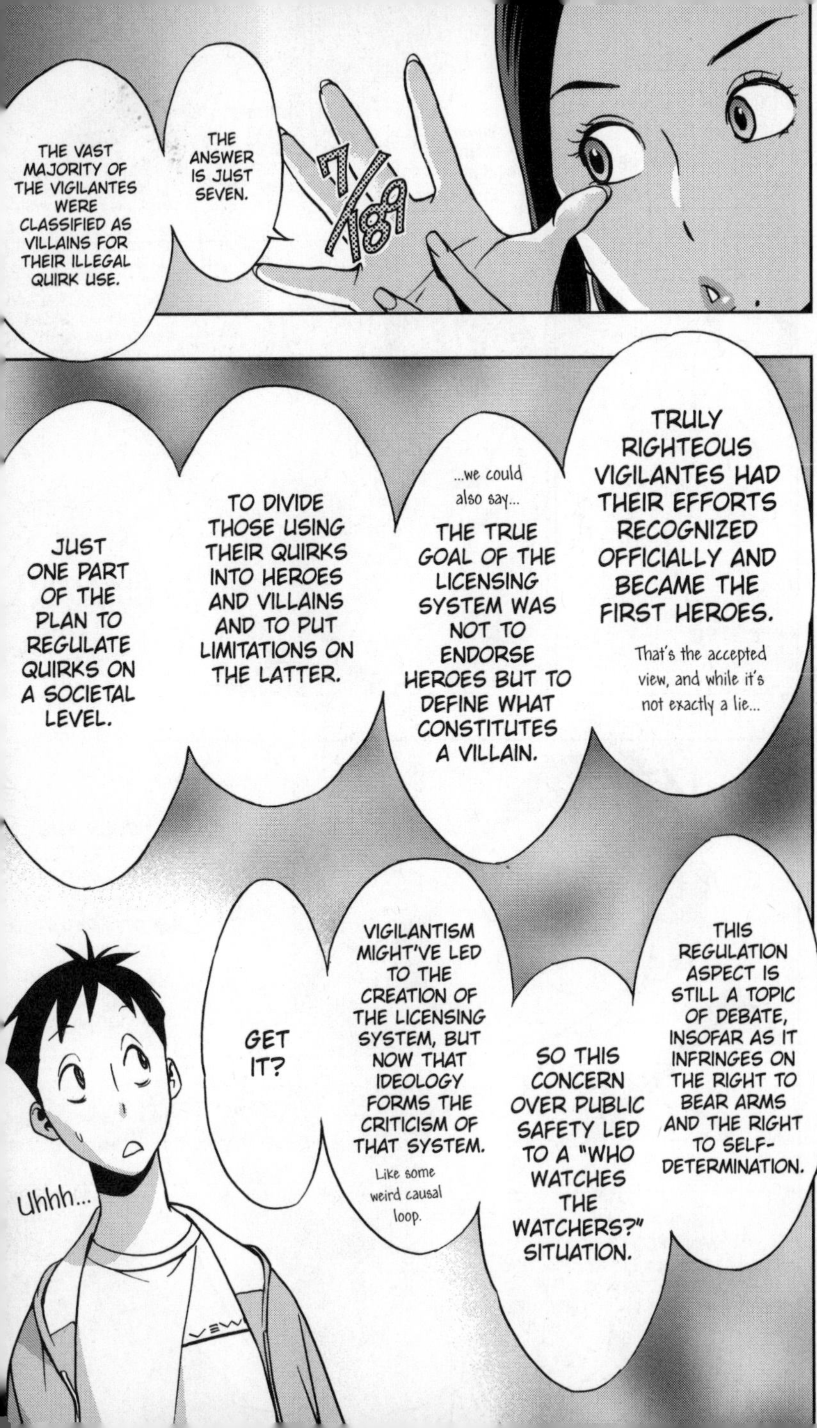
7/189
THE ANSWER IS JUST SEVEN.
THE VAST MAJORITY OF THE VIGILANTES WERE CLASSIFIED AS VILLAINS FOR THEIR ILLEGAL QUIRK USE.
TRULY RIGHTEOUS VIGILANTES HAD THEIR EFFORTS RECOGNIZED OFFICIALLY AND BECAME THE FIRST HEROES.
That's the accepted view, and while it's not exactly a lie...
...we could also say...
THE TRUE GOAL OF THE LICENSING SYSTEM WAS NOT TO ENDORSE HEROES BUT TO DEFINE WHAT CONSTITUTES A VILLAIN.
TO DIVIDE THOSE USING THEIR QUIRKS INTO HEROES AND VILLAINS AND TO PUT LIMITATIONS ON THE LATTER.
JUST ONE PART OF THE PLAN TO REGULATE QUIRKS ON A SOCIETAL LEVEL.
THIS REGULATION ASPECT IS STILL A TOPIC OF DEBATE, INSOFAR AS IT INFRINGES ON THE RIGHT TO BEAR ARMS AND THE RIGHT TO SELF-DETERMINATION.
SO THIS CONCERN OVER PUBLIC SAFETY LED TO A "WHO WATCHES THE WATCHERS?" SITUATION.
VIGILANTISM MIGHT'VE LED TO THE CREATION OF THE LICENSING SYSTEM, BUT NOW THAT IDEOLOGY FORMS THE CRITICISM OF THAT SYSTEM.
Like some weird causal loop.
GET IT?
Uhhh...

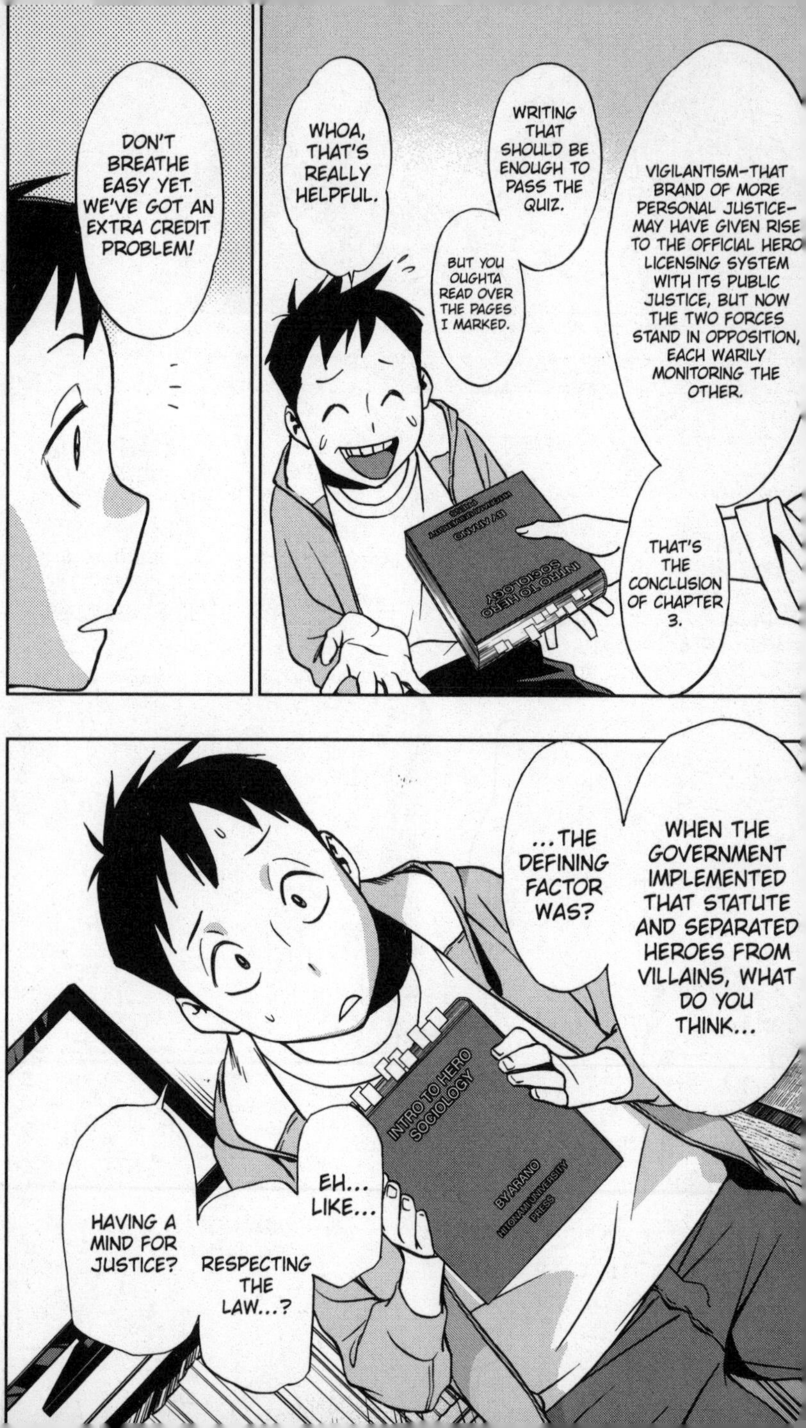
VIGILANTISM—THAT BRAND OF MORE PERSONAL JUSTICE—MAY HAVE GIVEN RISE TO THE OFFICIAL HERO LICENSING SYSTEM WITH ITS PUBLIC JUSTICE, BUT NOW THE TWO FORCES STAND IN OPPOSITION, EACH WARILY MONITORING THE OTHER.
THAT'S THE CONCLUSION OF CHAPTER 3.
WRITING THAT SHOULD BE ENOUGH TO PASS THE QUIZ.
BUT YOU OUGHTA READ OVER THE PAGES I MARKED.
WHOA, THAT'S REALLY HELPFUL.
DON'T BREATHE EASY YET. WE'VE GOT AN EXTRA CREDIT PROBLEM!
WHEN THE GOVERNMENT IMPLEMENTED THAT STATUTE AND SEPARATED HEROES FROM VILLAINS, WHAT DO YOU THINK...
...THE DEFINING FACTOR WAS?
INTRO TO HERO SOCIOLOGY
BY ARANO
EH... LIKE...
RESPECTING THE LAW...?
HAVING A MIND FOR JUSTICE?

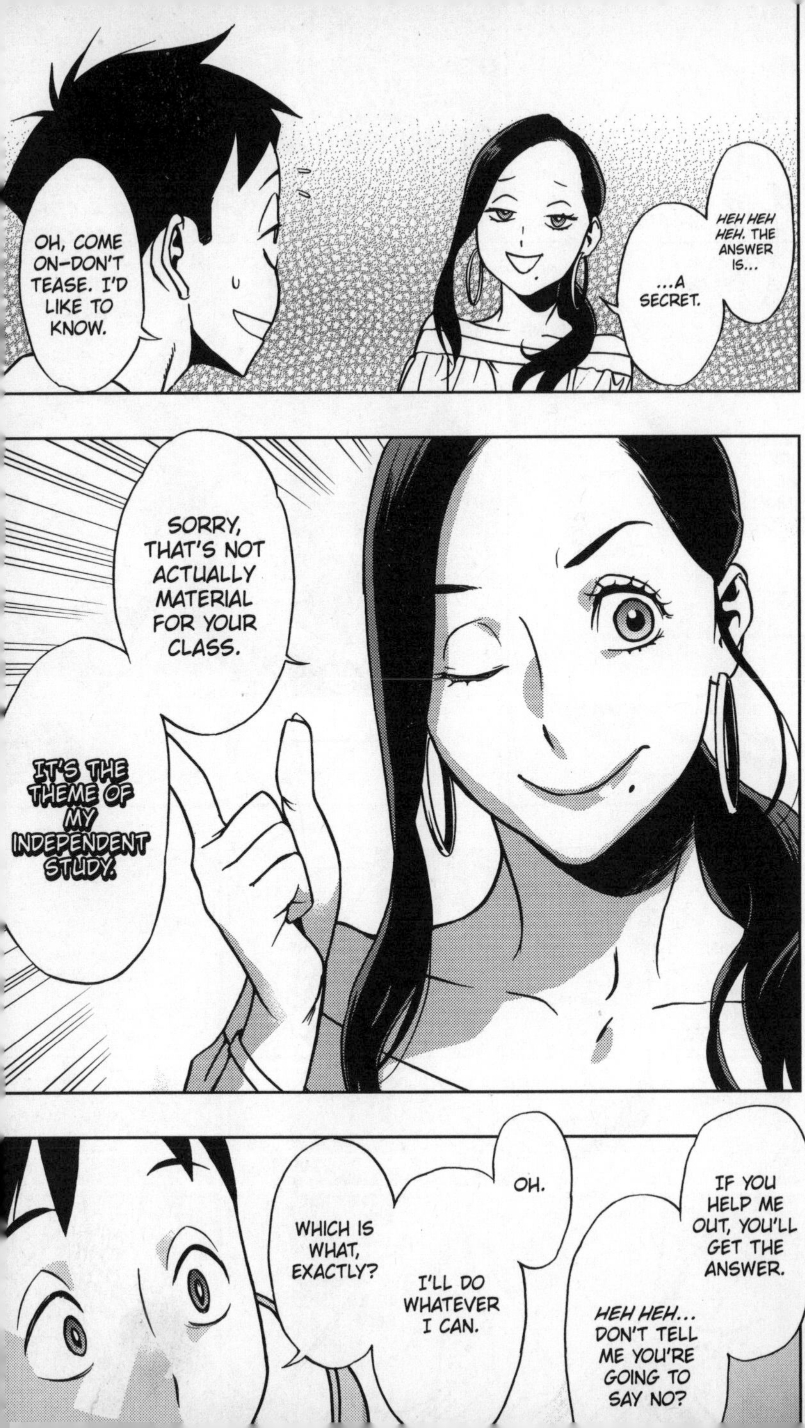
HEH HEH HEH. THE ANSWER IS...
...A SECRET.
OH, COME ON—DON'T TEASE. I'D LIKE TO KNOW.
SORRY, THAT'S NOT ACTUALLY MATERIAL FOR YOUR CLASS.
IT'S THE THEME OF MY INDEPENDENT STUDY.
IF YOU HELP ME OUT, YOU'LL GET THE ANSWER.
HEH HEH... DON'T TELL ME YOU'RE GOING TO SAY NO?
OH.
I'LL DO WHATEVER I CAN.
WHICH IS WHAT, EXACTLY?

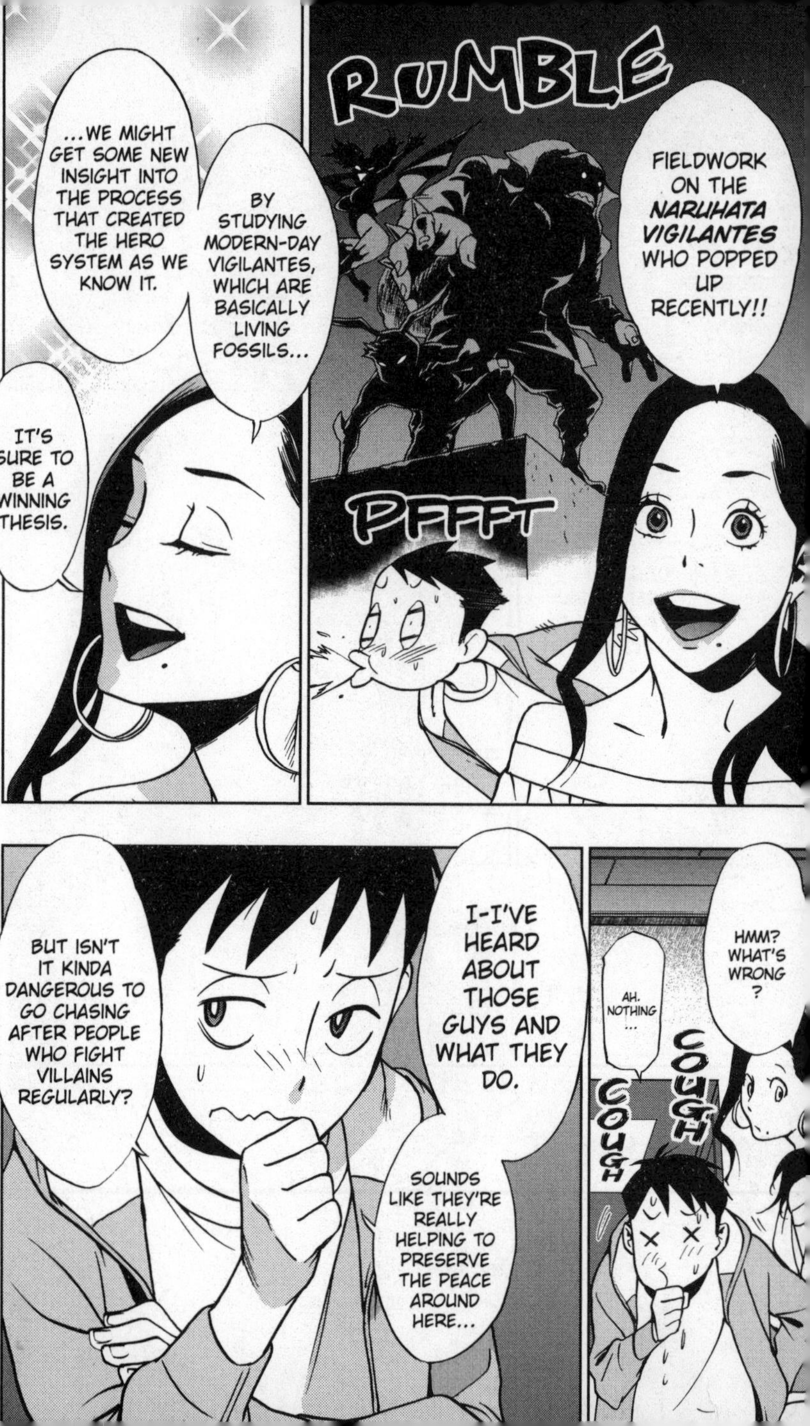
RUMBLE
FIELDWORK ON THE *NARUHATA VIGILANTES* WHO POPPED UP RECENTLY!!
PFFFT
BY STUDYING MODERN-DAY VIGILANTES, WHICH ARE BASICALLY LIVING FOSSILS...
...WE MIGHT GET SOME NEW INSIGHT INTO THE PROCESS THAT CREATED THE HERO SYSTEM AS WE KNOW IT.
IT'S SURE TO BE A WINNING THESIS.
HMM? WHAT'S WRONG?
AH. NOTHING...
COUGH
COUGH
I-I'VE HEARD ABOUT THOSE GUYS AND WHAT THEY DO.
SOUNDS LIKE THEY'RE REALLY HELPING TO PRESERVE THE PEACE AROUND HERE...
BUT ISN'T IT KINDA DANGEROUS TO GO CHASING AFTER PEOPLE WHO FIGHT VILLAINS REGULARLY?

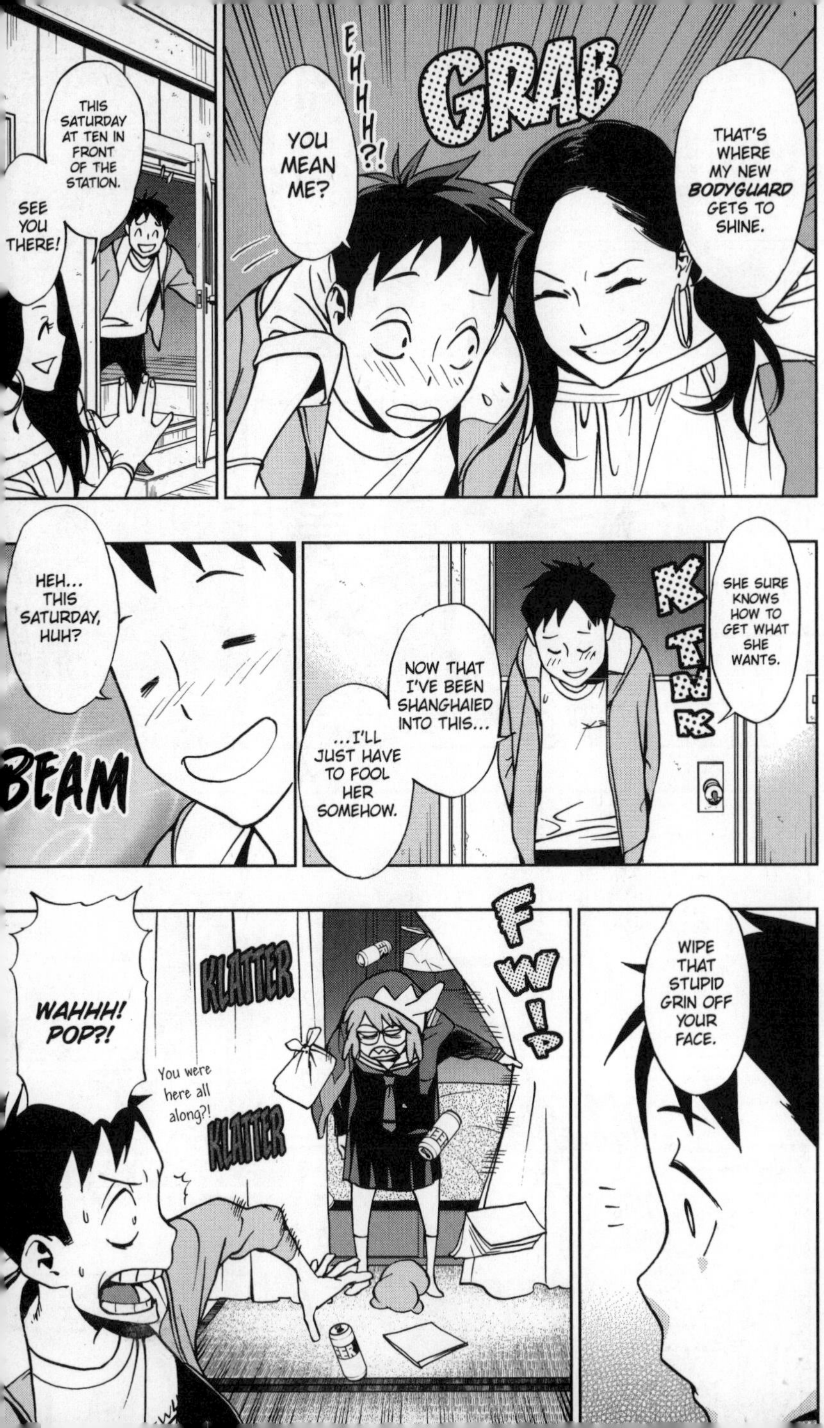
GRAB
THAT'S WHERE MY NEW BODYGUARD GETS TO SHINE.
EHHHH?!
YOU MEAN ME?
THIS SATURDAY AT TEN IN FRONT OF THE STATION.
SEE YOU THERE!
SHE SURE KNOWS HOW TO GET WHAT SHE WANTS.
NOW THAT I'VE BEEN SHANGHAIED INTO THIS...
...I'LL JUST HAVE TO FOOL HER SOMEHOW.
HEH... THIS SATURDAY, HUH?
BEAM
WIPE THAT STUPID GRIN OFF YOUR FACE.
FWIP
KLATTER
KLATTER
WAHHH! POP?!
You were here all along?!

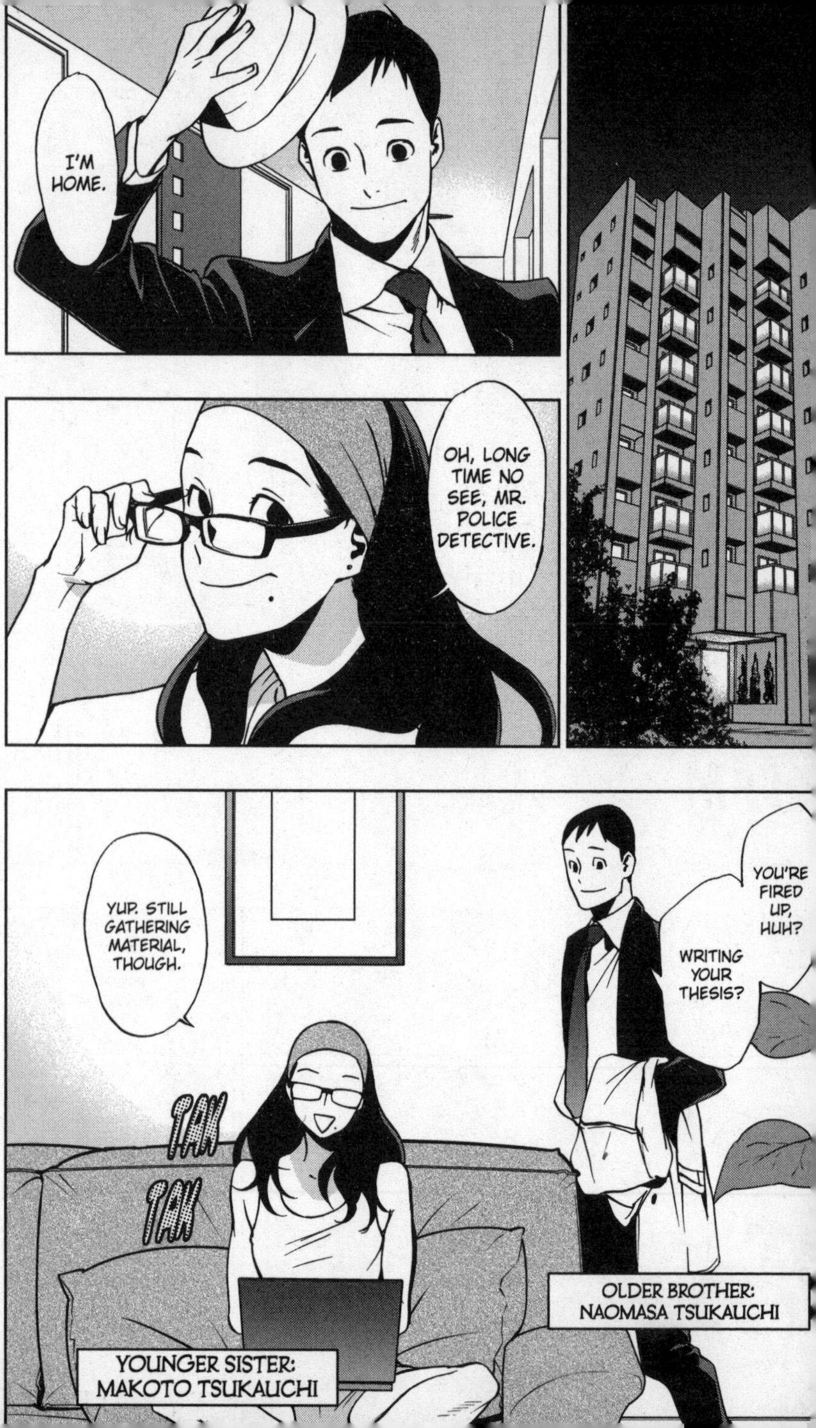
I'M HOME.
OH, LONG TIME NO SEE, MR. POLICE DETECTIVE.
YOU'RE FIRED UP, HUH?
WRITING YOUR THESIS?
YUP. STILL GATHERING MATERIAL, THOUGH.
TAK TAK
OLDER BROTHER: NAOMASA TSUKAUCHI
YOUNGER SISTER: MAKOTO TSUKAUCHI

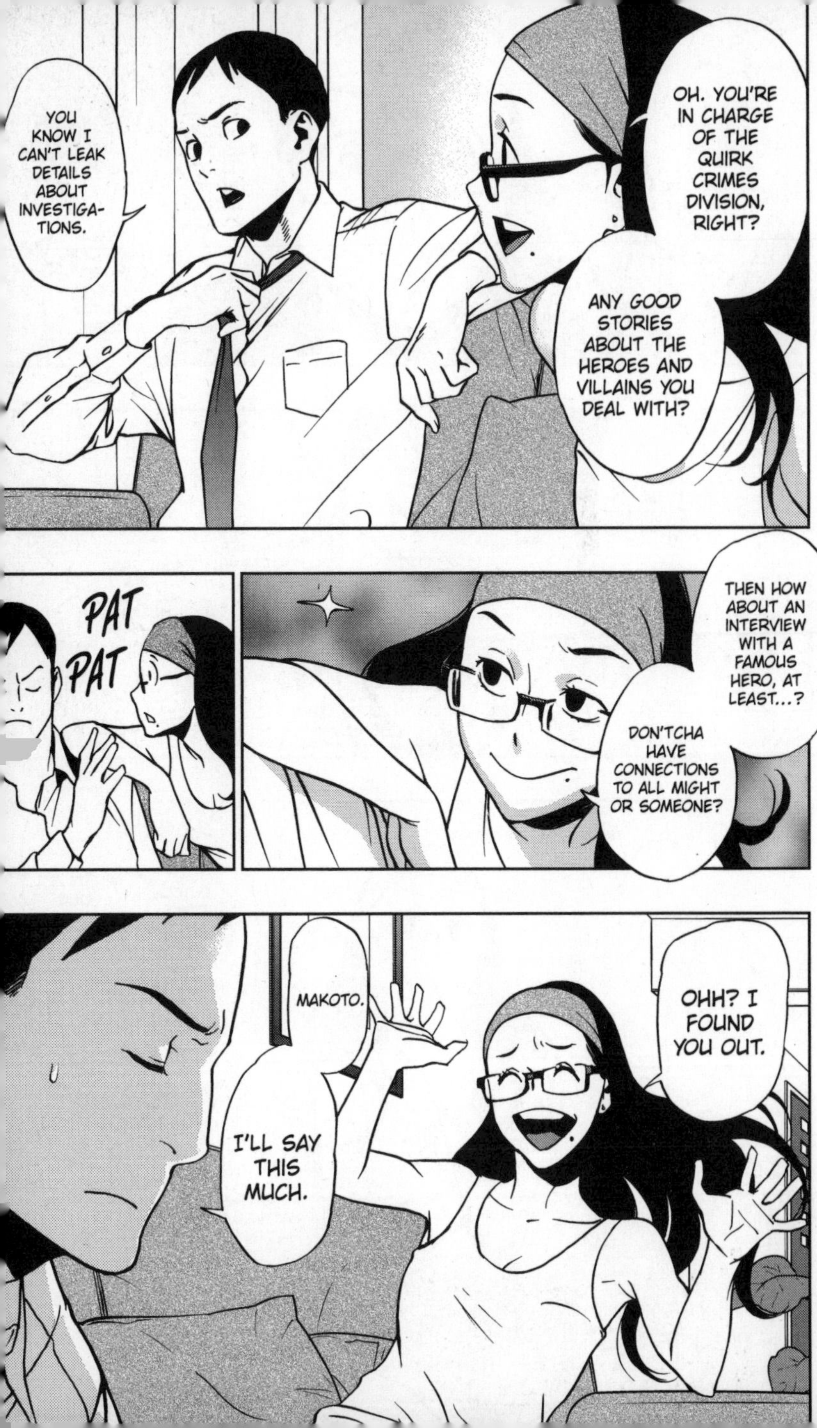
OH. YOU'RE IN CHARGE OF THE QUIRK CRIMES DIVISION, RIGHT?
ANY GOOD STORIES ABOUT THE HEROES AND VILLAINS YOU DEAL WITH?
YOU KNOW I CAN'T LEAK DETAILS ABOUT INVESTIGA-TIONS.
THEN HOW ABOUT AN INTERVIEW WITH A FAMOUS HERO, AT LEAST...?
DON'TCHA HAVE CONNECTIONS TO ALL MIGHT OR SOMEONE?
PAT PAT
OHH? I FOUND YOU OUT.
MAKOTO.
I'LL SAY THIS MUCH.

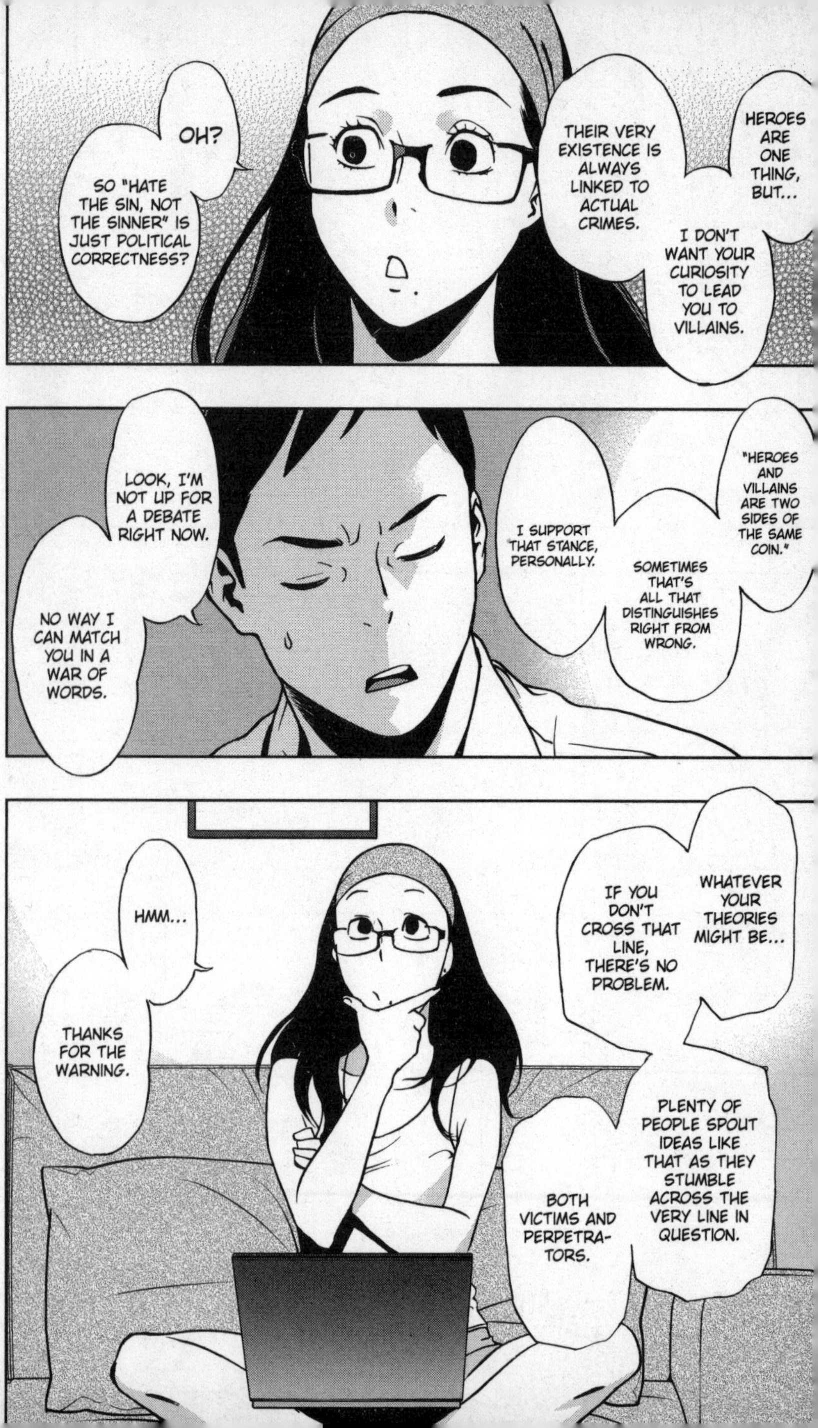
HEROES ARE ONE THING, BUT...
THEIR VERY EXISTENCE IS ALWAYS LINKED TO ACTUAL CRIMES.
I DON'T WANT YOUR CURIOSITY TO LEAD YOU TO VILLAINS.
OH?
SO "HATE THE SIN, NOT THE SINNER" IS JUST POLITICAL CORRECTNESS?
"HEROES AND VILLAINS ARE TWO SIDES OF THE SAME COIN."
SOMETIMES THAT'S ALL THAT DISTINGUISHES RIGHT FROM WRONG.
I SUPPORT THAT STANCE, PERSONALLY.
LOOK, I'M NOT UP FOR A DEBATE RIGHT NOW.
NO WAY I CAN MATCH YOU IN A WAR OF WORDS.
WHATEVER YOUR THEORIES MIGHT BE...
IF YOU DON'T CROSS THAT LINE, THERE'S NO PROBLEM.
PLENTY OF PEOPLE SPOUT IDEAS LIKE THAT AS THEY STUMBLE ACROSS THE VERY LINE IN QUESTION.
BOTH VICTIMS AND PERPETRATORS.
HMM...
THANKS FOR THE WARNING.

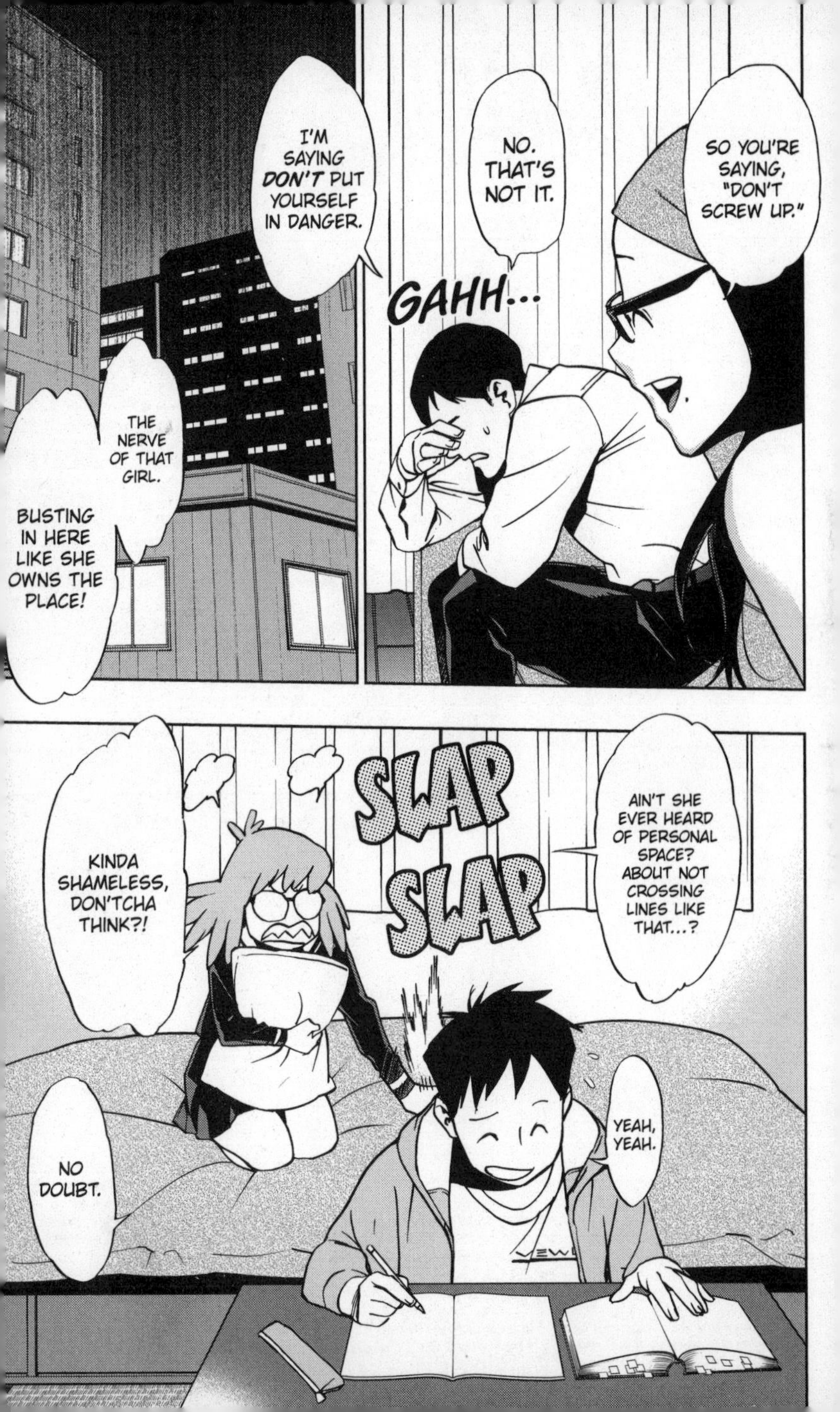
SO YOU'RE SAYING, "DON'T SCREW UP."
NO. THAT'S NOT IT.
GAHH...
I'M SAYING *DON'T* PUT YOURSELF IN DANGER.
THE NERVE OF THAT GIRL.
BUSTING IN HERE LIKE SHE OWNS THE PLACE!
AIN'T SHE EVER HEARD OF PERSONAL SPACE? ABOUT NOT CROSSING LINES LIKE THAT...?
SLAP
SLAP
KINDA SHAMELESS, DON'TCHA THINK?!
YEAH, YEAH.
NO DOUBT.

MAKOTO

THE ROUGH DESIGN

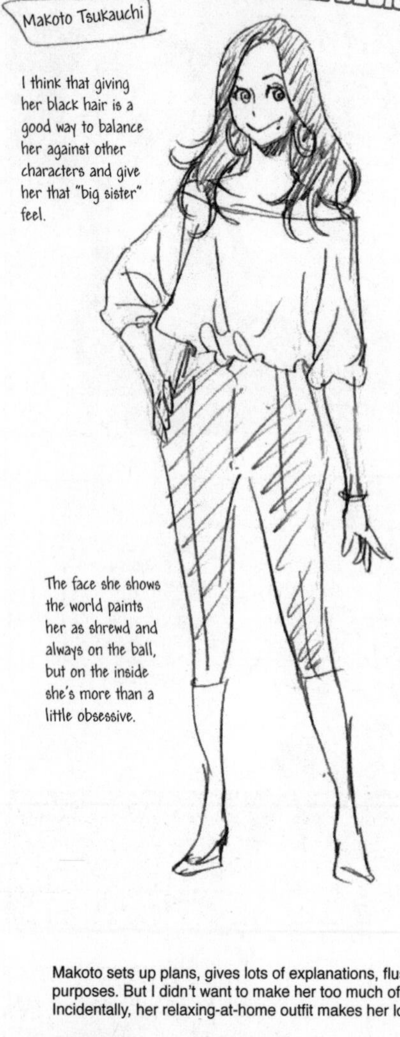
Makoto Tsukauchi
I think that giving her black hair is a good way to balance her against other characters and give her that "big sister" feel.
The face she shows the world paints her as shrewd and always on the ball, but on the inside she's more than a little obsessive.

REAL NAME: MAKOTO TSUKAUCHI

BIRTHDAY: 3/3

HEIGHT: 168 CM

FAVORITE THING: COFFEE

QUIRK: POLYGRAPH

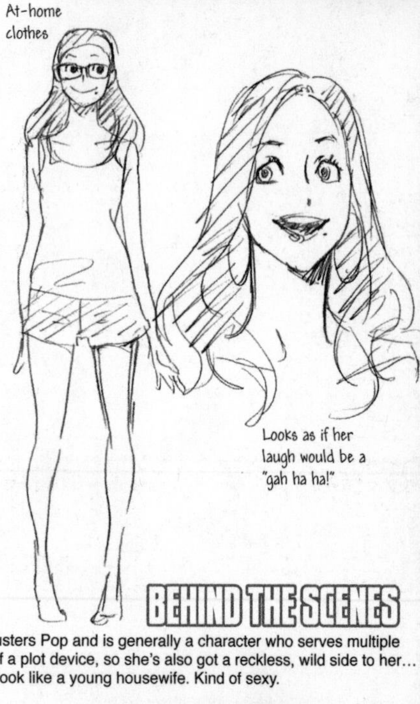
At-home clothes
Looks as if her laugh would be a "gah ha ha!"

BEHIND THE SCENES

Makoto sets up plans, gives lots of explanations, flusters Pop and is generally a character who serves multiple purposes. But I didn't want to make her too much of a plot device, so she's also got a reckless, wild side to her… Incidentally, her relaxing-at-home outfit makes her look like a young housewife. Kind of sexy.

—Furuhashi

I have an ideal image of how she should look, but I always have trouble putting that into the drawings. It's a constant process of trial and error, which means she's changed a lot since her debut…

—Betten

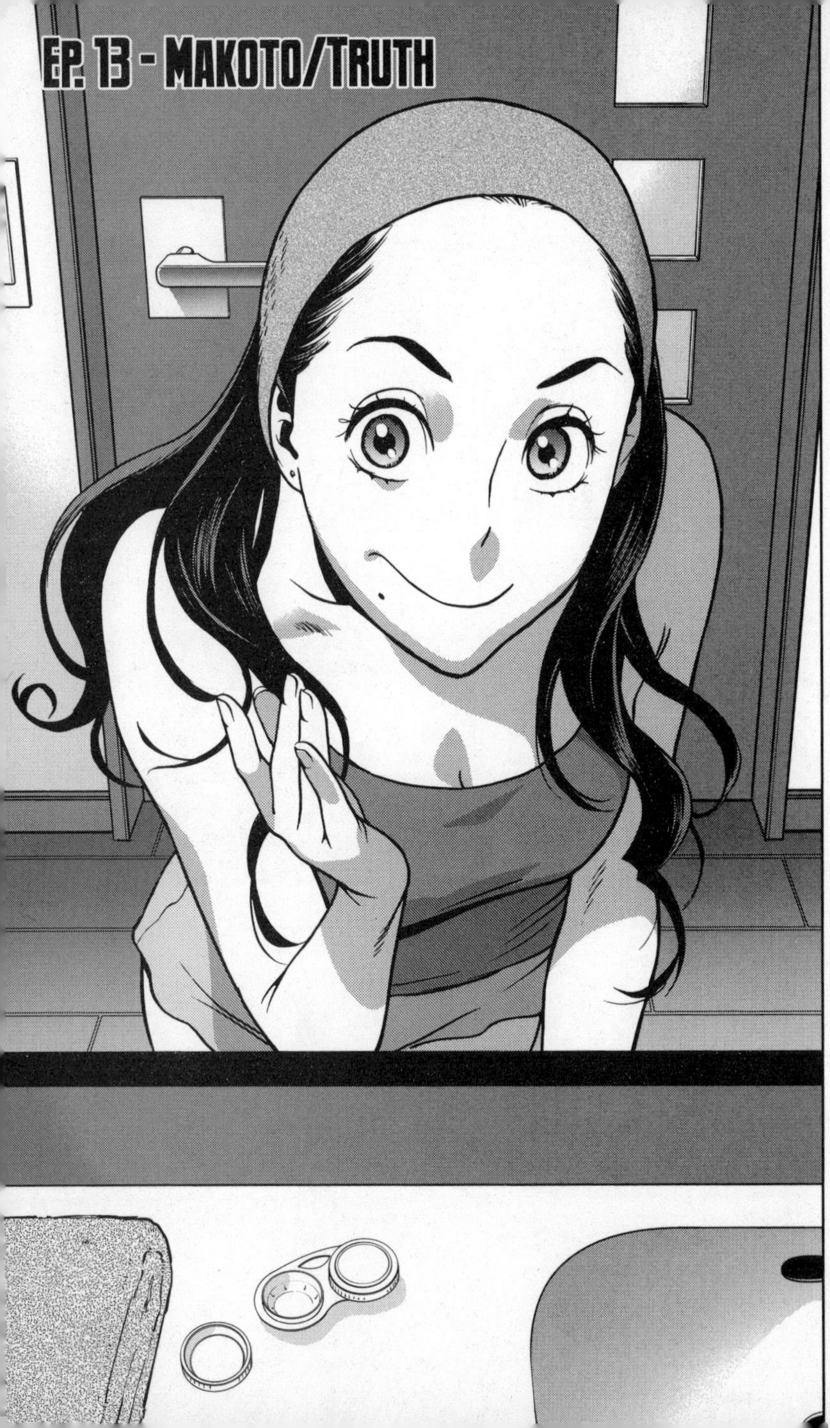
EP. 13 - MAKOTO/TRUTH

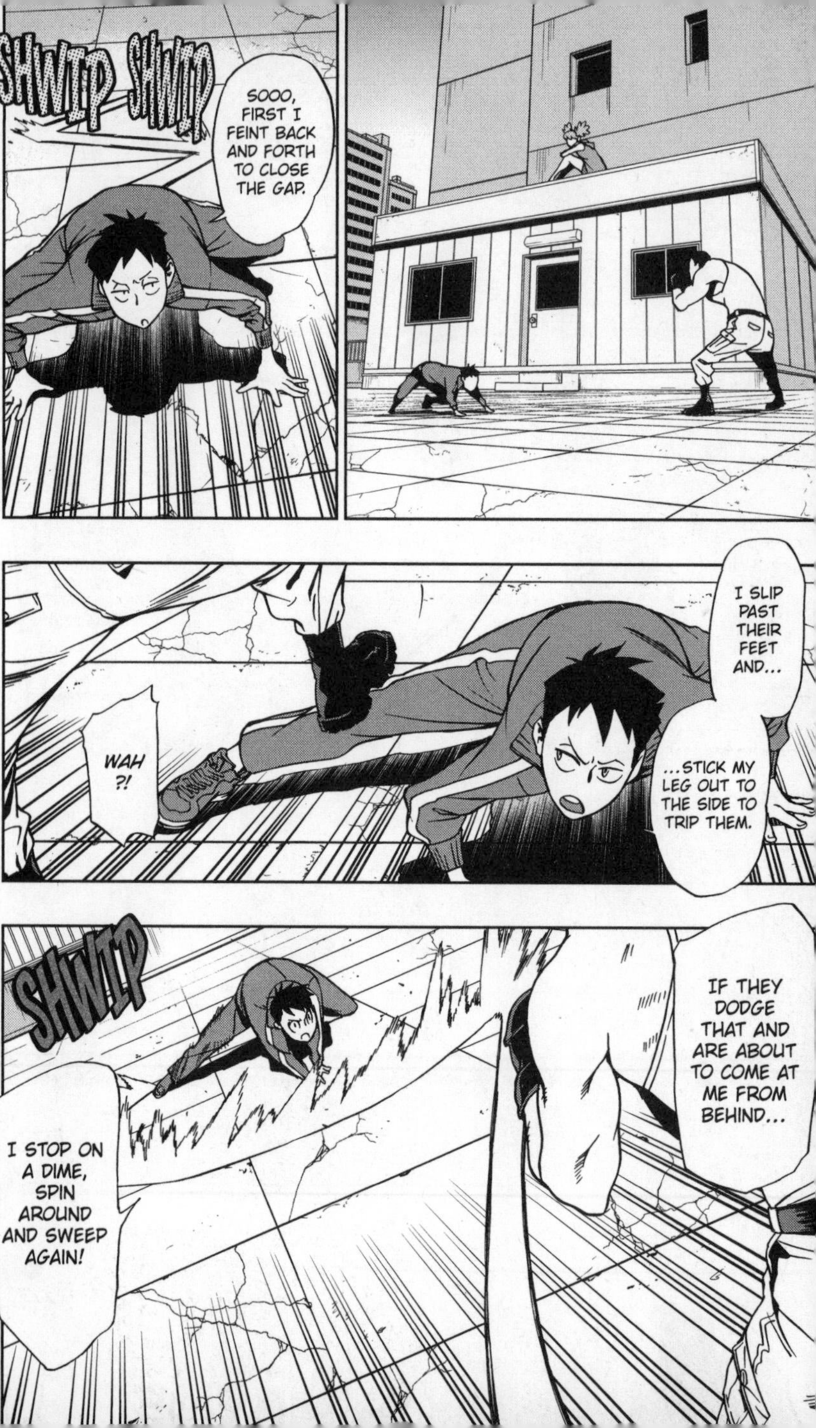
SHWIP SHWIP
SOOO, FIRST I FEINT BACK AND FORTH TO CLOSE THE GAP.
I SLIP PAST THEIR FEET AND...
...STICK MY LEG OUT TO THE SIDE TO TRIP THEM.
WAH ?!
IF THEY DODGE THAT AND ARE ABOUT TO COME AT ME FROM BEHIND...
I STOP ON A DIME, SPIN AROUND AND SWEEP AGAIN!
SHWIP

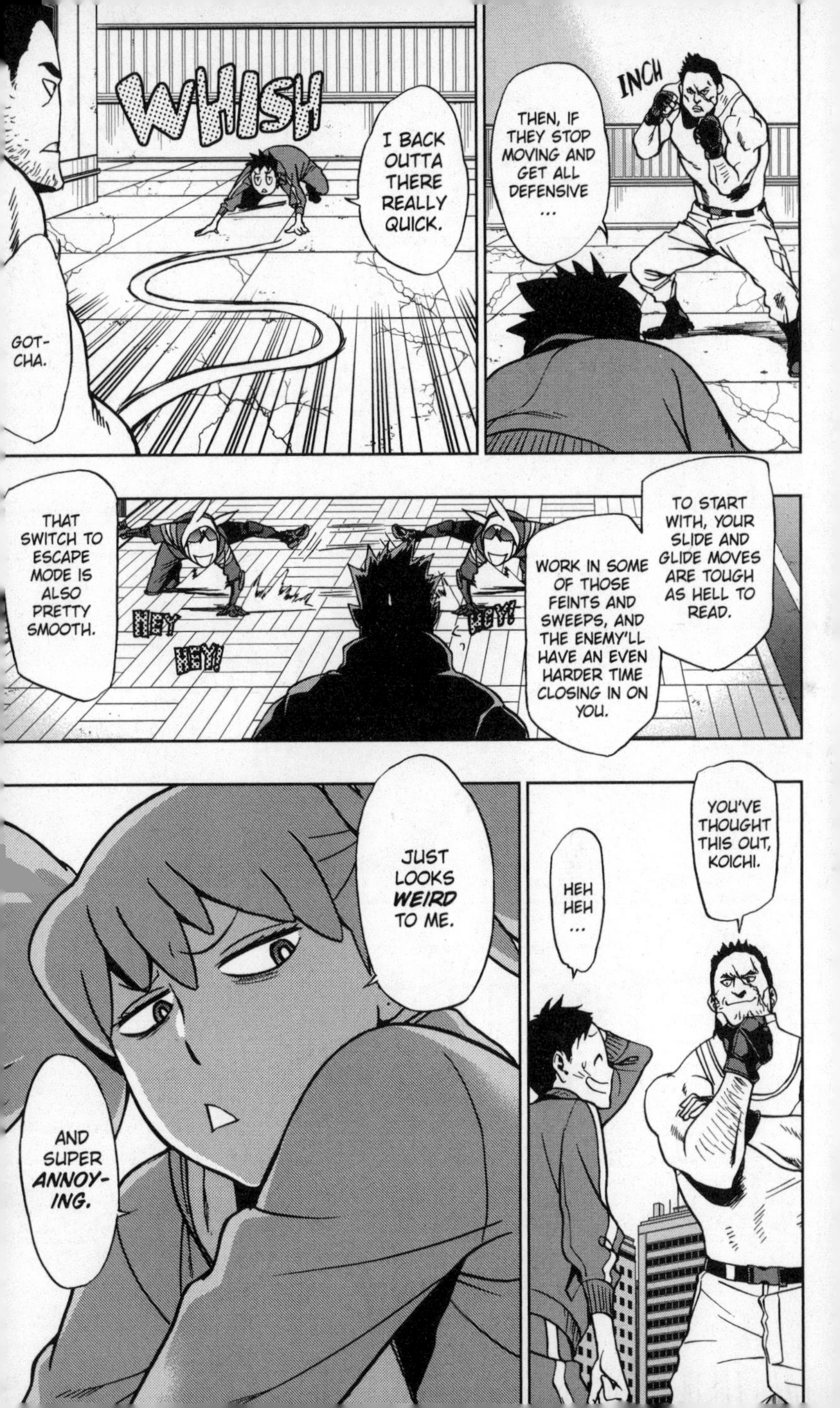
INCH
THEN, IF THEY STOP MOVING AND GET ALL DEFENSIVE ...
WHISH
I BACK OUTTA THERE REALLY QUICK.
GOT-CHA.
TO START WITH, YOUR SLIDE AND GLIDE MOVES ARE TOUGH AS HELL TO READ.
WORK IN SOME OF THOSE FEINTS AND SWEEPS, AND THE ENEMY'LL HAVE AN EVEN HARDER TIME CLOSING IN ON YOU.
HEY!
HEY!
HEY
THAT SWITCH TO ESCAPE MODE IS ALSO PRETTY SMOOTH.
YOU'VE THOUGHT THIS OUT, KOICHI.
HEH HEH ...
JUST LOOKS *WEIRD* TO ME.
AND SUPER *ANNOY-ING.*

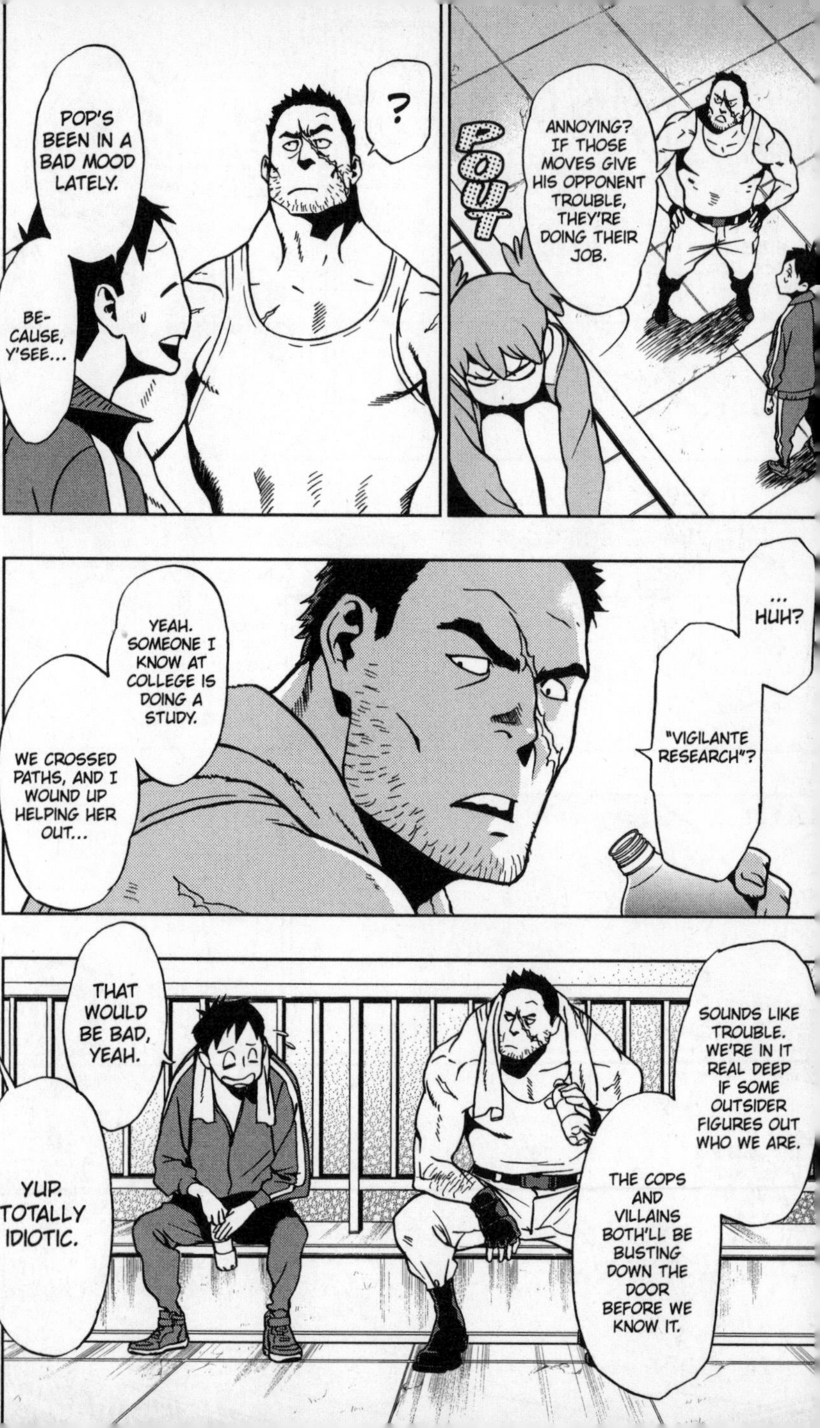

ANNOYING? IF THOSE MOVES GIVE HIS OPPONENT TROUBLE, THEY'RE DOING THEIR JOB.
POUT
?
POP'S BEEN IN A BAD MOOD LATELY.
BE-CAUSE, Y'SEE...
... HUH?
"VIGILANTE RESEARCH"?
YEAH. SOMEONE I KNOW AT COLLEGE IS DOING A STUDY.
WE CROSSED PATHS, AND I WOUND UP HELPING HER OUT...
SOUNDS LIKE TROUBLE. WE'RE IN IT REAL DEEP IF SOME OUTSIDER FIGURES OUT WHO WE ARE.
THE COPS AND VILLAINS BOTH'LL BE BUSTING DOWN THE DOOR BEFORE WE KNOW IT.
THAT WOULD BE BAD, YEAH.
YUP. TOTALLY IDIOTIC.

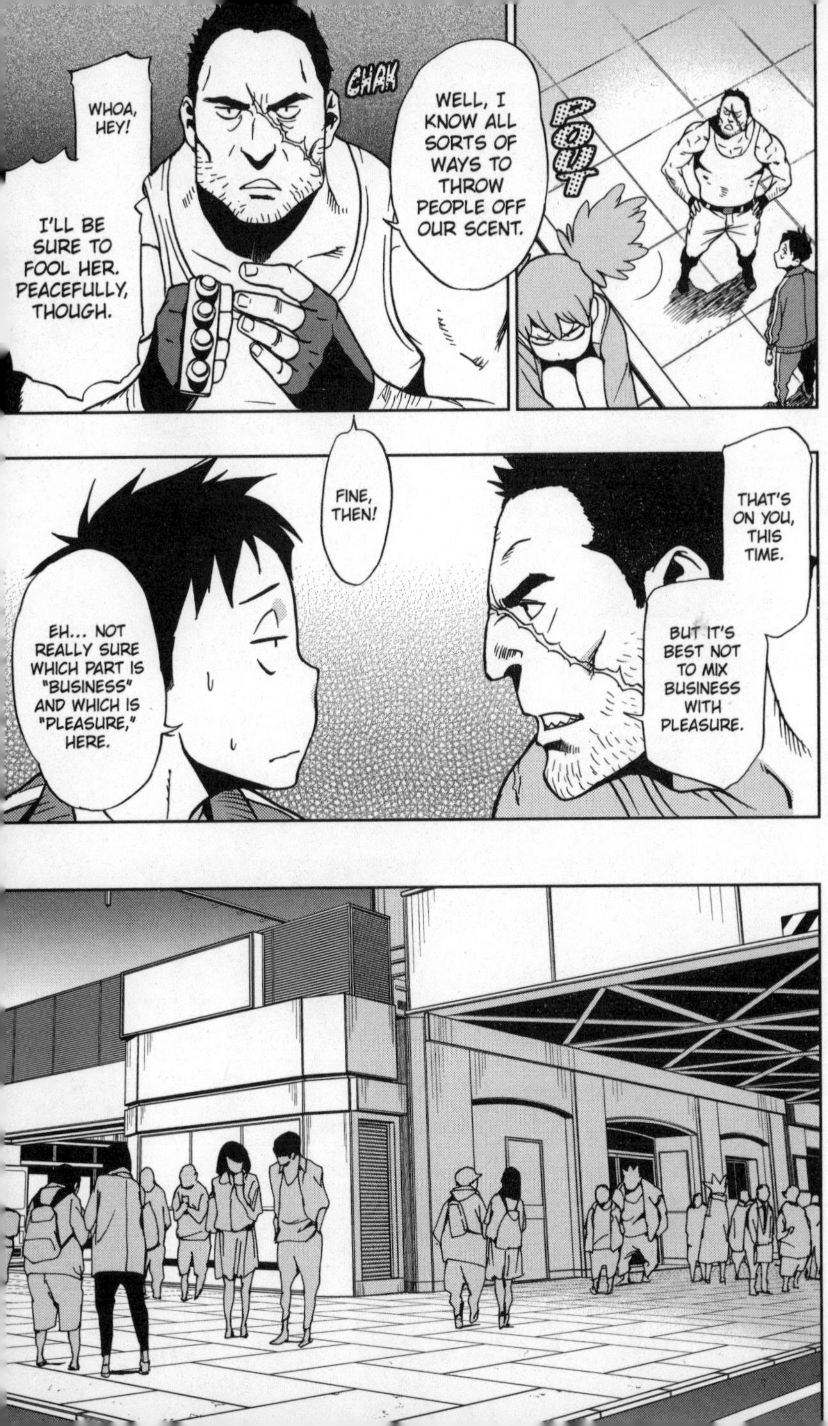
POUT
CHAK
WELL, I KNOW ALL SORTS OF WAYS TO THROW PEOPLE OFF OUR SCENT.
WHOA, HEY!
I'LL BE SURE TO FOOL HER. PEACEFULLY, THOUGH.
THAT'S ON YOU, THIS TIME.
BUT IT'S BEST NOT TO MIX BUSINESS WITH PLEASURE.
FINE, THEN!
EH... NOT REALLY SURE WHICH PART IS "BUSINESS" AND WHICH IS "PLEASURE," HERE.

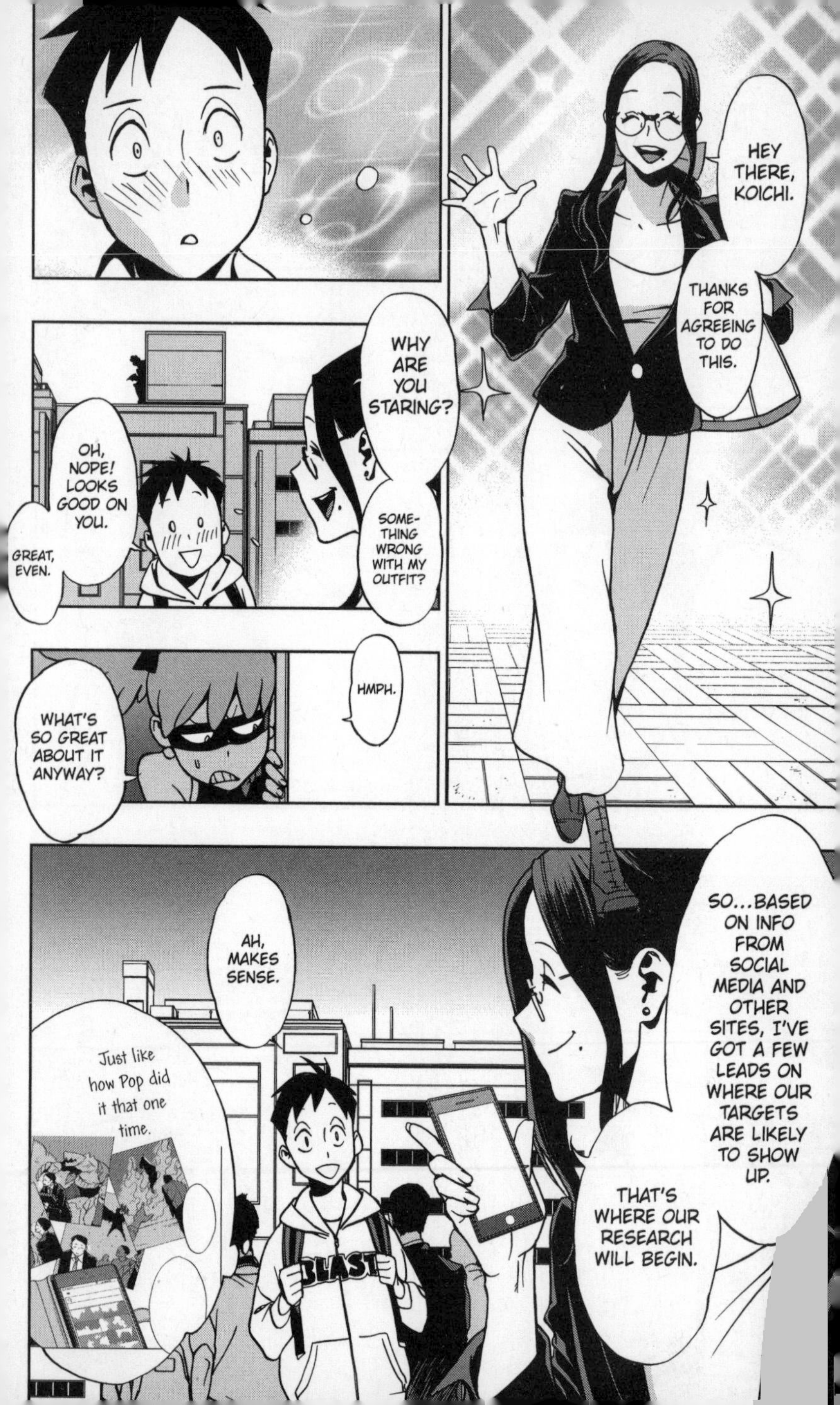
HEY THERE, KOICHI.
THANKS FOR AGREEING TO DO THIS.
WHY ARE YOU STARING?
SOME-THING WRONG WITH MY OUTFIT?
OH, NOPE! LOOKS GOOD ON YOU.
GREAT, EVEN.
HMPH.
WHAT'S SO GREAT ABOUT IT ANYWAY?
SO...BASED ON INFO FROM SOCIAL MEDIA AND OTHER SITES, I'VE GOT A FEW LEADS ON WHERE OUR TARGETS ARE LIKELY TO SHOW UP.
THAT'S WHERE OUR RESEARCH WILL BEGIN.
AH, MAKES SENSE.
Just like how Pop did it that one time.
BLAST

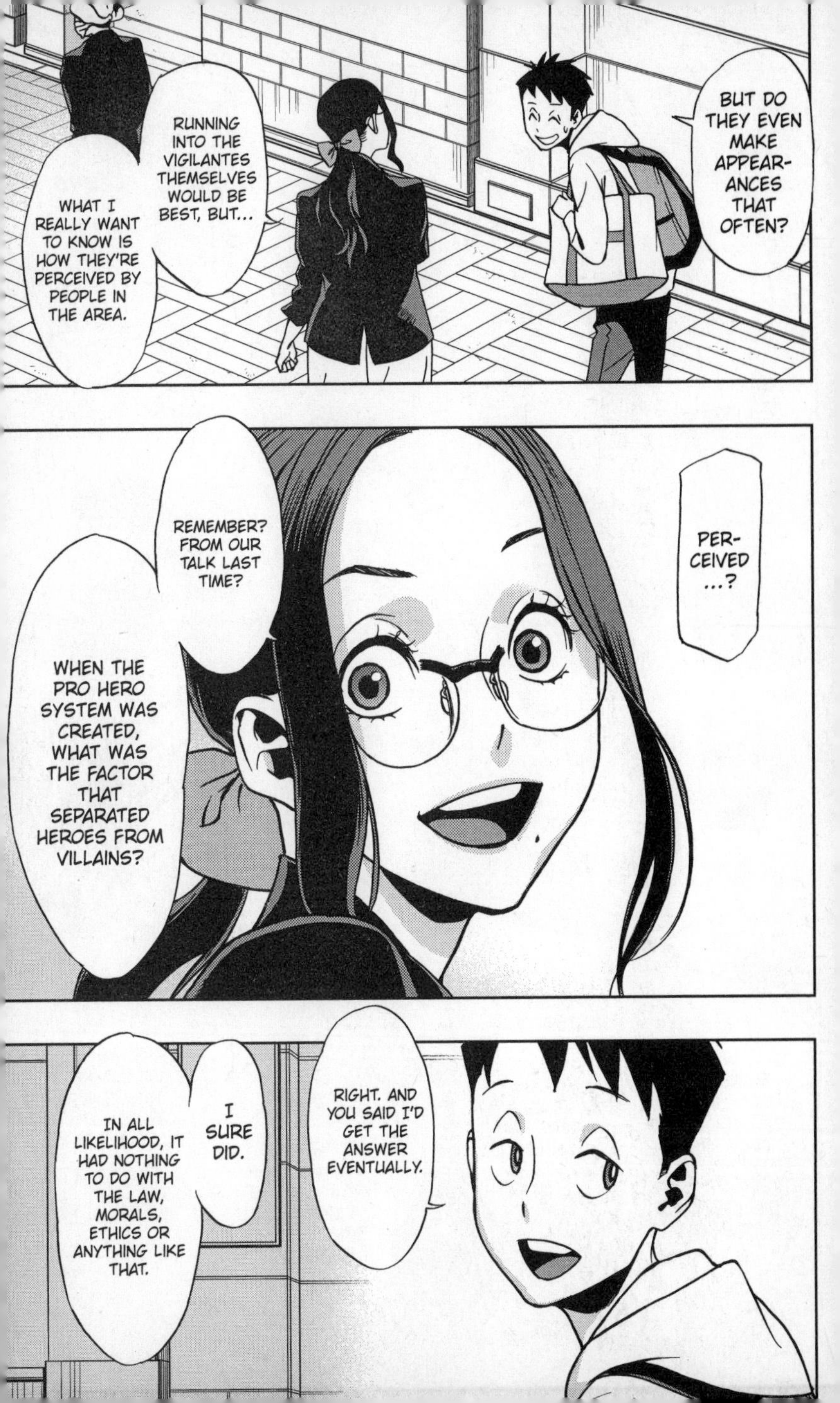
BUT DO THEY EVEN MAKE APPEARANCES THAT OFTEN?
RUNNING INTO THE VIGILANTES THEMSELVES WOULD BE BEST, BUT...
WHAT I REALLY WANT TO KNOW IS HOW THEY'RE PERCEIVED BY PEOPLE IN THE AREA.
PERCEIVED...?
REMEMBER? FROM OUR TALK LAST TIME?
WHEN THE PRO HERO SYSTEM WAS CREATED, WHAT WAS THE FACTOR THAT SEPARATED HEROES FROM VILLAINS?
RIGHT. AND YOU SAID I'D GET THE ANSWER EVENTUALLY.
I SURE DID.
IN ALL LIKELIHOOD, IT HAD NOTHING TO DO WITH THE LAW, MORALS, ETHICS OR ANYTHING LIKE THAT.

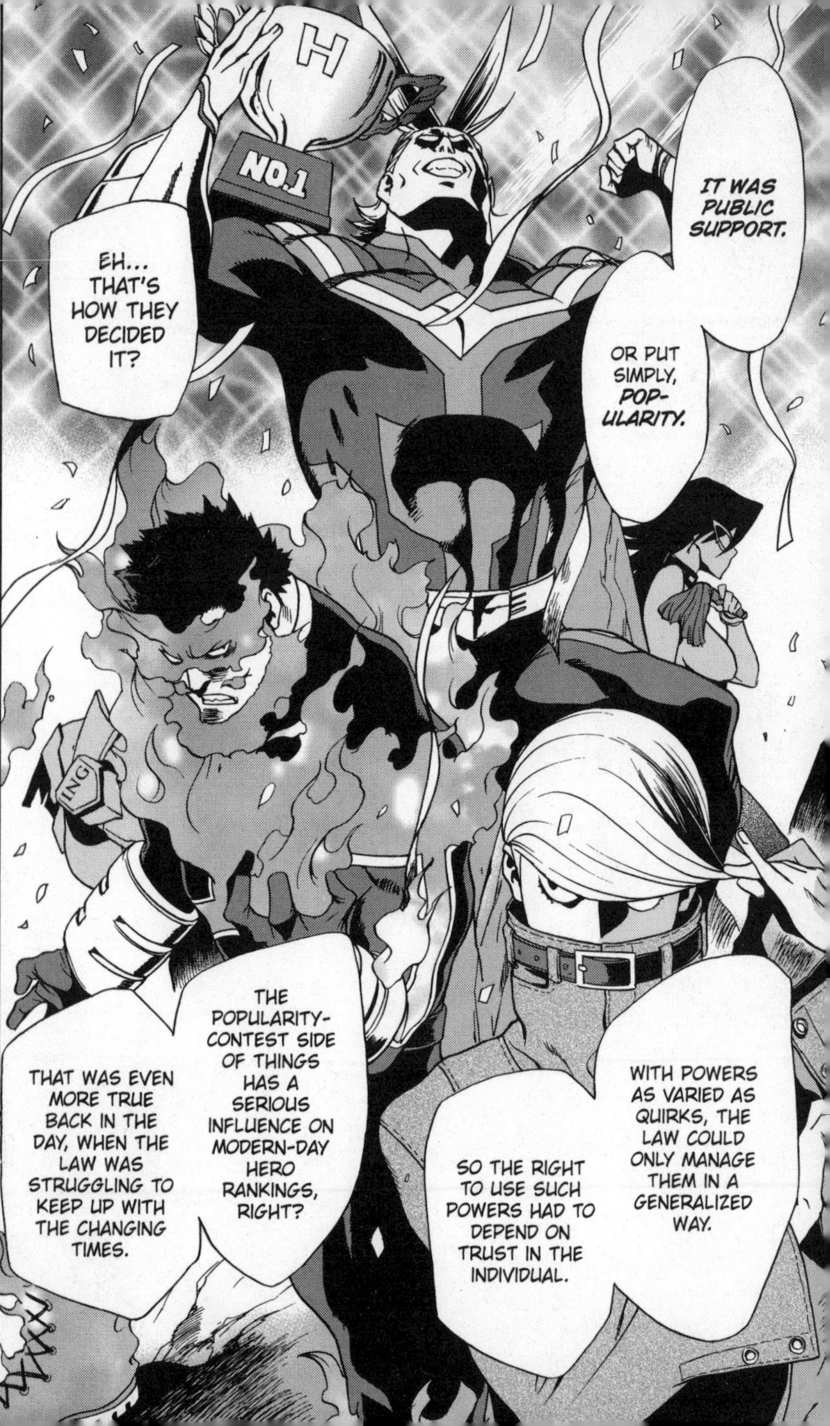

IT WAS PUBLIC SUPPORT.
OR PUT SIMPLY, POPULARITY.
EH... THAT'S HOW THEY DECIDED IT?
NO.1
WITH POWERS AS VARIED AS QUIRKS, THE LAW COULD ONLY MANAGE THEM IN A GENERALIZED WAY.
SO THE RIGHT TO USE SUCH POWERS HAD TO DEPEND ON TRUST IN THE INDIVIDUAL.
THE POPULARITY-CONTEST SIDE OF THINGS HAS A SERIOUS INFLUENCE ON MODERN-DAY HERO RANKINGS, RIGHT?
THAT WAS EVEN MORE TRUE BACK IN THE DAY, WHEN THE LAW WAS STRUGGLING TO KEEP UP WITH THE CHANGING TIMES.

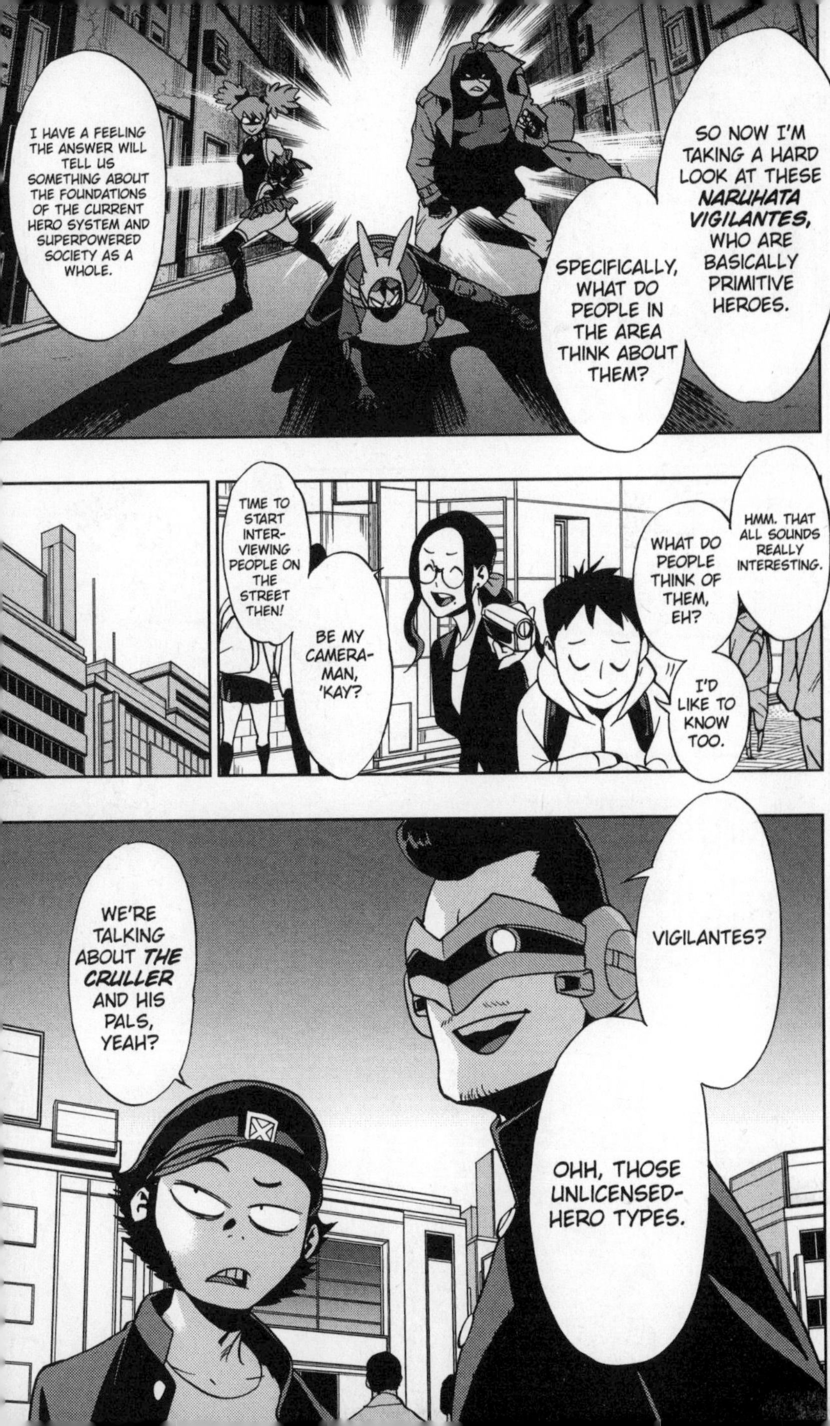
SO NOW I'M TAKING A HARD LOOK AT THESE *NARUHATA VIGILANTES,* WHO ARE BASICALLY PRIMITIVE HEROES.
SPECIFICALLY, WHAT DO PEOPLE IN THE AREA THINK ABOUT THEM?
I HAVE A FEELING THE ANSWER WILL TELL US SOMETHING ABOUT THE FOUNDATIONS OF THE CURRENT HERO SYSTEM AND SUPERPOWERED SOCIETY AS A WHOLE.
HMM. THAT ALL SOUNDS REALLY INTERESTING.
WHAT DO PEOPLE THINK OF THEM, EH?
I'D LIKE TO KNOW TOO.
TIME TO START INTER-VIEWING PEOPLE ON THE STREET THEN!
BE MY CAMERA-MAN, 'KAY?
VIGILANTES?
WE'RE TALKING ABOUT *THE CRULLER* AND HIS PALS, YEAH?
OHH, THOSE UNLICENSED-HERO TYPES.

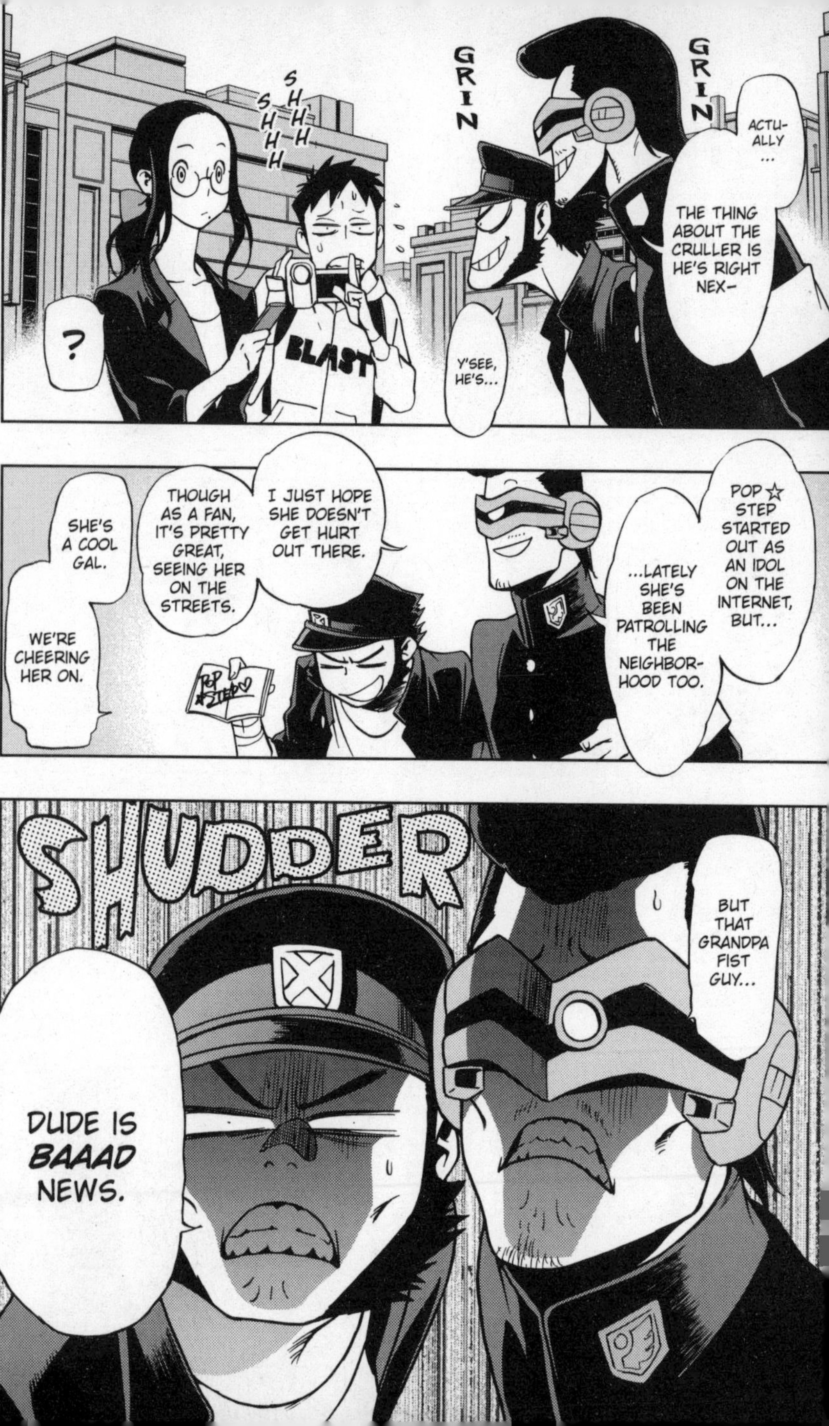
GRIN
ACTU-ALLY...
THE THING ABOUT THE CRULLER IS HE'S RIGHT NEX–
GRIN
Y'SEE, HE'S...
SHHHH SHHHH
?
POP☆STEP STARTED OUT AS AN IDOL ON THE INTERNET, BUT...
...LATELY SHE'S BEEN PATROLLING THE NEIGHBORHOOD TOO.
POP☆STEP♡
I JUST HOPE SHE DOESN'T GET HURT OUT THERE.
THOUGH AS A FAN, IT'S PRETTY GREAT, SEEING HER ON THE STREETS.
SHE'S A COOL GAL.
WE'RE CHEERING HER ON.
BUT THAT GRANDPA FIST GUY...
SHUDDER
DUDE IS *BAAAD* NEWS.

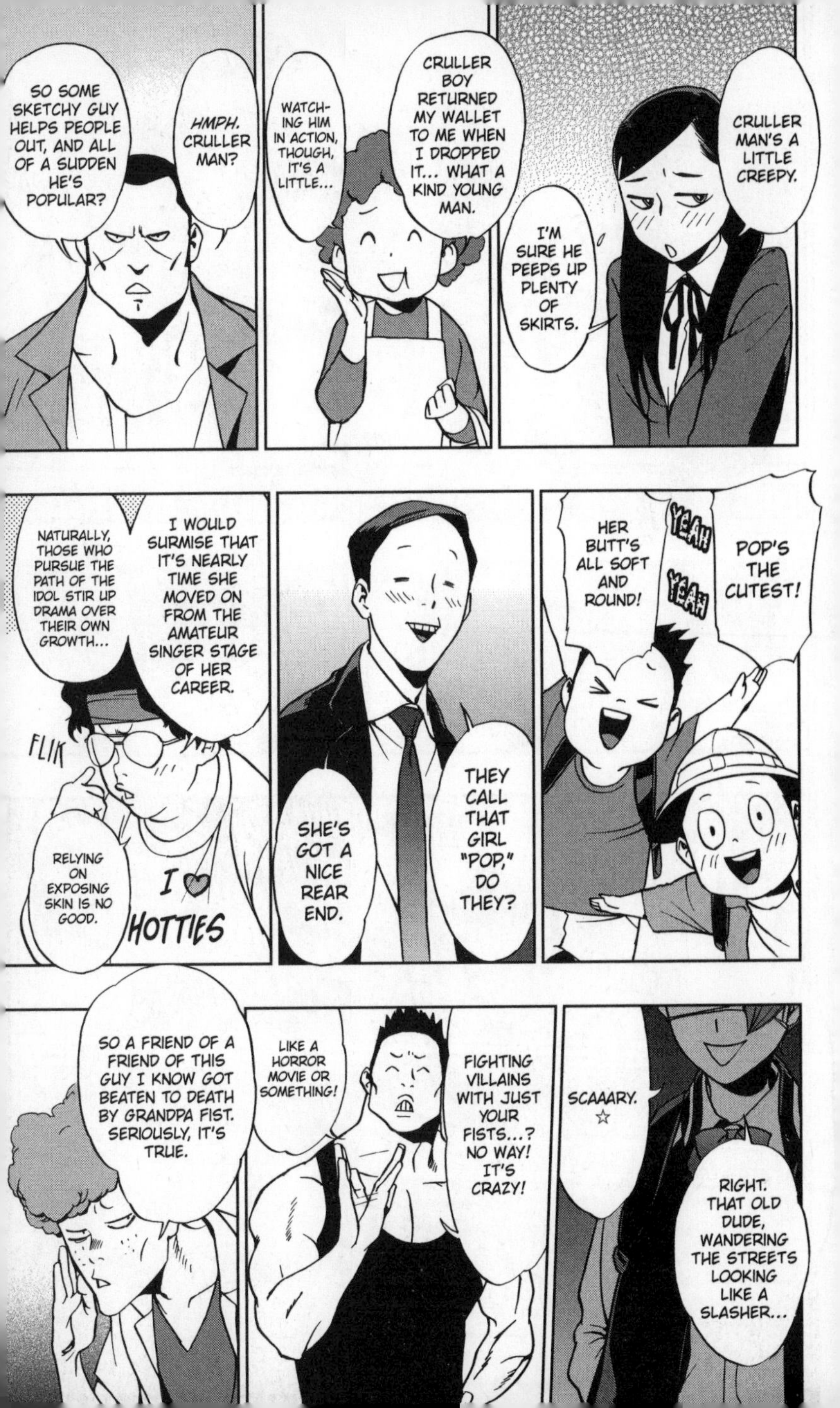
CRULLER MAN'S A LITTLE CREEPY.
I'M SURE HE PEEPS UP PLENTY OF SKIRTS.
CRULLER BOY RETURNED MY WALLET TO ME WHEN I DROPPED IT... WHAT A KIND YOUNG MAN.
WATCHING HIM IN ACTION, THOUGH, IT'S A LITTLE...
HMPH. CRULLER MAN?
SO SOME SKETCHY GUY HELPS PEOPLE OUT, AND ALL OF A SUDDEN HE'S POPULAR?
POP'S THE CUTEST!
YEAH
YEAH
HER BUTT'S ALL SOFT AND ROUND!
THEY CALL THAT GIRL "POP," DO THEY?
SHE'S GOT A NICE REAR END.
I WOULD SURMISE THAT IT'S NEARLY TIME SHE MOVED ON FROM THE AMATEUR SINGER STAGE OF HER CAREER.
NATURALLY, THOSE WHO PURSUE THE PATH OF THE IDOL STIR UP DRAMA OVER THEIR OWN GROWTH...
FLIK
RELYING ON EXPOSING SKIN IS NO GOOD.
I ♥ HOTTIES
SCAAARY. ☆
RIGHT. THAT OLD DUDE, WANDERING THE STREETS LOOKING LIKE A SLASHER...
FIGHTING VILLAINS WITH JUST YOUR FISTS...? NO WAY! IT'S CRAZY!
LIKE A HORROR MOVIE OR SOMETHING!
SO A FRIEND OF A FRIEND OF THIS GUY I KNOW GOT BEATEN TO DEATH BY GRANDPA FIST. SERIOUSLY, IT'S TRUE.

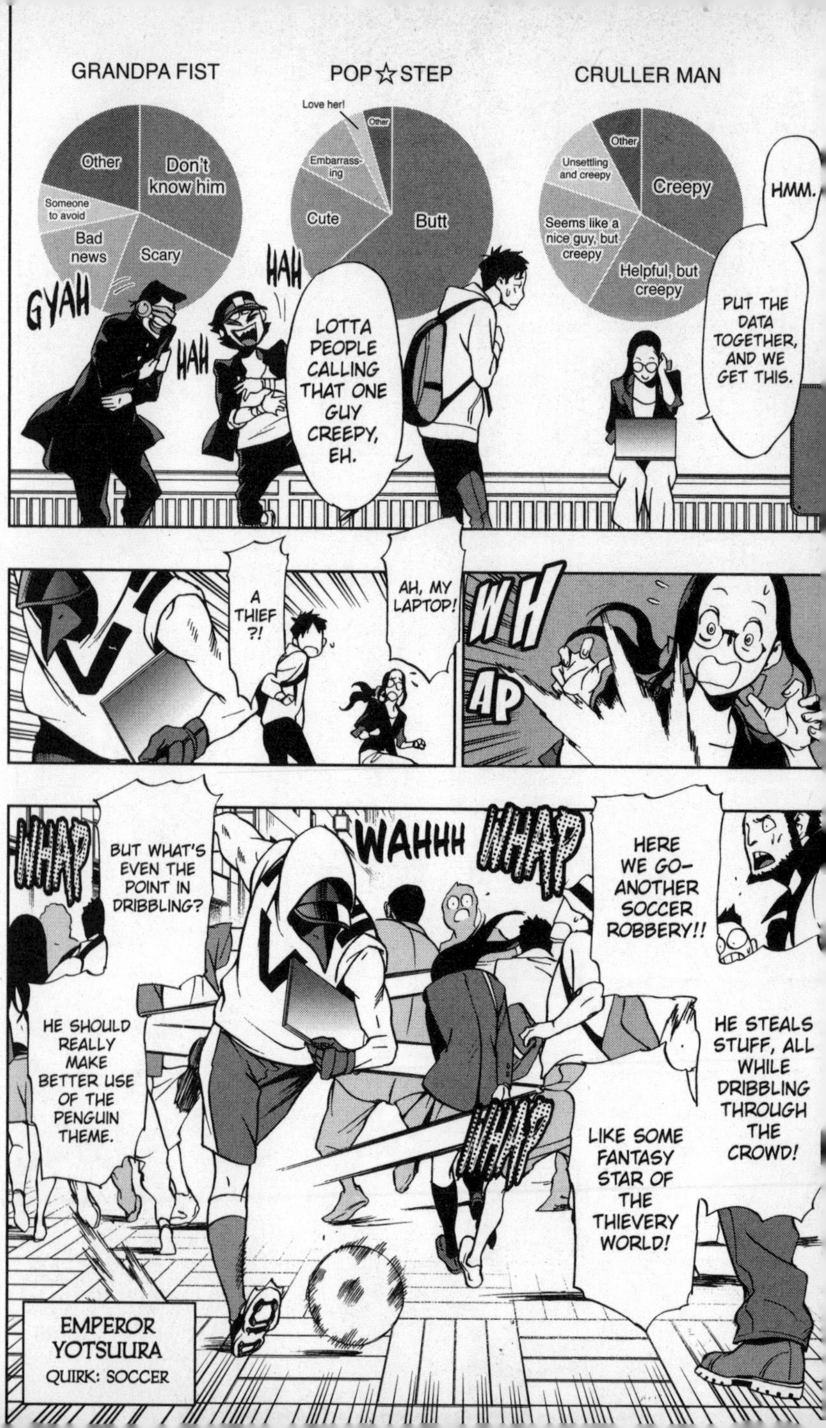
HMM.
PUT THE DATA TOGETHER, AND WE GET THIS.
CRULLER MAN
Creepy
Helpful, but creepy
Seems like a nice guy, but creepy
Unsettling and creepy
Other
POP☆STEP
Butt
Cute
Embarrass-ing
Love her!
Other
GRANDPA FIST
Don't know him
Scary
Bad news
Someone to avoid
Other
LOTTA PEOPLE CALLING THAT ONE GUY CREEPY, EH.
HAH
HAH
GYAH
WH
AP
AH, MY LAPTOP!
A THIEF ?!
HERE WE GO— ANOTHER SOCCER ROBBERY!!
HE STEALS STUFF, ALL WHILE DRIBBLING THROUGH THE CROWD!
LIKE SOME FANTASY STAR OF THE THIEVERY WORLD!
WHAP
WAHHH
WHAP
BUT WHAT'S EVEN THE POINT IN DRIBBLING?
HE SHOULD REALLY MAKE BETTER USE OF THE PENGUIN THEME.
WHAP
EMPEROR YOTSUURA
QUIRK: SOCCER

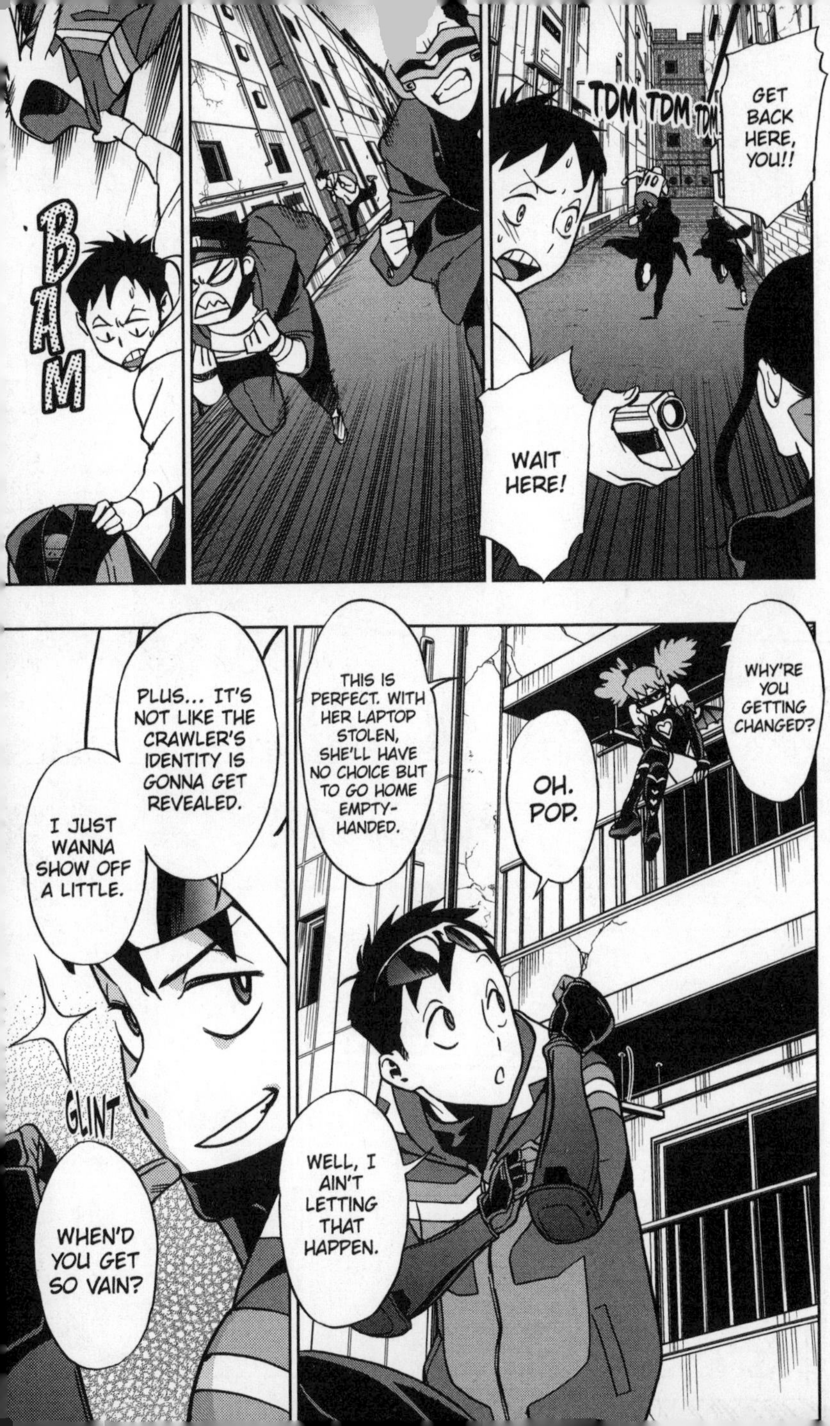
GET BACK HERE, YOU!!
TDM TDM TDM
WAIT HERE!
BAM
WHY'RE YOU GETTING CHANGED?
OH. POP.
THIS IS PERFECT. WITH HER LAPTOP STOLEN, SHE'LL HAVE NO CHOICE BUT TO GO HOME EMPTY-HANDED.
WELL, I AIN'T LETTING THAT HAPPEN.
PLUS... IT'S NOT LIKE THE CRAWLER'S IDENTITY IS GONNA GET REVEALED.
I JUST WANNA SHOW OFF A LITTLE.
GLINT
WHEN'D YOU GET SO VAIN?

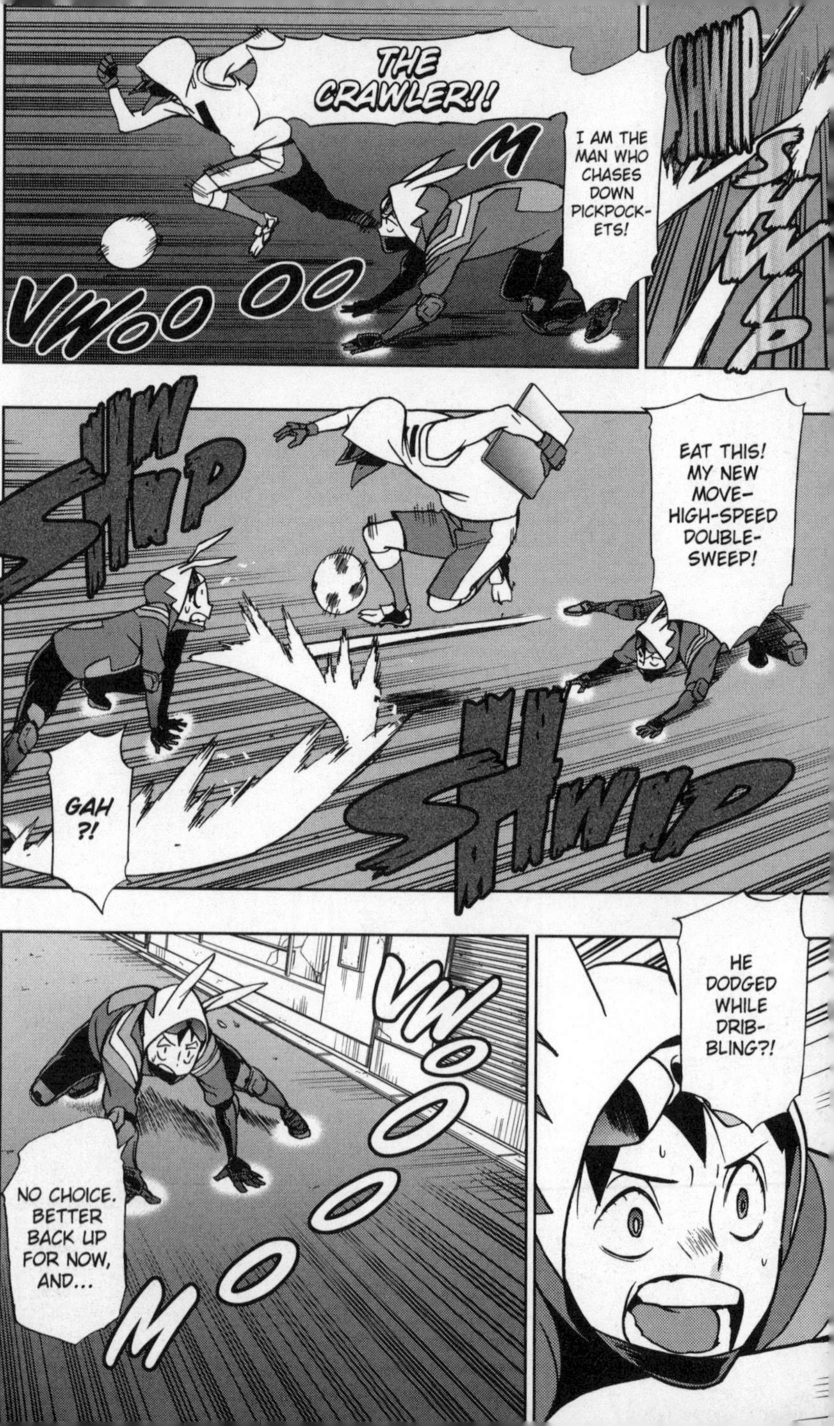
SHWIP
SHWIP
THE CRAWLER!!
I AM THE MAN WHO CHASES DOWN PICKPOCK-ETS!
VWOO OO M
SHWIP
EAT THIS! MY NEW MOVE-HIGH-SPEED DOUBLE-SWEEP!
GAH ?!
SHWIP
HE DODGED WHILE DRIB-BLING?!
VWOOOOOM
NO CHOICE. BETTER BACK UP FOR NOW, AND...

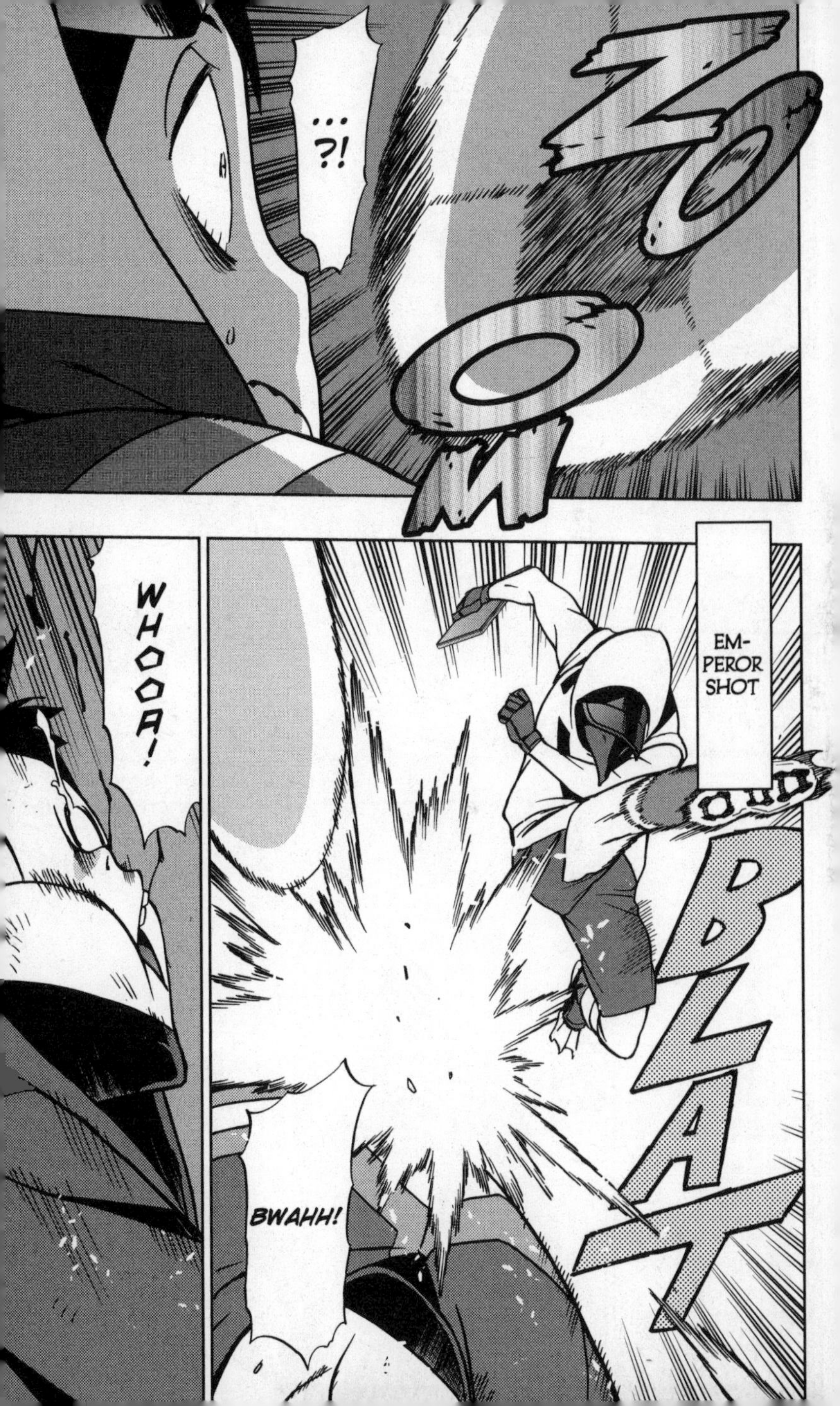

...?!
ZOOM
EMPEROR SHOT
BLAT
BWAHH!
WHOOA!

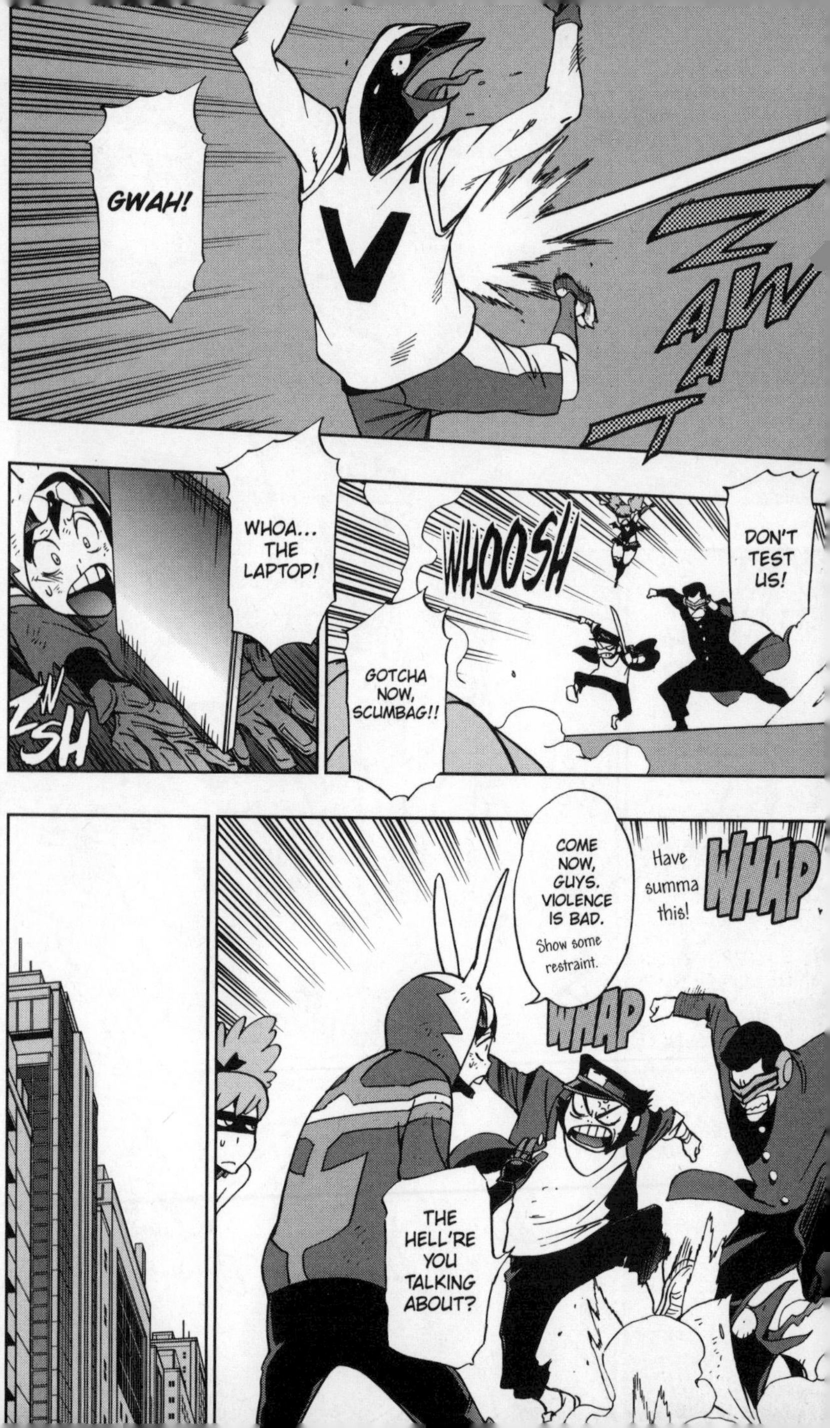
GWAH!
ZAWAT
DON'T TEST US!
WHOOSH
GOTCHA NOW, SCUMBAG!!
WHOA... THE LAPTOP!
WHAP
Have summa this!
COME NOW, GUYS. VIOLENCE IS BAD.
Show some restraint.
WHAP
THE HELL'RE YOU TALKING ABOUT?

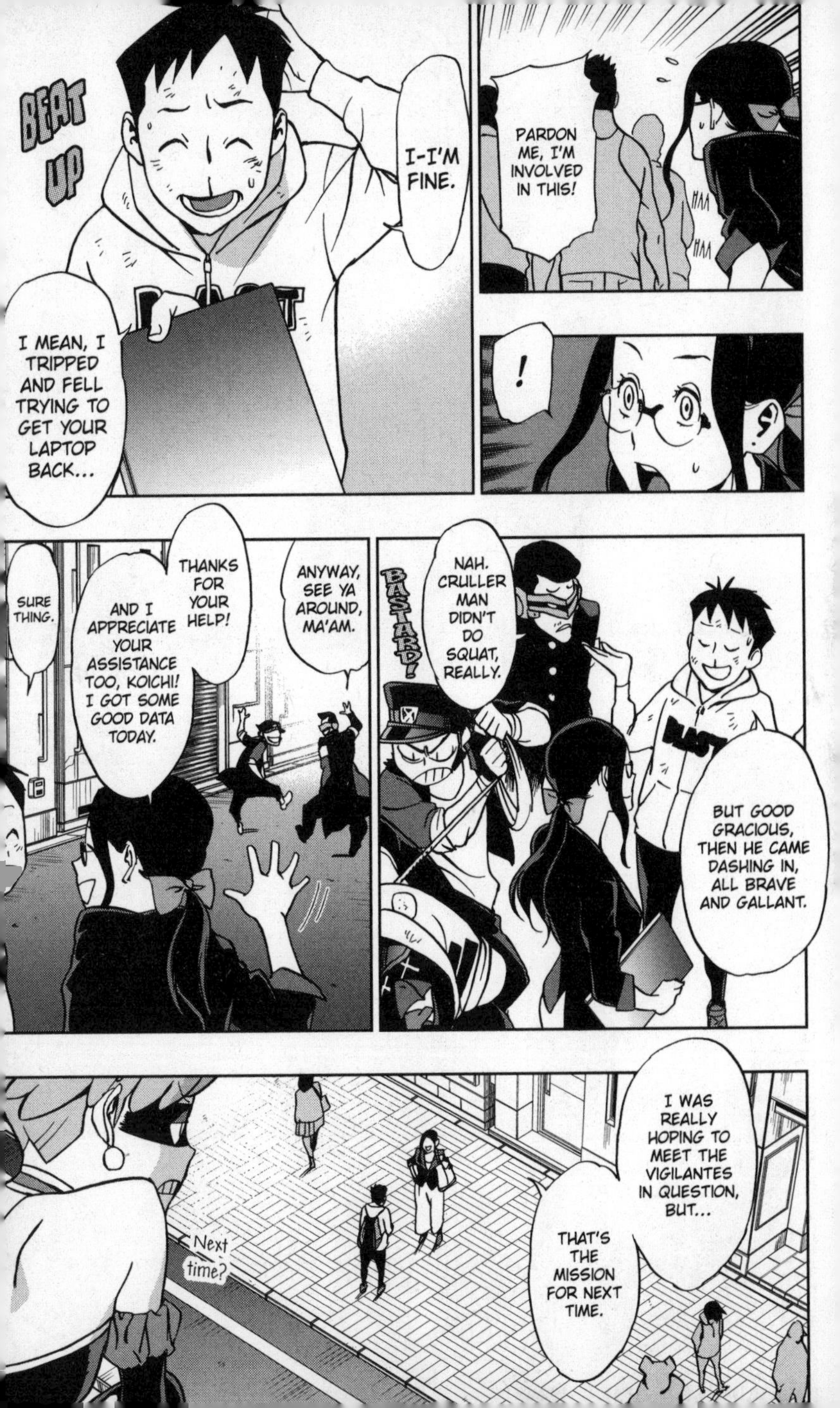
PARDON ME, I'M INVOLVED IN THIS!
HAA
HAA
!
BEAT UP
I-I'M FINE.
I MEAN, I TRIPPED AND FELL TRYING TO GET YOUR LAPTOP BACK...
NAH. CRULLER MAN DIDN'T DO SQUAT, REALLY.
BASTARD!
BUT GOOD GRACIOUS, THEN HE CAME DASHING IN, ALL BRAVE AND GALLANT.
ANYWAY, SEE YA AROUND, MA'AM.
THANKS FOR YOUR HELP!
AND I APPRECIATE YOUR ASSISTANCE TOO, KOICHI! I GOT SOME GOOD DATA TODAY.
SURE THING.
I WAS REALLY HOPING TO MEET THE VIGILANTES IN QUESTION, BUT...
THAT'S THE MISSION FOR NEXT TIME.
Next time?

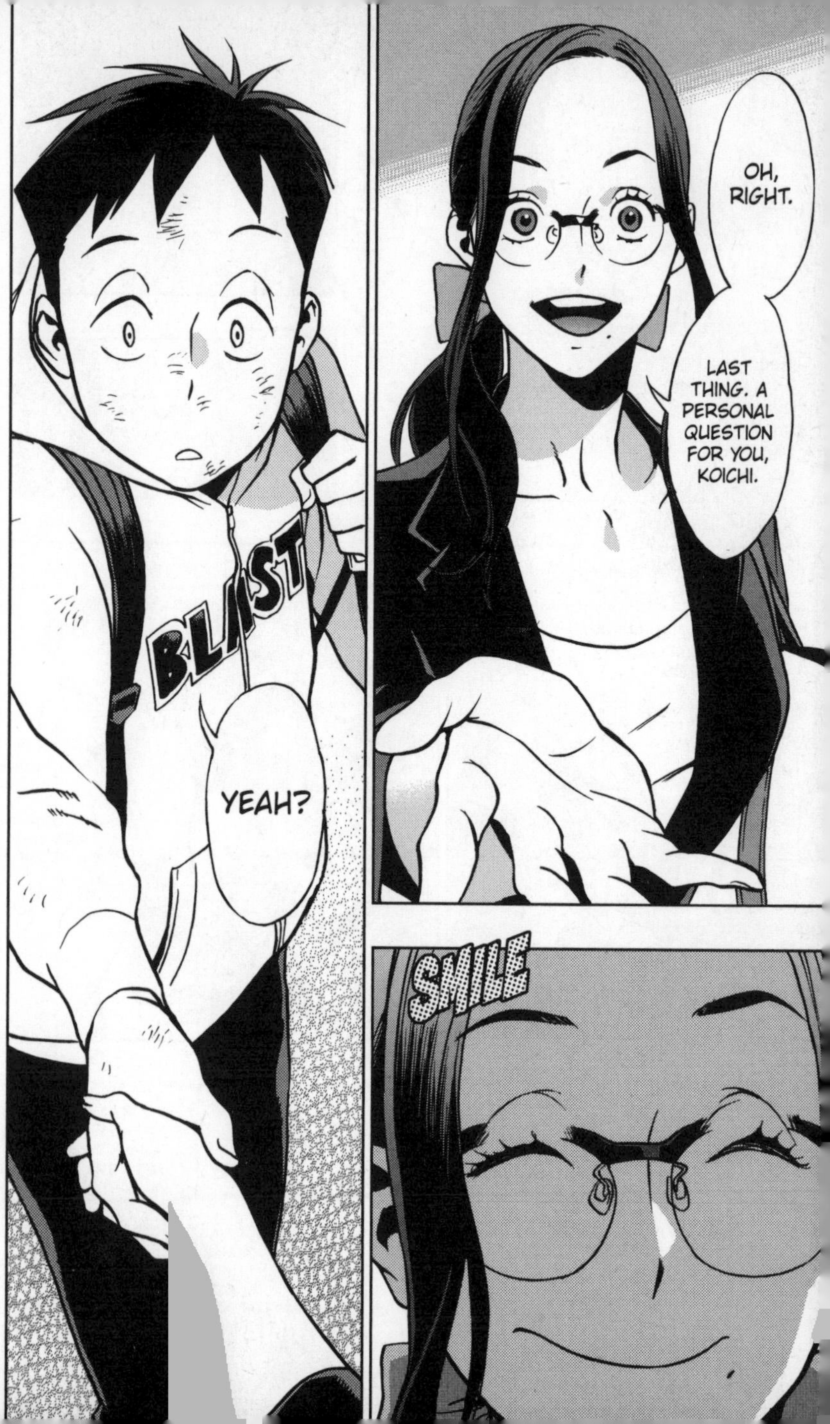
OH, RIGHT.
LAST THING. A PERSONAL QUESTION FOR YOU, KOICHI.
SMILE
YEAH?

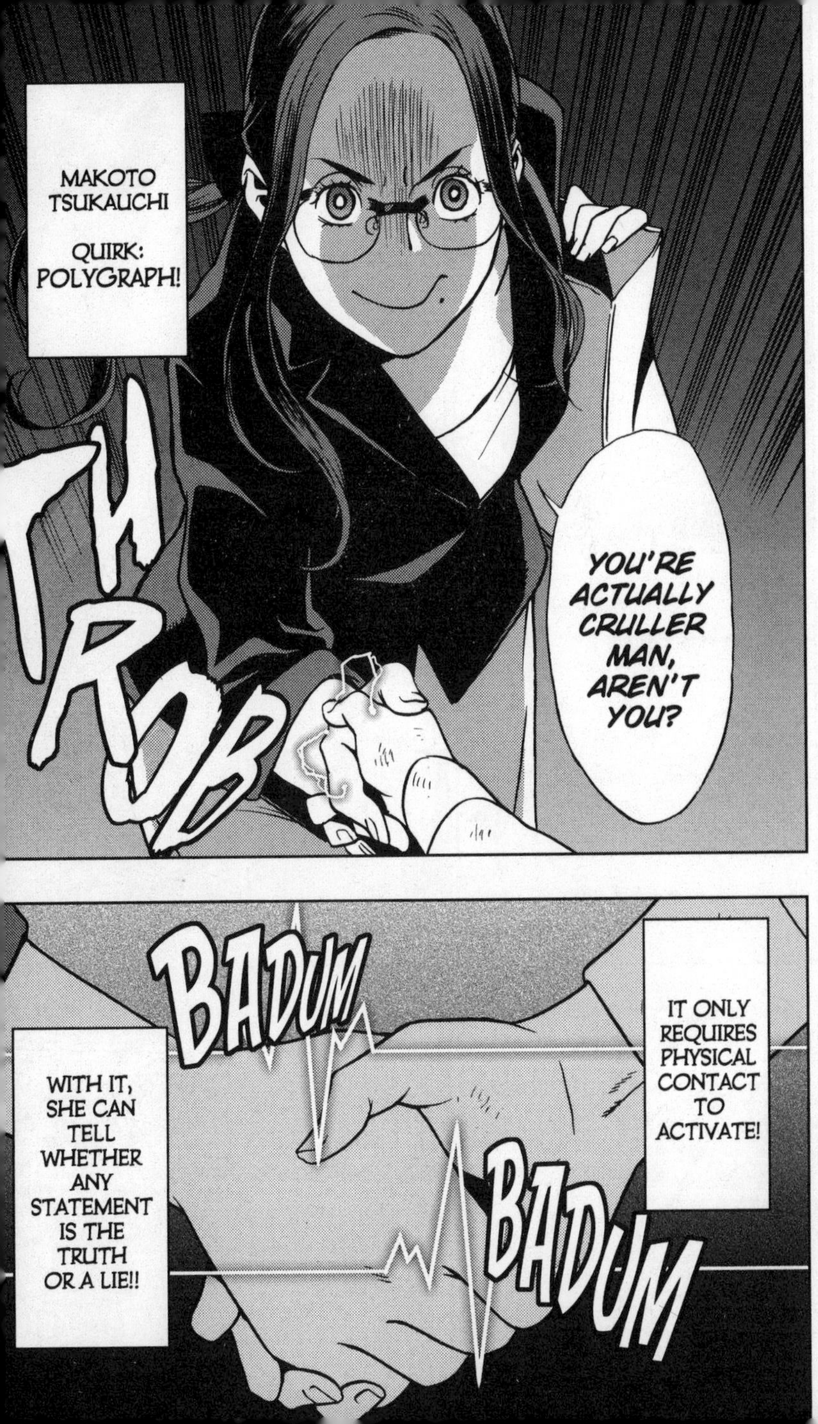
MAKOTO TSUKAUCHI

QUIRK: POLYGRAPH!
YOU'RE ACTUALLY CRULLER MAN, AREN'T YOU?
THROB
IT ONLY REQUIRES PHYSICAL CONTACT TO ACTIVATE!
BADUM
WITH IT, SHE CAN TELL WHETHER ANY STATEMENT IS THE TRUTH OR A LIE!!
BADUM

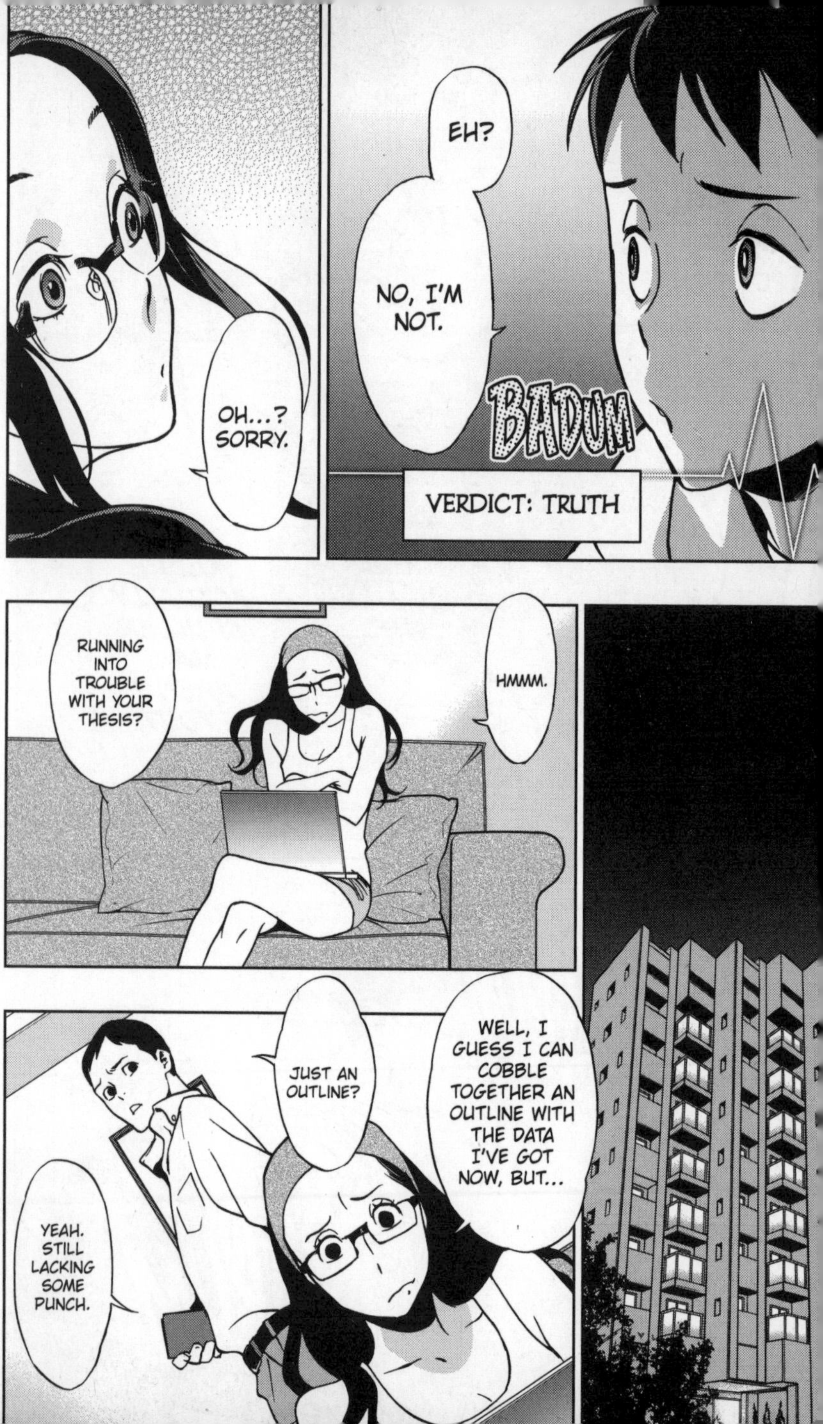
EH?
NO, I'M NOT.
BADUM
VERDICT: TRUTH
OH...? SORRY.
RUNNING INTO TROUBLE WITH YOUR THESIS?
HMMM.
WELL, I GUESS I CAN COBBLE TOGETHER AN OUTLINE WITH THE DATA I'VE GOT NOW, BUT...
JUST AN OUTLINE?
YEAH. STILL LACKING SOME PUNCH.

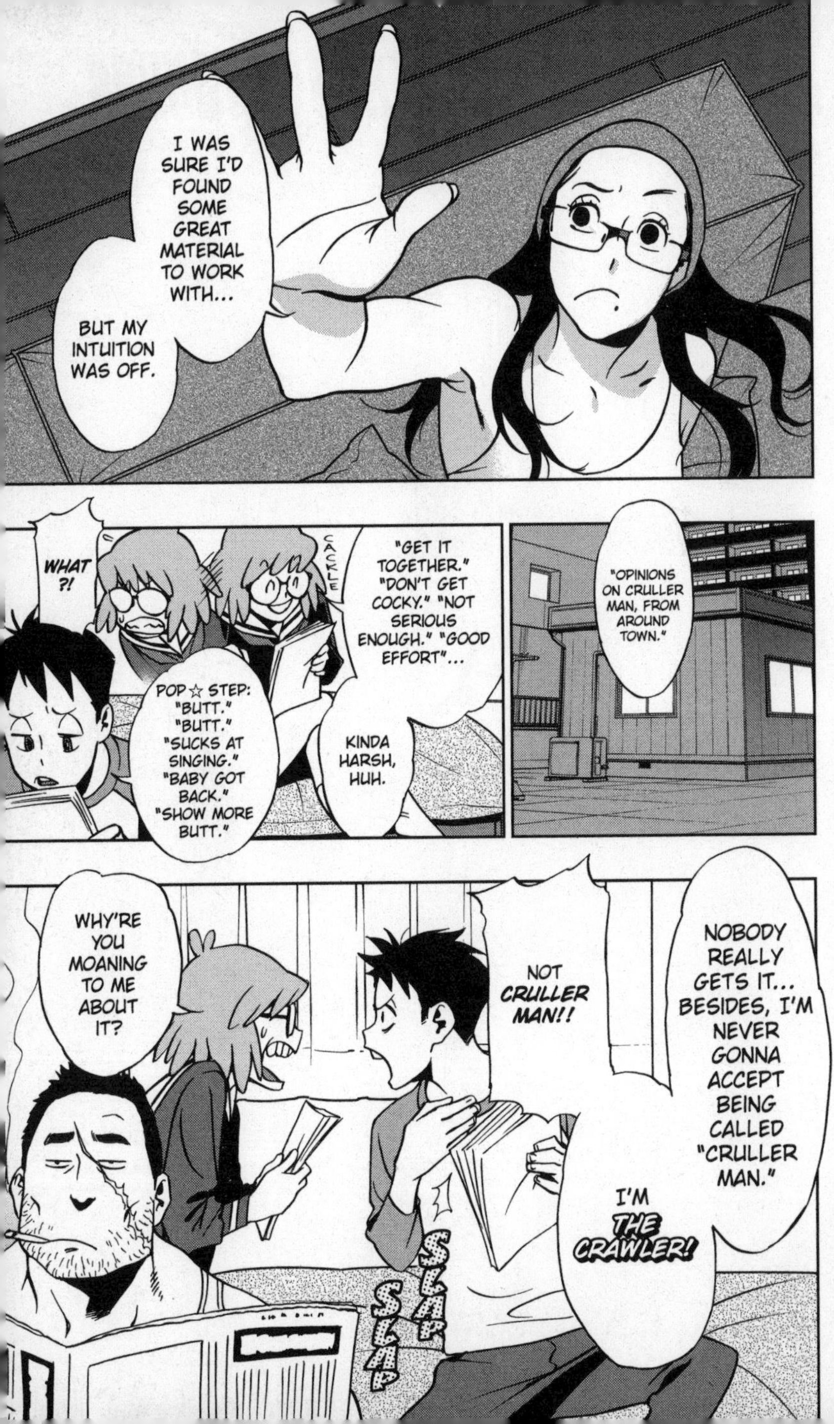
I WAS SURE I'D FOUND SOME GREAT MATERIAL TO WORK WITH...
BUT MY INTUITION WAS OFF.
"OPINIONS ON CRULLER MAN, FROM AROUND TOWN."
"GET IT TOGETHER." "DON'T GET COCKY." "NOT SERIOUS ENOUGH." "GOOD EFFORT"...
CACKLE
KINDA HARSH, HUH.
WHAT ?!
POP☆STEP: "BUTT." "BUTT." "SUCKS AT SINGING." "BABY GOT BACK." "SHOW MORE BUTT."
NOBODY REALLY GETS IT... BESIDES, I'M NEVER GONNA ACCEPT BEING CALLED "CRULLER MAN."
I'M THE CRAWLER!
NOT CRULLER MAN!!
WHY'RE YOU MOANING TO ME ABOUT IT?
SLAP
SLAP

SOCCER VILLAIN/EMPEROR YOTSUURA

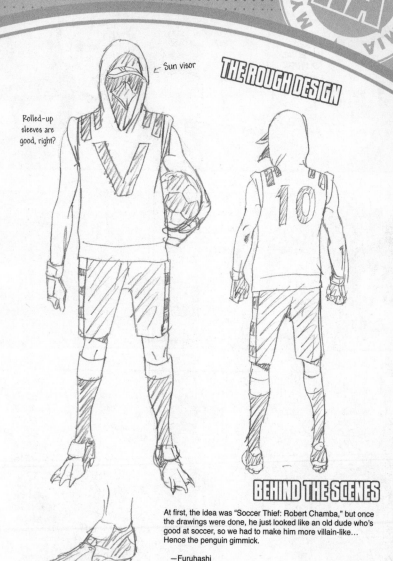

THE ROUGH DESIGN

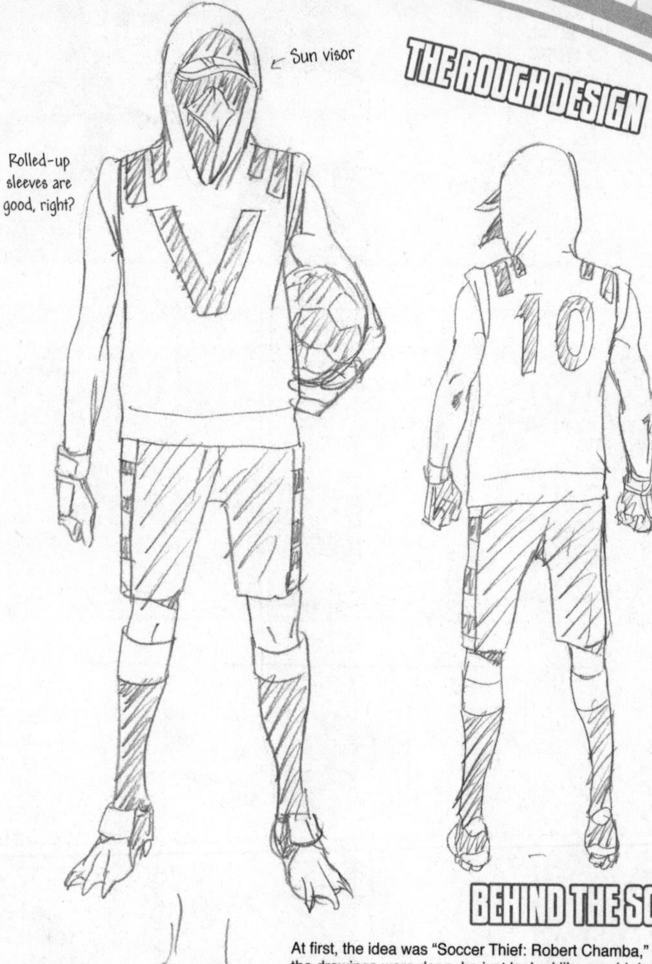
Sun visor
Rolled-up sleeves are good, right?

BEHIND THE SCENES

At first, the idea was "Soccer Thief: Robert Chamba," but once the drawings were done, he just looked like an old dude who's good at soccer, so we had to make him more villain-like… Hence the penguin gimmick.

—Furuhashi

This character went through a lot of redesigns. (LOL) From his name alone, I'm picturing a soccer-based character from some old fighting game.

—Betten

EP. 14 - MAJOR

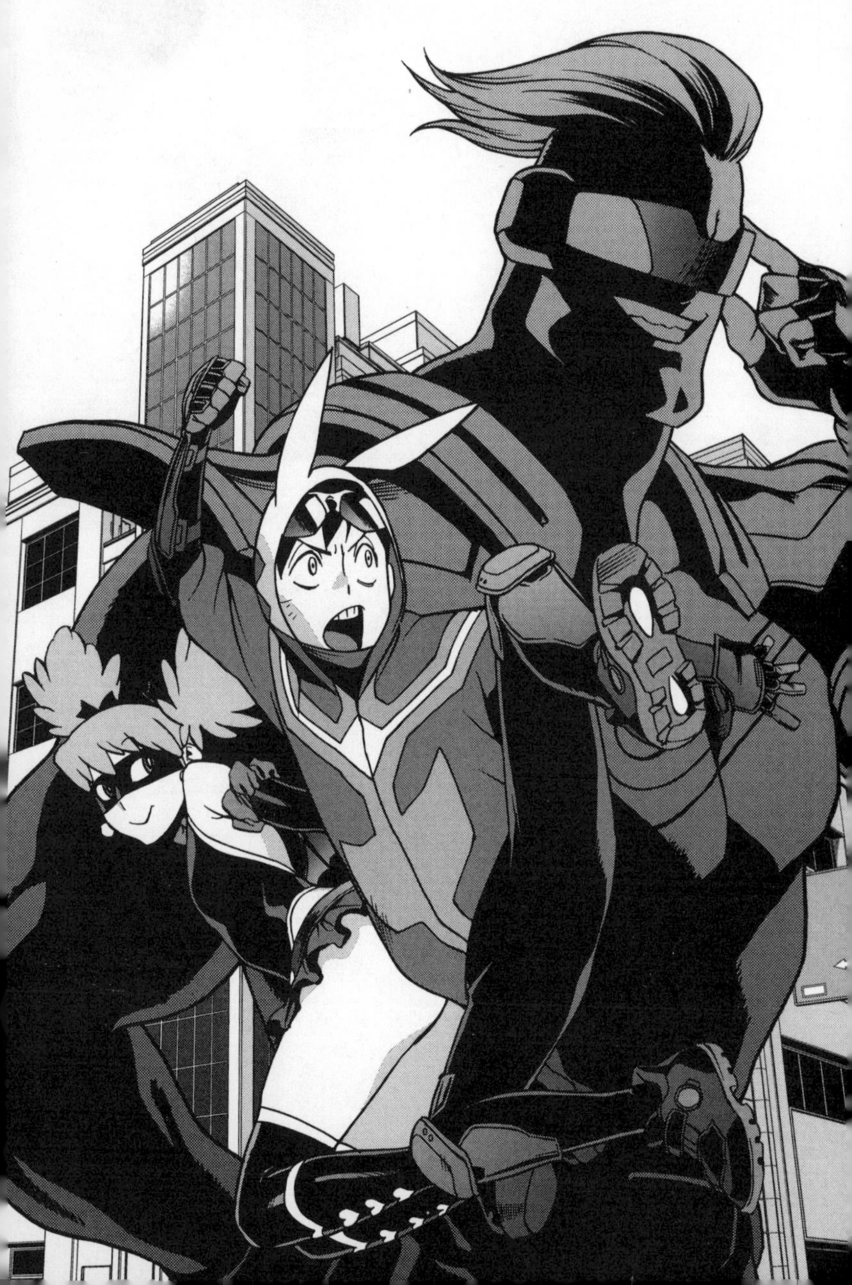

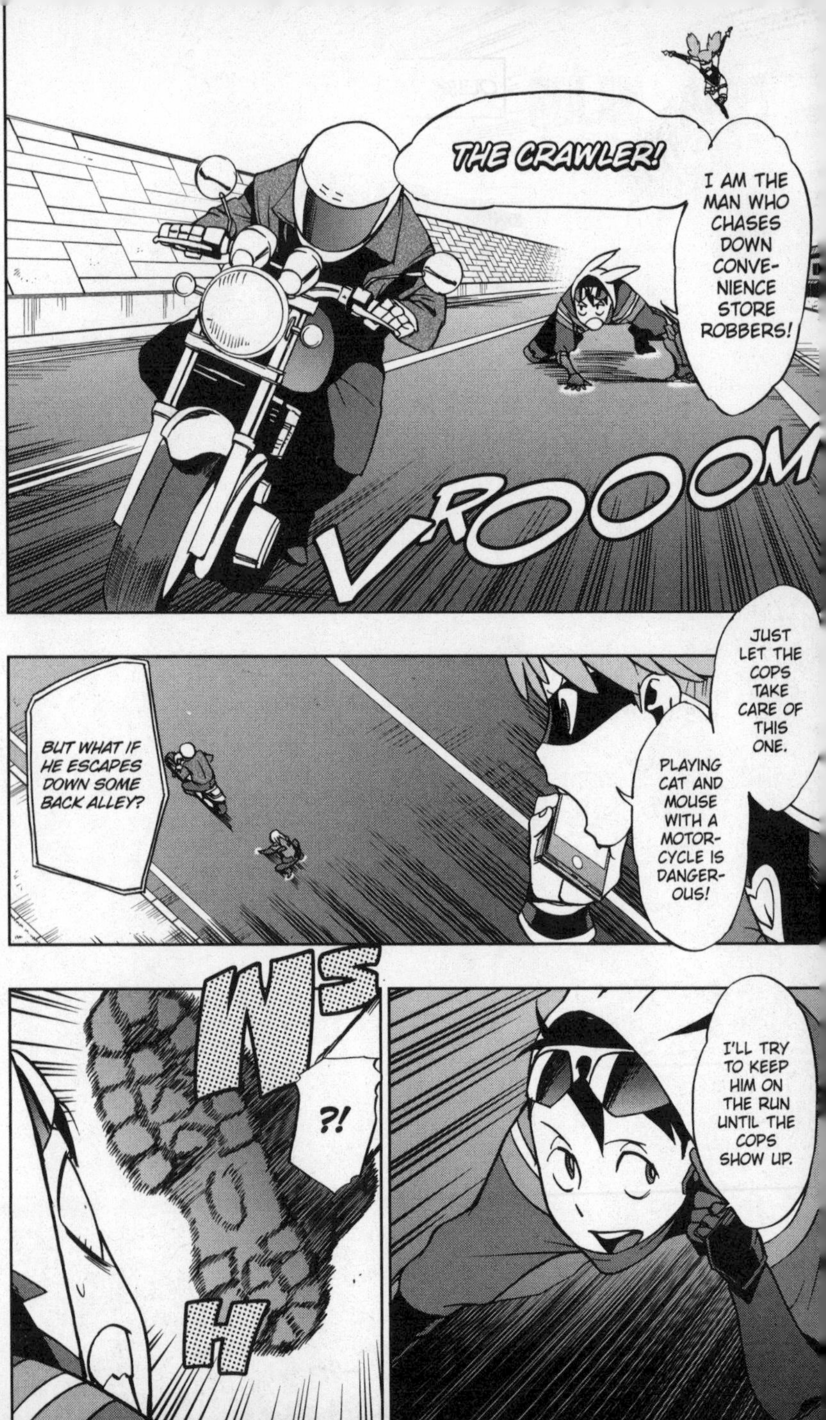
I AM THE MAN WHO CHASES DOWN CONVENIENCE STORE ROBBERS!
THE CRAWLER!
VROOOOM
JUST LET THE COPS TAKE CARE OF THIS ONE.
PLAYING CAT AND MOUSE WITH A MOTORCYCLE IS DANGEROUS!
BUT WHAT IF HE ESCAPES DOWN SOME BACK ALLEY?
I'LL TRY TO KEEP HIM ON THE RUN UNTIL THE COPS SHOW UP.
WISH
?!

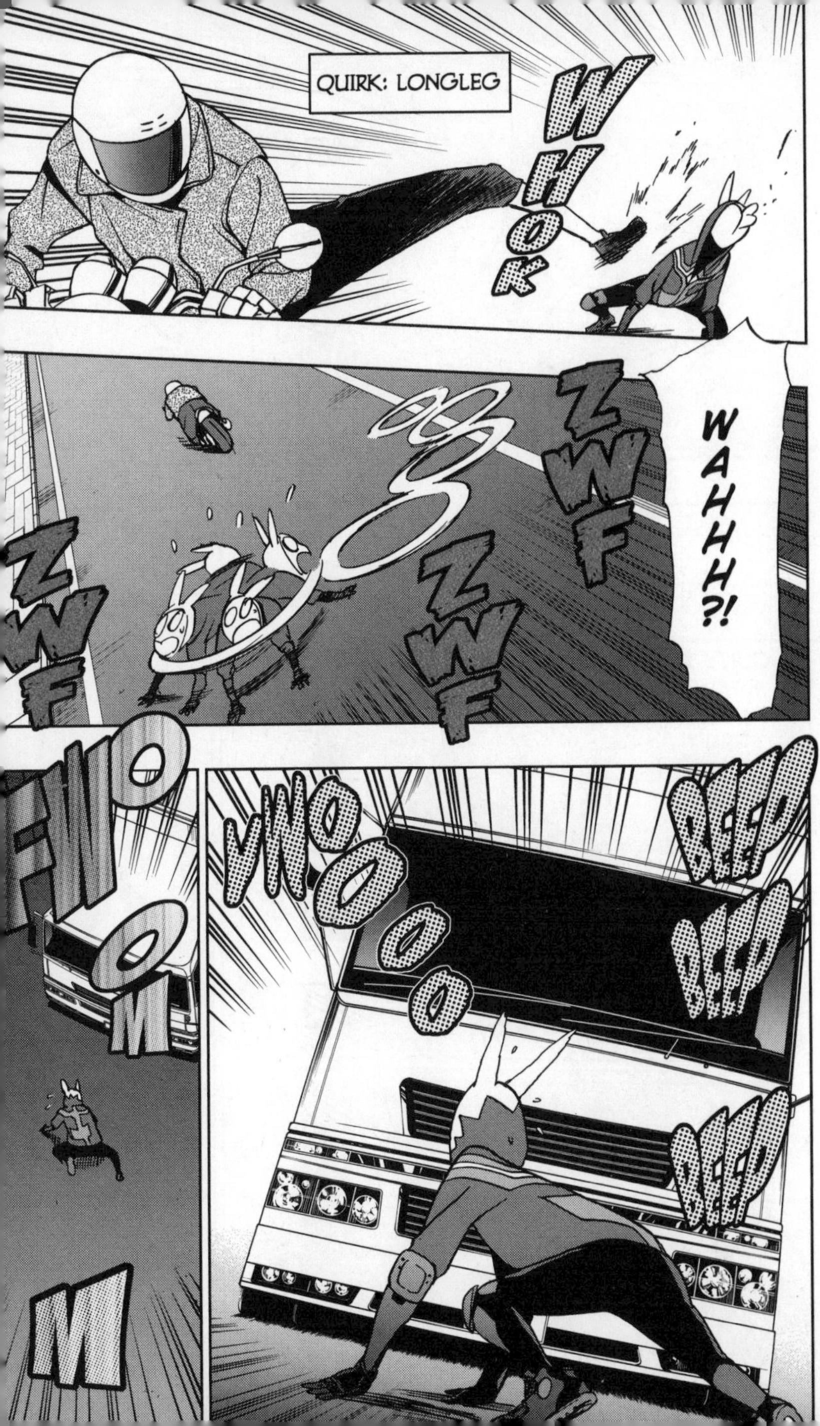
QUIRK: LONGLEG
WHHOK
WAHHHH?!
ZWF
ZWF
ZWF
BEEP
BEEP
BEEP
VWOOOOO
FWOOMM

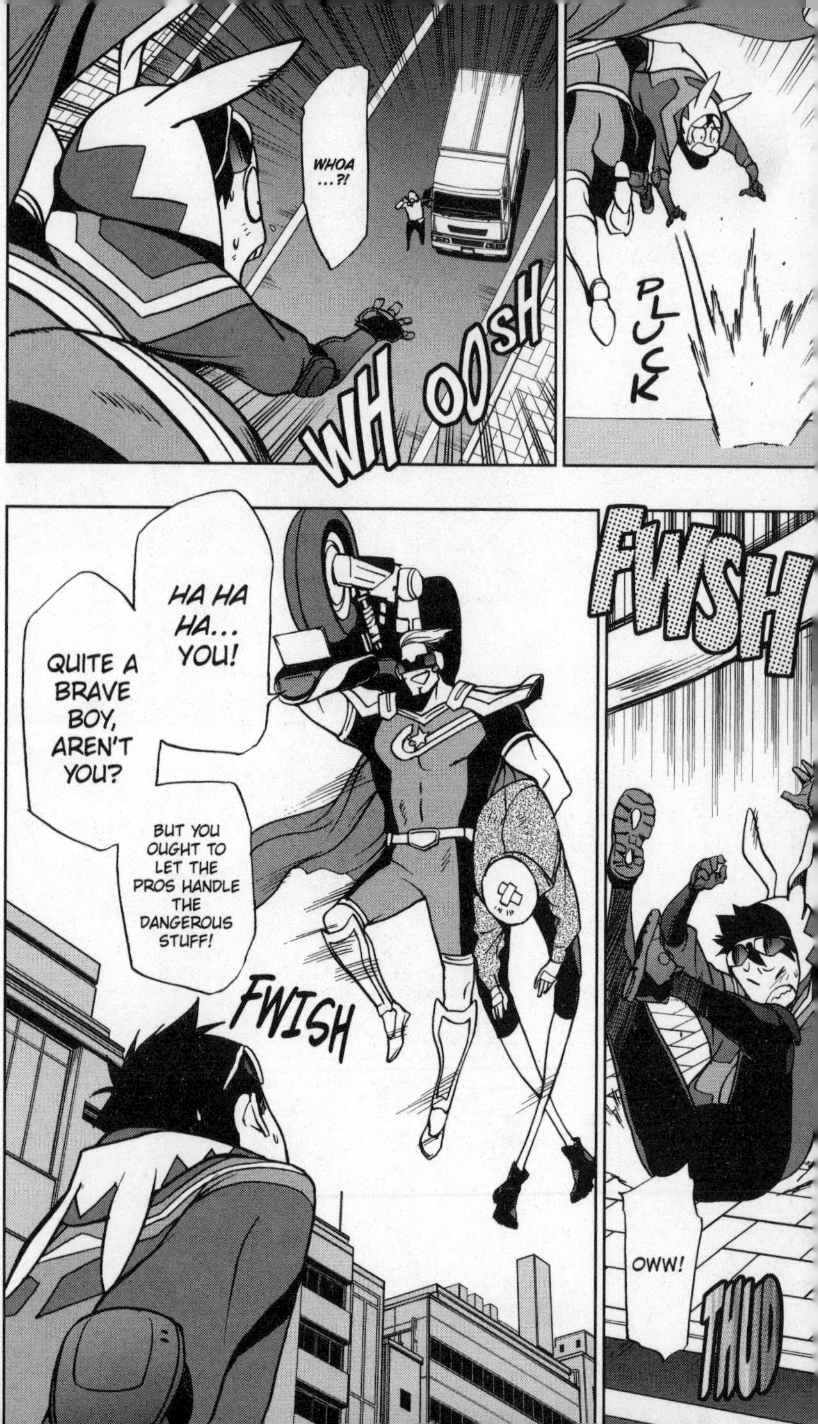
PLUCK
WHOA ...?!
WHOOSH
FWSH
OWW!
THUD
HA HA HA... YOU!
QUITE A BRAVE BOY, AREN'T YOU?
BUT YOU OUGHT TO LET THE PROS HANDLE THE DANGEROUS STUFF!
FWISH

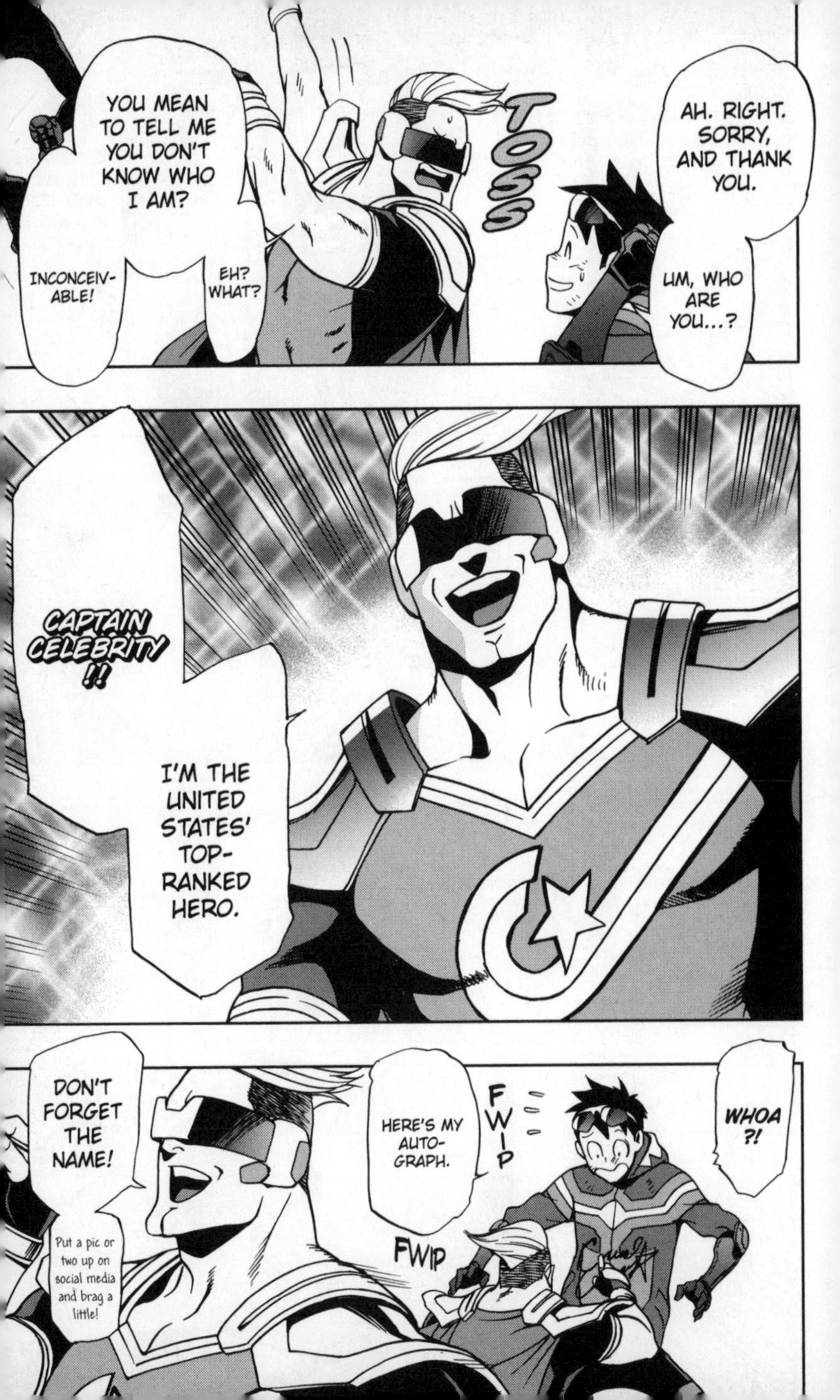
AH. RIGHT. SORRY, AND THANK YOU.
UM, WHO ARE YOU...?
TOSS
YOU MEAN TO TELL ME YOU DON'T KNOW WHO I AM?
EH? WHAT?
INCONCEIV-ABLE!
I'M THE UNITED STATES' TOP-RANKED HERO.
CAPTAIN CELEBRITY!!
WHOA?!
FWIP
HERE'S MY AUTO-GRAPH.
FWIP
DON'T FORGET THE NAME!
Put a pic or two up on social media and brag a little!

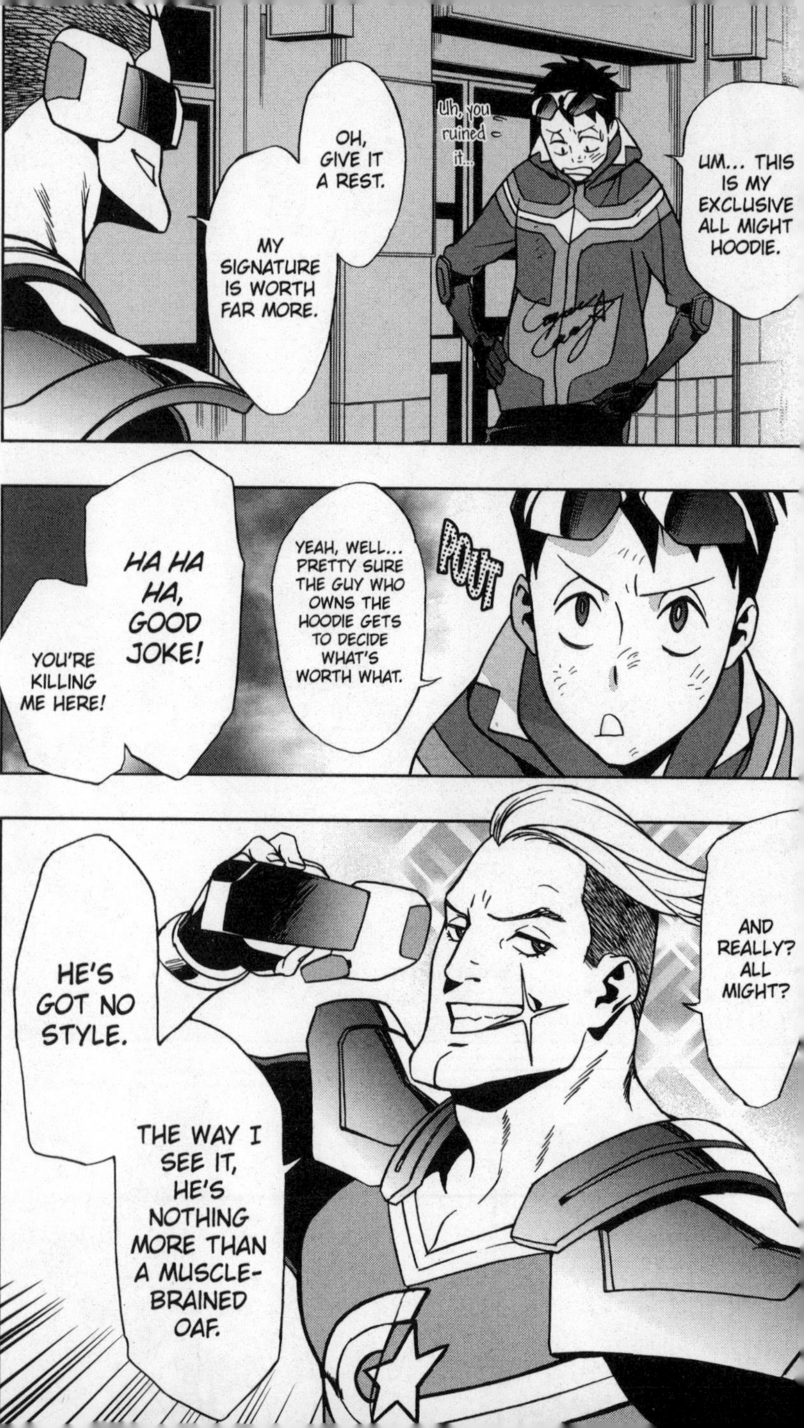
UM... THIS IS MY EXCLUSIVE ALL MIGHT HOODIE.
Uh, you ruined it...
OH, GIVE IT A REST.
MY SIGNATURE IS WORTH FAR MORE.
POUT
YEAH, WELL... PRETTY SURE THE GUY WHO OWNS THE HOODIE GETS TO DECIDE WHAT'S WORTH WHAT.
HA HA HA, GOOD JOKE!
YOU'RE KILLING ME HERE!
AND REALLY? ALL MIGHT?
HE'S GOT NO STYLE.
THE WAY I SEE IT, HE'S NOTHING MORE THAN A MUSCLE-BRAINED OAF.

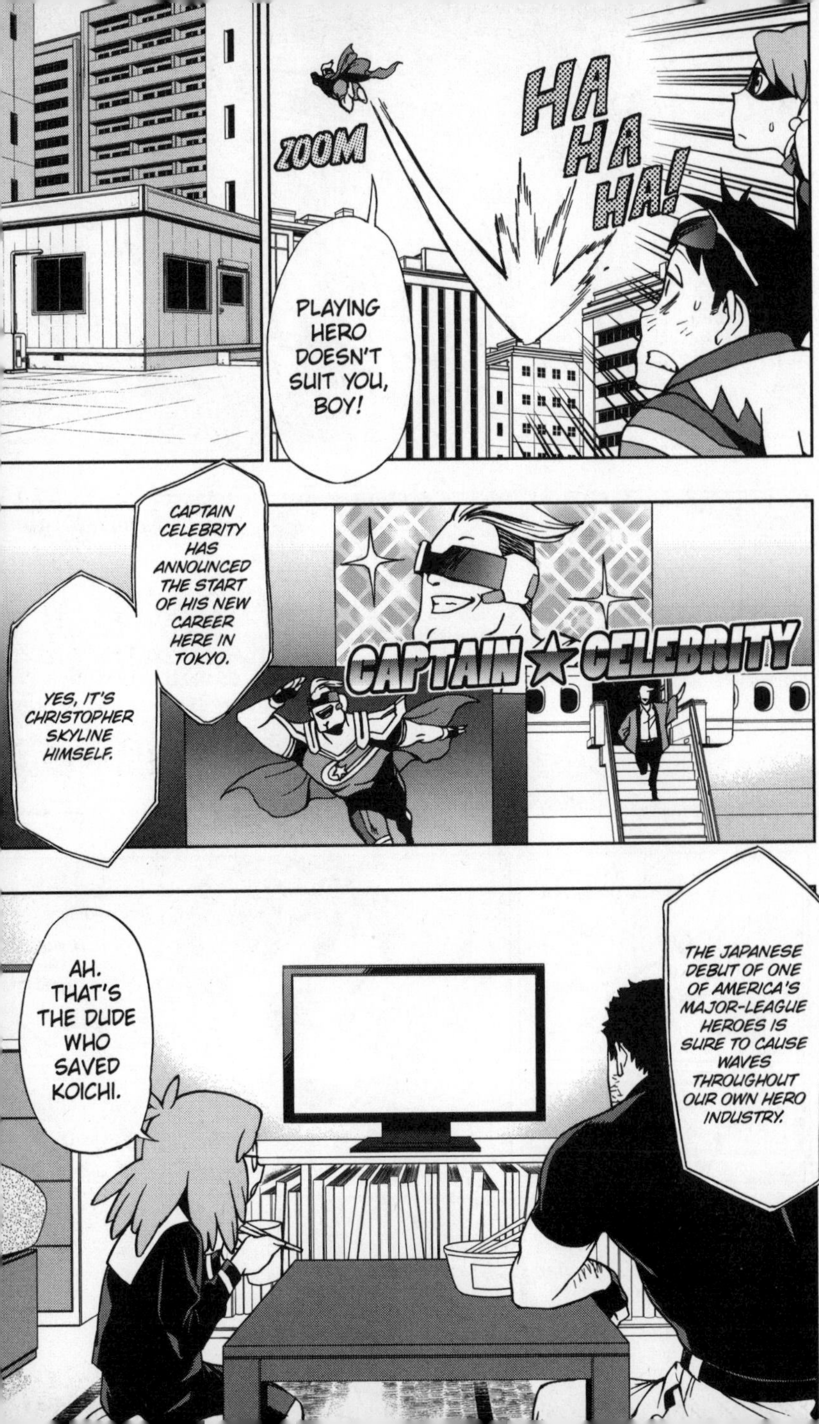
HA HA HA!
ZOOM
PLAYING HERO DOESN'T SUIT YOU, BOY!
CAPTAIN CELEBRITY HAS ANNOUNCED THE START OF HIS NEW CAREER HERE IN TOKYO.
CAPTAIN ☆ CELEBRITY
YES, IT'S CHRISTOPHER SKYLINE HIMSELF.
THE JAPANESE DEBUT OF ONE OF AMERICA'S MAJOR-LEAGUE HEROES IS SURE TO CAUSE WAVES THROUGHOUT OUR OWN HERO INDUSTRY.
AH. THAT'S THE DUDE WHO SAVED KOICHI.

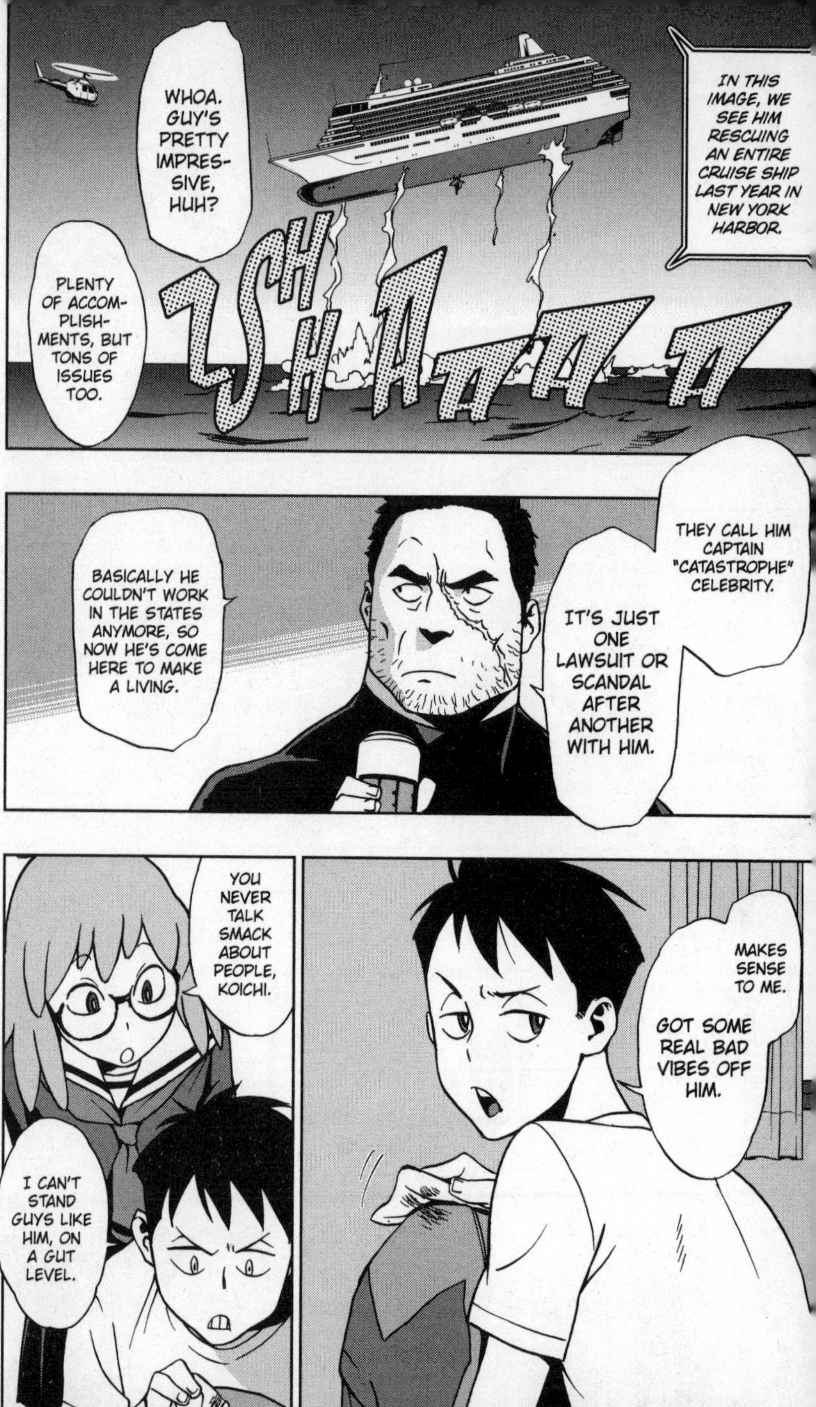

IN THIS IMAGE, WE SEE HIM RESCUING AN ENTIRE CRUISE SHIP LAST YEAR IN NEW YORK HARBOR.
WHOA. GUY'S PRETTY IMPRES-SIVE, HUH?
PLENTY OF ACCOM-PLISH-MENTS, BUT TONS OF ISSUES TOO.
THEY CALL HIM CAPTAIN "CATASTROPHE" CELEBRITY.
IT'S JUST ONE LAWSUIT OR SCANDAL AFTER ANOTHER WITH HIM.
BASICALLY HE COULDN'T WORK IN THE STATES ANYMORE, SO NOW HE'S COME HERE TO MAKE A LIVING.
MAKES SENSE TO ME.
GOT SOME REAL BAD VIBES OFF HIM.
YOU NEVER TALK SMACK ABOUT PEOPLE, KOICHI.
I CAN'T STAND GUYS LIKE HIM, ON A GUT LEVEL.

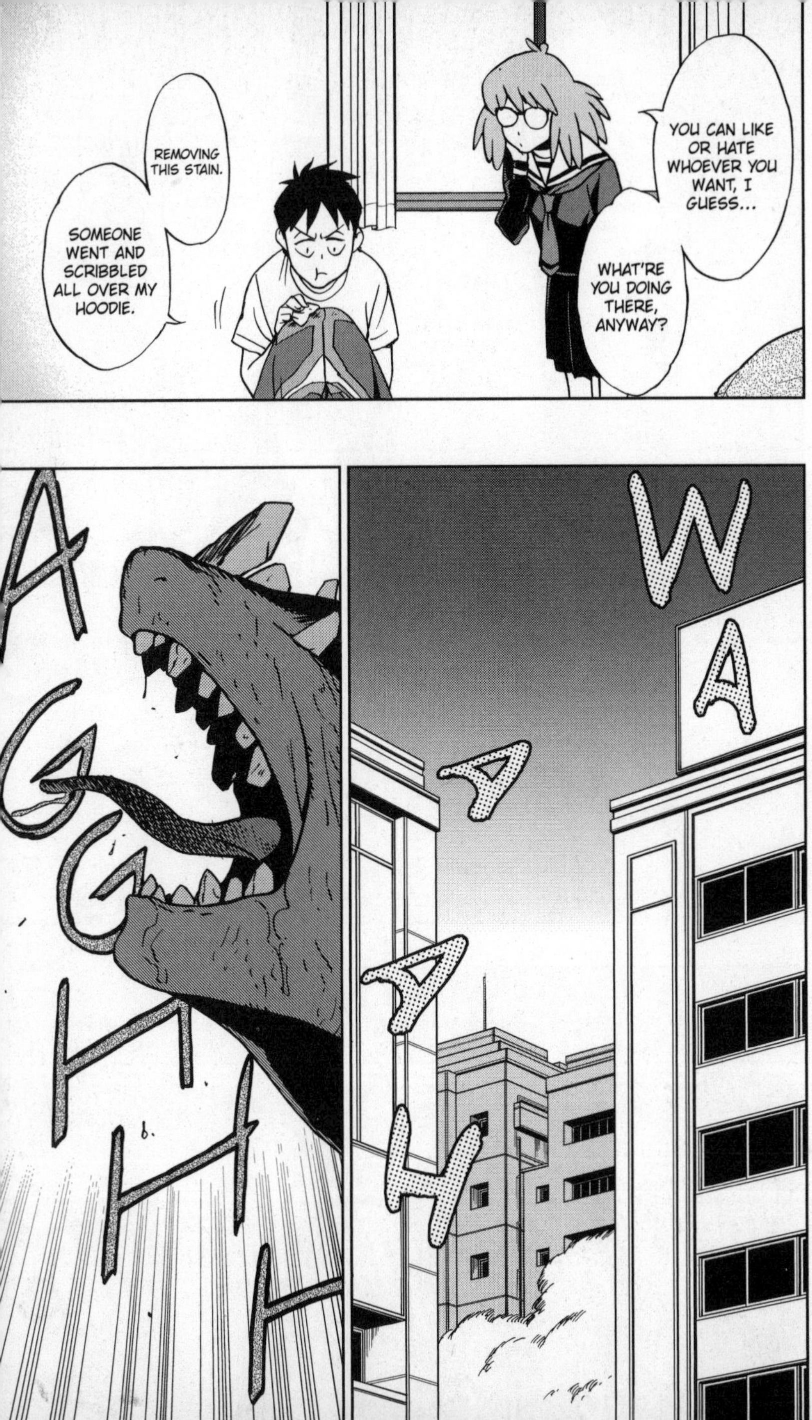
YOU CAN LIKE OR HATE WHOEVER YOU WANT, I GUESS...
WHAT'RE YOU DOING THERE, ANYWAY?
REMOVING THIS STAIN.
SOMEONE WENT AND SCRIBBLED ALL OVER MY HOODIE.
WAAAH
AGGHHH

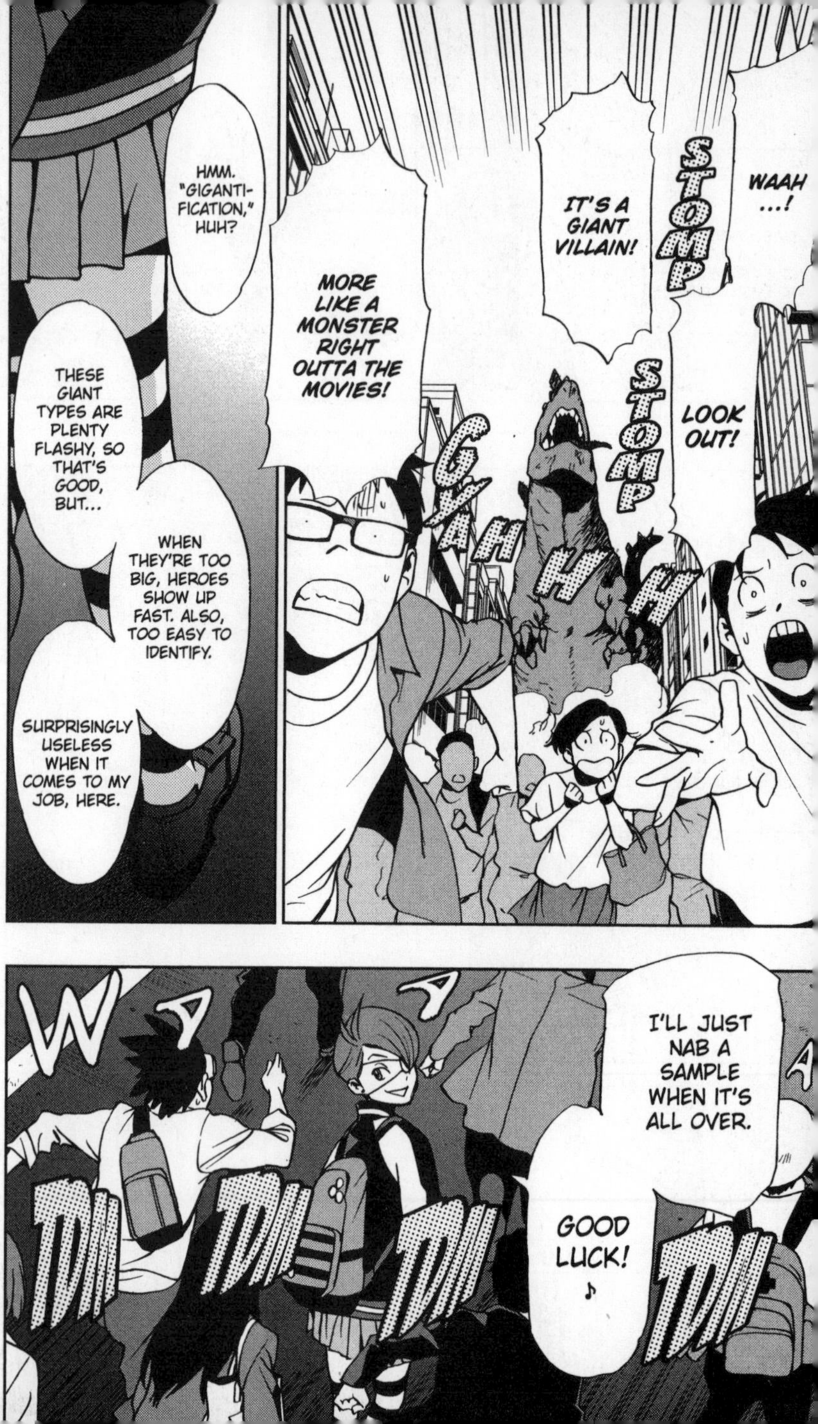
WAAH ...!
STOMP
IT'S A GIANT VILLAIN!
LOOK OUT!
STOMP
MORE LIKE A MONSTER RIGHT OUTTA THE MOVIES!
GYAHHHH
HMM. "GIGANTI-FICATION," HUH?
THESE GIANT TYPES ARE PLENTY FLASHY, SO THAT'S GOOD, BUT...
WHEN THEY'RE TOO BIG, HEROES SHOW UP FAST. ALSO, TOO EASY TO IDENTIFY.
SURPRISINGLY USELESS WHEN IT COMES TO MY JOB, HERE.
WAA
I'LL JUST NAB A SAMPLE WHEN IT'S ALL OVER.
GOOD LUCK! ♪

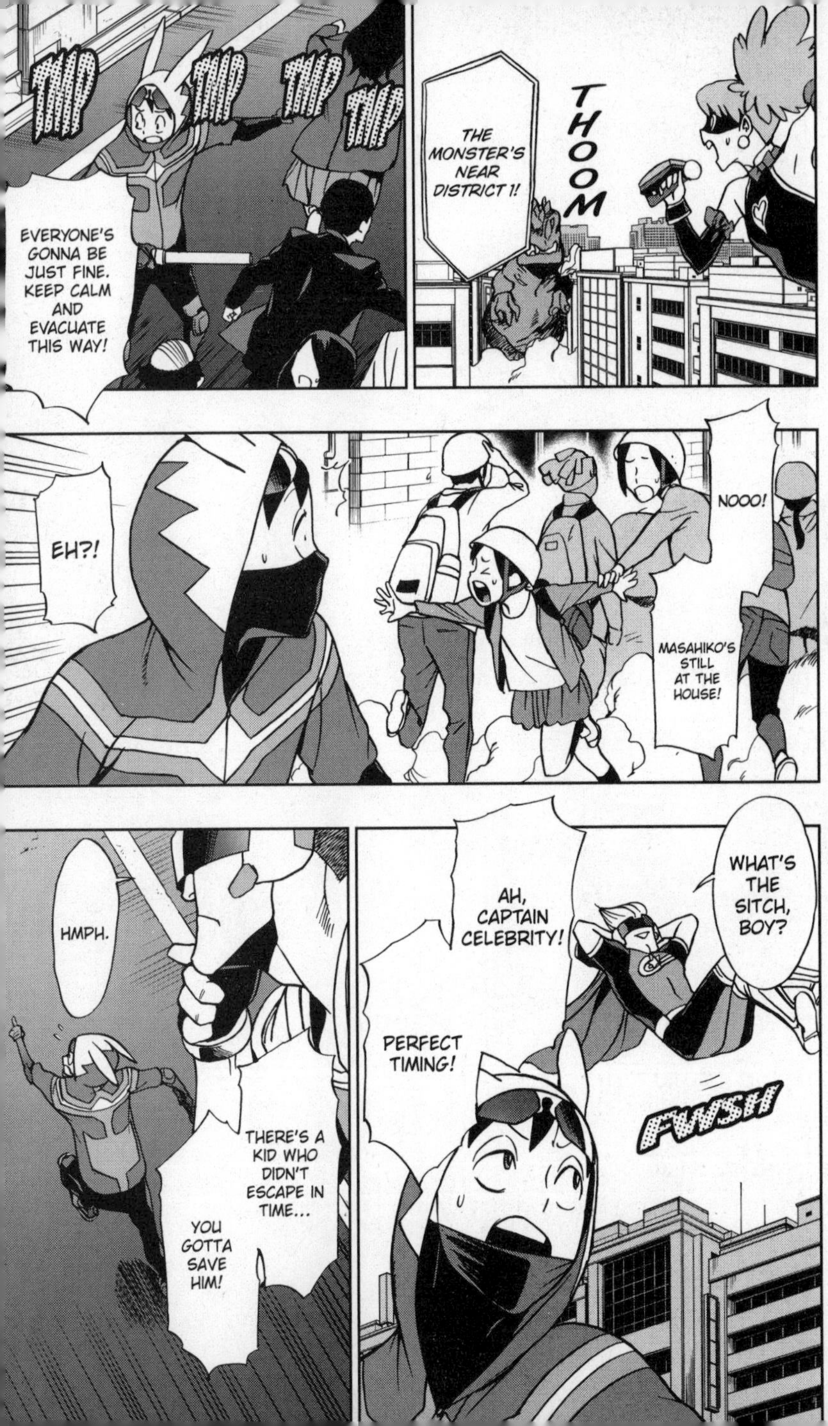
THOOM
THE MONSTER'S NEAR DISTRICT 1!
THP THP THP THP
EVERYONE'S GONNA BE JUST FINE. KEEP CALM AND EVACUATE THIS WAY!
NOOO!
MASAHIKO'S STILL AT THE HOUSE!
EH?!
WHAT'S THE SITCH, BOY?
AH, CAPTAIN CELEBRITY!
PERFECT TIMING!
FWSH
HMPH.
THERE'S A KID WHO DIDN'T ESCAPE IN TIME...
YOU GOTTA SAVE HIM!

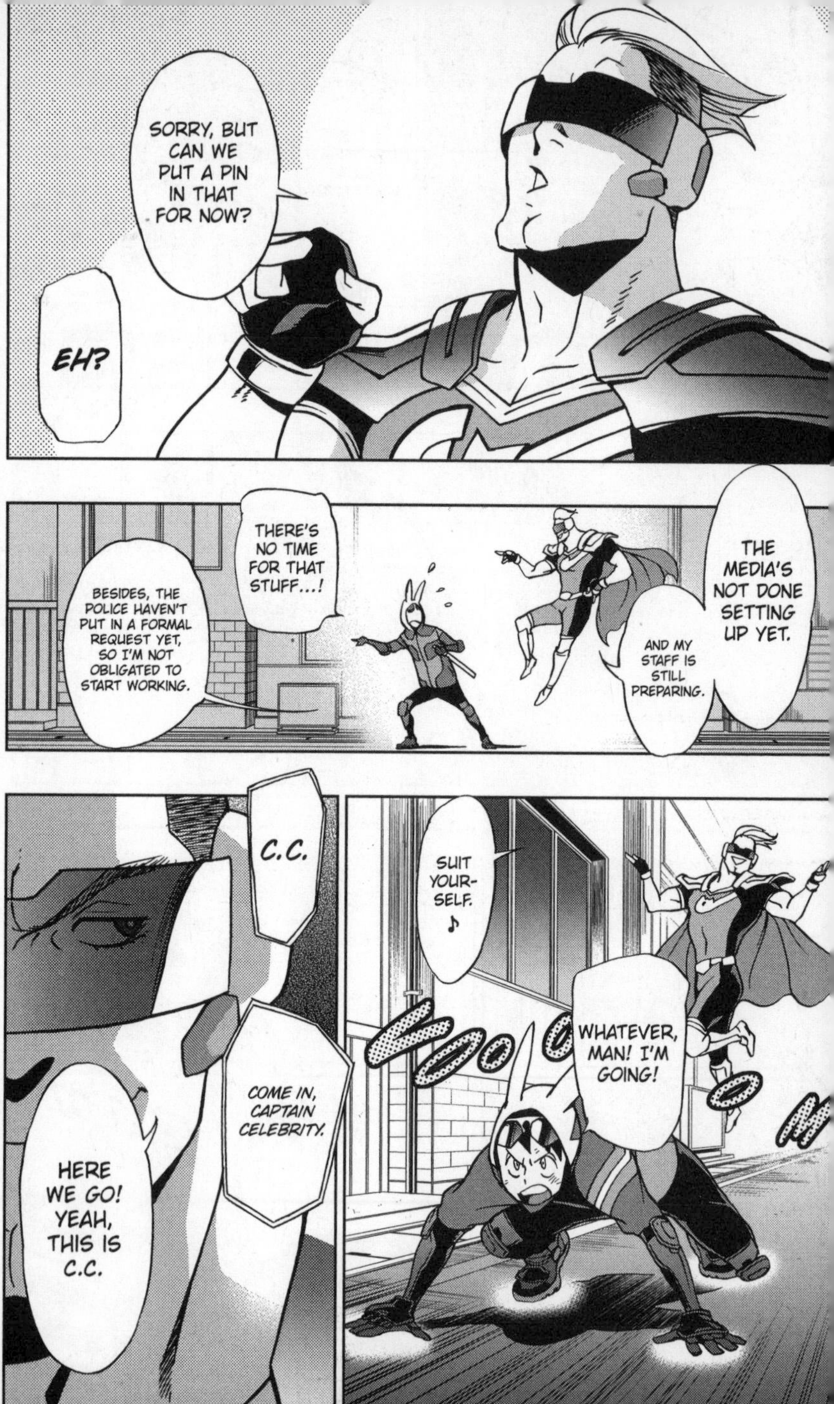
SORRY, BUT CAN WE PUT A PIN IN THAT FOR NOW?
EH?
THE MEDIA'S NOT DONE SETTING UP YET.
AND MY STAFF IS STILL PREPARING.
THERE'S NO TIME FOR THAT STUFF...!
BESIDES, THE POLICE HAVEN'T PUT IN A FORMAL REQUEST YET, SO I'M NOT OBLIGATED TO START WORKING.
SUIT YOURSELF. ♪
WHATEVER, MAN! I'M GOING!
C.C.
COME IN, CAPTAIN CELEBRITY.
HERE WE GO! YEAH, THIS IS C.C.

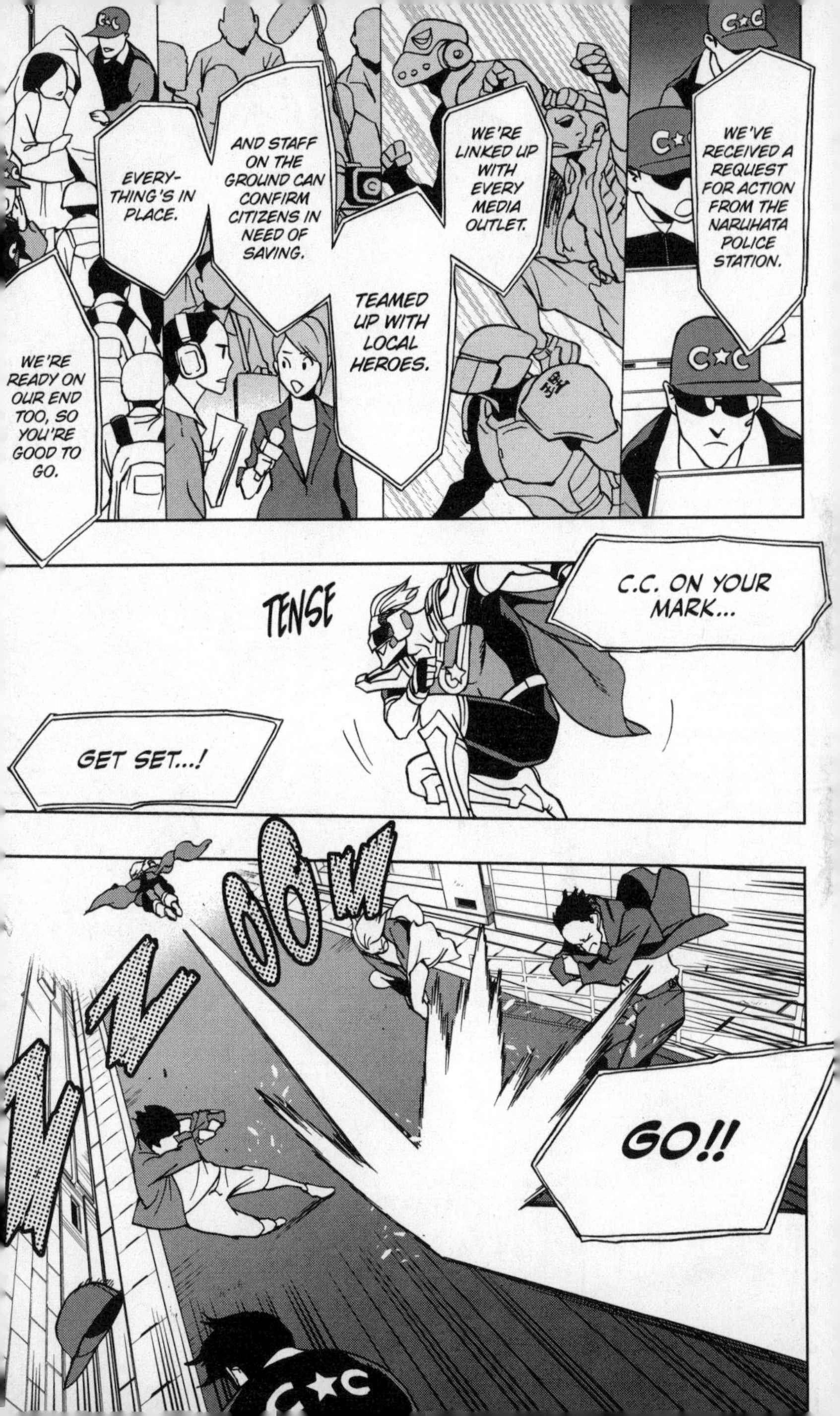
WE'VE RECEIVED A REQUEST FOR ACTION FROM THE NARUHATA POLICE STATION.
WE'RE LINKED UP WITH EVERY MEDIA OUTLET.
TEAMED UP WITH LOCAL HEROES.
AND STAFF ON THE GROUND CAN CONFIRM CITIZENS IN NEED OF SAVING.
EVERYTHING'S IN PLACE.
WE'RE READY ON OUR END TOO, SO YOU'RE GOOD TO GO.
C.C. ON YOUR MARK...
TENSE
GET SET...!
GO!!
ZOOOM

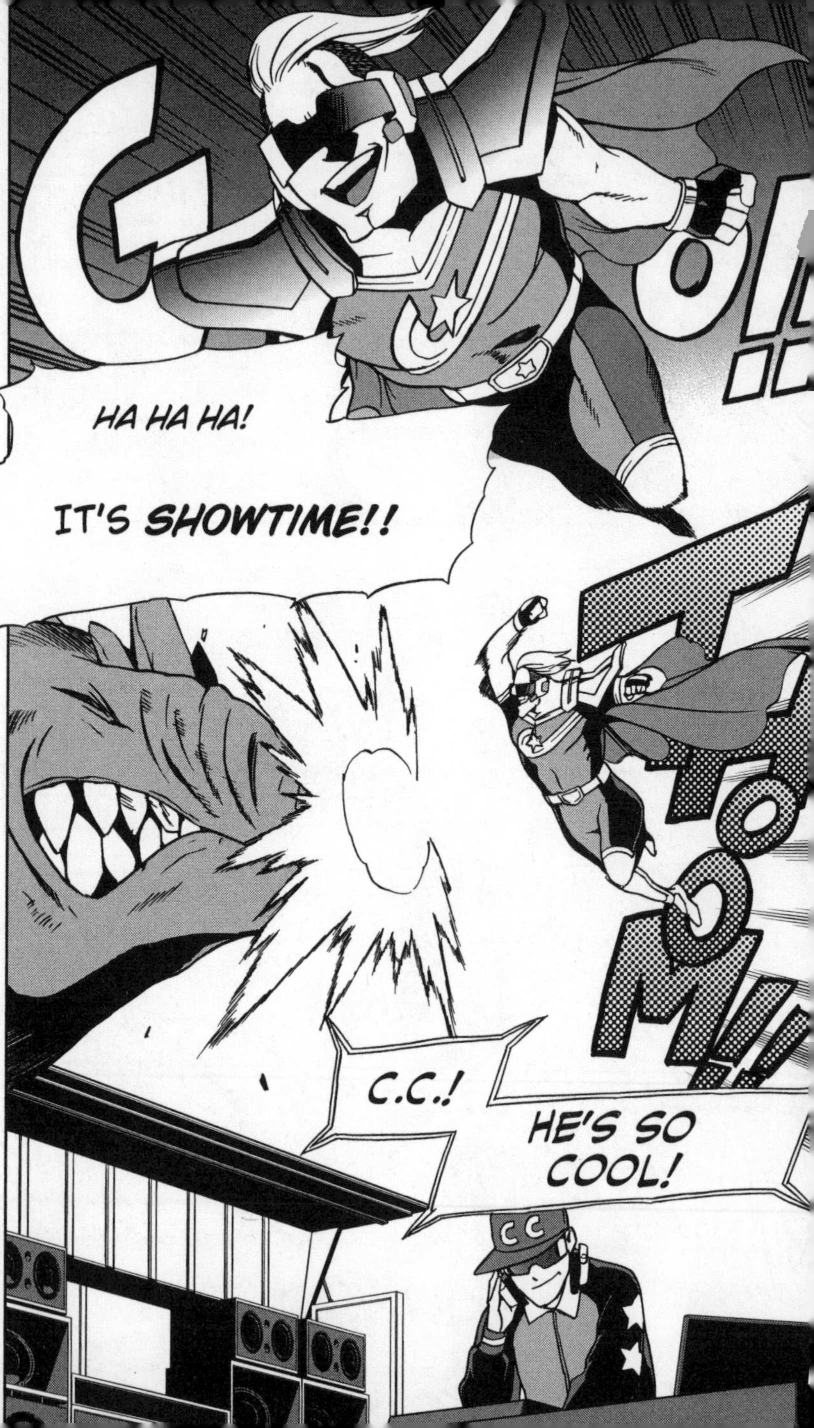
HA HA HA!
IT'S SHOWTIME!!
TOOM!!
HE'S SO COOL!
C.C.!

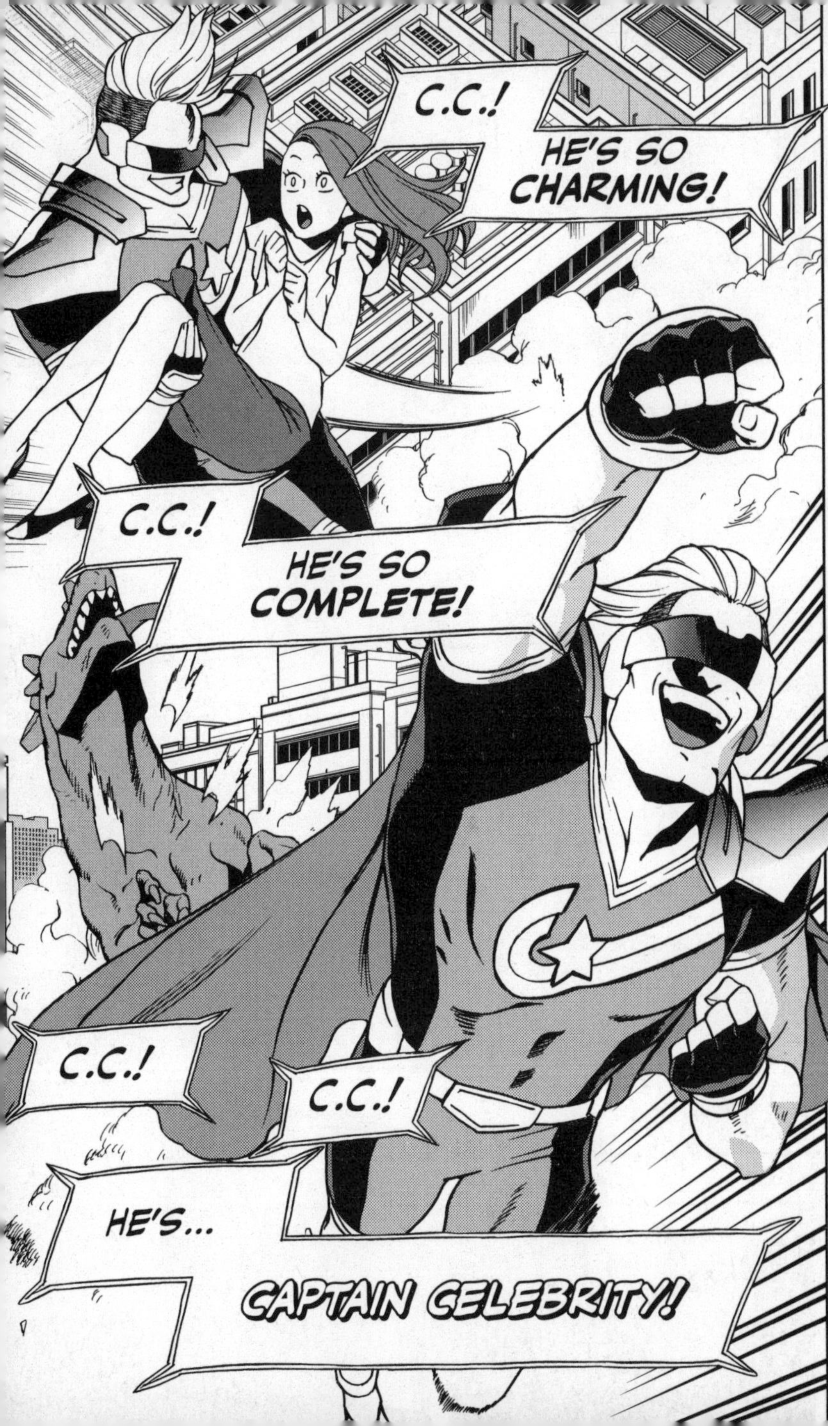
C.C.!
HE'S SO CHARMING!
C.C.!
HE'S SO COMPLETE!
C.C.!
C.C.!
HE'S...
CAPTAIN CELEBRITY!

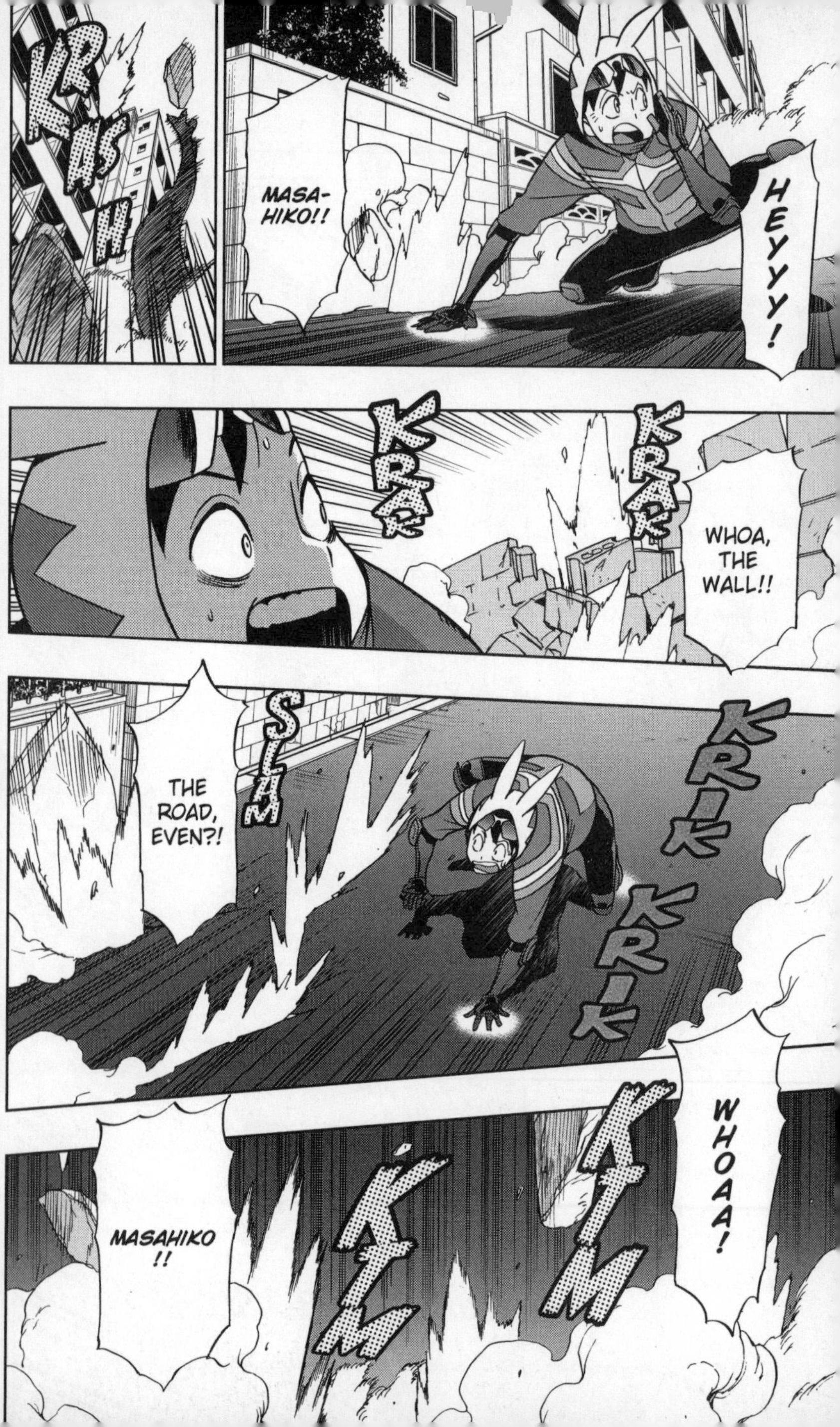
HEYYY!
MASA-HIKO!!
KRASH
WHOA, THE WALL!!
KRAK
KRAK
KRIK
KRIK
SLAM
THE ROAD, EVEN?!
WHOAA!
KTM
KTM
MASAHIKO!!

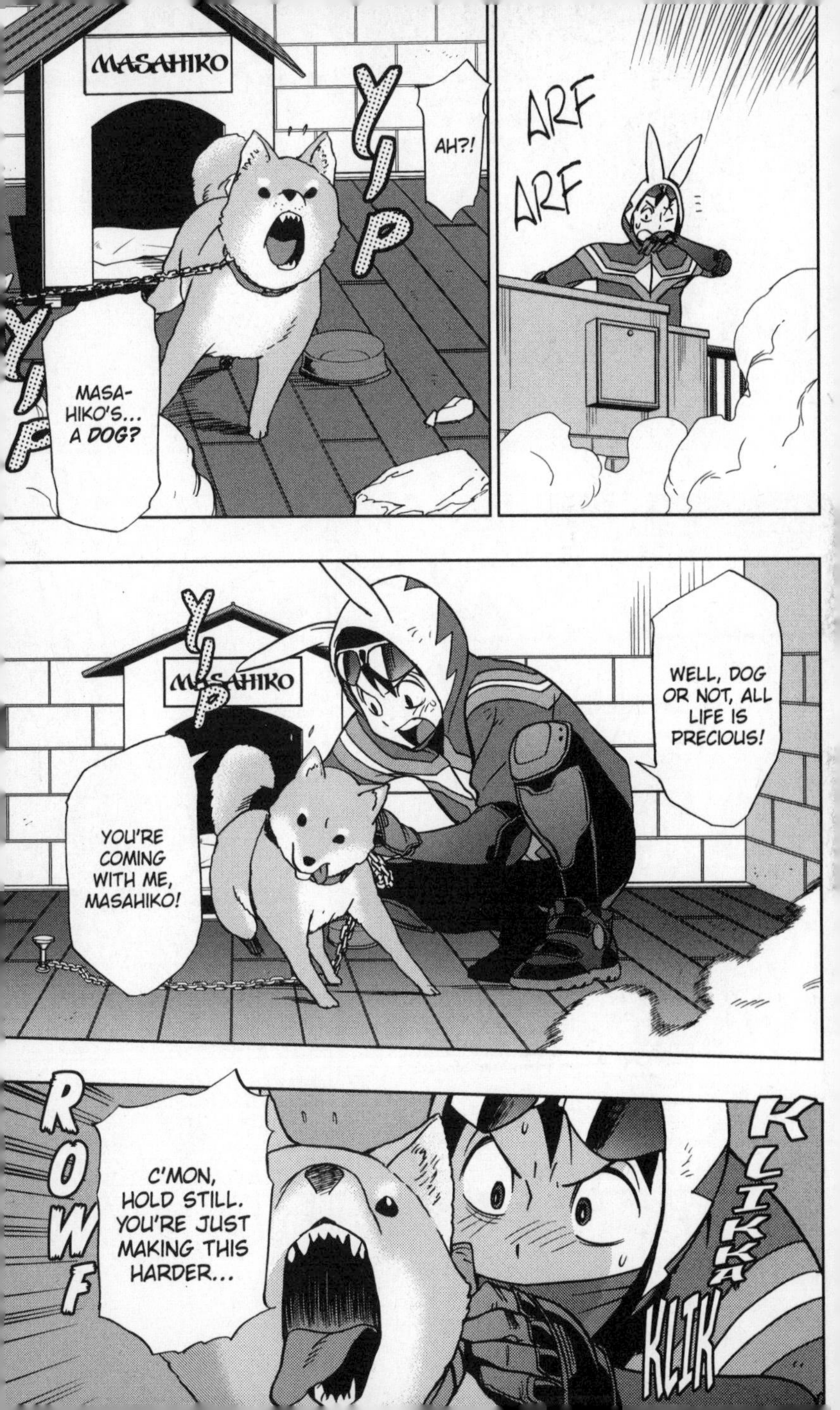
ARF
ARF
AH?!
YIP
MASAHIKO
YIP
MASA-HIKO'S... A *DOG*?
WELL, DOG OR NOT, ALL LIFE IS PRECIOUS!
YIP
MASAHIKO
YOU'RE COMING WITH ME, MASAHIKO!
KLIKKA
KLIK
C'MON, HOLD STILL. YOU'RE JUST MAKING THIS HARDER...
ROWF

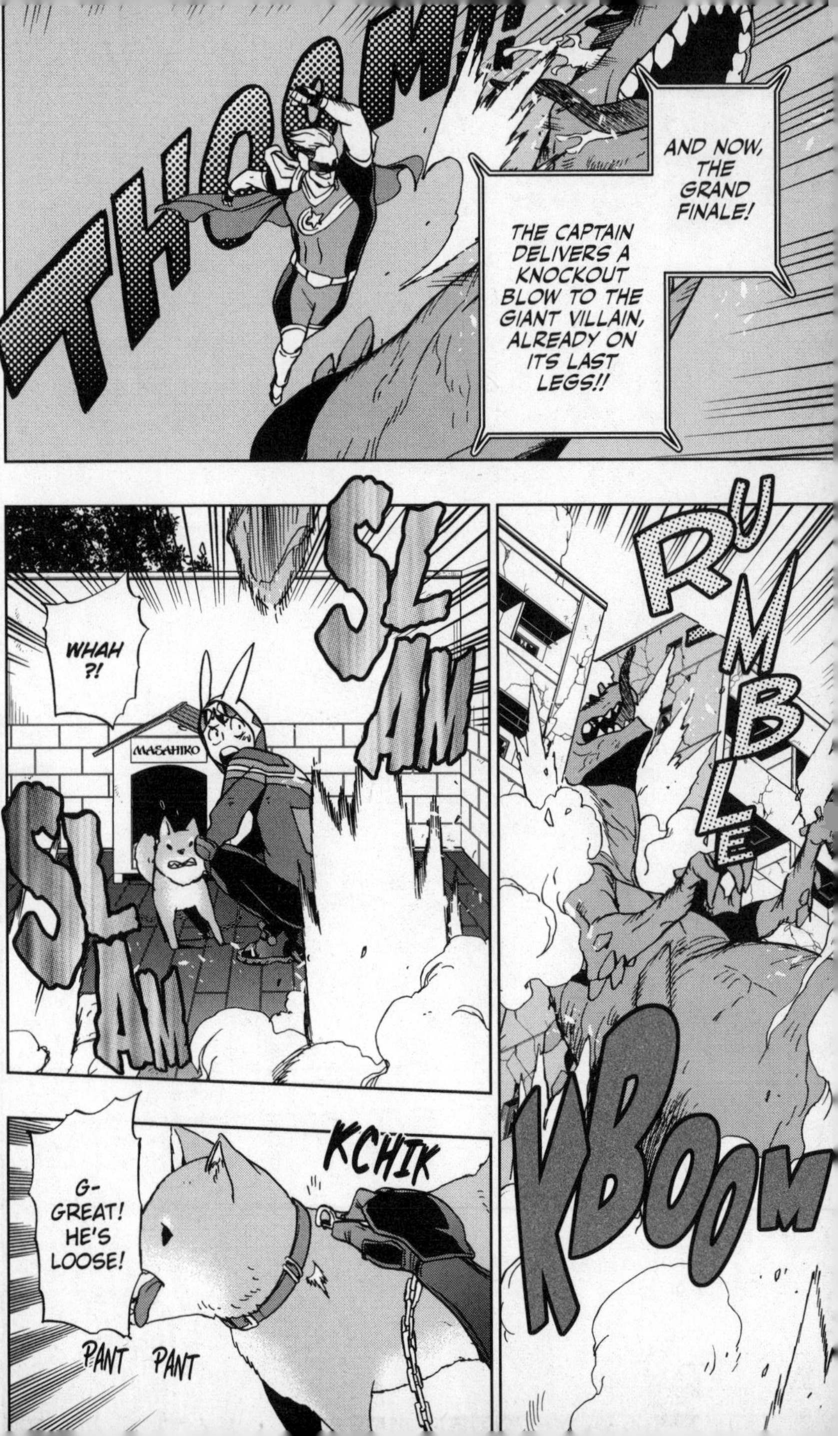
AND NOW, THE GRAND FINALE!
THE CAPTAIN DELIVERS A KNOCKOUT BLOW TO THE GIANT VILLAIN, ALREADY ON ITS LAST LEGS!!
THOOM!!
RUMBLE
KBOOM
SLAM
WHAH?!
MASAHIKO
SLAM
KCHIK
G-GREAT! HE'S LOOSE!
PANT PANT

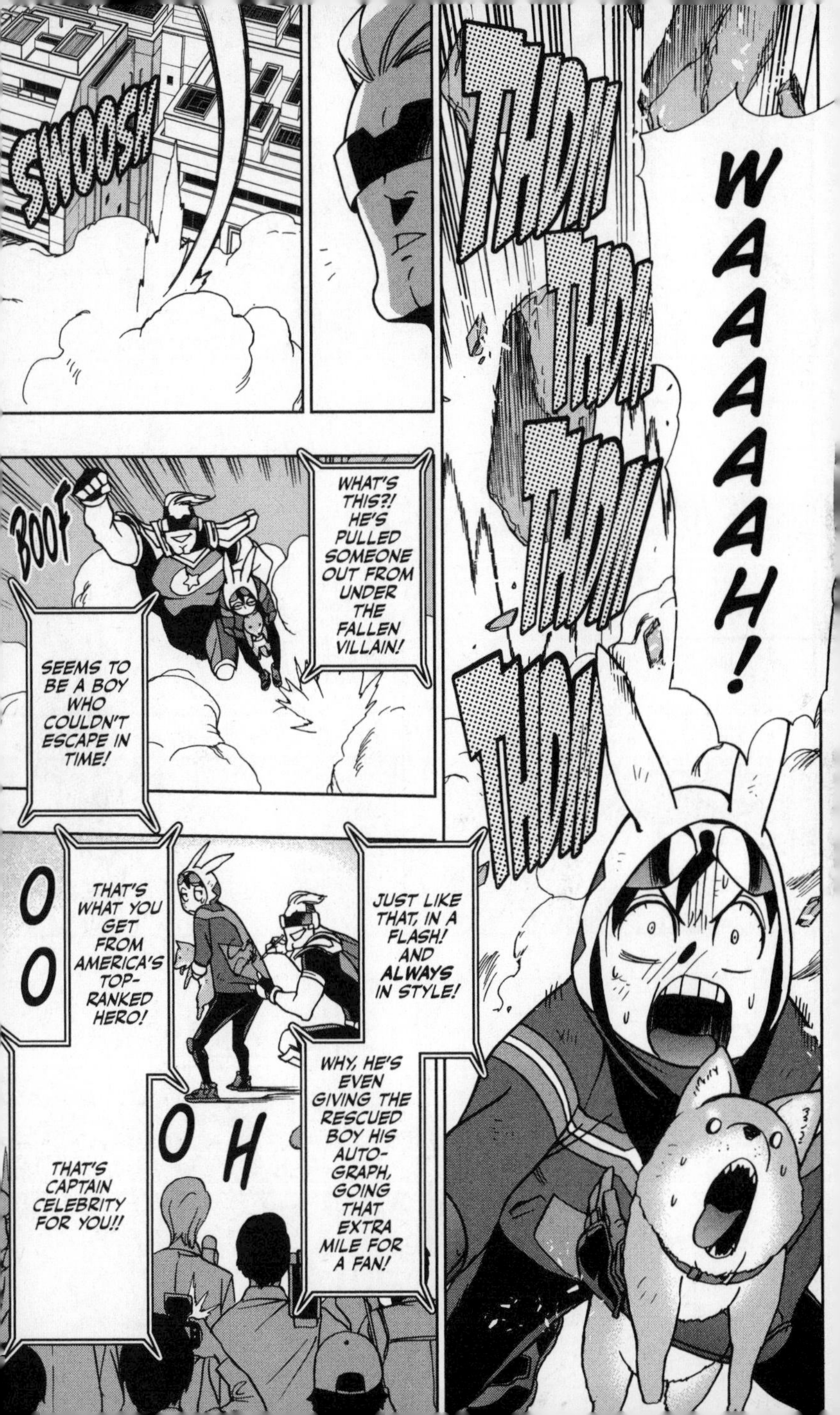
THOM
THOM
THOM
THOM
WAAAAAH!
SWOOSH
BOOF
WHAT'S THIS?! HE'S PULLED SOMEONE OUT FROM UNDER THE FALLEN VILLAIN!
SEEMS TO BE A BOY WHO COULDN'T ESCAPE IN TIME!
JUST LIKE THAT, IN A FLASH! AND **ALWAYS** IN STYLE!
THAT'S WHAT YOU GET FROM AMERICA'S TOP-RANKED HERO!
OOOH
WHY, HE'S EVEN GIVING THE RESCUED BOY HIS AUTO-GRAPH, GOING THAT EXTRA MILE FOR A FAN!
THAT'S CAPTAIN CELEBRITY FOR YOU!!

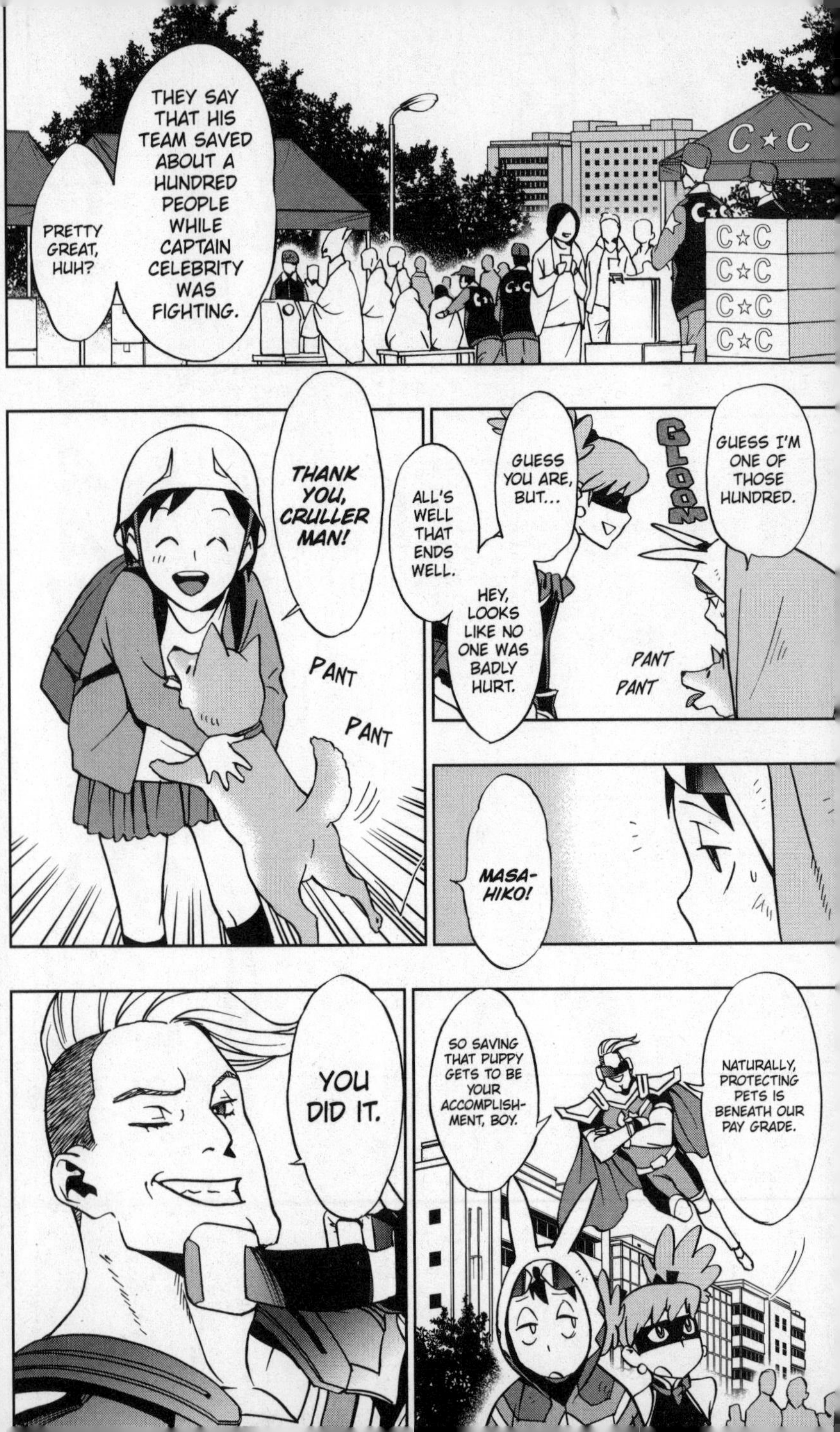
C★C
THEY SAY THAT HIS TEAM SAVED ABOUT A HUNDRED PEOPLE WHILE CAPTAIN CELEBRITY WAS FIGHTING.
PRETTY GREAT, HUH?
C★C
C★C
C★C
C★C
GUESS I'M ONE OF THOSE HUNDRED.
GLOOM
GUESS YOU ARE, BUT...
ALL'S WELL THAT ENDS WELL.
HEY, LOOKS LIKE NO ONE WAS BADLY HURT.
PANT PANT
MASA-HIKO!
THANK YOU, CRULLER MAN!
PANT
PANT
NATURALLY, PROTECTING PETS IS BENEATH OUR PAY GRADE.
SO SAVING THAT PUPPY GETS TO BE YOUR ACCOMPLISHMENT, BOY.
YOU DID IT.

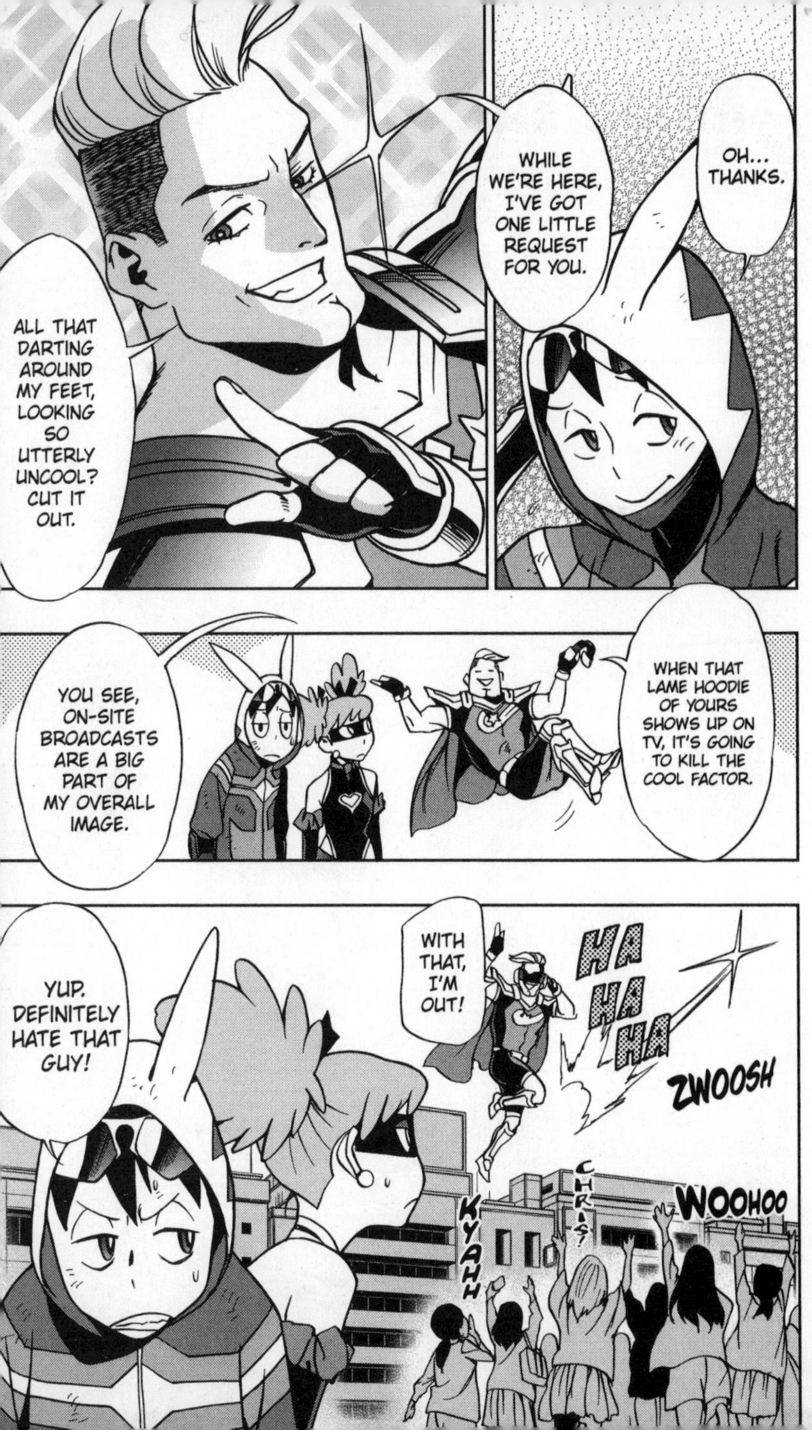

OH... THANKS.
WHILE WE'RE HERE, I'VE GOT ONE LITTLE REQUEST FOR YOU.
ALL THAT DARTING AROUND MY FEET, LOOKING SO UTTERLY UNCOOL? CUT IT OUT.
WHEN THAT LAME HOODIE OF YOURS SHOWS UP ON TV, IT'S GOING TO KILL THE COOL FACTOR.
YOU SEE, ON-SITE BROADCASTS ARE A BIG PART OF MY OVERALL IMAGE.
HA HA HA
WITH THAT, I'M OUT!
ZWOOSH
WOOHOO
CHRIS!
KYAHH
YUP. DEFINITELY HATE THAT GUY!

KAIJU VILLAIN

BEHIND THE SCENES

This big guy was perfect for showing off Captain Celebrity's power and organizational might in his debut chapter. The monster itself has no background to speak of and is more of a natural disaster than a character. One that causes a ridiculous amount of destruction. Effects of the "Naruhata monster incident" reverberate throughout the chapters to come.

—Furuhashi

I'm not that great at drawing giant monsters. (LOL) But I tried hard with this guy.

—Betten

THE ROUGH DESIGN

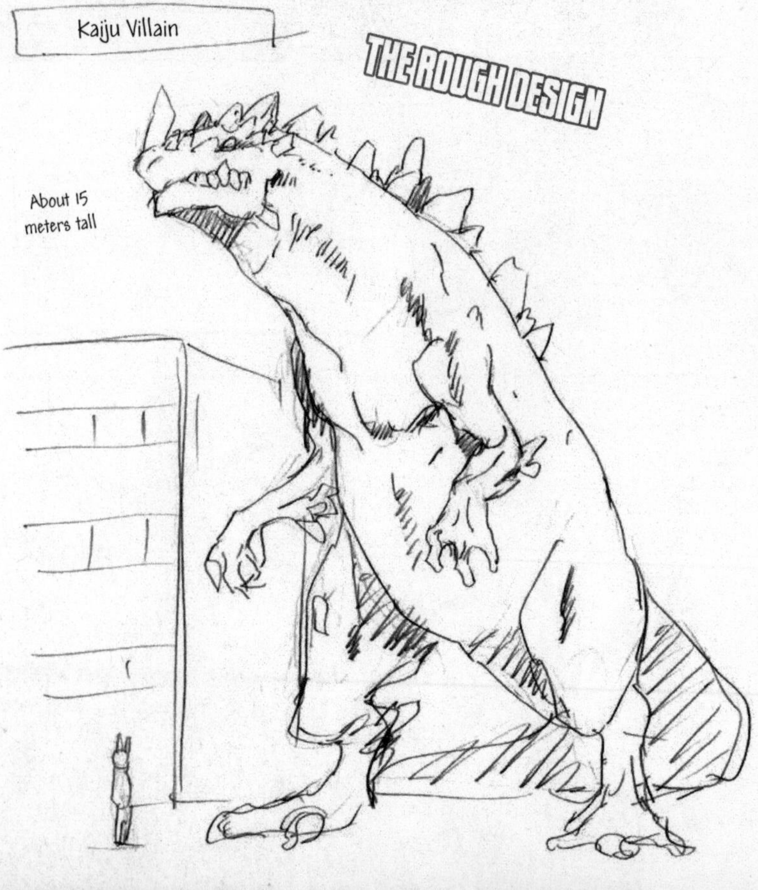

Kaiju Villain
About 15 meters tall

EP. 15 - PLAYBOY

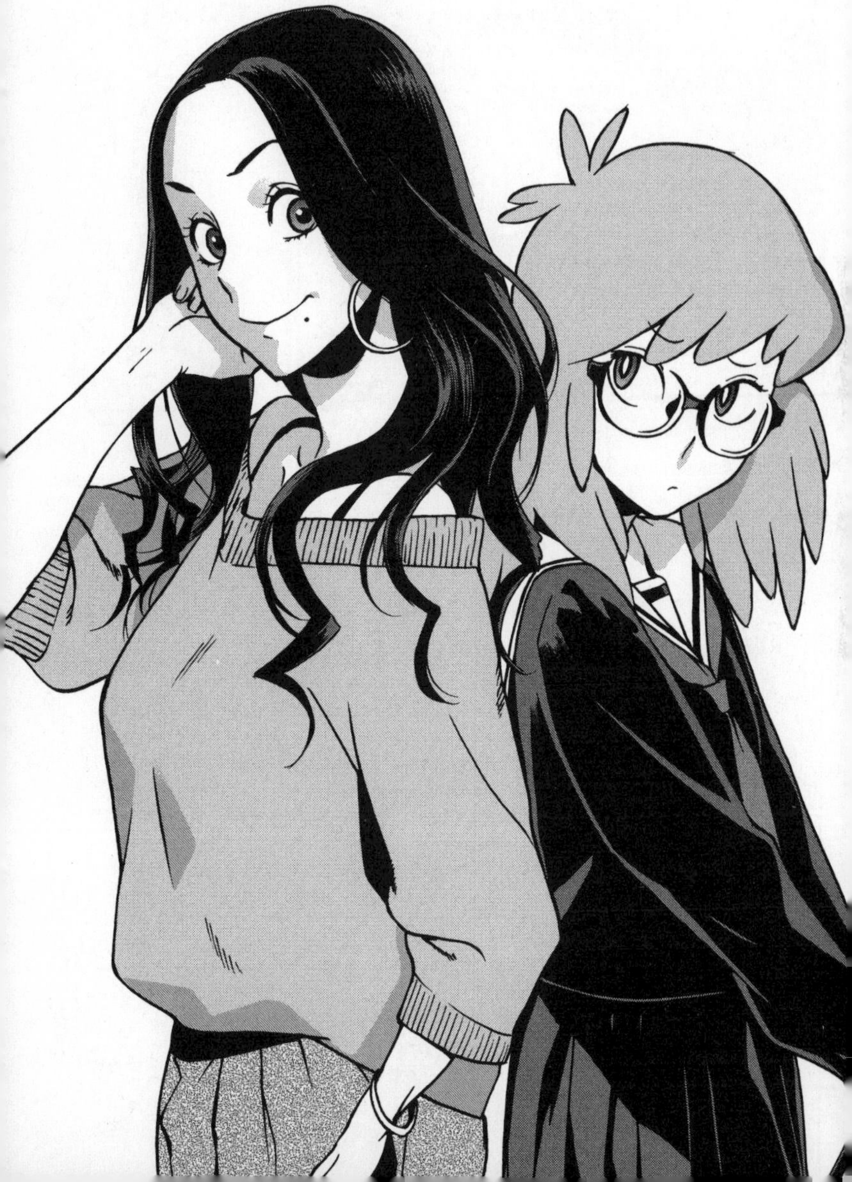

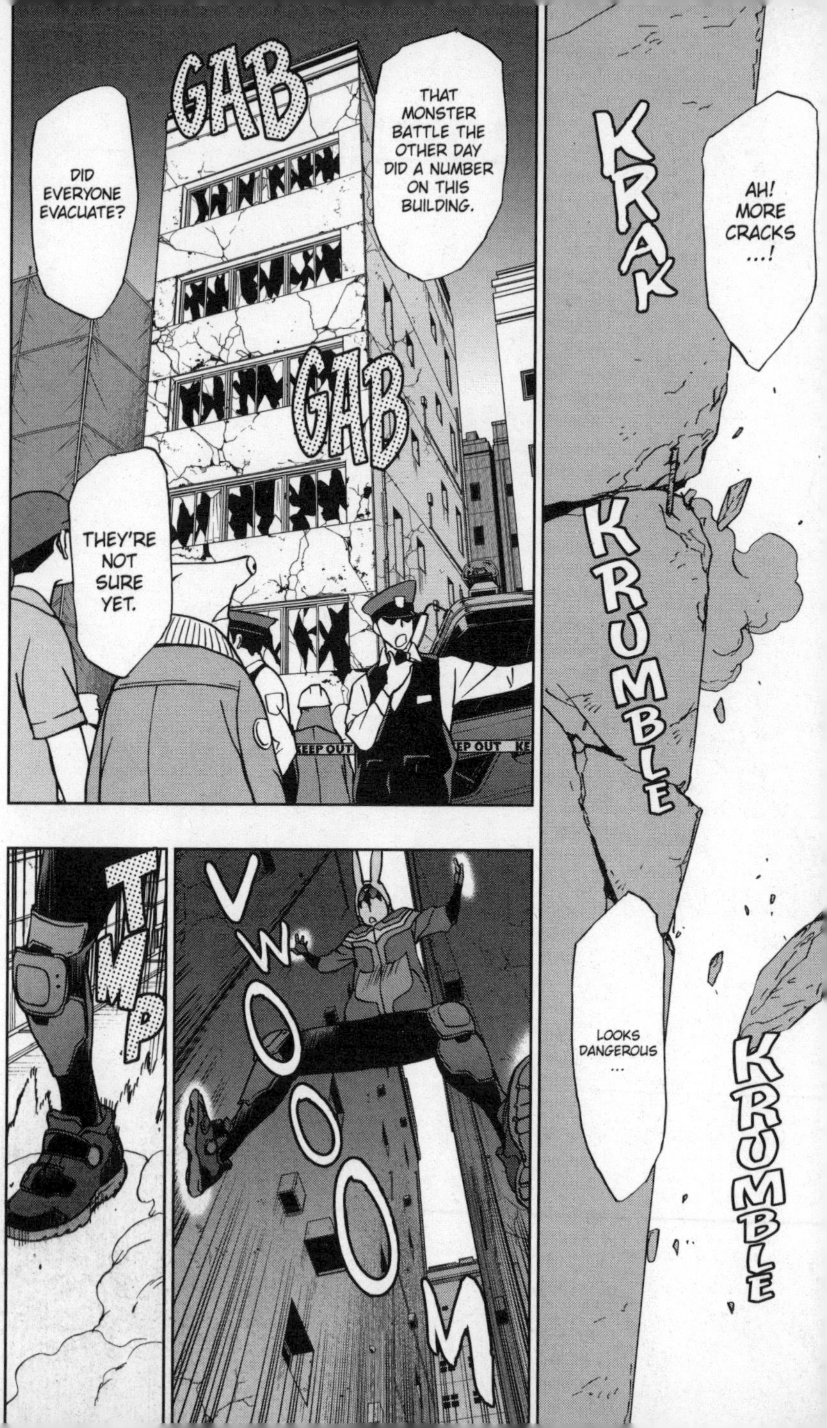
AH! MORE CRACKS ...!
KRAK
KRUMBLE
KRUMBLE
LOOKS DANGEROUS ...
GAB
THAT MONSTER BATTLE THE OTHER DAY DID A NUMBER ON THIS BUILDING.
DID EVERYONE EVACUATE?
GAB
THEY'RE NOT SURE YET.
VWOOOOM
TMP

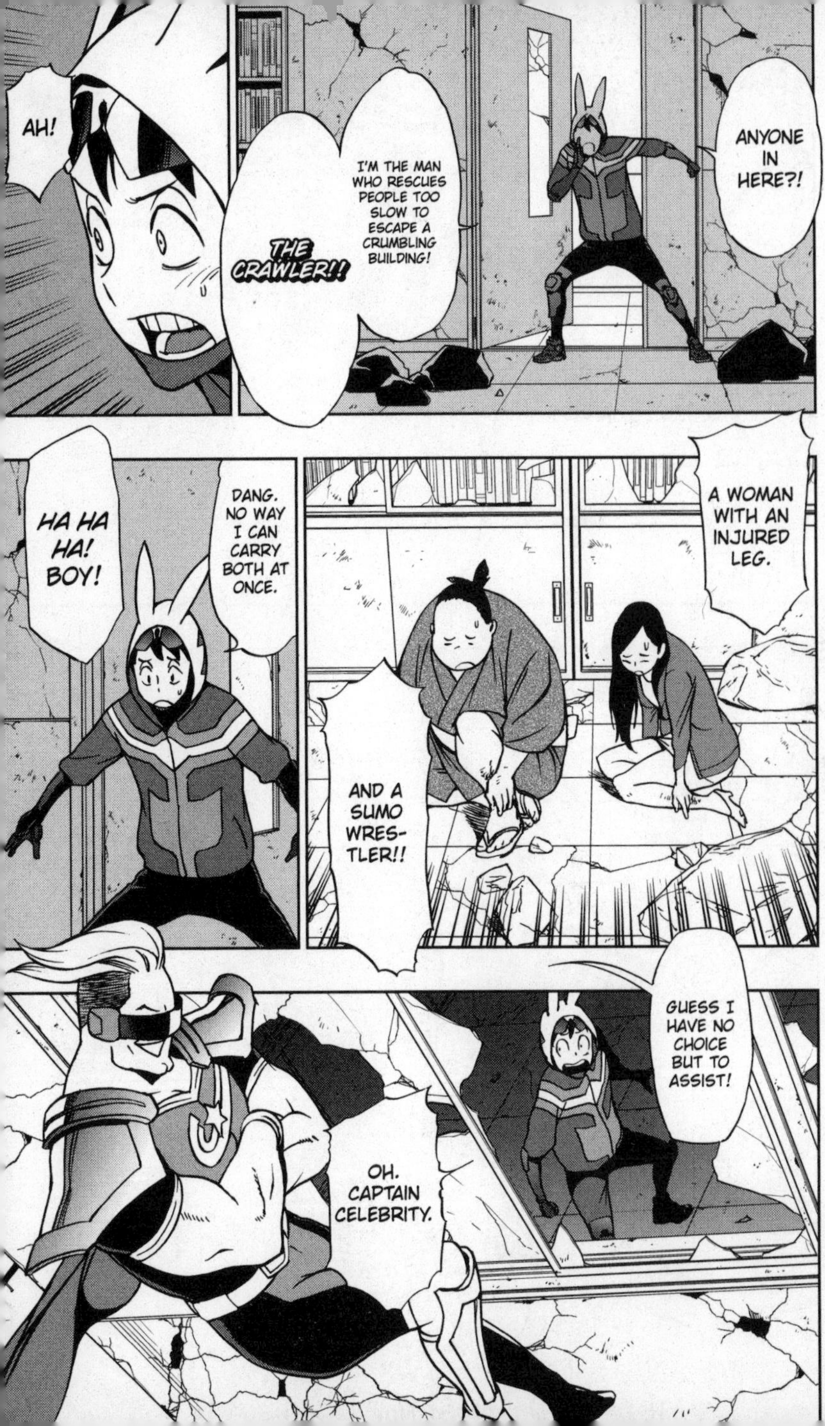
ANYONE IN HERE?!
I'M THE MAN WHO RESCUES PEOPLE TOO SLOW TO ESCAPE A CRUMBLING BUILDING!
THE CRAWLER!!
AH!
A WOMAN WITH AN INJURED LEG.
AND A SUMO WRES-TLER!!
DANG. NO WAY I CAN CARRY BOTH AT ONCE.
HA HA HA! BOY!
GUESS I HAVE NO CHOICE BUT TO ASSIST!
OH. CAPTAIN CELEBRITY.

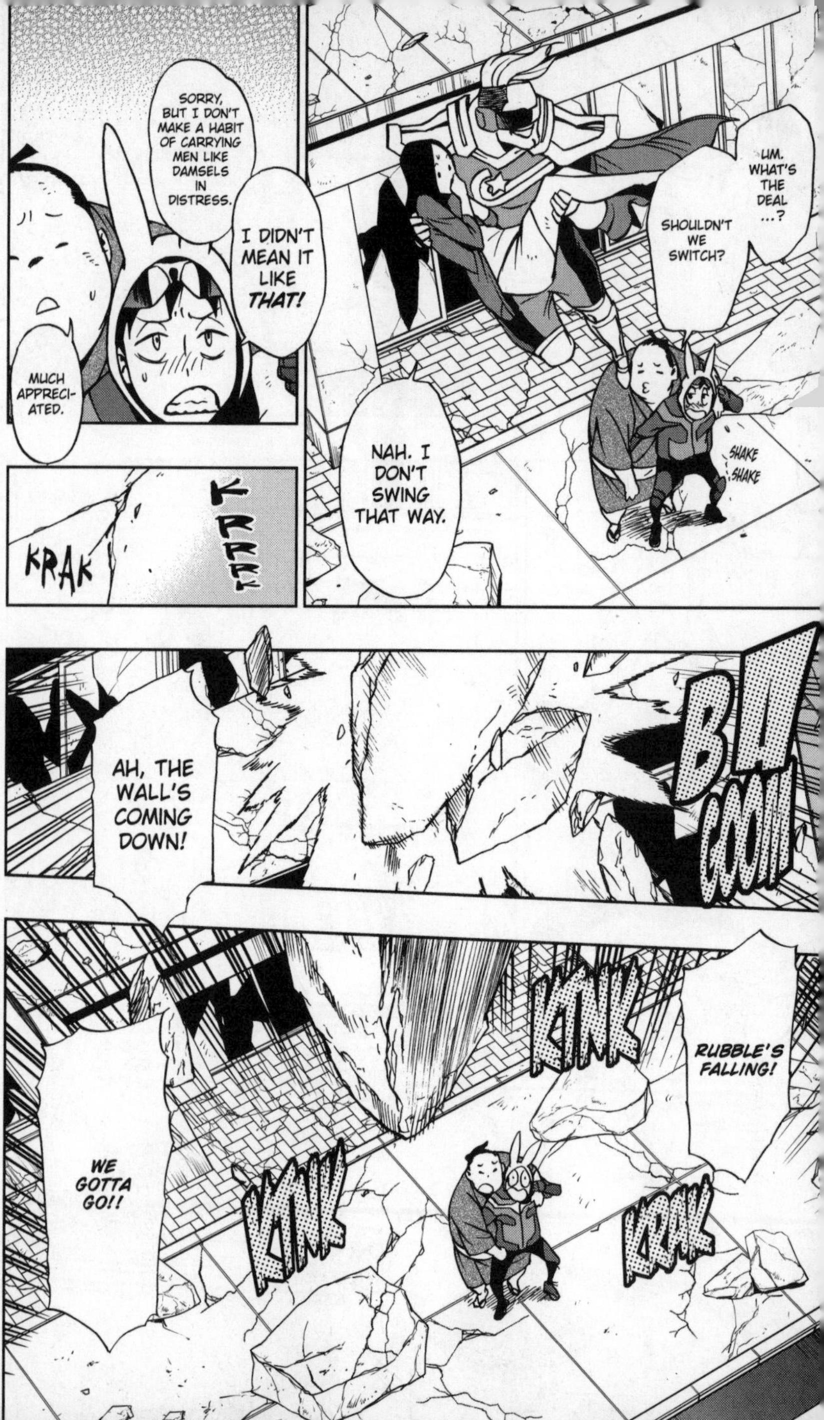
UM. WHAT'S THE DEAL ...?
SHOULDN'T WE SWITCH?
NAH. I DON'T SWING THAT WAY.
SHAKE SHAKE
I DIDN'T MEAN IT LIKE *THAT!*
SORRY, BUT I DON'T MAKE A HABIT OF CARRYING MEN LIKE DAMSELS IN DISTRESS.
MUCH APPRECIATED.
KRRRK
KRAK
BA-COOM
AH, THE WALL'S COMING DOWN!
KTINK
RUBBLE'S FALLING!
KRAK
KTINK
WE GOTTA GO!!

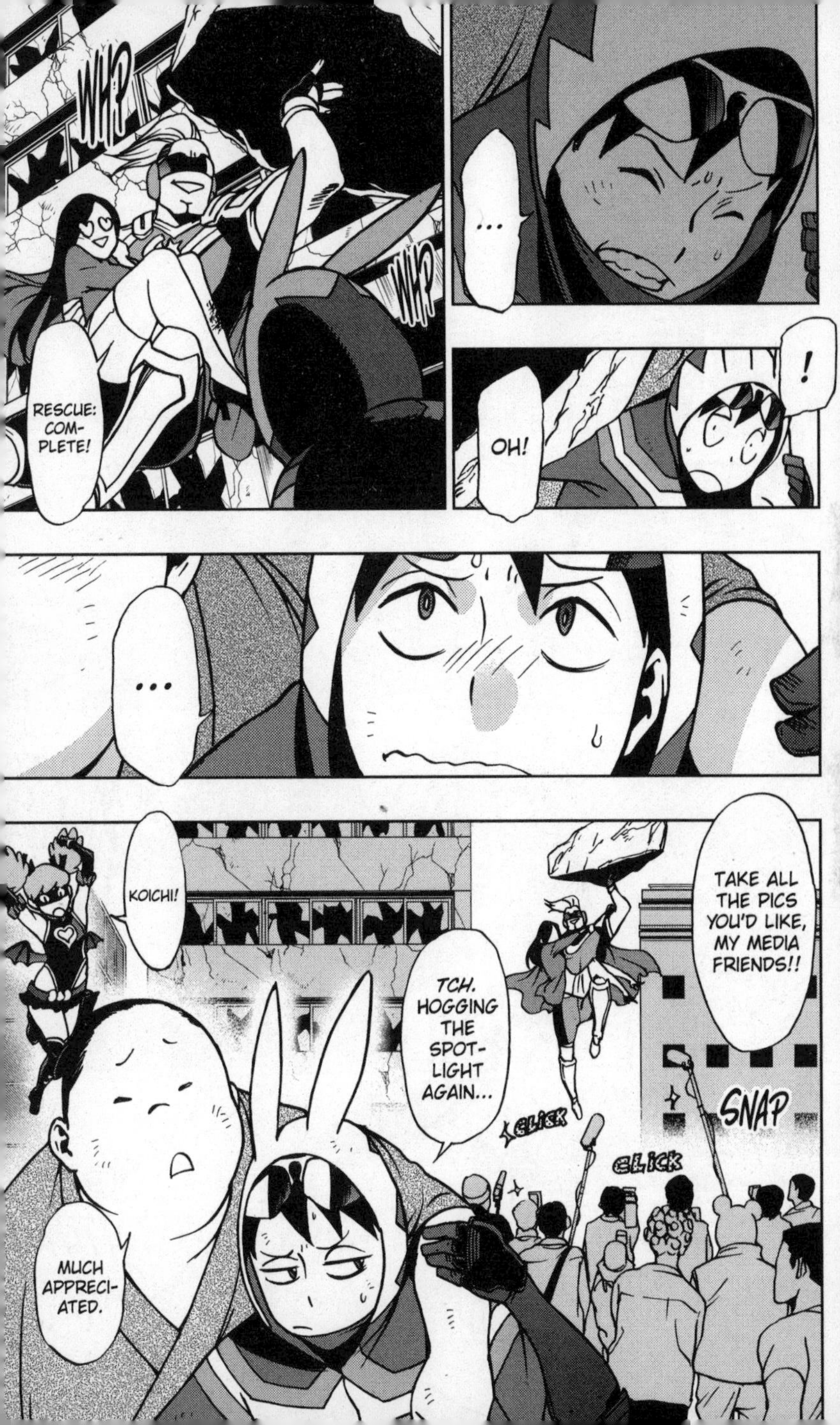
...
OH!
!
WHP
WHP
RESCUE: COMPLETE!
...
TAKE ALL THE PICS YOU'D LIKE, MY MEDIA FRIENDS!!
SNAP
CLICK
CLICK
TCH. HOGGING THE SPOTLIGHT AGAIN...
KOICHI!
MUCH APPRECIATED.

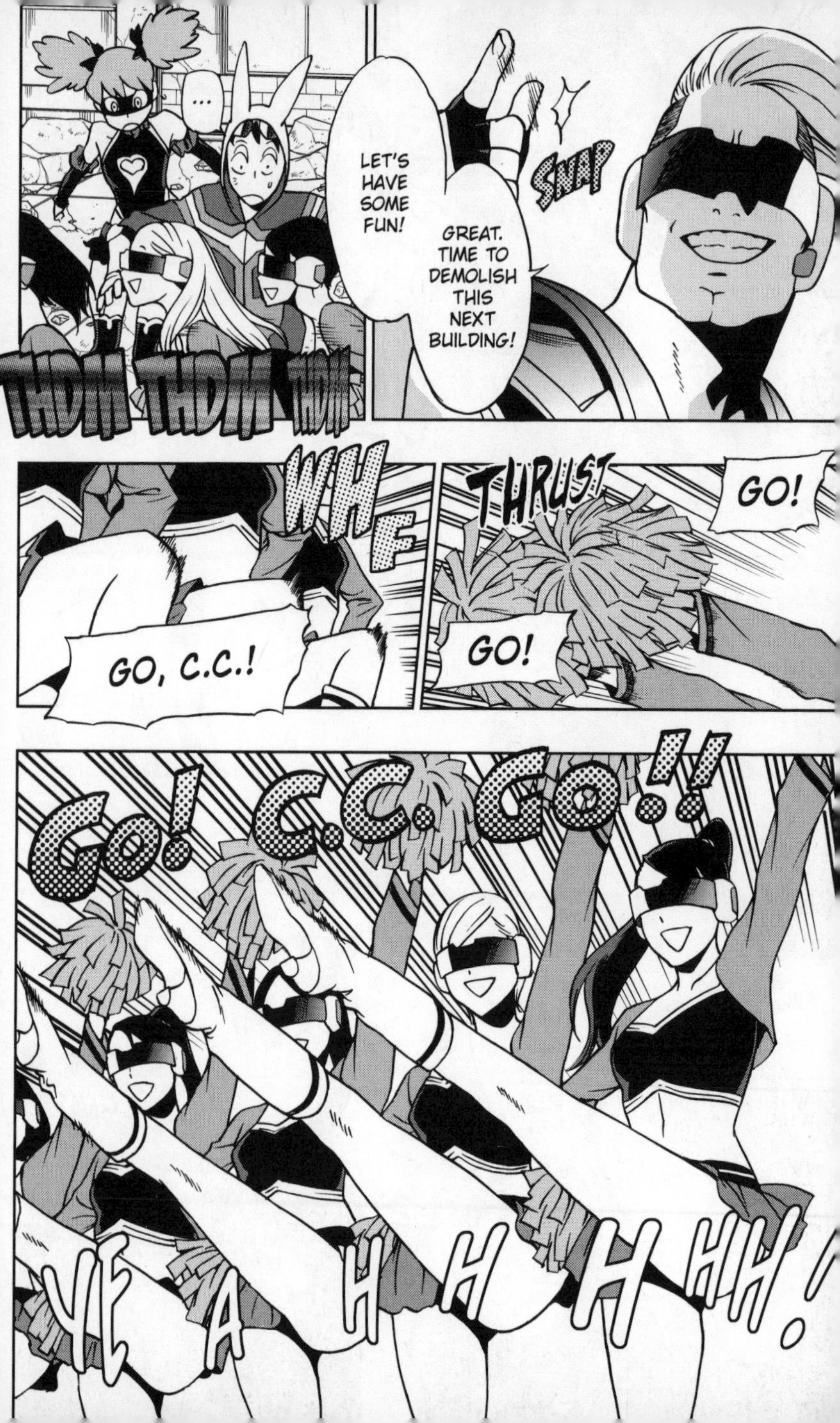
SNAP
LET'S HAVE SOME FUN!
GREAT. TIME TO DEMOLISH THIS NEXT BUILDING!
...
THDM THDM THDM
THRUST
GO!
GO!
WHF
GO, C.C.!
GO! C.C. GO!!
YEAHHHHHH!

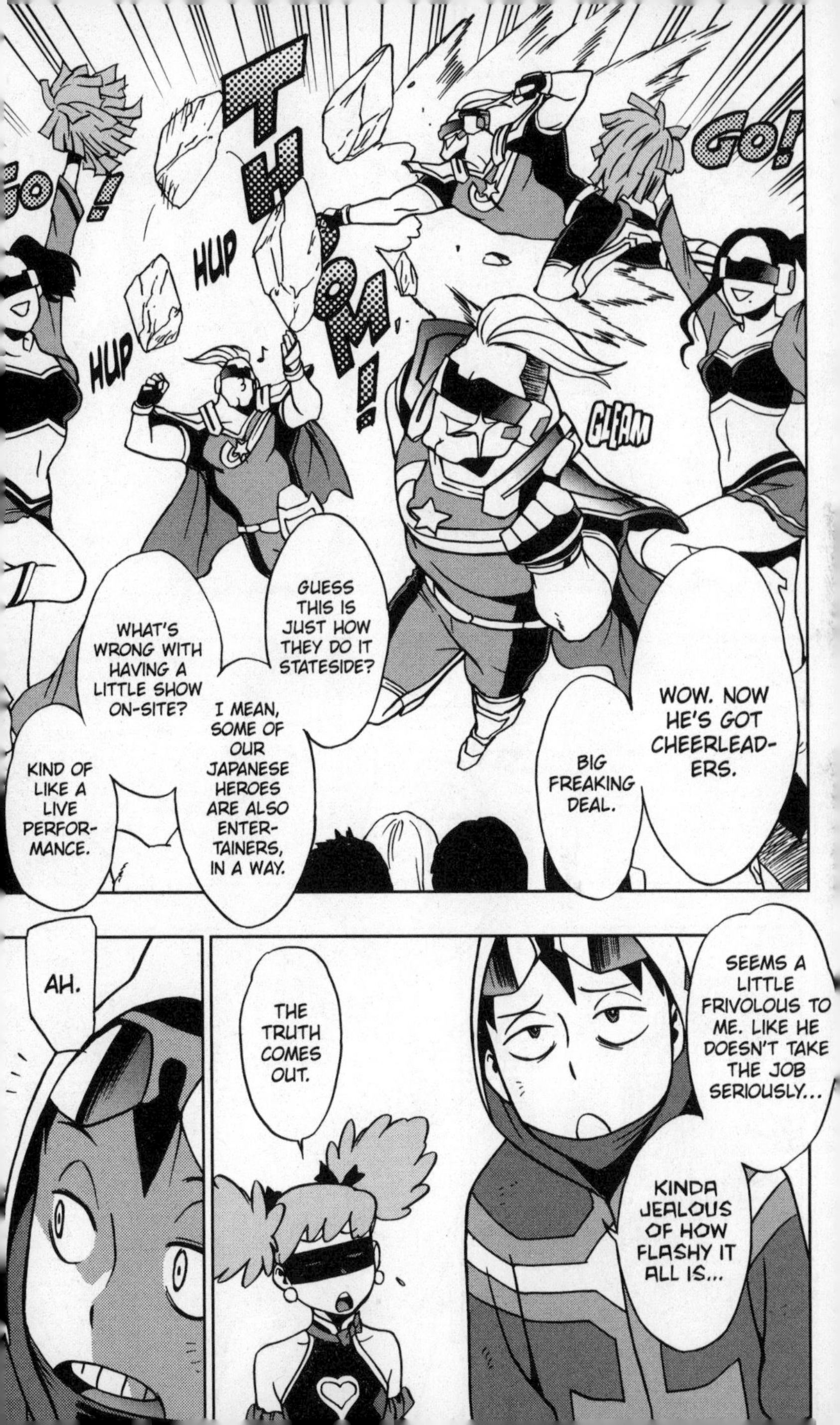
GO!
THOOM!
GLEAM
HUP HUP
GO!
WOW. NOW HE'S GOT CHEERLEADERS.
BIG FREAKING DEAL.
GUESS THIS IS JUST HOW THEY DO IT STATESIDE?
I MEAN, SOME OF OUR JAPANESE HEROES ARE ALSO ENTERTAINERS, IN A WAY.
WHAT'S WRONG WITH HAVING A LITTLE SHOW ON-SITE?
KIND OF LIKE A LIVE PERFORMANCE.
SEEMS A LITTLE FRIVOLOUS TO ME. LIKE HE DOESN'T TAKE THE JOB SERIOUSLY...
KINDA JEALOUS OF HOW FLASHY IT ALL IS...
THE TRUTH COMES OUT.
AH.

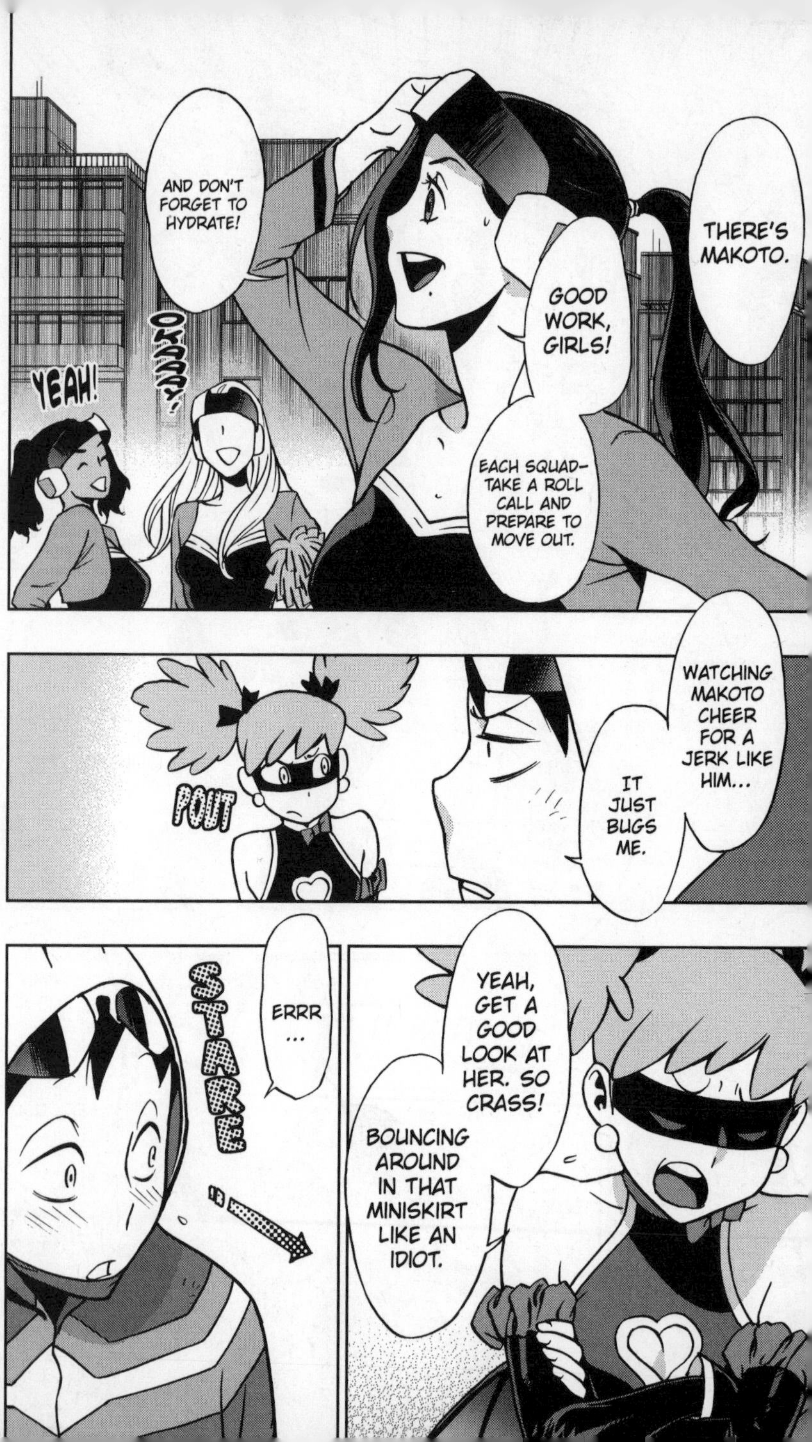
THERE'S MAKOTO.
GOOD WORK, GIRLS!
EACH SQUAD-TAKE A ROLL CALL AND PREPARE TO MOVE OUT.
AND DON'T FORGET TO HYDRATE!
OKAAAY!
YEAH!
WATCHING MAKOTO CHEER FOR A JERK LIKE HIM...
IT JUST BUGS ME.
POUT
YEAH, GET A GOOD LOOK AT HER. SO CRASS!
BOUNCING AROUND IN THAT MINISKIRT LIKE AN IDIOT.
ERRR ...
STARE

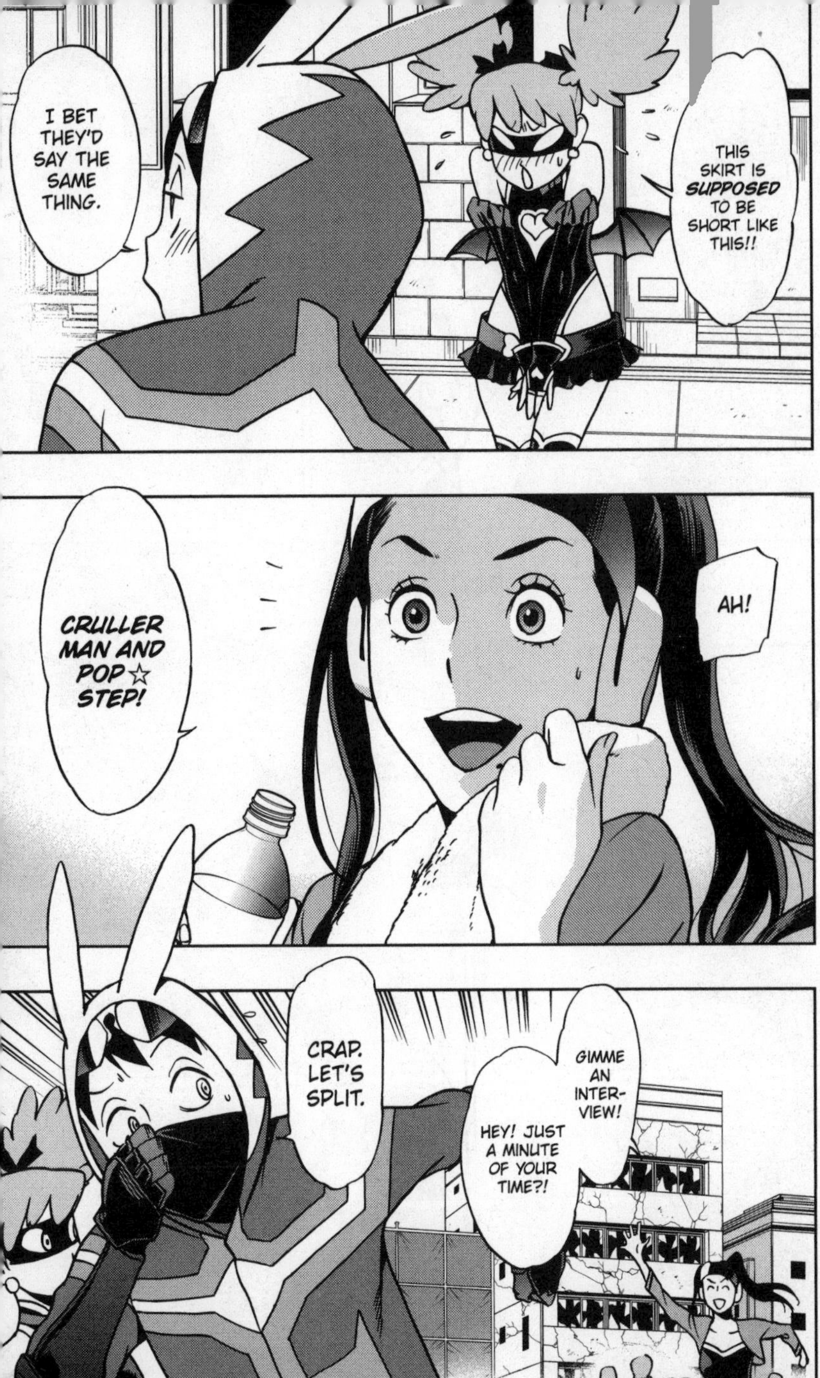
THIS SKIRT IS SUPPOSED TO BE SHORT LIKE THIS!!
I BET THEY'D SAY THE SAME THING.
AH!
CRULLER MAN AND POP☆STEP!
GIMME AN INTER-VIEW!
HEY! JUST A MINUTE OF YOUR TIME?!
CRAP. LET'S SPLIT.

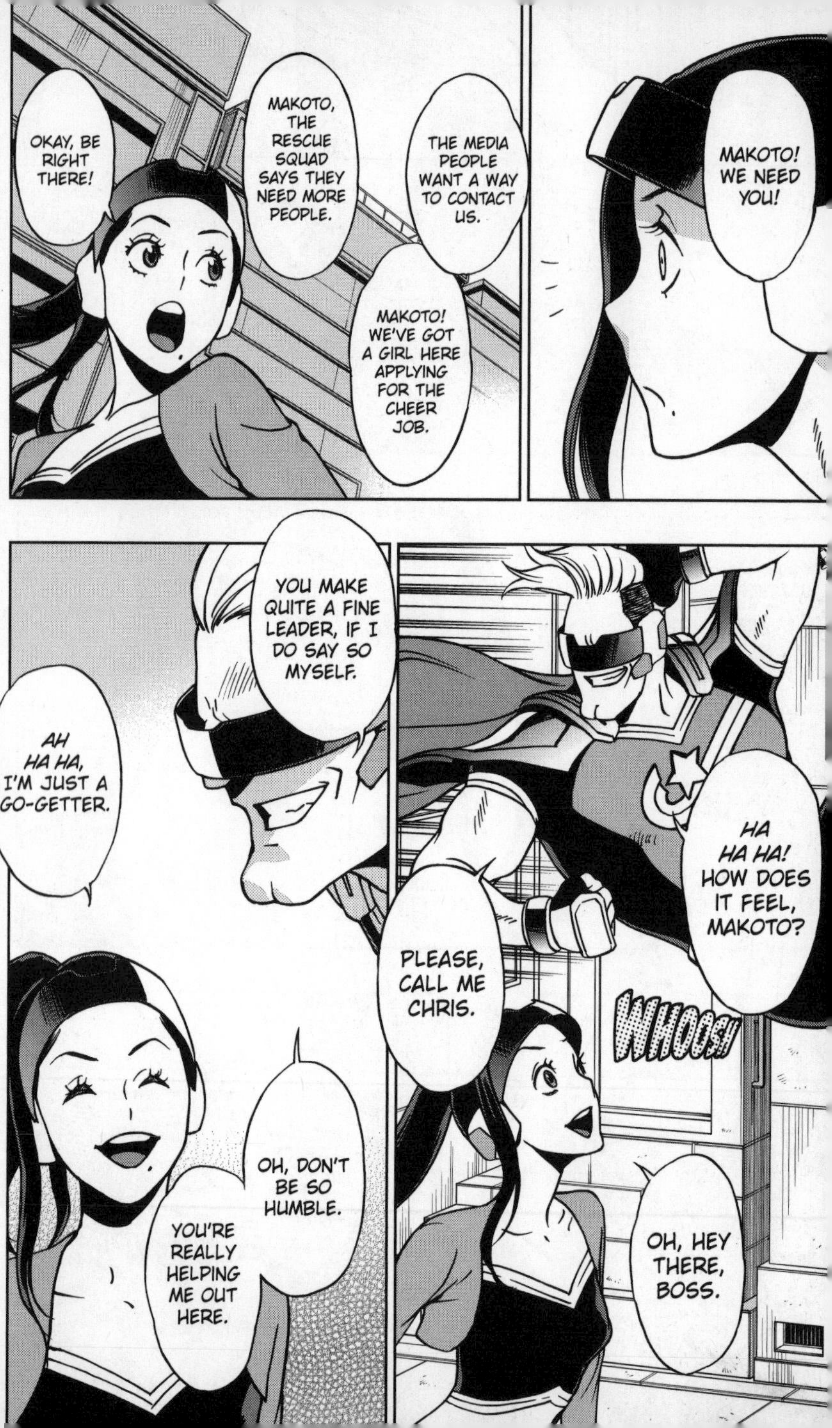
MAKOTO! WE NEED YOU!
THE MEDIA PEOPLE WANT A WAY TO CONTACT US.
MAKOTO, THE RESCUE SQUAD SAYS THEY NEED MORE PEOPLE.
MAKOTO! WE'VE GOT A GIRL HERE APPLYING FOR THE CHEER JOB.
OKAY, BE RIGHT THERE!
HA HA HA! HOW DOES IT FEEL, MAKOTO?
WHOOSH
OH, HEY THERE, BOSS.
PLEASE, CALL ME CHRIS.
YOU MAKE QUITE A FINE LEADER, IF I DO SAY SO MYSELF.
AH HA HA, I'M JUST A GO-GETTER.
OH, DON'T BE SO HUMBLE.
YOU'RE REALLY HELPING ME OUT HERE.

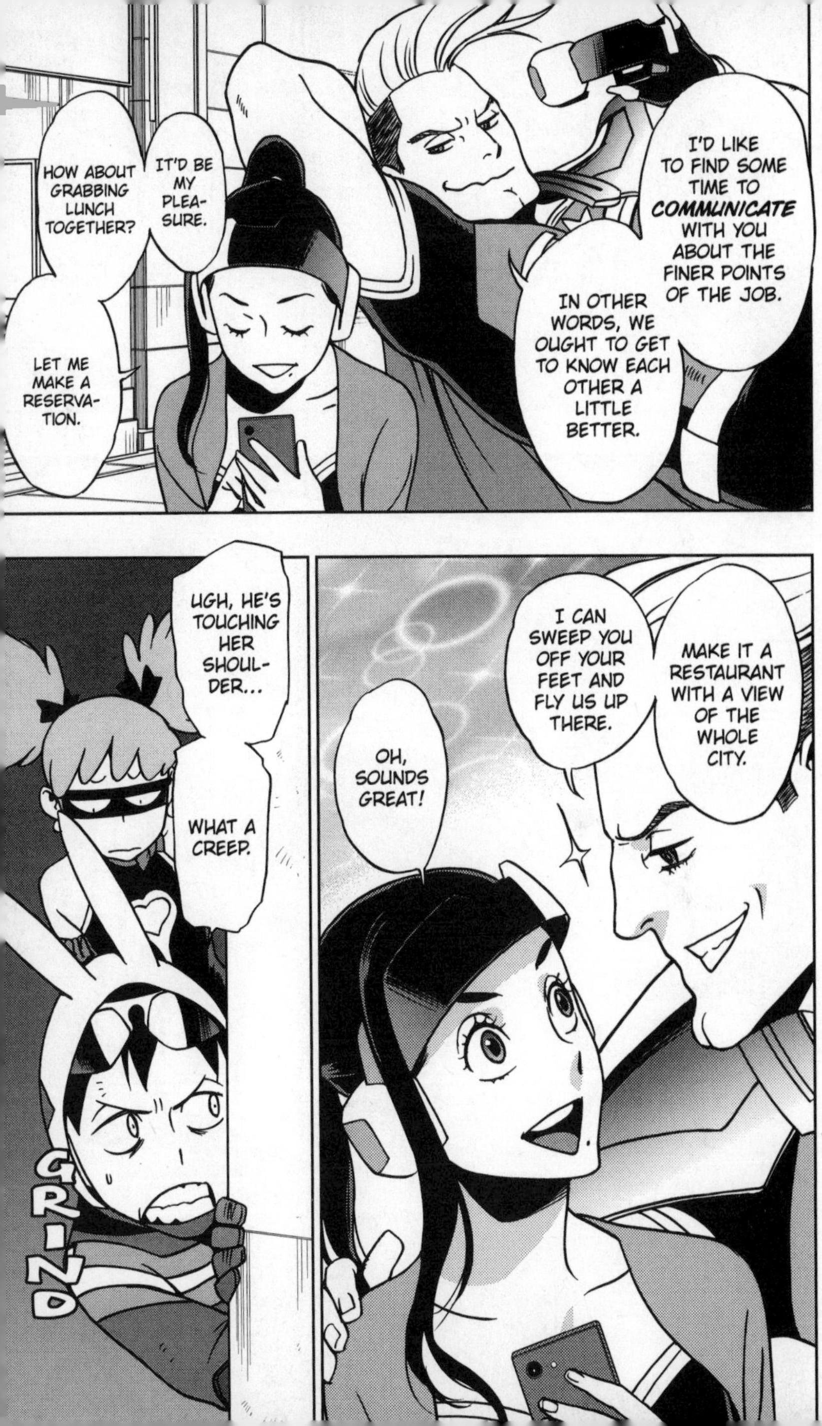
I'D LIKE TO FIND SOME TIME TO **COMMUNICATE** WITH YOU ABOUT THE FINER POINTS OF THE JOB.
IN OTHER WORDS, WE OUGHT TO GET TO KNOW EACH OTHER A LITTLE BETTER.
IT'D BE MY PLEA-SURE.
HOW ABOUT GRABBING LUNCH TOGETHER?
LET ME MAKE A RESERVA-TION.
MAKE IT A RESTAURANT WITH A VIEW OF THE WHOLE CITY.
I CAN SWEEP YOU OFF YOUR FEET AND FLY US UP THERE.
OH, SOUNDS GREAT!
UGH, HE'S TOUCHING HER SHOUL-DER...
WHAT A CREEP.
GRIND

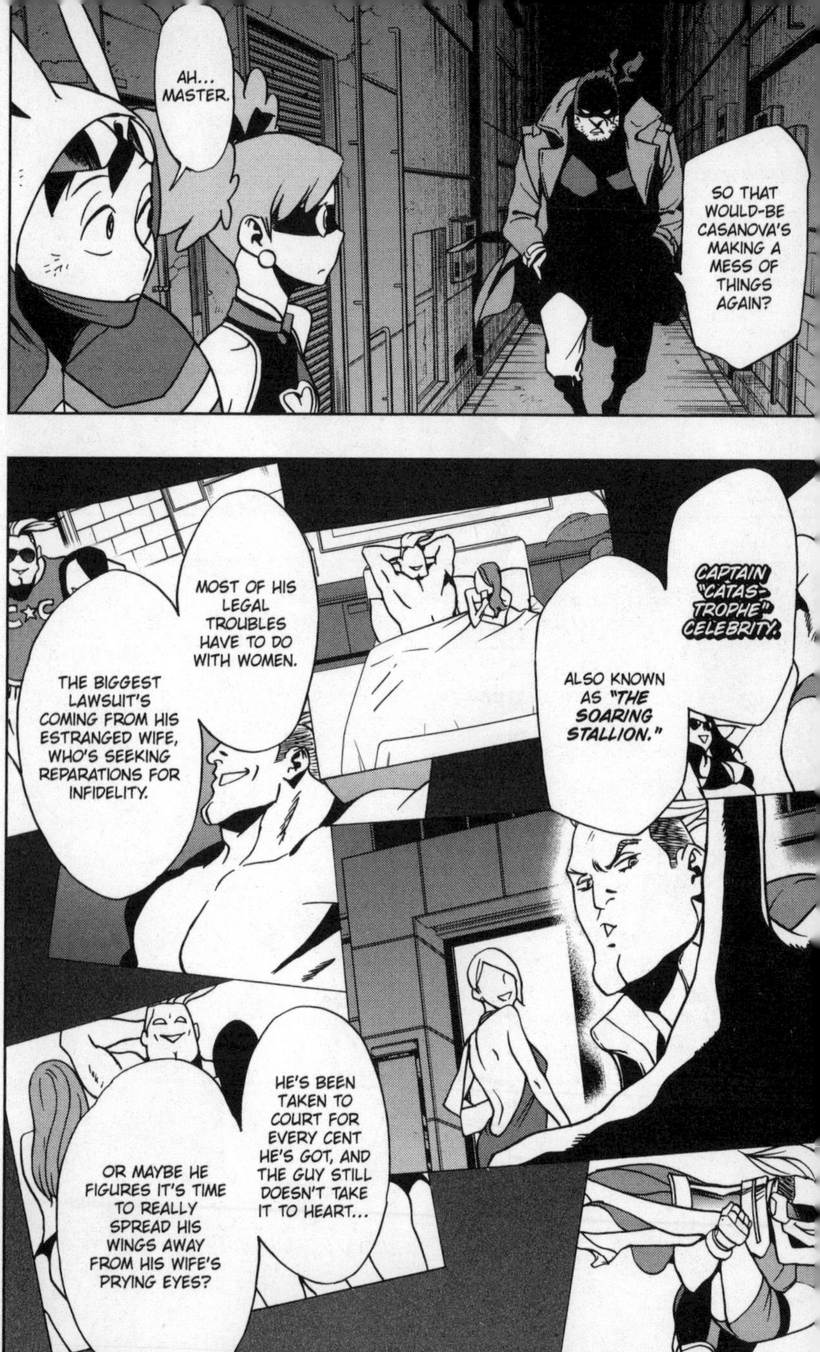
SO THAT WOULD-BE CASANOVA'S MAKING A MESS OF THINGS AGAIN?
AH... MASTER.
CAPTAIN "CATASTROPHE" CELEBRITY.
ALSO KNOWN AS "THE SOARING STALLION."
MOST OF HIS LEGAL TROUBLES HAVE TO DO WITH WOMEN.
THE BIGGEST LAWSUIT'S COMING FROM HIS ESTRANGED WIFE, WHO'S SEEKING REPARATIONS FOR INFIDELITY.
HE'S BEEN TAKEN TO COURT FOR EVERY CENT HE'S GOT, AND THE GUY STILL DOESN'T TAKE IT TO HEART...
OR MAYBE HE FIGURES IT'S TIME TO REALLY SPREAD HIS WINGS AWAY FROM HIS WIFE'S PRYING EYES?

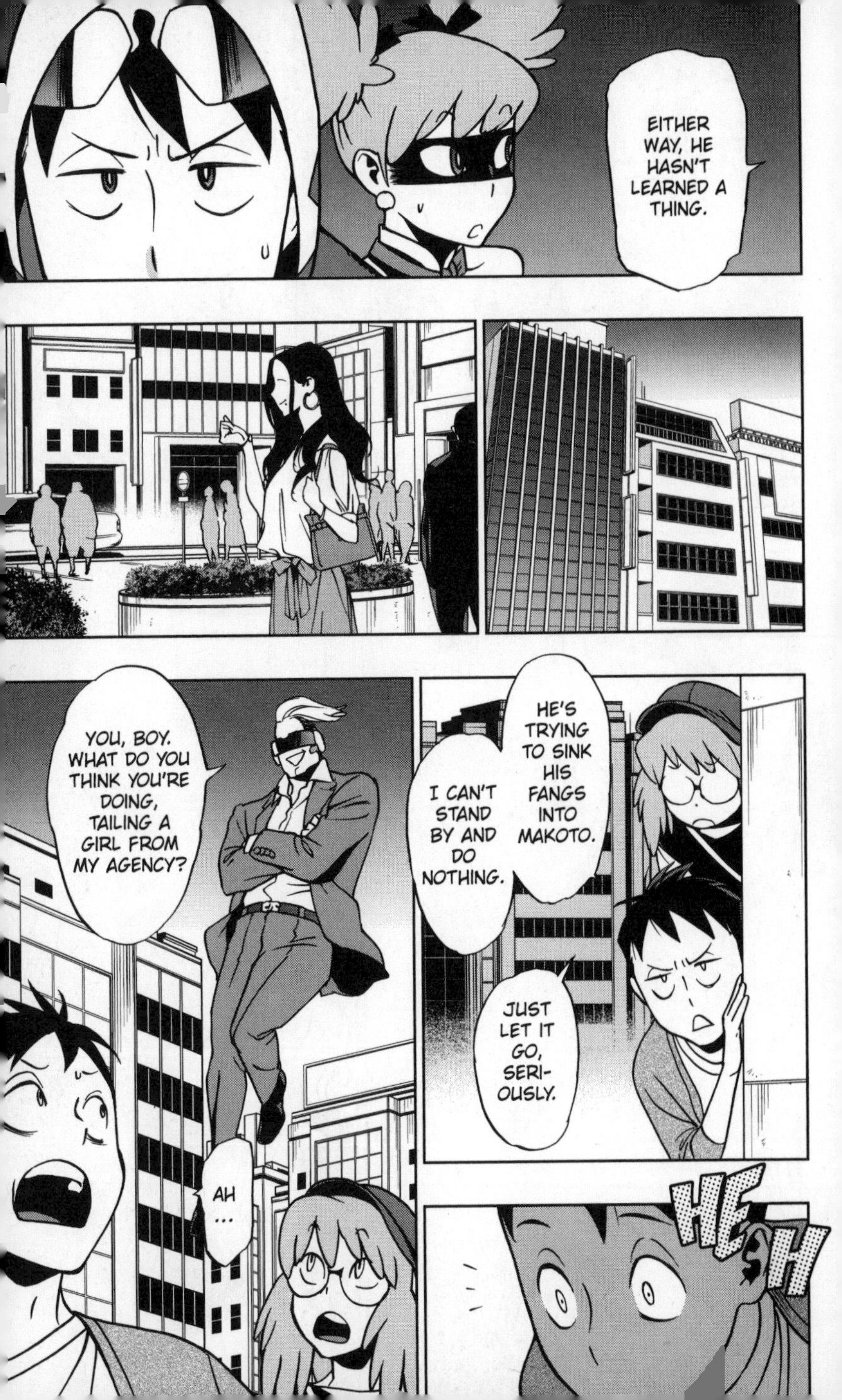
EITHER WAY, HE HASN'T LEARNED A THING.
HE'S TRYING TO SINK HIS FANGS INTO MAKOTO.
I CAN'T STAND BY AND DO NOTHING.
JUST LET IT GO, SERIOUSLY.
HEH
YOU, BOY. WHAT DO YOU THINK YOU'RE DOING, TAILING A GIRL FROM MY AGENCY?
AH ...

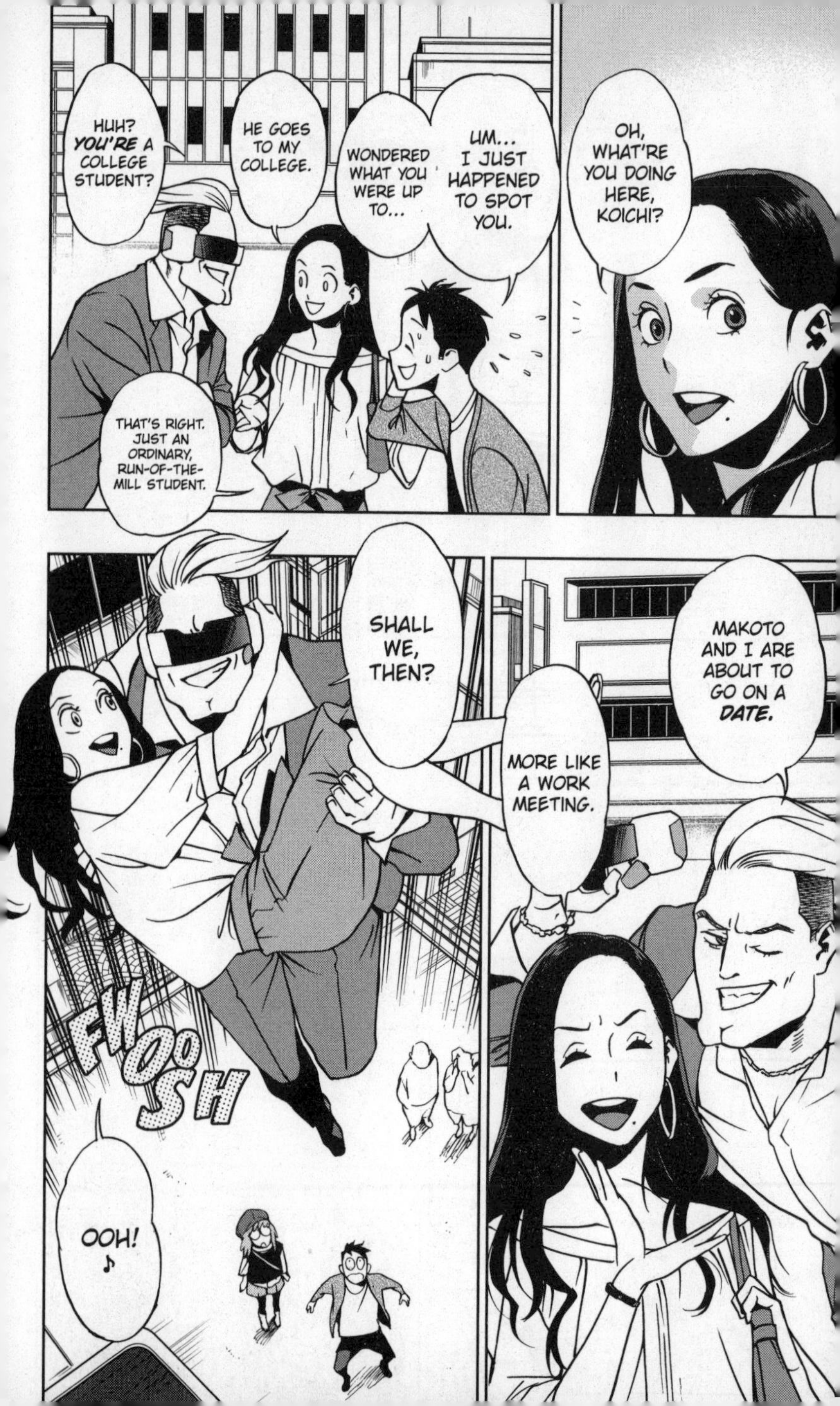
OH, WHAT'RE YOU DOING HERE, KOICHI?
UM... I JUST HAPPENED TO SPOT YOU.
WONDERED WHAT YOU WERE UP TO...
HE GOES TO MY COLLEGE.
HUH? ***YOU'RE*** A COLLEGE STUDENT?
THAT'S RIGHT. JUST AN ORDINARY, RUN-OF-THE-MILL STUDENT.
MAKOTO AND I ARE ABOUT TO GO ON A ***DATE.***
MORE LIKE A WORK MEETING.
SHALL WE, THEN?
FWOOSH
OOH! ♪

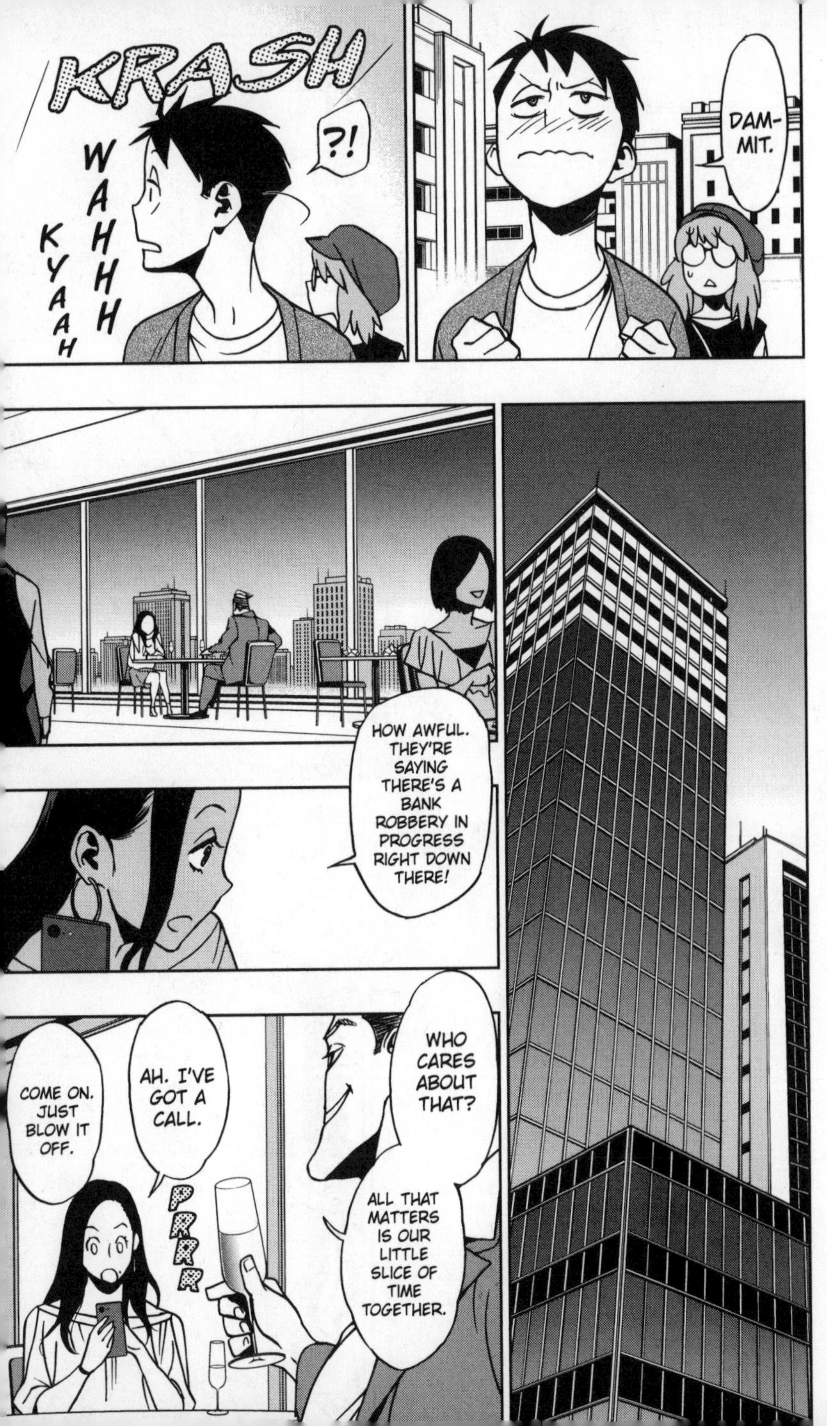
DAM-MIT.
KRASH
?!
WAHHHH
KYAAH
HOW AWFUL. THEY'RE SAYING THERE'S A BANK ROBBERY IN PROGRESS RIGHT DOWN THERE!
WHO CARES ABOUT THAT?
ALL THAT MATTERS IS OUR LITTLE SLICE OF TIME TOGETHER.
AH. I'VE GOT A CALL.
PRRR
COME ON. JUST BLOW IT OFF.

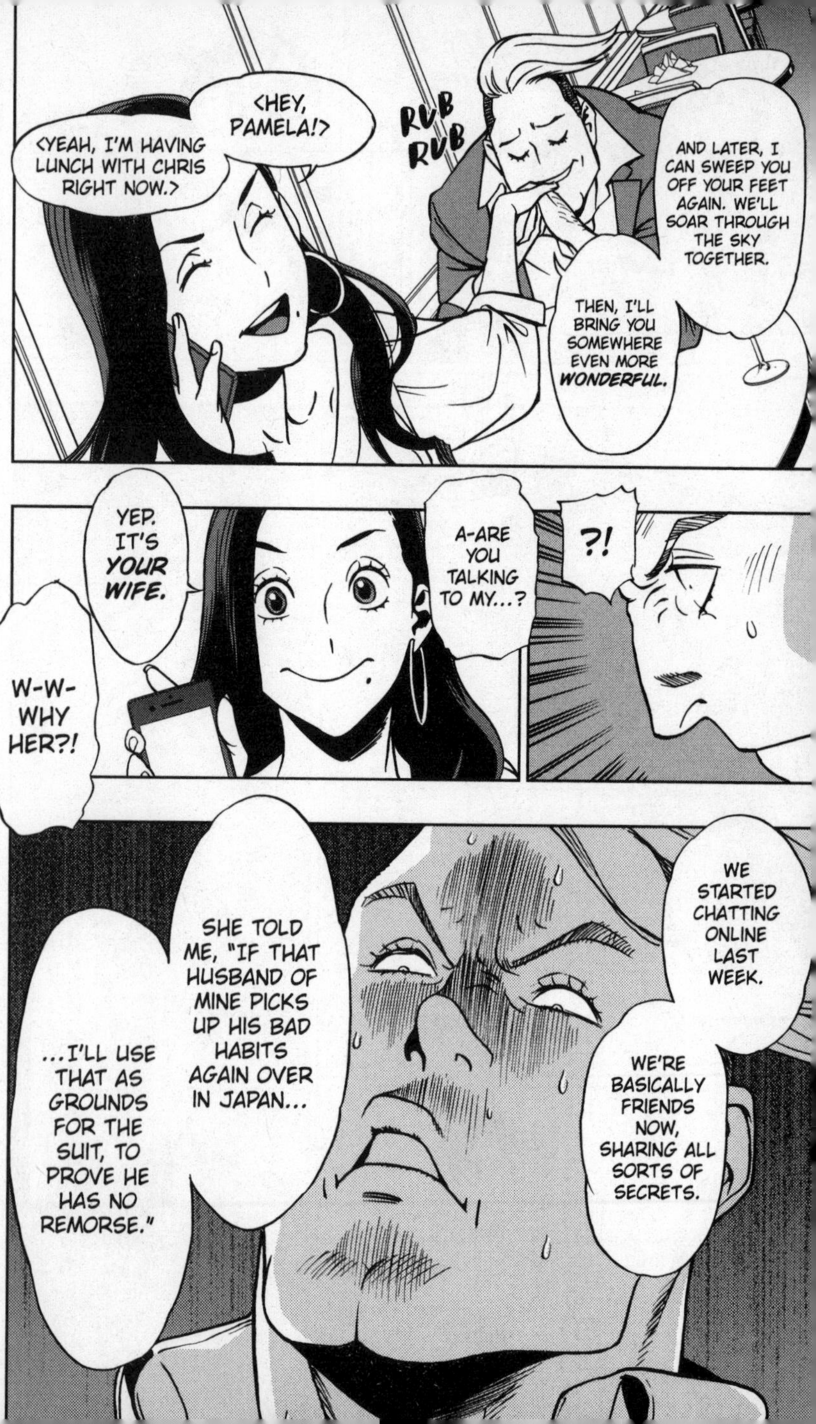
THEN, I'LL BRING YOU SOMEWHERE EVEN MORE **WONDERFUL.**
AND LATER, I CAN SWEEP YOU OFF YOUR FEET AGAIN. WE'LL SOAR THROUGH THE SKY TOGETHER.
RUB RUB
<HEY, PAMELA!>
<YEAH, I'M HAVING LUNCH WITH CHRIS RIGHT NOW.>
?!
A-ARE YOU TALKING TO MY...?
YEP. IT'S ***YOUR WIFE.***
W-W-WHY HER?!
WE STARTED CHATTING ONLINE LAST WEEK.
WE'RE BASICALLY FRIENDS NOW, SHARING ALL SORTS OF SECRETS.
SHE TOLD ME, "IF THAT HUSBAND OF MINE PICKS UP HIS BAD HABITS AGAIN OVER IN JAPAN...
...I'LL USE THAT AS GROUNDS FOR THE SUIT, TO PROVE HE HAS NO REMORSE."

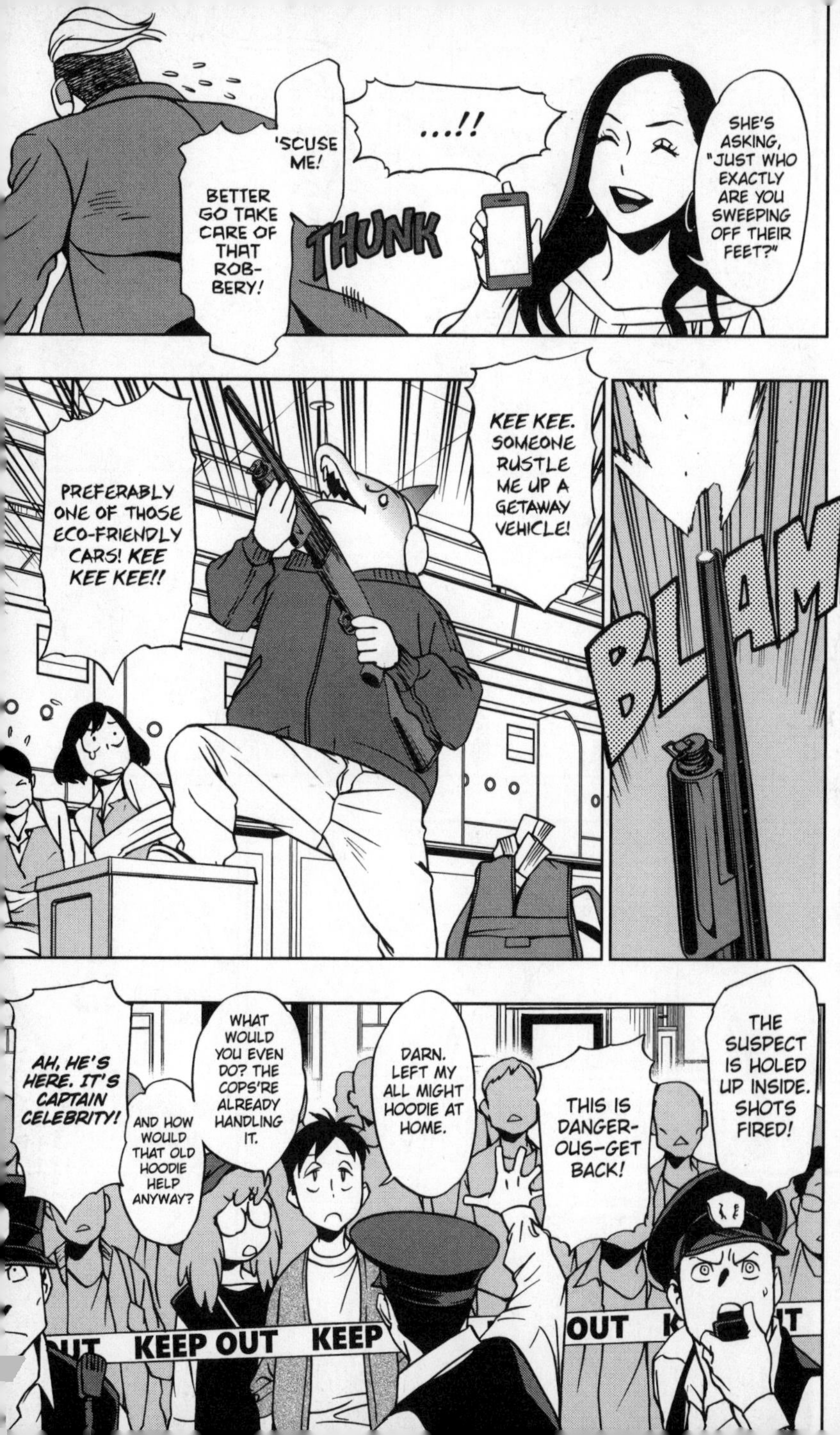
SHE'S ASKING, "JUST WHO EXACTLY ARE YOU SWEEPING OFF THEIR FEET?"
...!!
THUNK
'SCUSE ME!
BETTER GO TAKE CARE OF THAT ROB-BERY!
BLAM!
KEE KEE. SOMEONE RUSTLE ME UP A GETAWAY VEHICLE!
PREFERABLY ONE OF THOSE ECO-FRIENDLY CARS! KEE KEE KEE!!
THE SUSPECT IS HOLED UP INSIDE. SHOTS FIRED!
THIS IS DANGER-OUS—GET BACK!
DARN. LEFT MY ALL MIGHT HOODIE AT HOME.
WHAT WOULD YOU EVEN DO? THE COPS'RE ALREADY HANDLING IT.
AND HOW WOULD THAT OLD HOODIE HELP ANYWAY?
AH, HE'S HERE. IT'S CAPTAIN CELEBRITY!
KEEP OUT

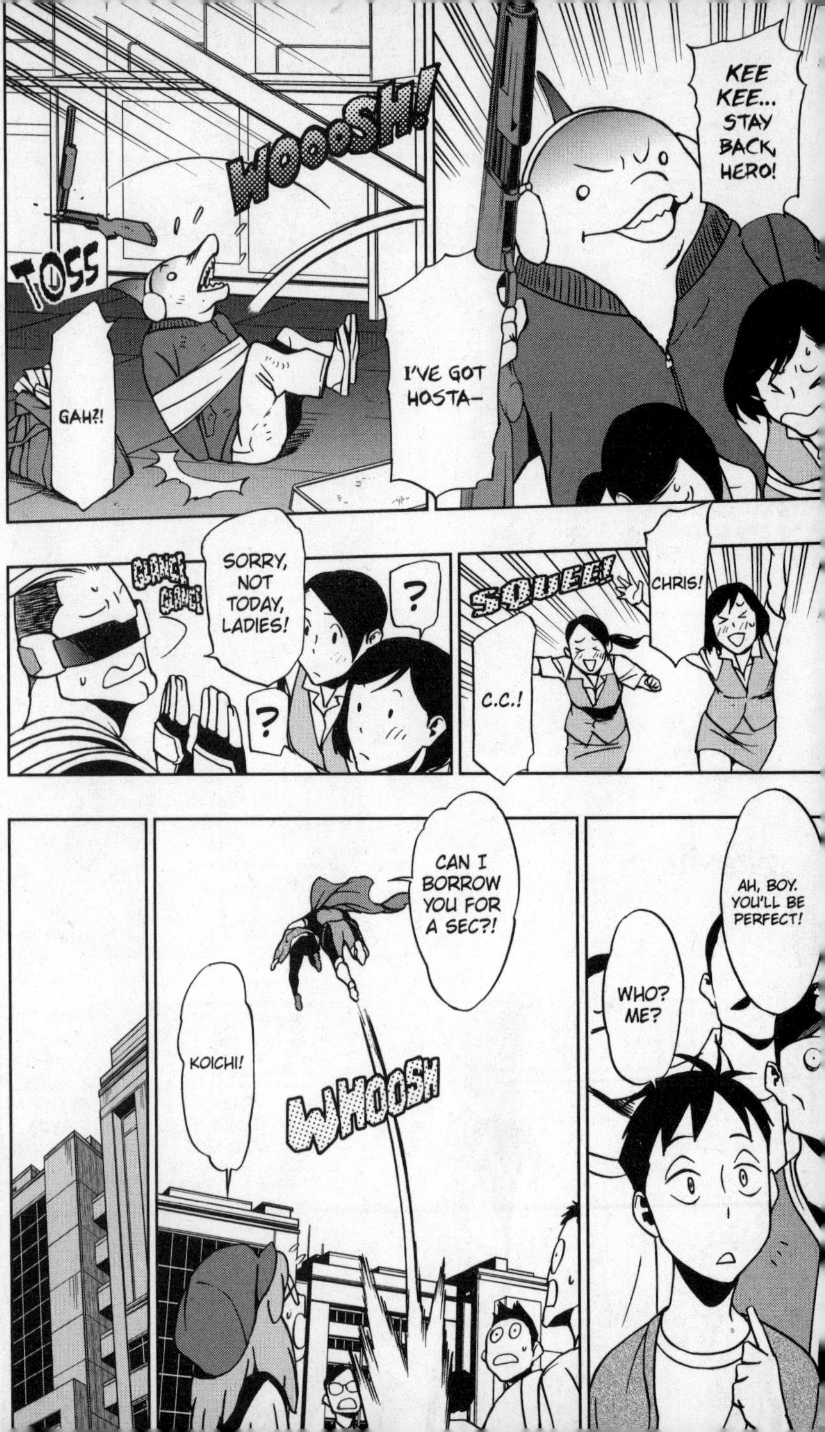
KEE KEE... STAY BACK, HERO!
I'VE GOT HOSTA-
WOOSH!
TOSS
GAH?!
CHRIS!
SQUEE!
C.C.!
SORRY, NOT TODAY, LADIES!
?
?
GLANCE GLANCE
AH, BOY. YOU'LL BE PERFECT!
WHO? ME?
CAN I BORROW YOU FOR A SEC?!
WHOOSH
KOICHI!

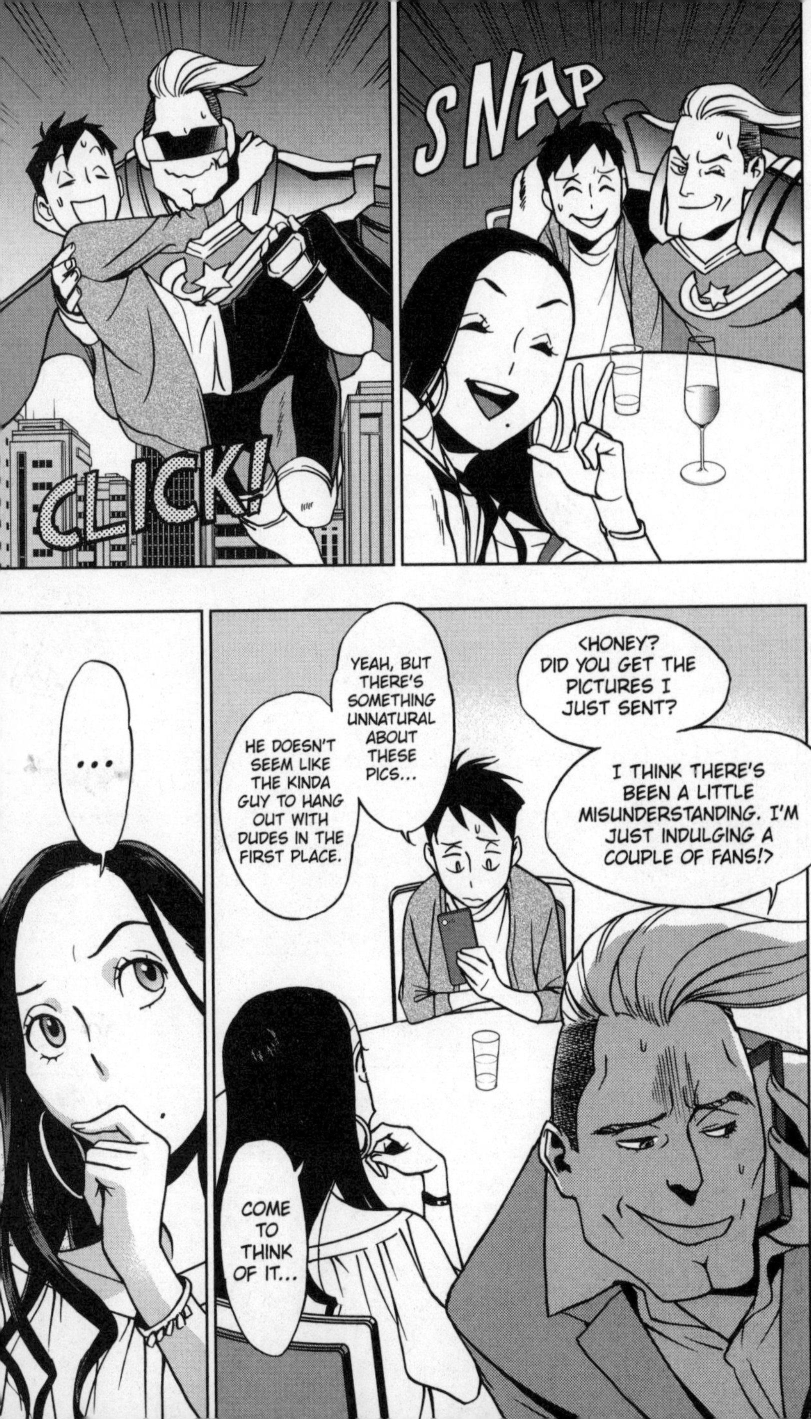
SNAP
CLICK!
<HONEY? DID YOU GET THE PICTURES I JUST SENT?
I THINK THERE'S BEEN A LITTLE MISUNDERSTANDING. I'M JUST INDULGING A COUPLE OF FANS!>
YEAH, BUT THERE'S SOMETHING UNNATURAL ABOUT THESE PICS...
HE DOESN'T SEEM LIKE THE KINDA GUY TO HANG OUT WITH DUDES IN THE FIRST PLACE.
COME TO THINK OF IT...
...

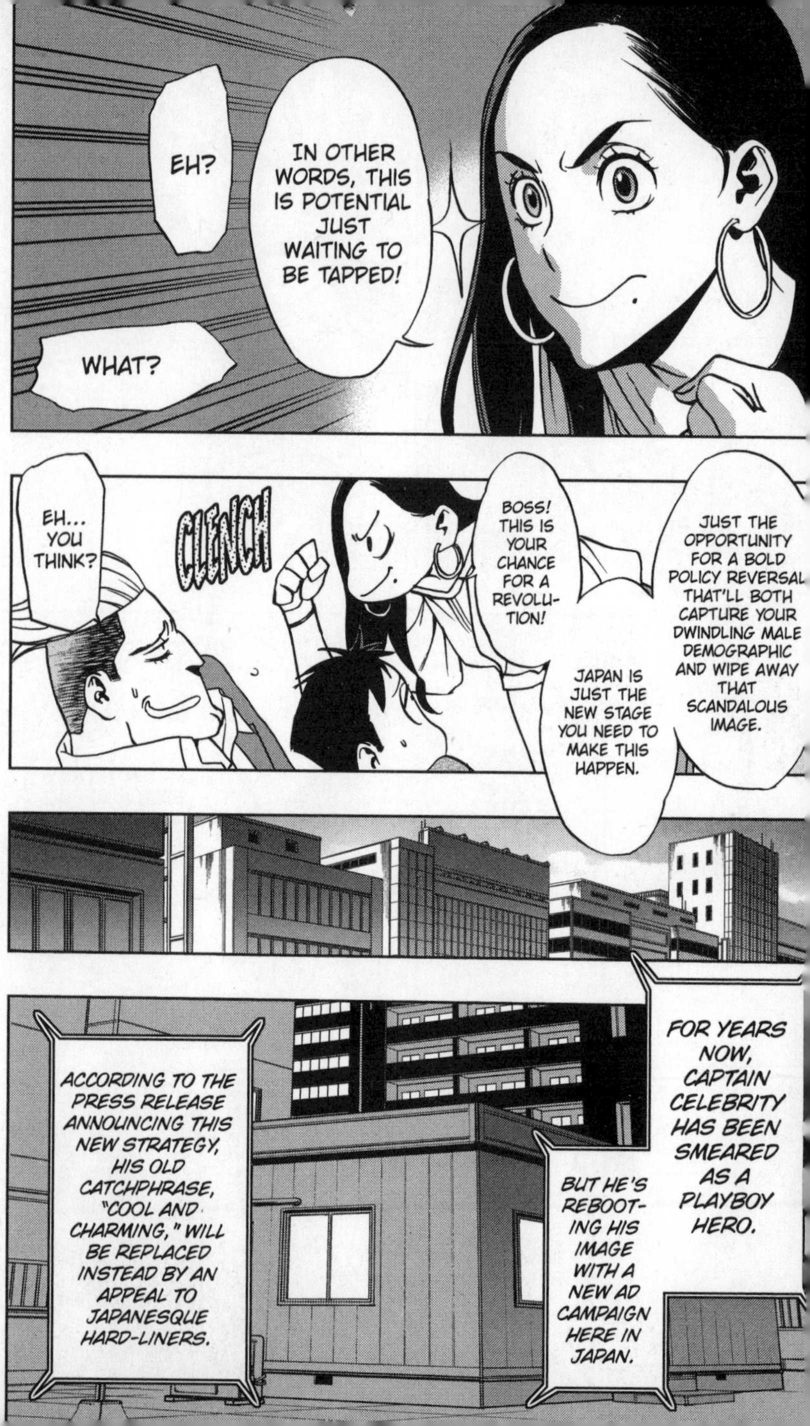
IN OTHER WORDS, THIS IS POTENTIAL JUST WAITING TO BE TAPPED!
EH?
WHAT?
JUST THE OPPORTUNITY FOR A BOLD POLICY REVERSAL THAT'LL BOTH CAPTURE YOUR DWINDLING MALE DEMOGRAPHIC AND WIPE AWAY THAT SCANDALOUS IMAGE.
BOSS! THIS IS YOUR CHANCE FOR A REVOLU-TION!
JAPAN IS JUST THE NEW STAGE YOU NEED TO MAKE THIS HAPPEN.
CLENCH
EH... YOU THINK?
FOR YEARS NOW, CAPTAIN CELEBRITY HAS BEEN SMEARED AS A PLAYBOY HERO.
BUT HE'S REBOOT-ING HIS IMAGE WITH A NEW AD CAMPAIGN HERE IN JAPAN.
ACCORDING TO THE PRESS RELEASE ANNOUNCING THIS NEW STRATEGY, HIS OLD CATCHPHRASE, "COOL AND CHARMING," WILL BE REPLACED INSTEAD BY AN APPEAL TO JAPANESQUE HARD-LINERS.

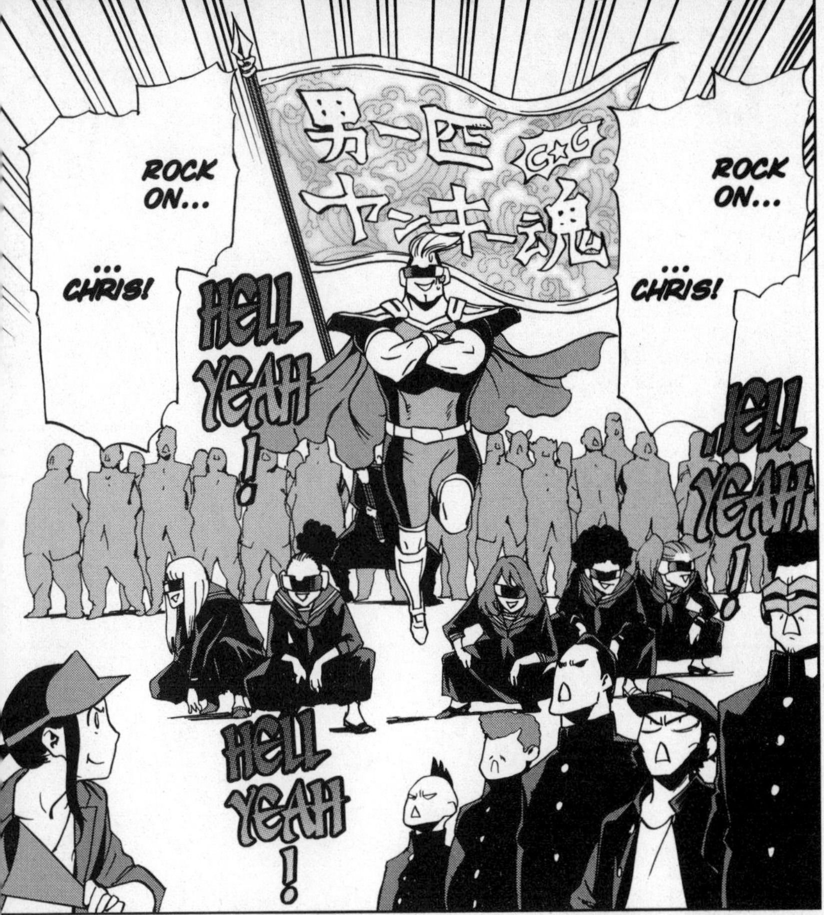
ROCK ON... ...CHRIS!
男一匹 C☆C ヤンキー魂
ROCK ON... ...CHRIS!
HELL YEAH!
HELL YEAH!
HELL YEAH!
*FLAG: A MAN'S MAN YANKEE SPIRIT

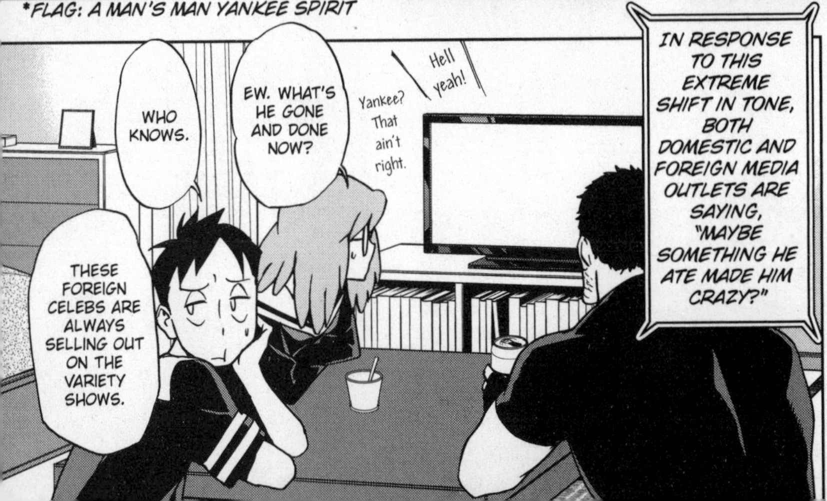
IN RESPONSE TO THIS EXTREME SHIFT IN TONE, BOTH DOMESTIC AND FOREIGN MEDIA OUTLETS ARE SAYING, "MAYBE SOMETHING HE ATE MADE HIM CRAZY?"
Hell yeah!
Yankee? That ain't right.
EW. WHAT'S HE GONE AND DONE NOW?
WHO KNOWS.
THESE FOREIGN CELEBS ARE ALWAYS SELLING OUT ON THE VARIETY SHOWS.

CAPTAIN CELEBRITY

THE ROUGH DESIGN

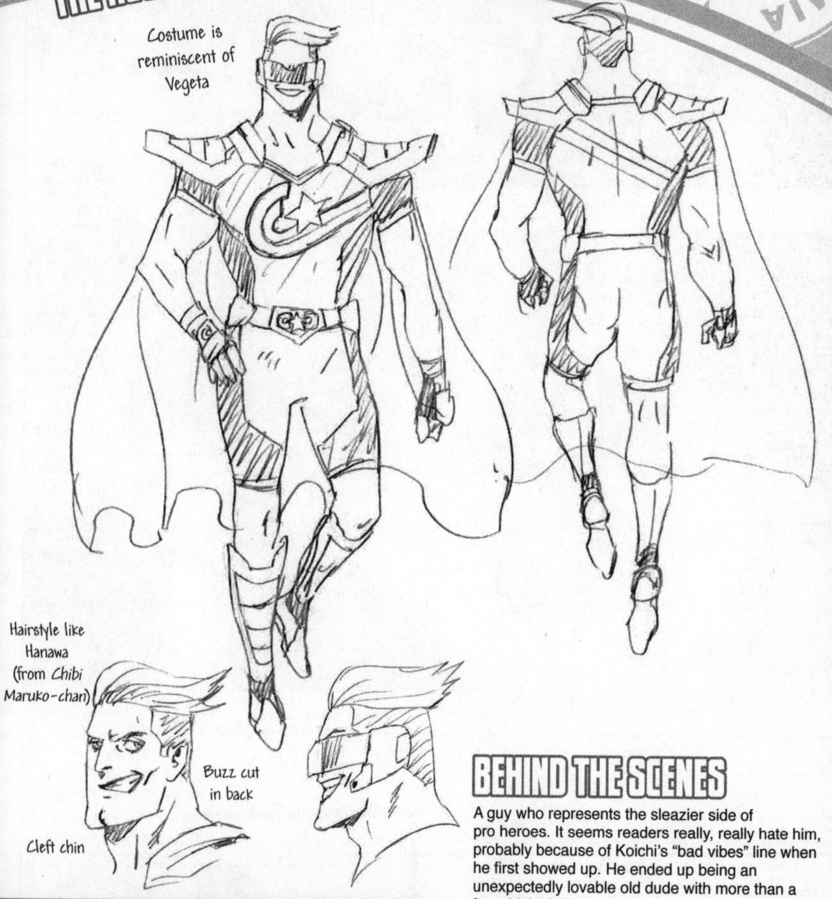

Costume is reminiscent of Vegeta
Hairstyle like Hanawa (from Chibi Maruko-chan)
Buzz cut in back
Cleft chin

BEHIND THE SCENES

A guy who represents the sleazier side of pro heroes. It seems readers really, really hate him, probably because of Koichi's "bad vibes" line when he first showed up. He ended up being an unexpectedly lovable old dude with more than a few chinks in his armor, but, well, first impressions are everything.

—Furuhashi

Think cleft chin + Freeza's army + Knights of the Zodiac + Hanawa hair. That's the image, here.

—Betten

REAL NAME: CHRISTOPHER SKYLINE

BIRTHDAY: 7/4

HEIGHT: 200 CM

FAVORITE THINGS: HAMBURGERS, STEAKS

QUIRK: FLIGHT

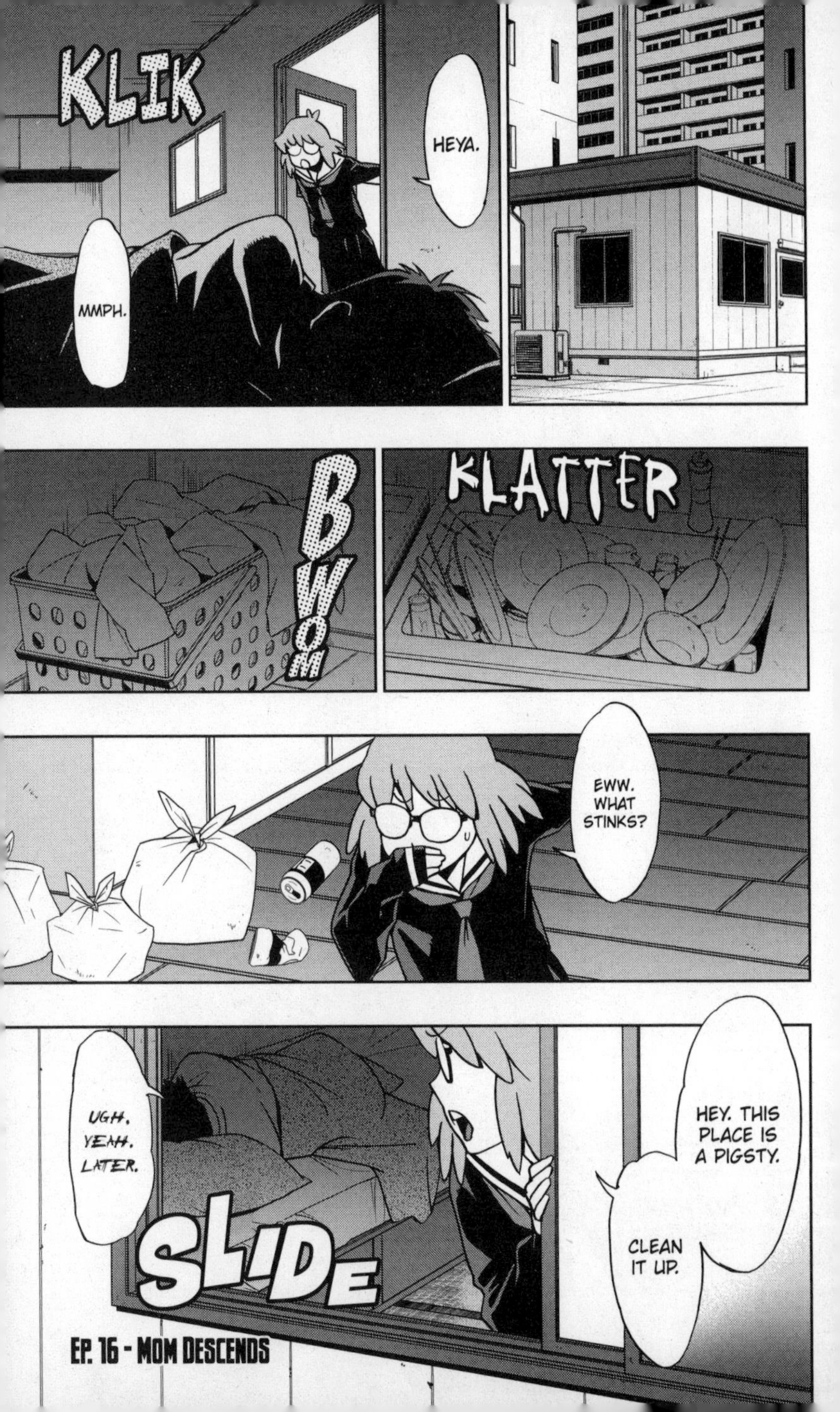
KLIK
HEYA.
MMPH.
KLATTER
BWOM
EWW. WHAT STINKS?
HEY. THIS PLACE IS A PIGSTY.
CLEAN IT UP.
SLIDE
UGH. YEAH. LATER.
EP. 16 - MOM DESCENDS

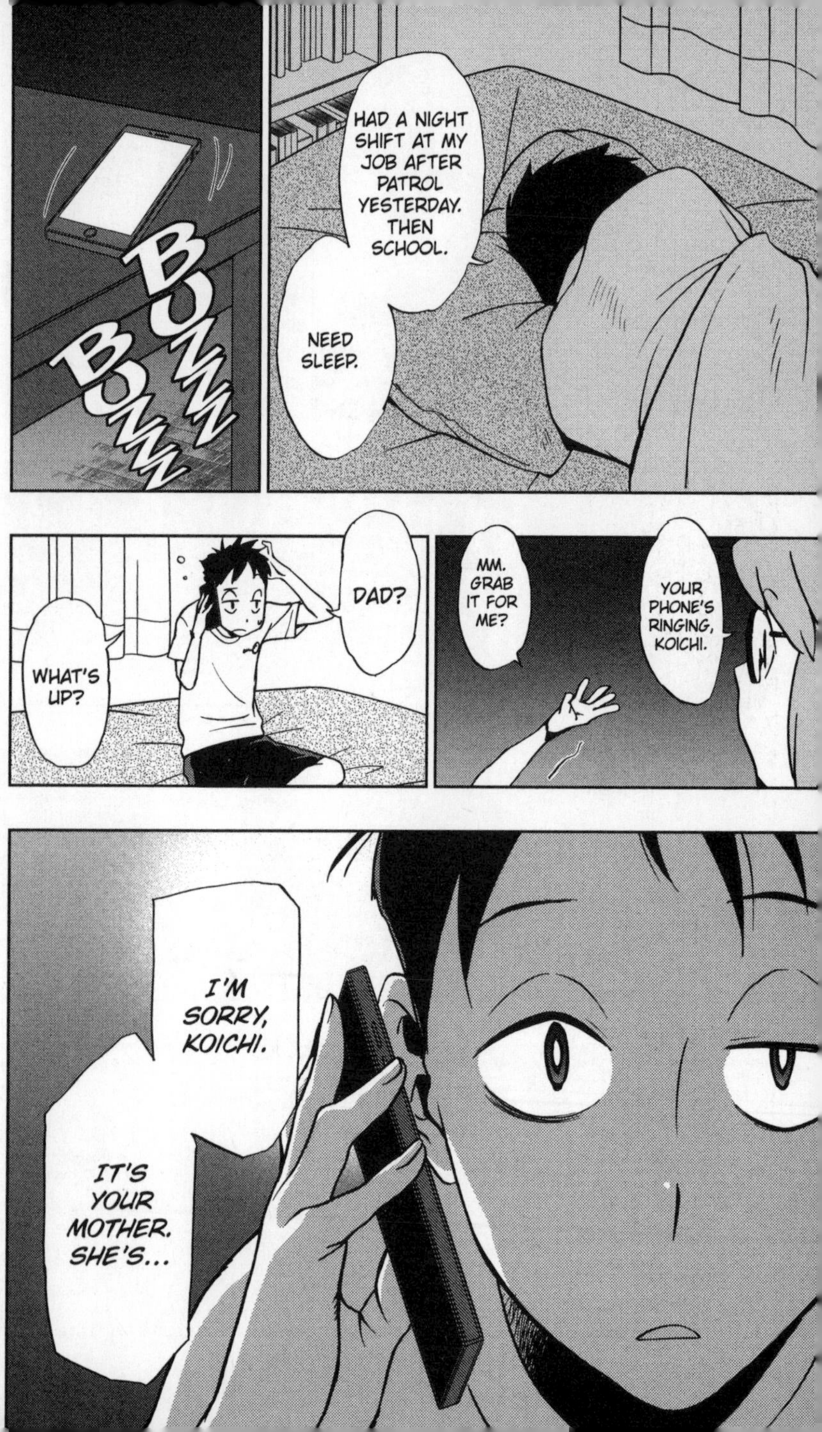

HAD A NIGHT SHIFT AT MY JOB AFTER PATROL YESTERDAY. THEN SCHOOL.
NEED SLEEP.
BUMM
BUMM
YOUR PHONE'S RINGING, KOICHI.
MM. GRAB IT FOR ME?
DAD?
WHAT'S UP?
I'M SORRY, KOICHI.
IT'S YOUR MOTHER. SHE'S...

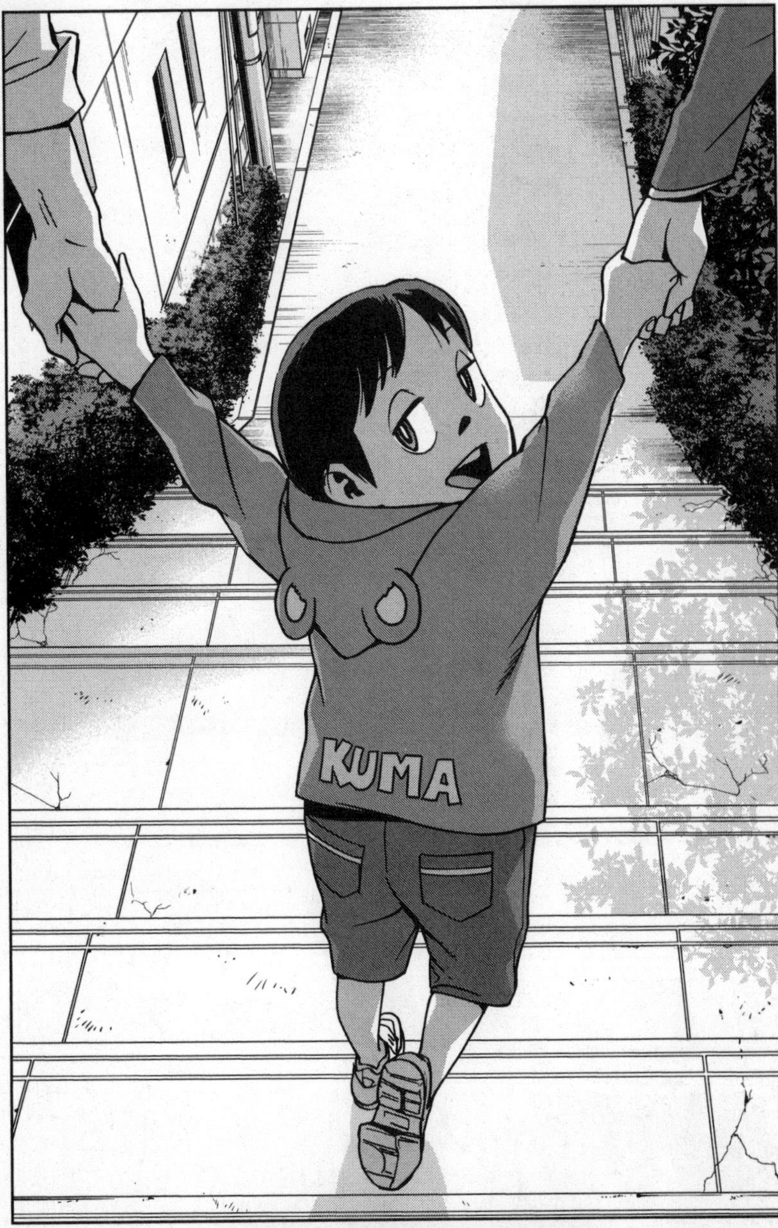
KUMA

EP. 16 - MOM DESCENDS

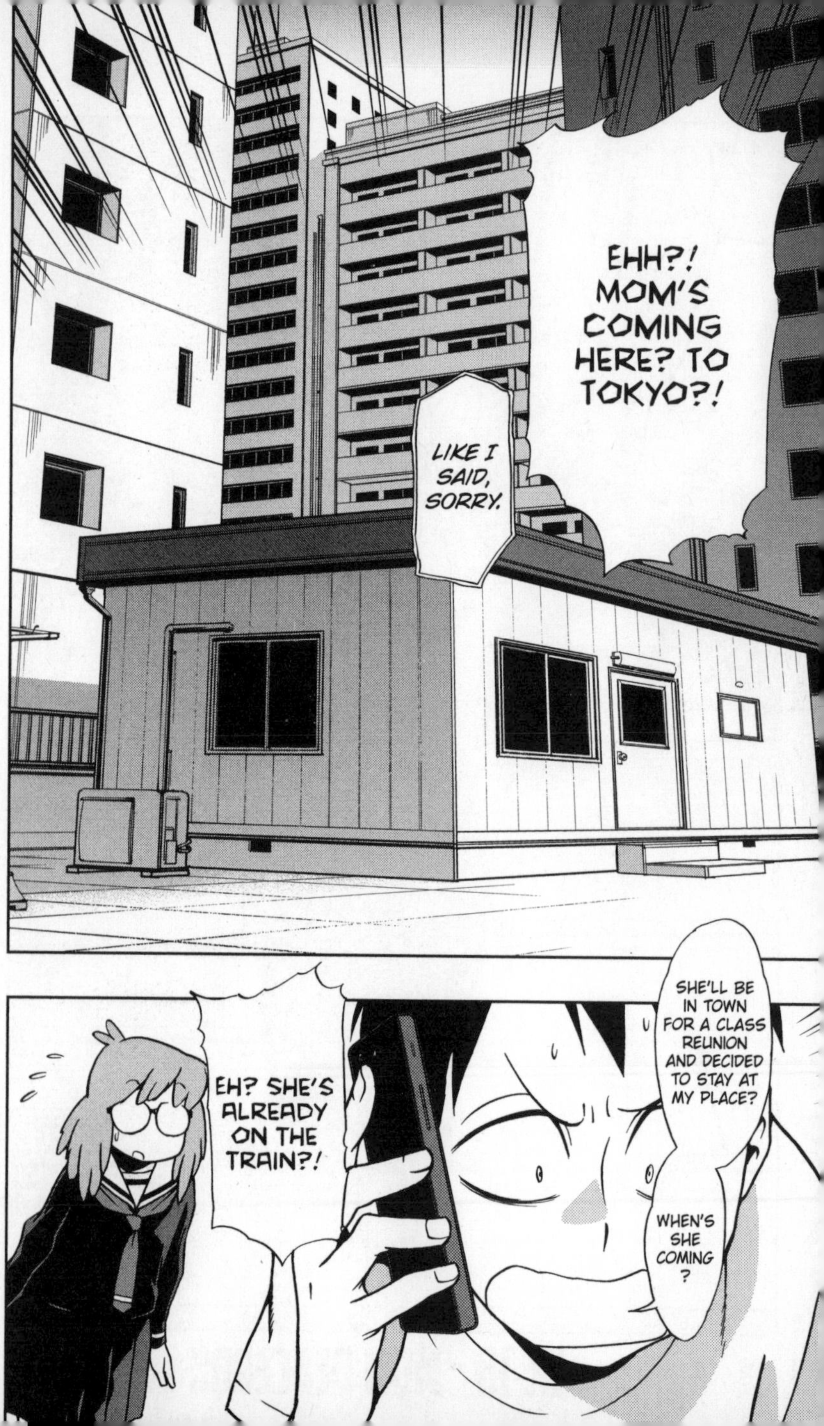
EHH?! MOM'S COMING HERE? TO TOKYO?!
LIKE I SAID, SORRY.
SHE'LL BE IN TOWN FOR A CLASS REUNION AND DECIDED TO STAY AT MY PLACE?
WHEN'S SHE COMING?
EH? SHE'S ALREADY ON THE TRAIN?!

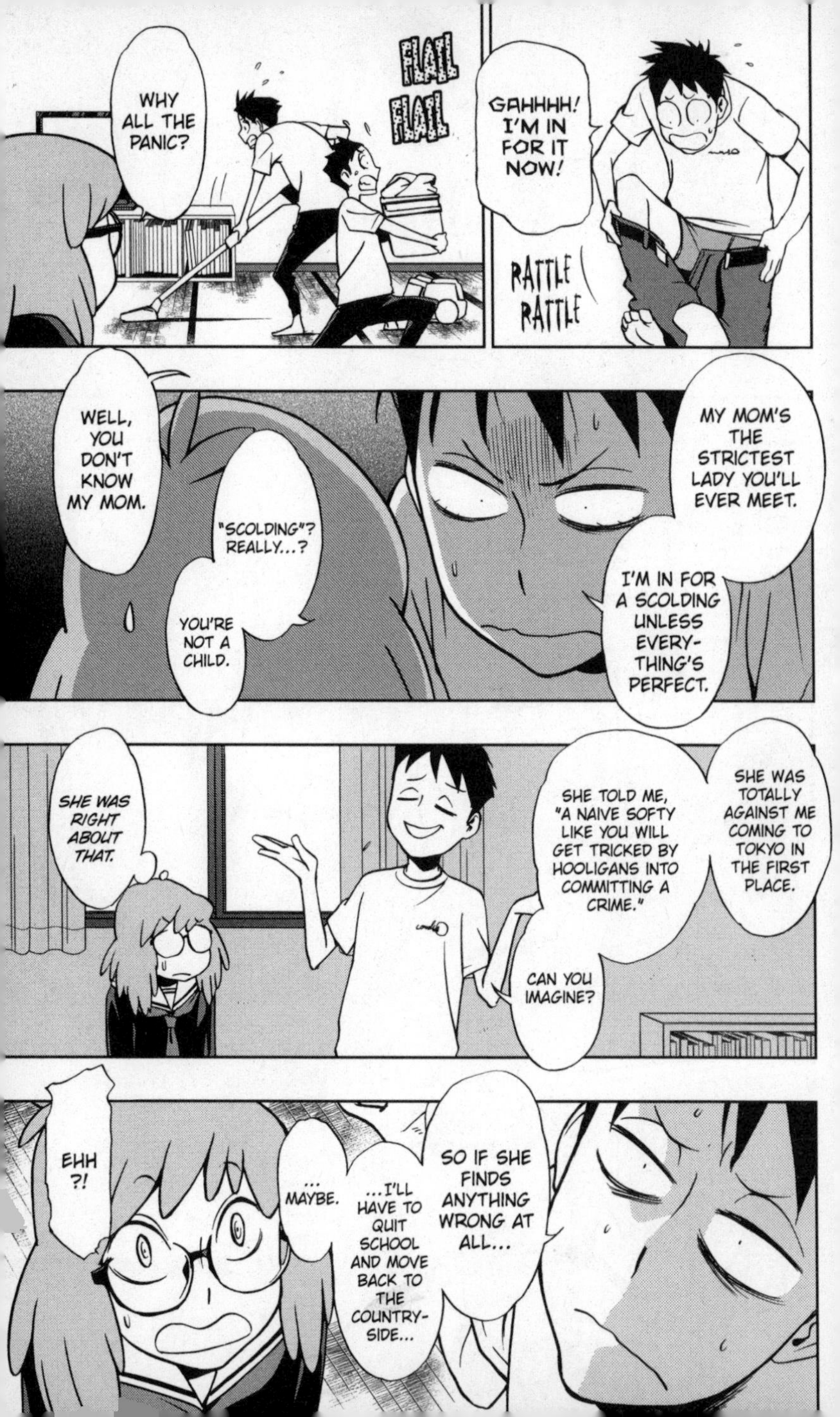
GAHHHH! I'M IN FOR IT NOW!
RATTLE RATTLE
FLAIL FLAIL
WHY ALL THE PANIC?
MY MOM'S THE STRICTEST LADY YOU'LL EVER MEET.
I'M IN FOR A SCOLDING UNLESS EVERY-THING'S PERFECT.
"SCOLDING"? REALLY...?
YOU'RE NOT A CHILD.
WELL, YOU DON'T KNOW MY MOM.
SHE WAS TOTALLY AGAINST ME COMING TO TOKYO IN THE FIRST PLACE.
SHE TOLD ME, "A NAIVE SOFTY LIKE YOU WILL GET TRICKED BY HOOLIGANS INTO COMMITTING A CRIME."
CAN YOU IMAGINE?
SHE WAS RIGHT ABOUT THAT.
SO IF SHE FINDS ANYTHING WRONG AT ALL...
...I'LL HAVE TO QUIT SCHOOL AND MOVE BACK TO THE COUNTRY-SIDE...
... MAYBE.
EHH ?!

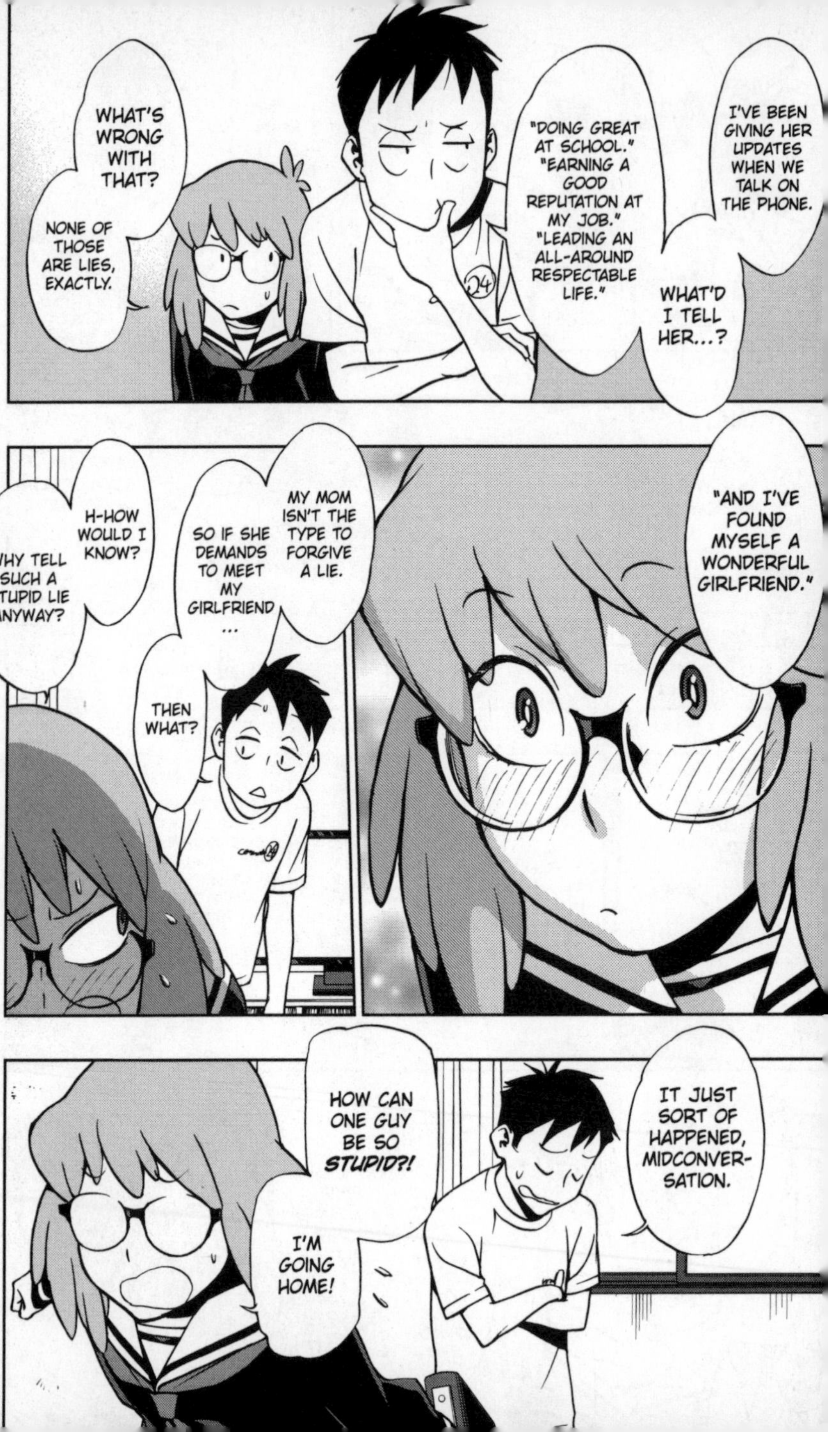
I'VE BEEN GIVING HER UPDATES WHEN WE TALK ON THE PHONE.
WHAT'D I TELL HER...?
"DOING GREAT AT SCHOOL." "EARNING A GOOD REPUTATION AT MY JOB." "LEADING AN ALL-AROUND RESPECTABLE LIFE."
NONE OF THOSE ARE LIES, EXACTLY.
WHAT'S WRONG WITH THAT?
"AND I'VE FOUND MYSELF A WONDERFUL GIRLFRIEND."
MY MOM ISN'T THE TYPE TO FORGIVE A LIE.
SO IF SHE DEMANDS TO MEET MY GIRLFRIEND...
THEN WHAT?
H-HOW WOULD I KNOW?
WHY TELL SUCH A STUPID LIE ANYWAY?
IT JUST SORT OF HAPPENED, MIDCONVERSATION.
HOW CAN ONE GUY BE SO *STUPID*?!
I'M GOING HOME!

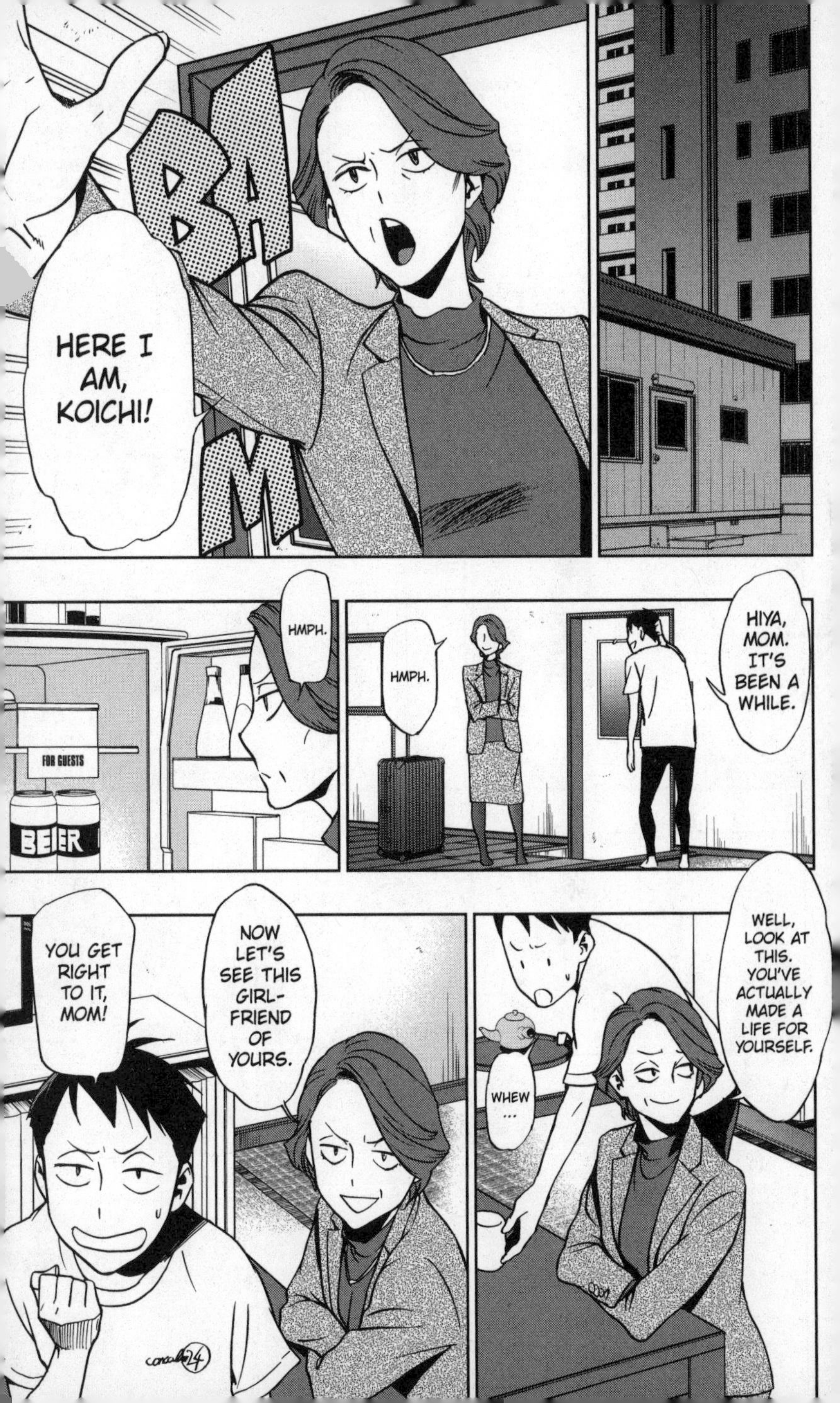
BAM
HERE I AM, KOICHI!
HIYA, MOM. IT'S BEEN A WHILE.
HMPH.
HMPH.
FOR GUESTS
BEER
WELL, LOOK AT THIS. YOU'VE ACTUALLY MADE A LIFE FOR YOURSELF.
WHEW ...
NOW LET'S SEE THIS GIRLFRIEND OF YOURS.
YOU GET RIGHT TO IT, MOM!

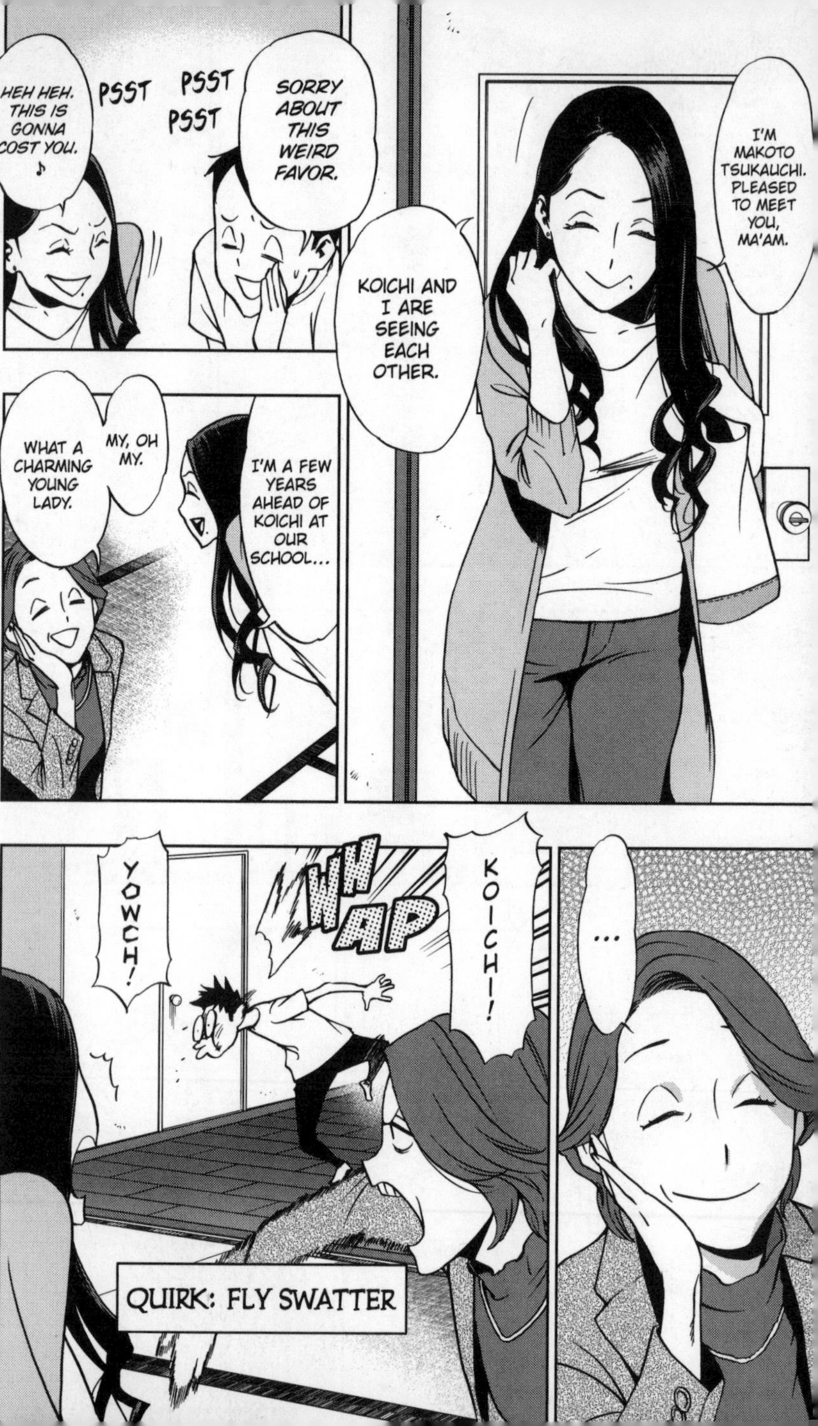
I'M MAKOTO TSUKAUCHI. PLEASED TO MEET YOU, MA'AM.
KOICHI AND I ARE SEEING EACH OTHER.
SORRY ABOUT THIS WEIRD FAVOR.
PSST PSST
PSST
HEH HEH. THIS IS GONNA COST YOU. ♪
I'M A FEW YEARS AHEAD OF KOICHI AT OUR SCHOOL...
MY, OH MY.
WHAT A CHARMING YOUNG LADY.
...
KOICHI!
WHAP
YOWCH!
QUIRK: FLY SWATTER

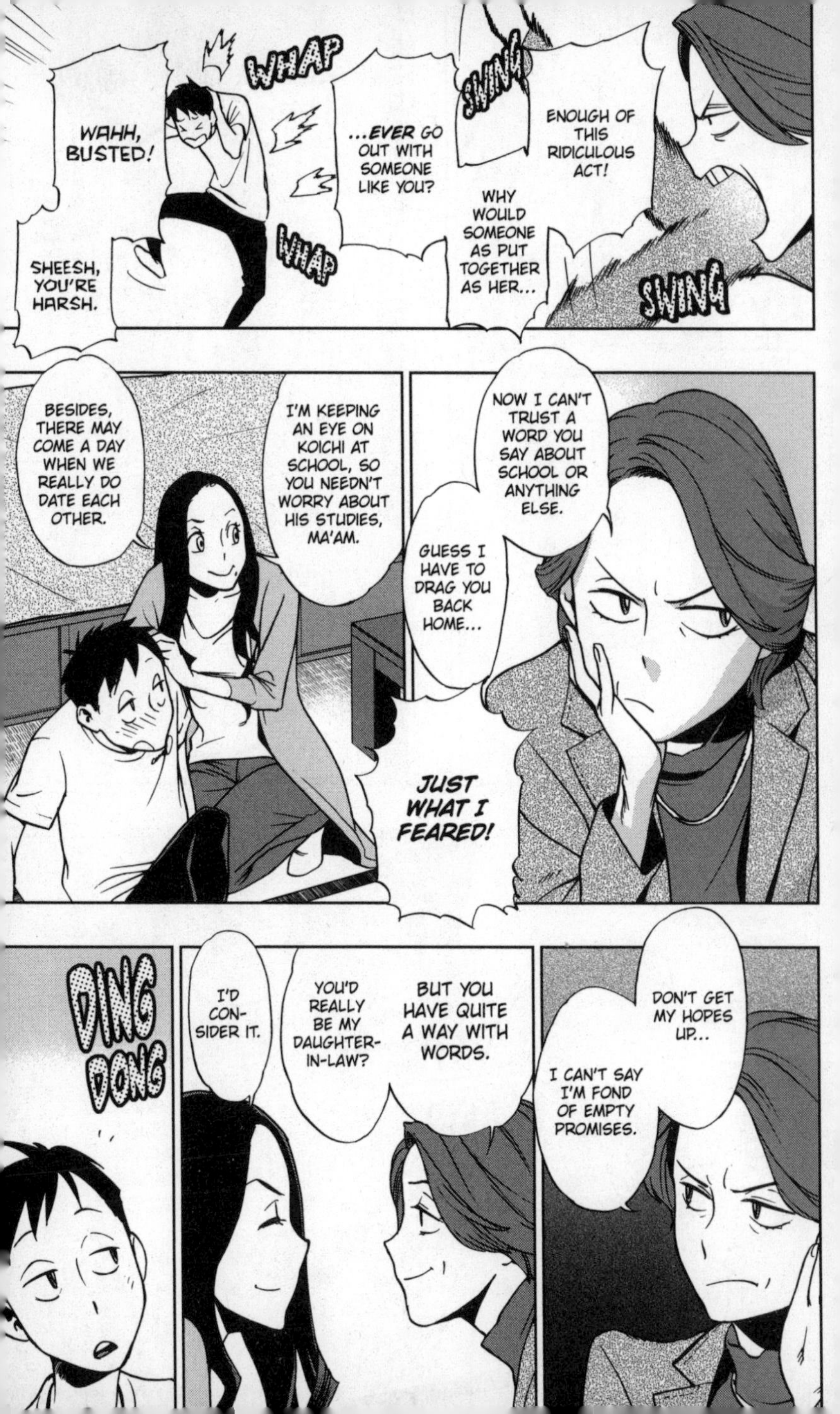
ENOUGH OF THIS RIDICULOUS ACT!
SWING
SWING
WHY WOULD SOMEONE AS PUT TOGETHER AS HER...
...*EVER* GO OUT WITH SOMEONE LIKE YOU?
WHAP
WHAP
WAHH, BUSTED!
SHEESH, YOU'RE HARSH.
NOW I CAN'T TRUST A WORD YOU SAY ABOUT SCHOOL OR ANYTHING ELSE.
GUESS I HAVE TO DRAG YOU BACK HOME...
JUST WHAT I FEARED!
I'M KEEPING AN EYE ON KOICHI AT SCHOOL, SO YOU NEEDN'T WORRY ABOUT HIS STUDIES, MA'AM.
BESIDES, THERE MAY COME A DAY WHEN WE REALLY DO DATE EACH OTHER.
DON'T GET MY HOPES UP...
I CAN'T SAY I'M FOND OF EMPTY PROMISES.
BUT YOU HAVE QUITE A WAY WITH WORDS.
YOU'D REALLY BE MY DAUGHTER-IN-LAW?
I'D CON-SIDER IT.
DING DONG

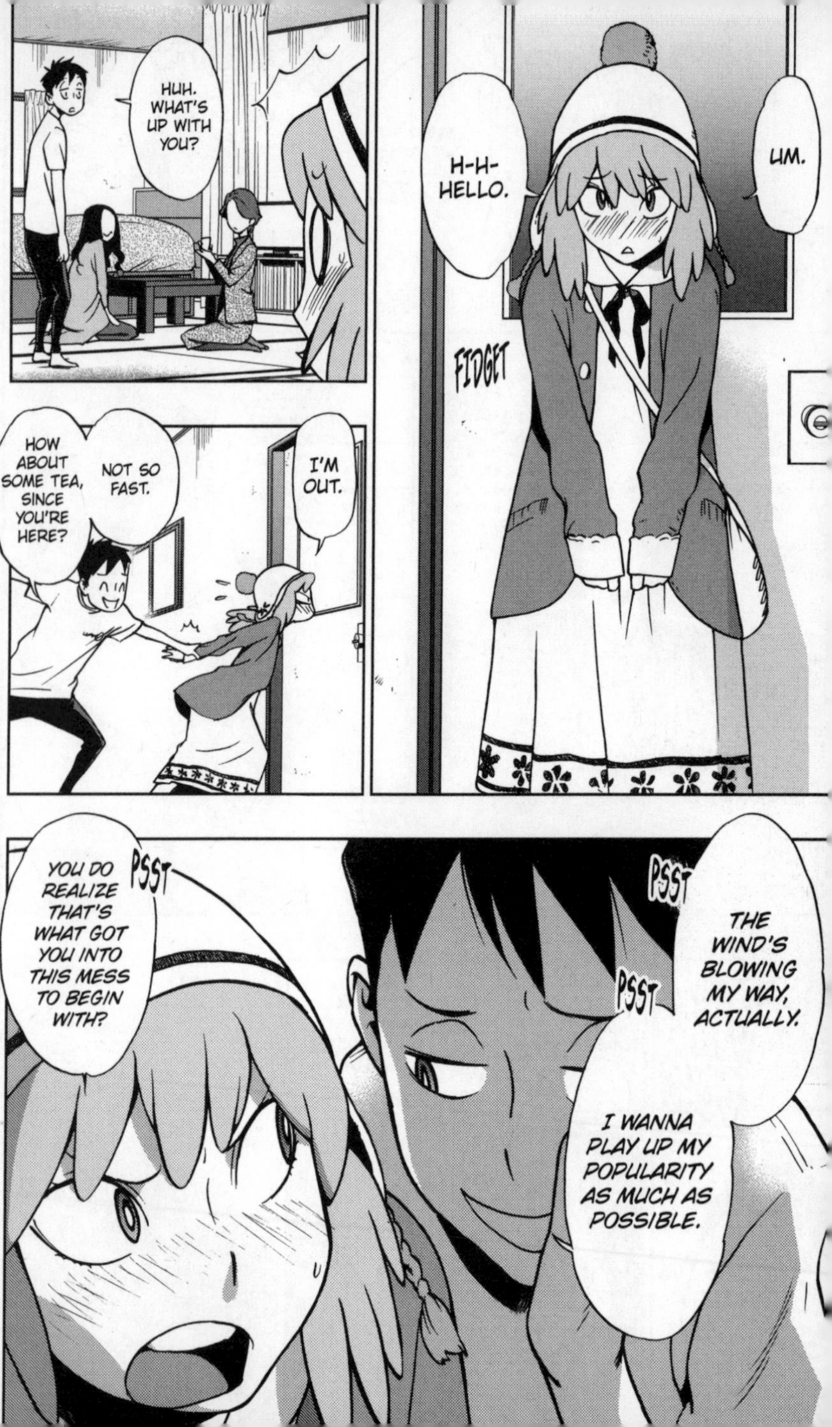
UM.
H-H-HELLO.
FIDGET
HUH. WHAT'S UP WITH YOU?
I'M OUT.
NOT SO FAST.
HOW ABOUT SOME TEA, SINCE YOU'RE HERE?
PSST
THE WIND'S BLOWING MY WAY, ACTUALLY.
PSST
I WANNA PLAY UP MY POPULARITY AS MUCH AS POSSIBLE.
PSST
YOU DO REALIZE THAT'S WHAT GOT YOU INTO THIS MESS TO BEGIN WITH?

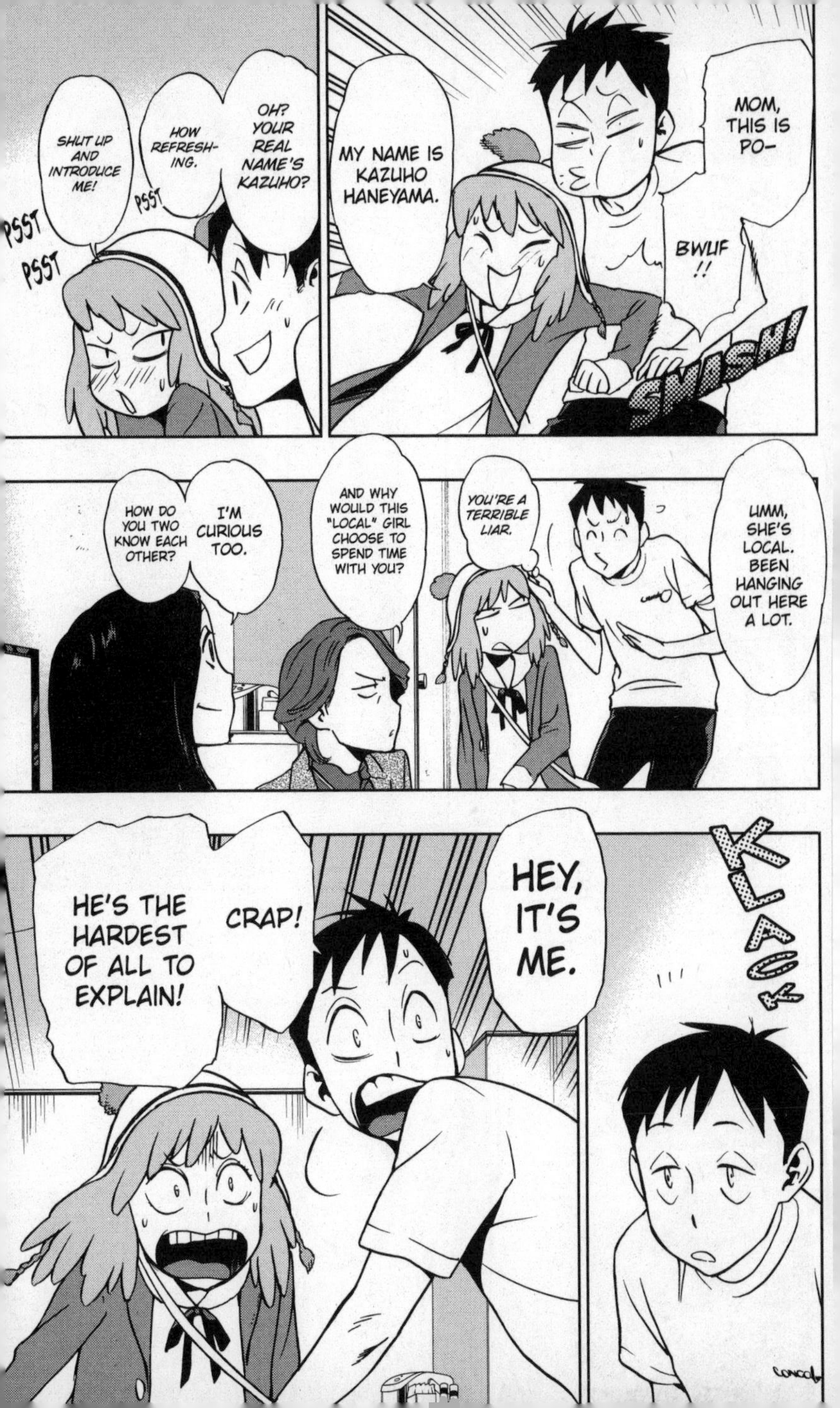
MOM, THIS IS PO-
BWUF!!
SWISH!
MY NAME IS KAZUHO HANEYAMA.
OH? YOUR REAL NAME'S KAZUHO?
HOW REFRESH-ING.
PSST
SHUT UP AND INTRODUCE ME!
PSST PSST
UMM, SHE'S LOCAL. BEEN HANGING OUT HERE A LOT.
YOU'RE A TERRIBLE LIAR.
AND WHY WOULD THIS "LOCAL" GIRL CHOOSE TO SPEND TIME WITH YOU?
I'M CURIOUS TOO.
HOW DO YOU TWO KNOW EACH OTHER?
KLACK
HEY, IT'S ME.
CRAP!
HE'S THE HARDEST OF ALL TO EXPLAIN!

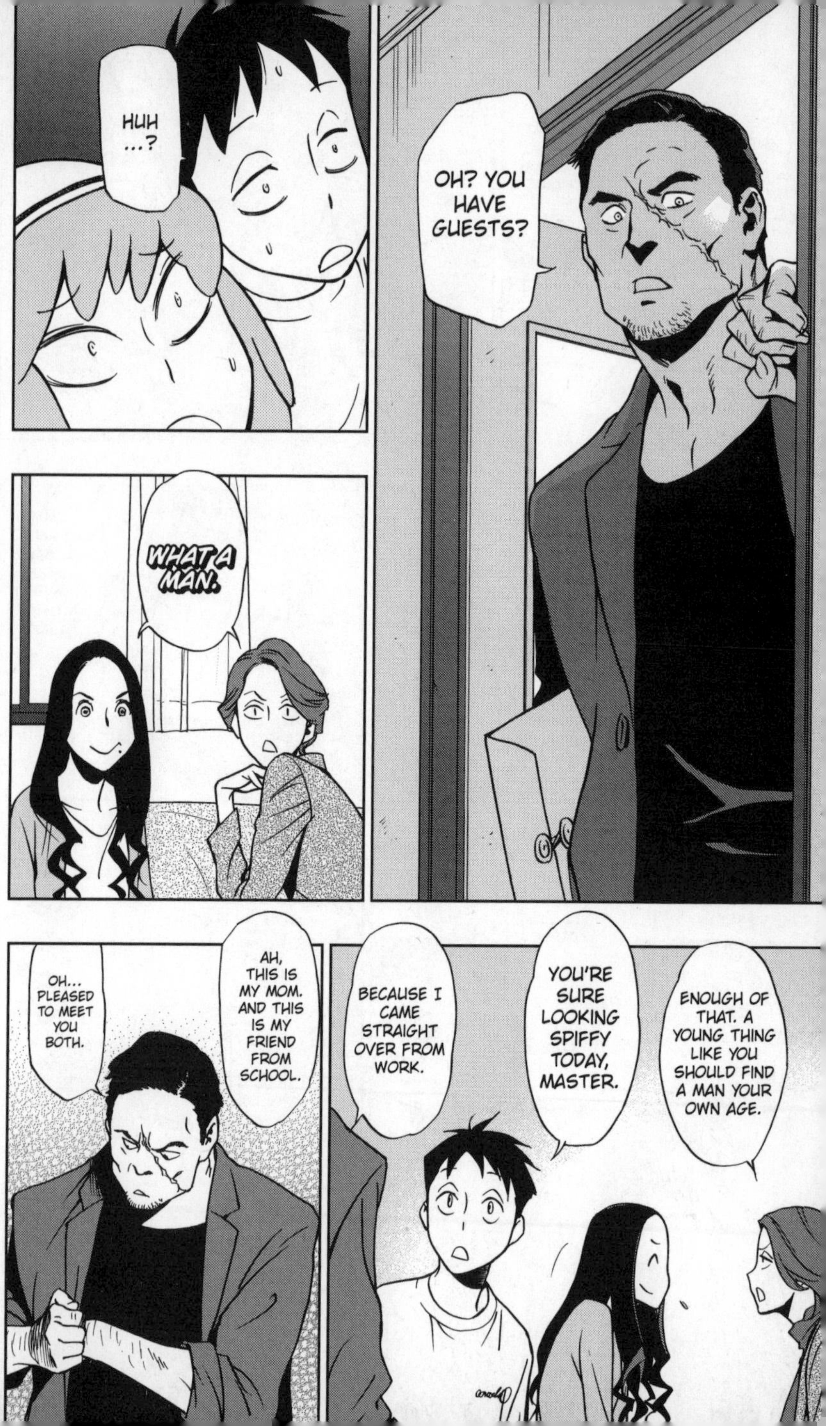
OH? YOU HAVE GUESTS?
HUH ...?
WHAT A MAN.
ENOUGH OF THAT. A YOUNG THING LIKE YOU SHOULD FIND A MAN YOUR OWN AGE.
YOU'RE SURE LOOKING SPIFFY TODAY, MASTER.
BECAUSE I CAME STRAIGHT OVER FROM WORK.
AH, THIS IS MY MOM. AND THIS IS MY FRIEND FROM SCHOOL.
OH... PLEASED TO MEET YOU BOTH.

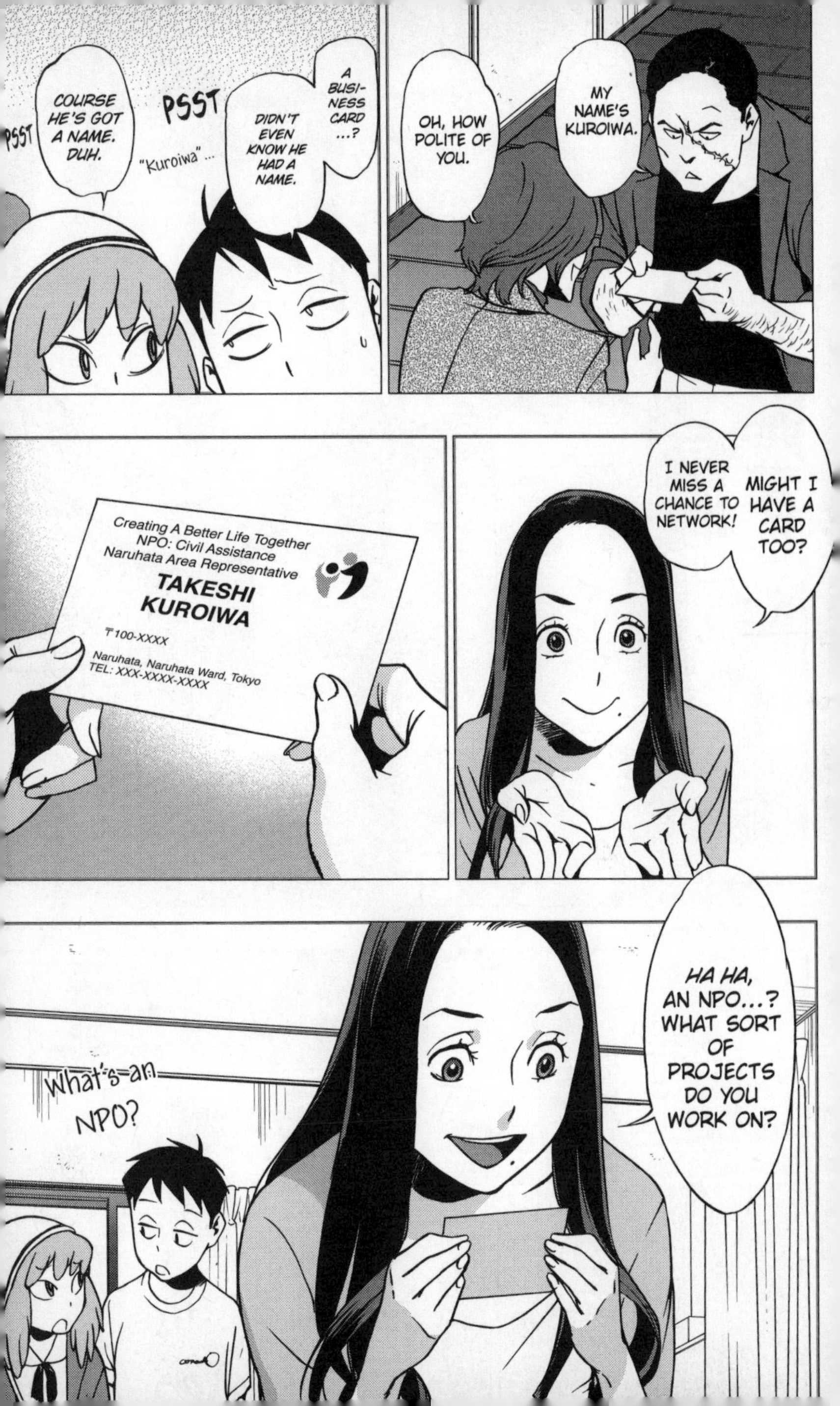
MY NAME'S KUROIWA.
OH, HOW POLITE OF YOU.
A BUSI-NESS CARD ...?
DIDN'T EVEN KNOW HE HAD A NAME.
PSST
"Kuroiwa"...
COURSE HE'S GOT A NAME. DUH.
PSST
MIGHT I HAVE A CARD TOO?
I NEVER MISS A CHANCE TO NETWORK!
Creating A Better Life Together
NPO: Civil Assistance
Naruhata Area Representative
TAKESHI KUROIWA
〒100-XXXX
Naruhata, Naruhata Ward, Tokyo
TEL: XXX-XXXX-XXXX
HA HA, AN NPO...? WHAT SORT OF PROJECTS DO YOU WORK ON?
What's an NPO?

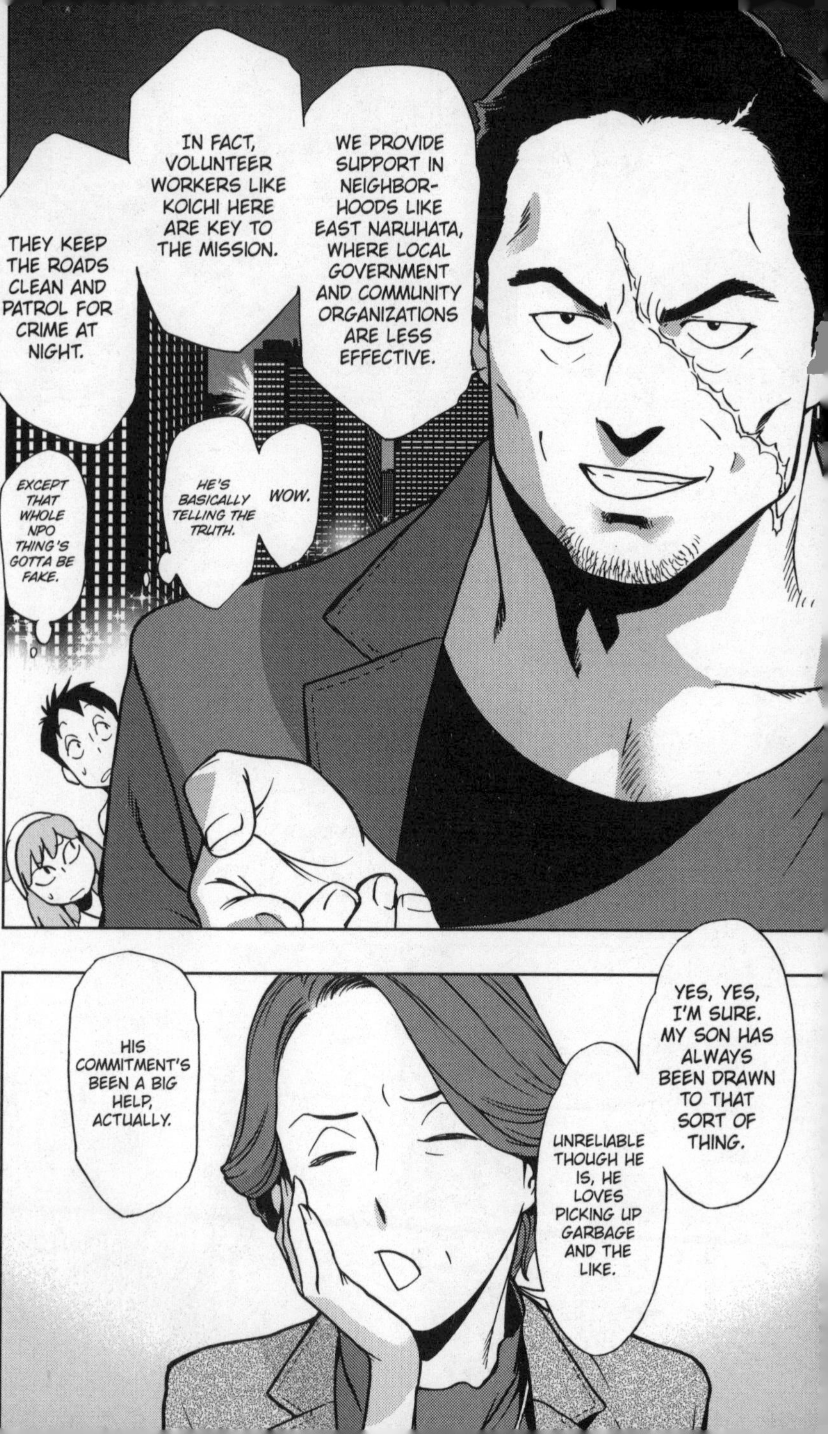
WE PROVIDE SUPPORT IN NEIGHBOR-HOODS LIKE EAST NARUHATA, WHERE LOCAL GOVERNMENT AND COMMUNITY ORGANIZATIONS ARE LESS EFFECTIVE.
IN FACT, VOLUNTEER WORKERS LIKE KOICHI HERE ARE KEY TO THE MISSION.
THEY KEEP THE ROADS CLEAN AND PATROL FOR CRIME AT NIGHT.
WOW.
HE'S BASICALLY TELLING THE TRUTH.
EXCEPT THAT WHOLE NPO THING'S GOTTA BE FAKE.
YES, YES, I'M SURE. MY SON HAS ALWAYS BEEN DRAWN TO THAT SORT OF THING.
UNRELIABLE THOUGH HE IS, HE LOVES PICKING UP GARBAGE AND THE LIKE.
HIS COMMITMENT'S BEEN A BIG HELP, ACTUALLY.

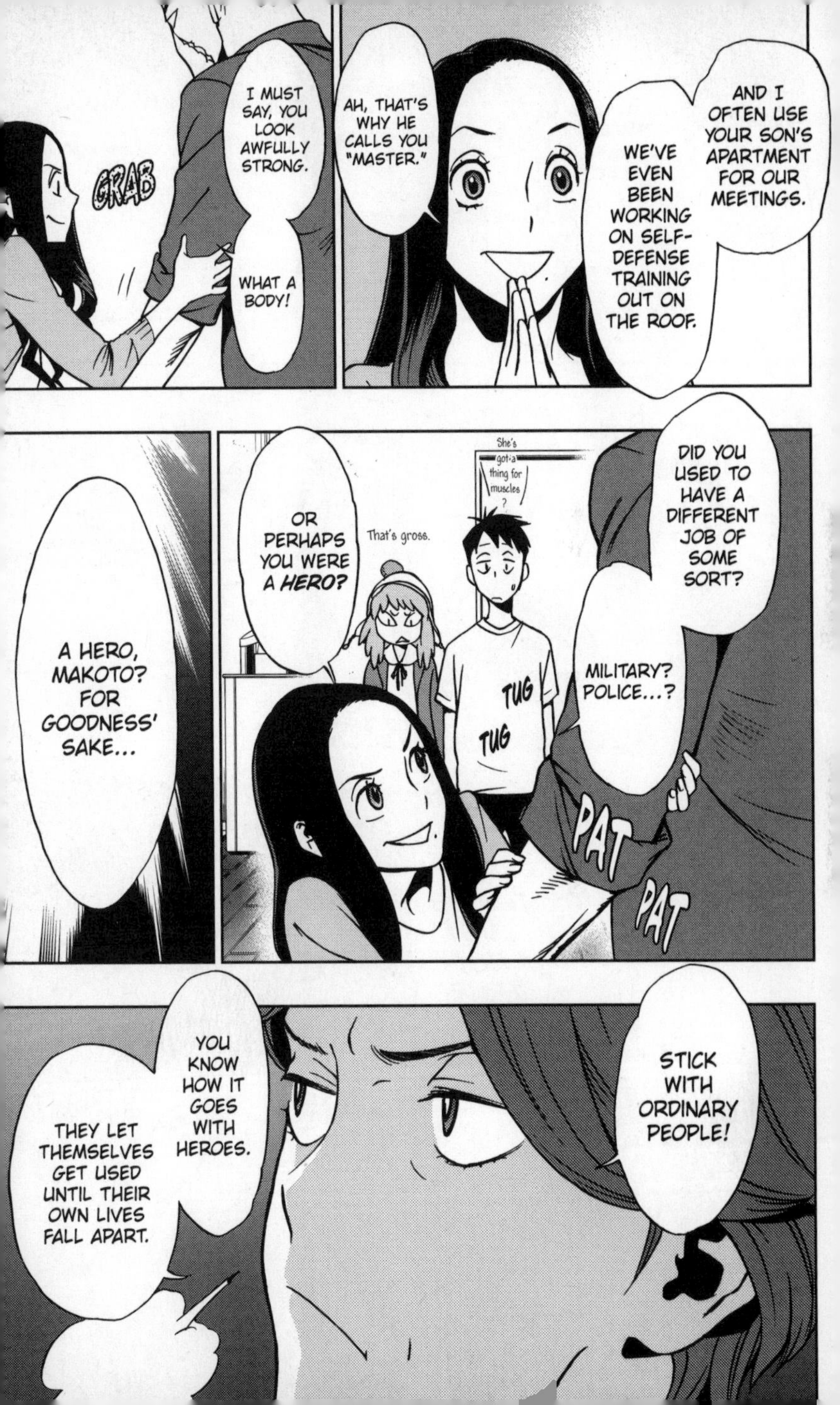
AND I OFTEN USE YOUR SON'S APARTMENT FOR OUR MEETINGS.
WE'VE EVEN BEEN WORKING ON SELF-DEFENSE TRAINING OUT ON THE ROOF.
AH, THAT'S WHY HE CALLS YOU "MASTER."
I MUST SAY, YOU LOOK AWFULLY STRONG.
GRAB
WHAT A BODY!
DID YOU USED TO HAVE A DIFFERENT JOB OF SOME SORT?
MILITARY? POLICE...?
PAT
PAT
TUG
TUG
She's got a thing for muscles?
That's gross.
OR PERHAPS YOU WERE A *HERO*?
A HERO, MAKOTO? FOR GOODNESS' SAKE...
STICK WITH ORDINARY PEOPLE!
YOU KNOW HOW IT GOES WITH HEROES.
THEY LET THEMSELVES GET USED UNTIL THEIR OWN LIVES FALL APART.

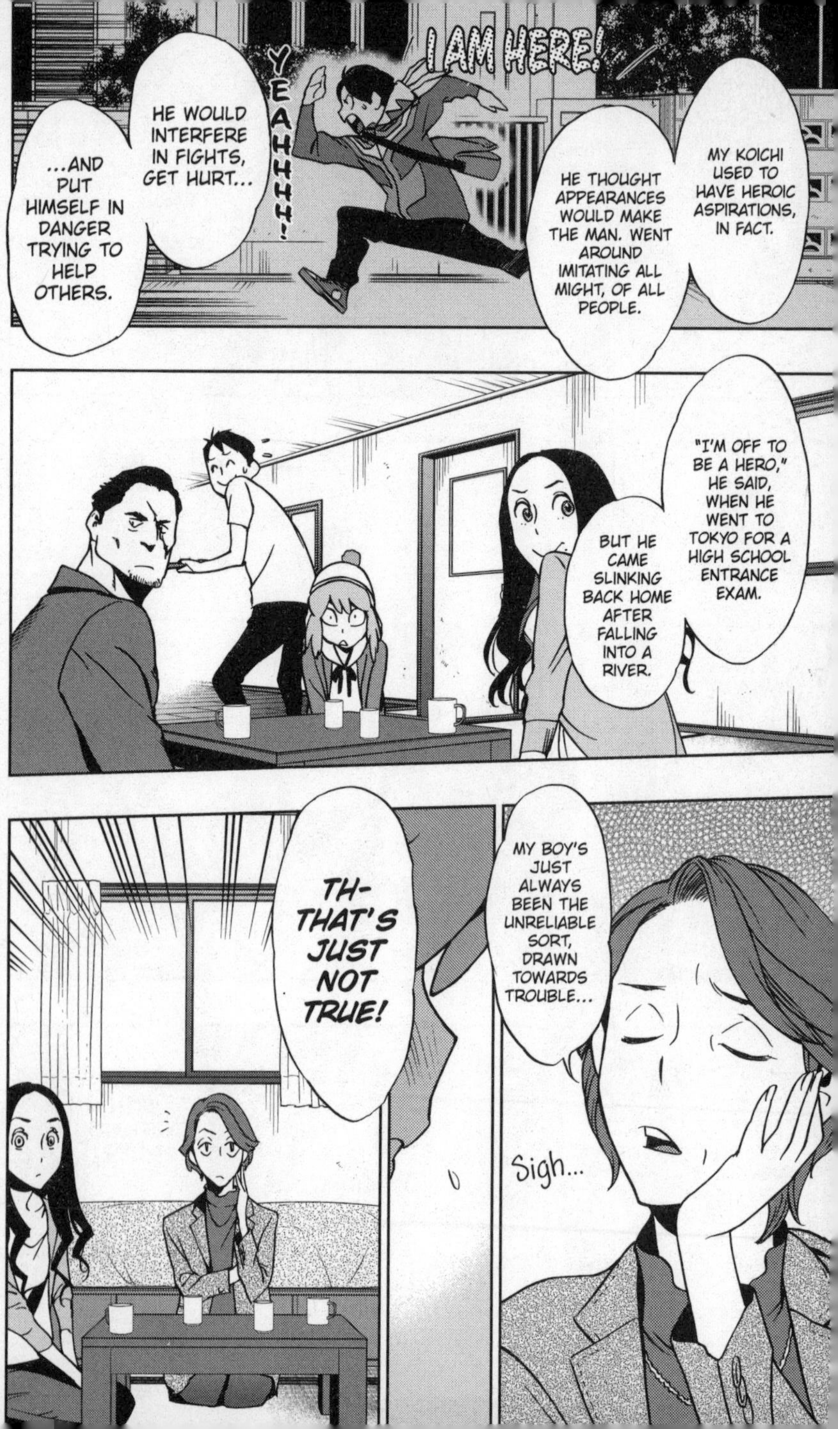
MY KOICHI USED TO HAVE HEROIC ASPIRATIONS, IN FACT.
HE THOUGHT APPEARANCES WOULD MAKE THE MAN. WENT AROUND IMITATING ALL MIGHT, OF ALL PEOPLE.
I AM HERE!
YEAHHHHH!
HE WOULD INTERFERE IN FIGHTS, GET HURT...
...AND PUT HIMSELF IN DANGER TRYING TO HELP OTHERS.
"I'M OFF TO BE A HERO," HE SAID, WHEN HE WENT TO TOKYO FOR A HIGH SCHOOL ENTRANCE EXAM.
BUT HE CAME SLINKING BACK HOME AFTER FALLING INTO A RIVER.
MY BOY'S JUST ALWAYS BEEN THE UNRELIABLE SORT, DRAWN TOWARDS TROUBLE...
Sigh...
TH- THAT'S JUST NOT TRUE!

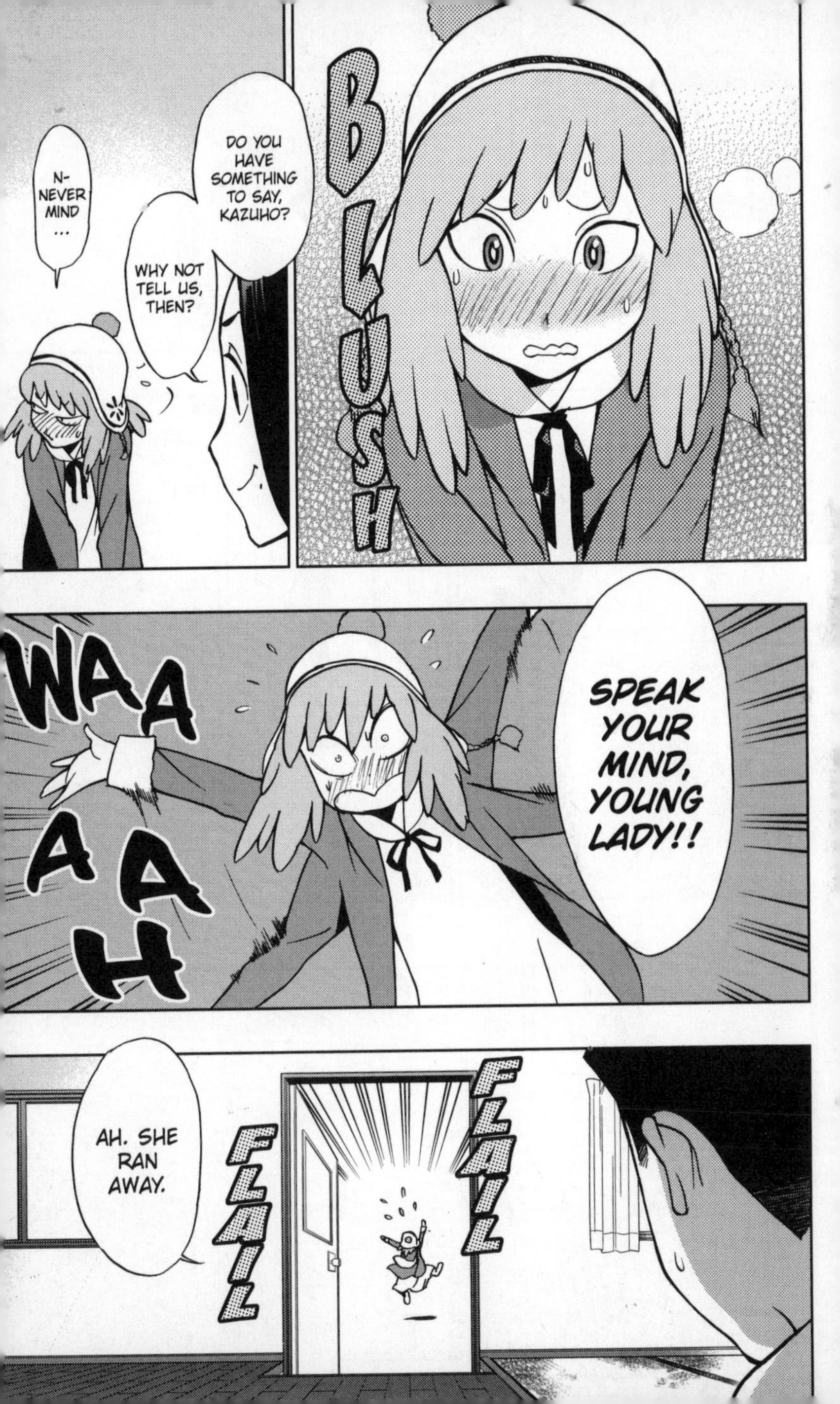
BLUSH
DO YOU HAVE SOMETHING TO SAY, KAZUHO?
WHY NOT TELL US, THEN?
N-NEVER MIND...
SPEAK YOUR MIND, YOUNG LADY!!
WAAAAAH
FLAIL
FLAIL
AH. SHE RAN AWAY.

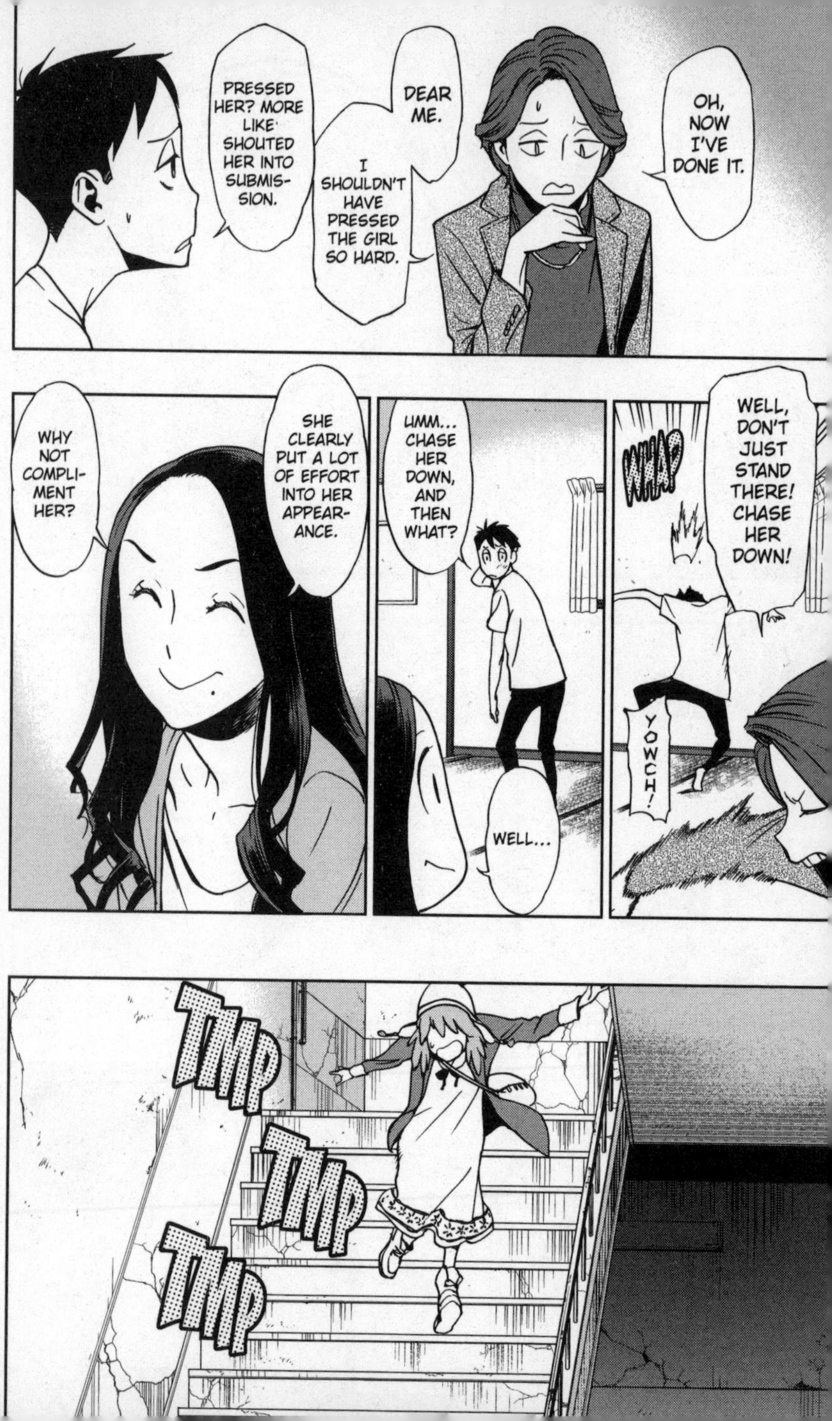
OH, NOW I'VE DONE IT.
DEAR ME.
I SHOULDN'T HAVE PRESSED THE GIRL SO HARD.
PRESSED HER? MORE LIKE SHOUTED HER INTO SUBMISSION.
WELL, DON'T JUST STAND THERE! CHASE HER DOWN!
WHAP
YOWCH!
UMM... CHASE HER DOWN, AND THEN WHAT?
WELL...
SHE CLEARLY PUT A LOT OF EFFORT INTO HER APPEARANCE.
WHY NOT COMPLIMENT HER?
TMP
TMP
TMP

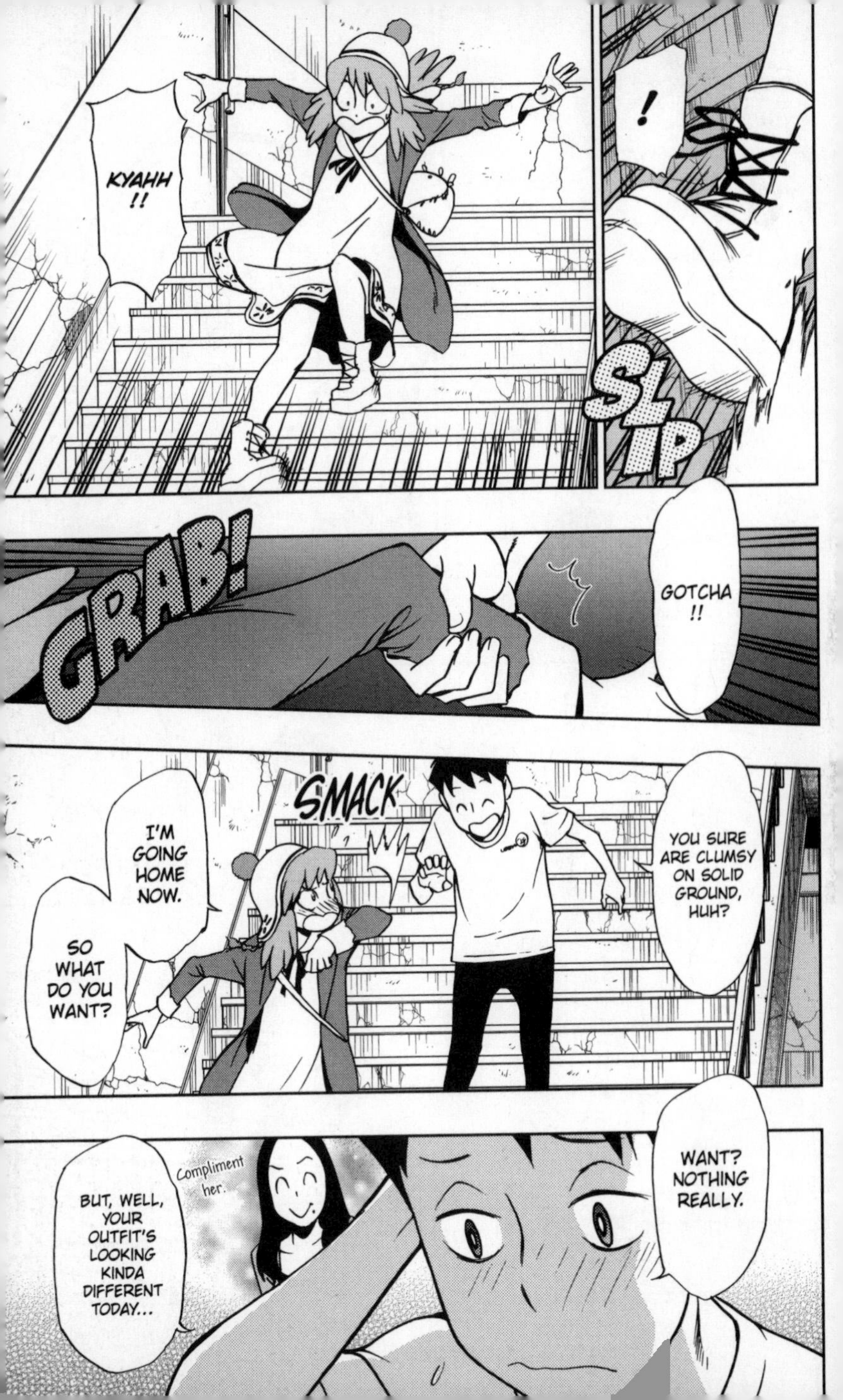
!
SLIP
KYAHH !!
GOTCHA !!
GRAB!
YOU SURE ARE CLUMSY ON SOLID GROUND, HUH?
SMACK
I'M GOING HOME NOW.
SO WHAT DO YOU WANT?
WANT? NOTHING REALLY.
Compliment her.
BUT, WELL, YOUR OUTFIT'S LOOKING KINDA DIFFERENT TODAY...

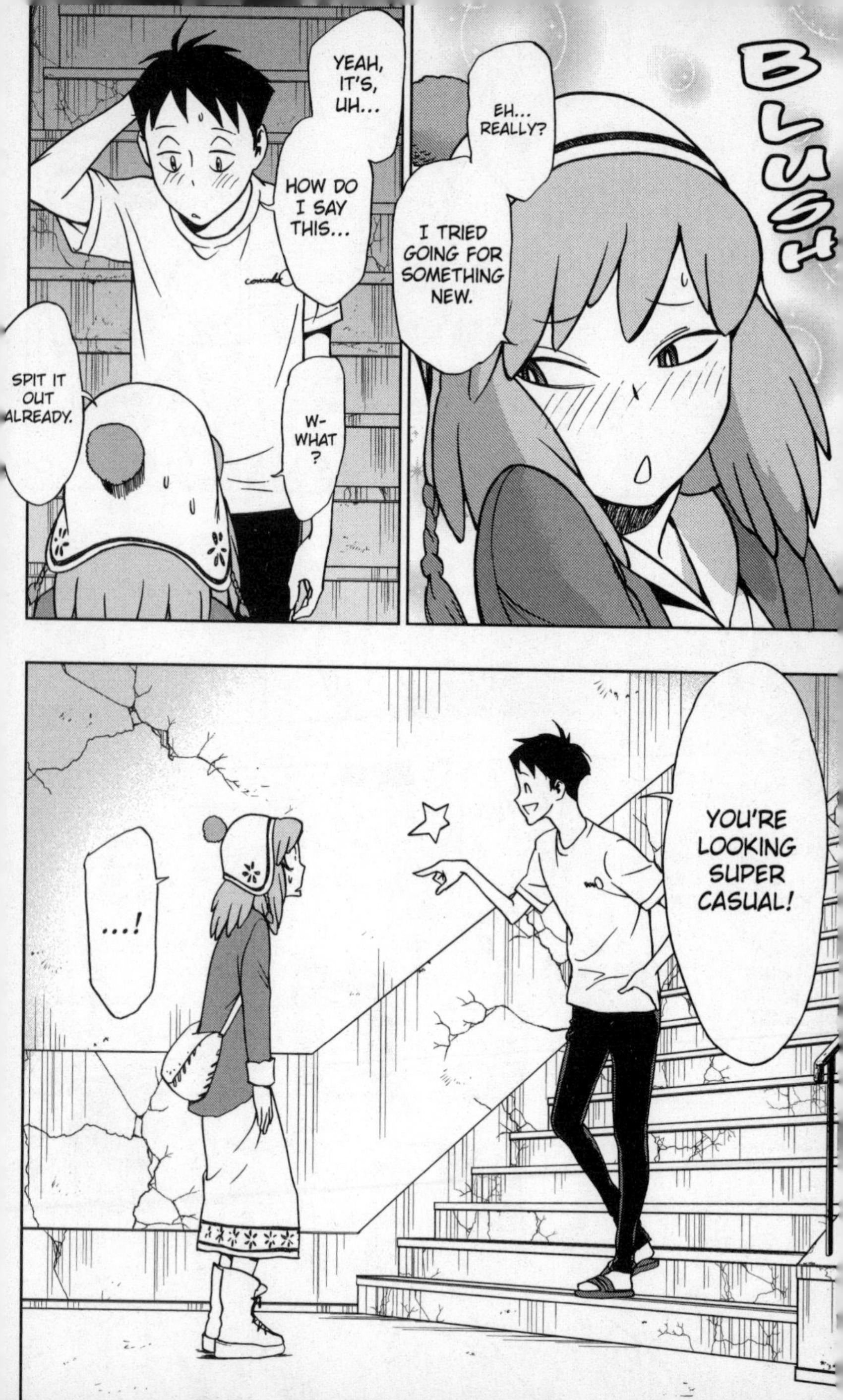
BLUSH
EH... REALLY?
I TRIED GOING FOR SOMETHING NEW.
YEAH, IT'S, UH...
HOW DO I SAY THIS...
W-WHAT?
SPIT IT OUT ALREADY.
YOU'RE LOOKING SUPER CASUAL!
...!

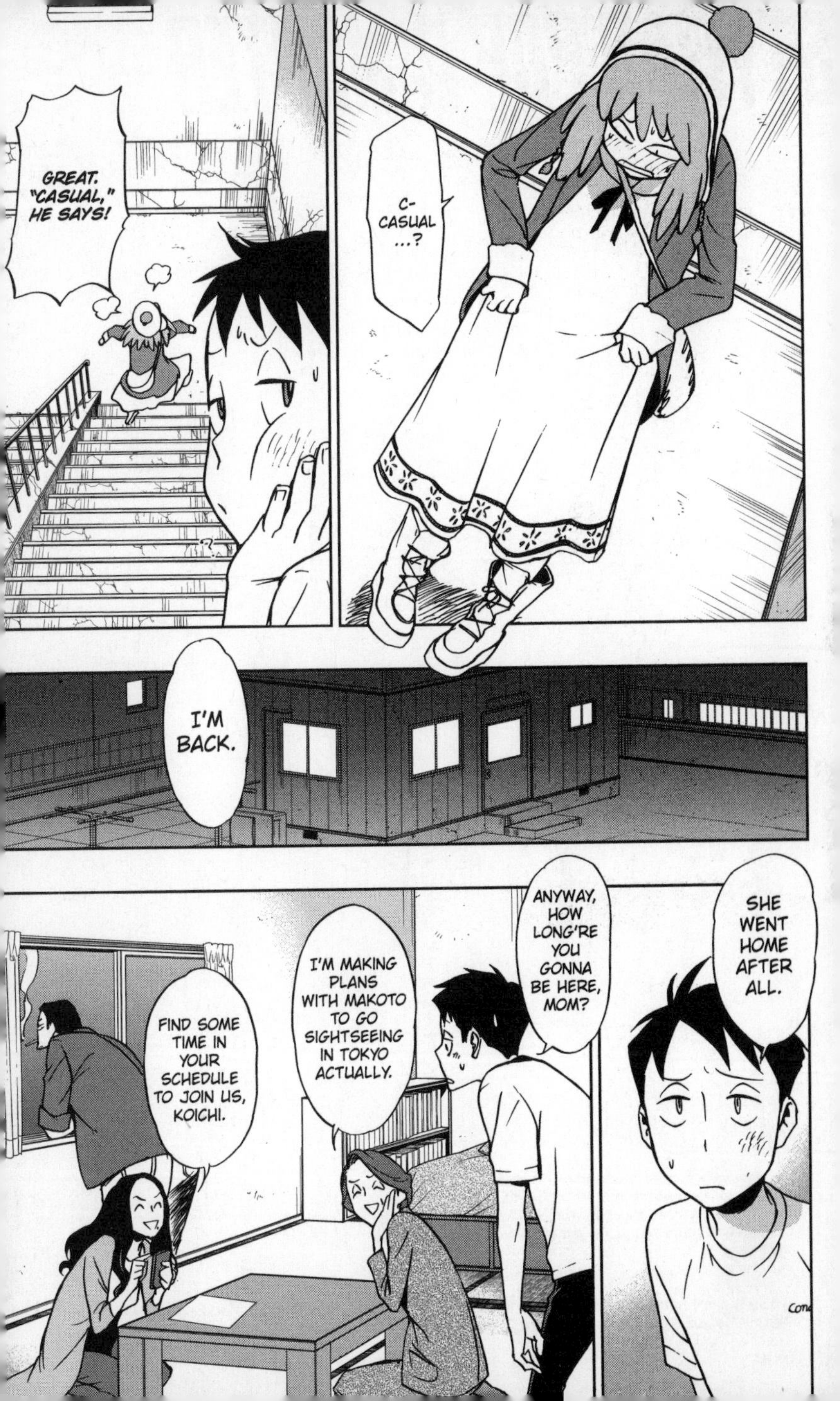
C-CASUAL ...?
GREAT. "CASUAL," HE SAYS!
I'M BACK.
SHE WENT HOME AFTER ALL.
ANYWAY, HOW LONG'RE YOU GONNA BE HERE, MOM?
I'M MAKING PLANS WITH MAKOTO TO GO SIGHTSEEING IN TOKYO ACTUALLY.
FIND SOME TIME IN YOUR SCHEDULE TO JOIN US, KOICHI.

STYLISH POP & MASTER

THE ROUGH DESIGN

Master

Scruff, only on chin

Dressed-up Pop

Absence of glasses shows how hard she's trying...

This is Pop's idea of getting all dolled up... or something?

Style like City Hunter

The "cleaner" (assassin) one

Envelope doesn't carry a bag

BEHIND THE SCENES

As you might have noticed, the heart of this chapter was Pop going home to change. Her outfit shows you how hard she's trying, which is really cute. Master is about to have a serious arc of his own, so I wanted to portray this side of him in advance—how he's also a put-together guy with a life of his own.

—Furuhashi

The request from Furuhashi-san for Pop was "a nature girl…" With Master, I thought there was good synergy between his "Janitor of the Fist" thing and the "cleaner" look. (LOL)

—Betten

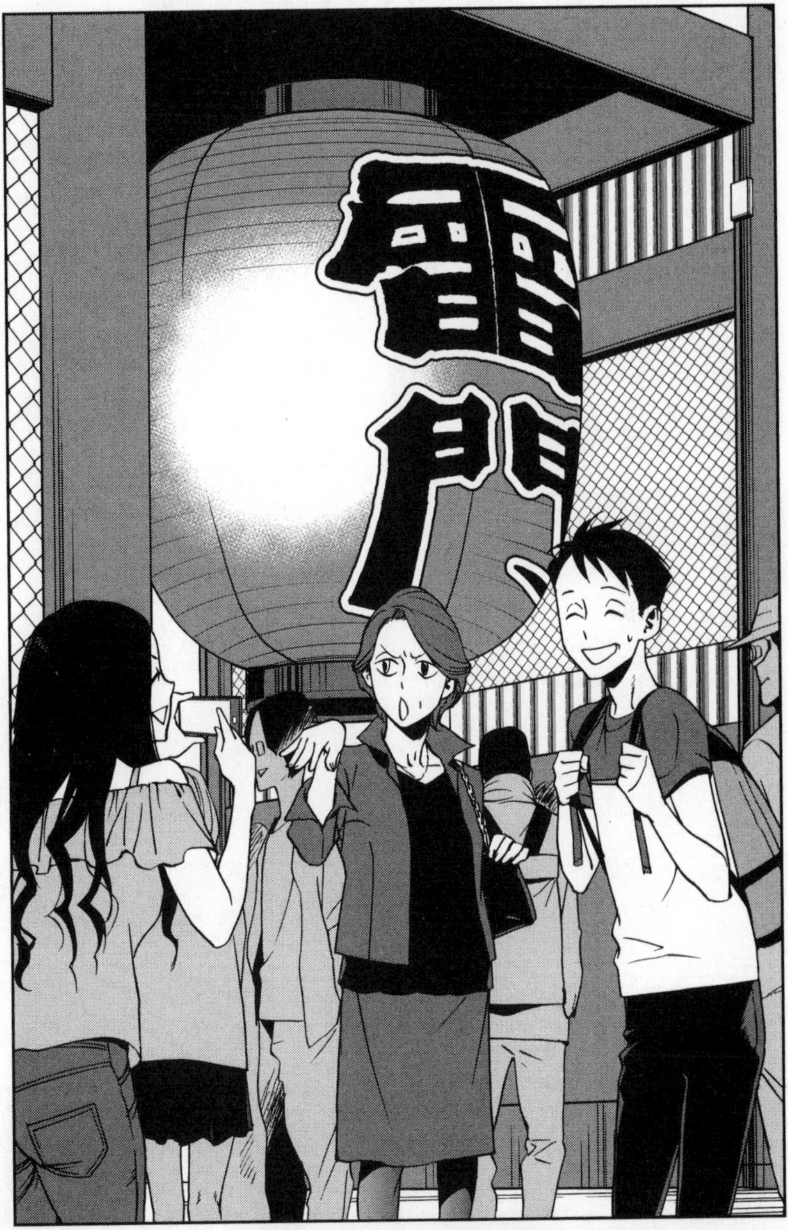
雷門

EP. 17 - TAG TEAM!

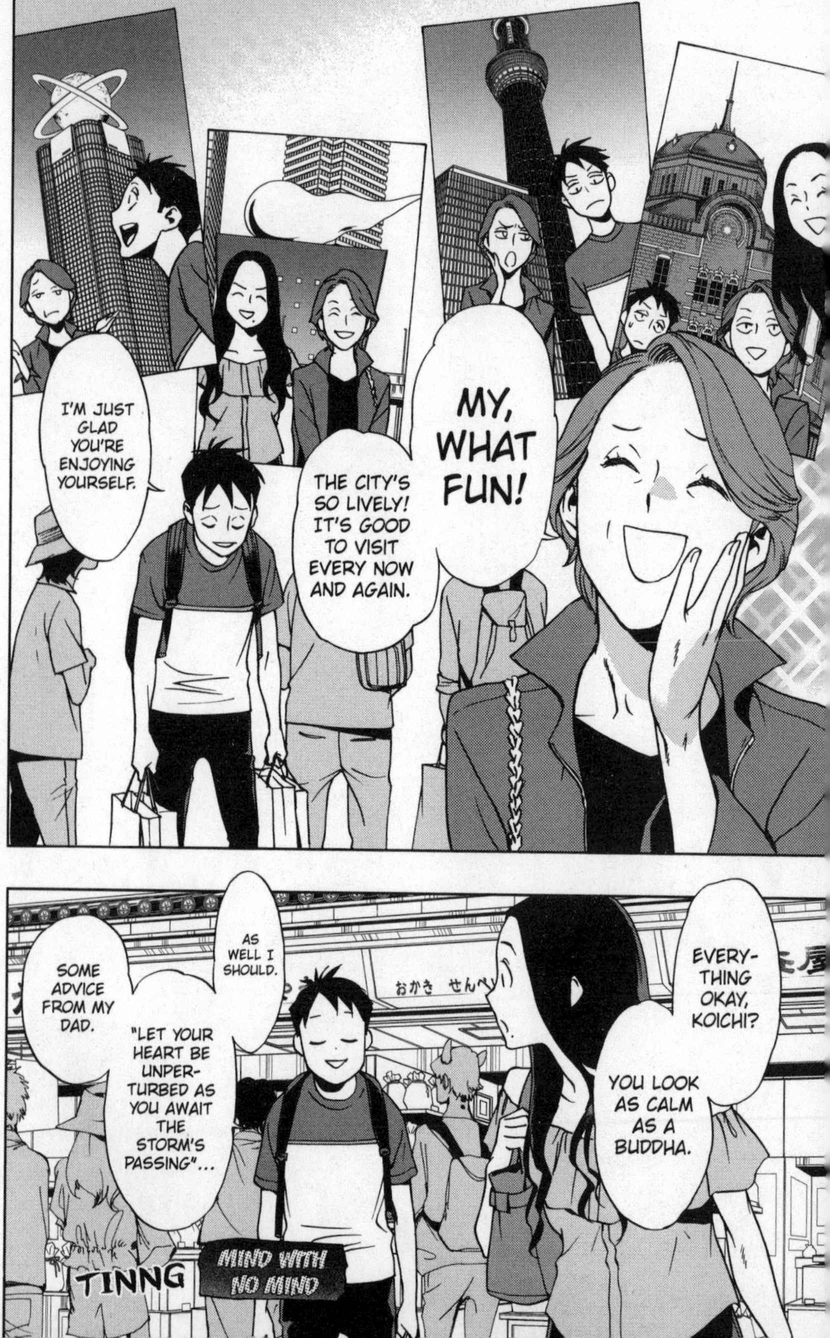
MY, WHAT FUN!
THE CITY'S SO LIVELY! IT'S GOOD TO VISIT EVERY NOW AND AGAIN.
I'M JUST GLAD YOU'RE ENJOYING YOURSELF.
EVERY-THING OKAY, KOICHI?
YOU LOOK AS CALM AS A BUDDHA.
おかき
AS WELL I SHOULD.
SOME ADVICE FROM MY DAD.
"LET YOUR HEART BE UNPER-TURBED AS YOU AWAIT THE STORM'S PASSING"...
MIND WITH NO MIND
TINNG

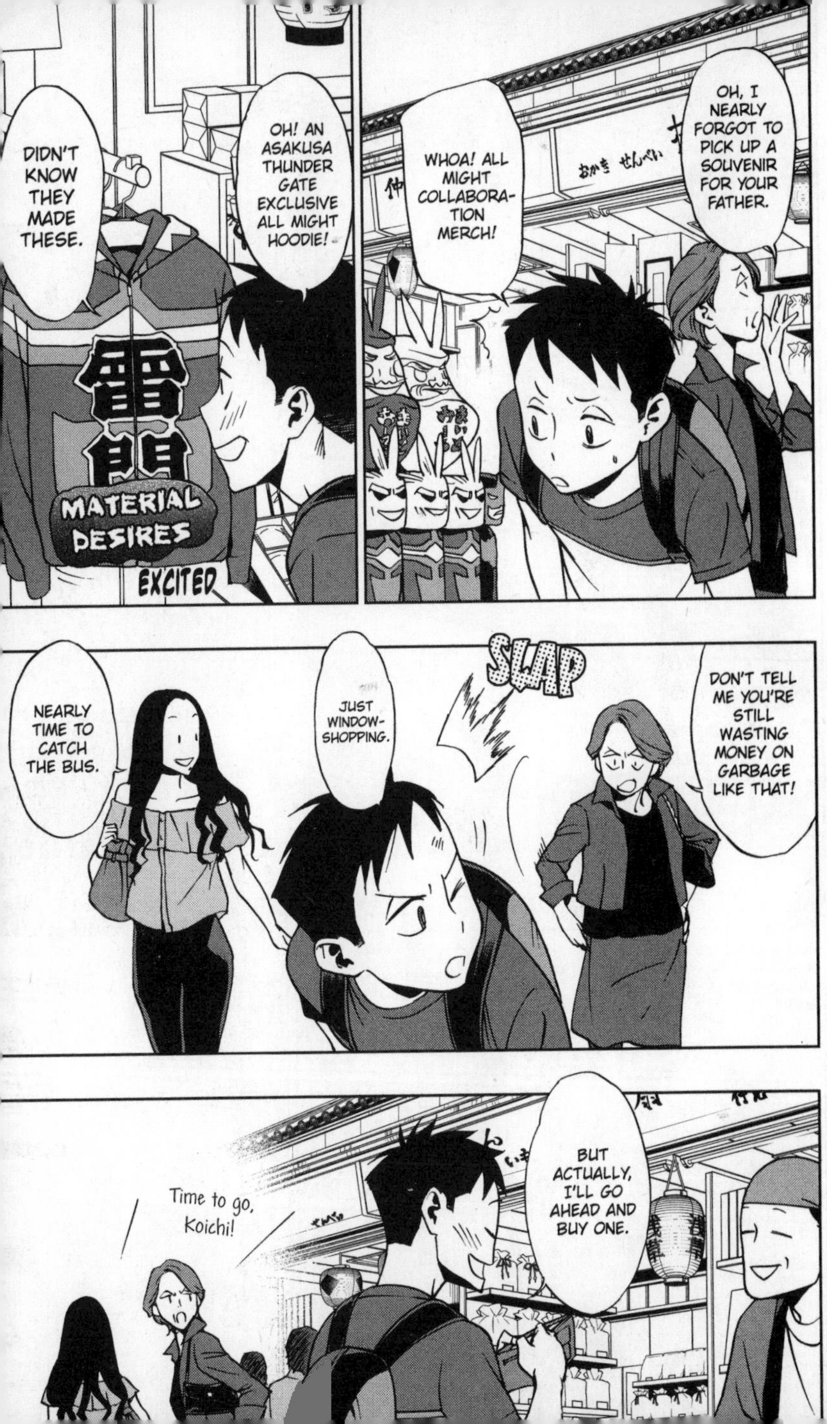

OH, I NEARLY FORGOT TO PICK UP A SOUVENIR FOR YOUR FATHER.
おかき せんべい
WHOA! ALL MIGHT COLLABORA-TION MERCH!
OH! AN ASAKUSA THUNDER GATE EXCLUSIVE ALL MIGHT HOODIE!
DIDN'T KNOW THEY MADE THESE.
雷門
MATERIAL DESIRES
EXCITED
DON'T TELL ME YOU'RE STILL WASTING MONEY ON GARBAGE LIKE THAT!
SLAP
JUST WINDOW-SHOPPING.
NEARLY TIME TO CATCH THE BUS.
BUT ACTUALLY, I'LL GO AHEAD AND BUY ONE.
Time to go, Koichi!

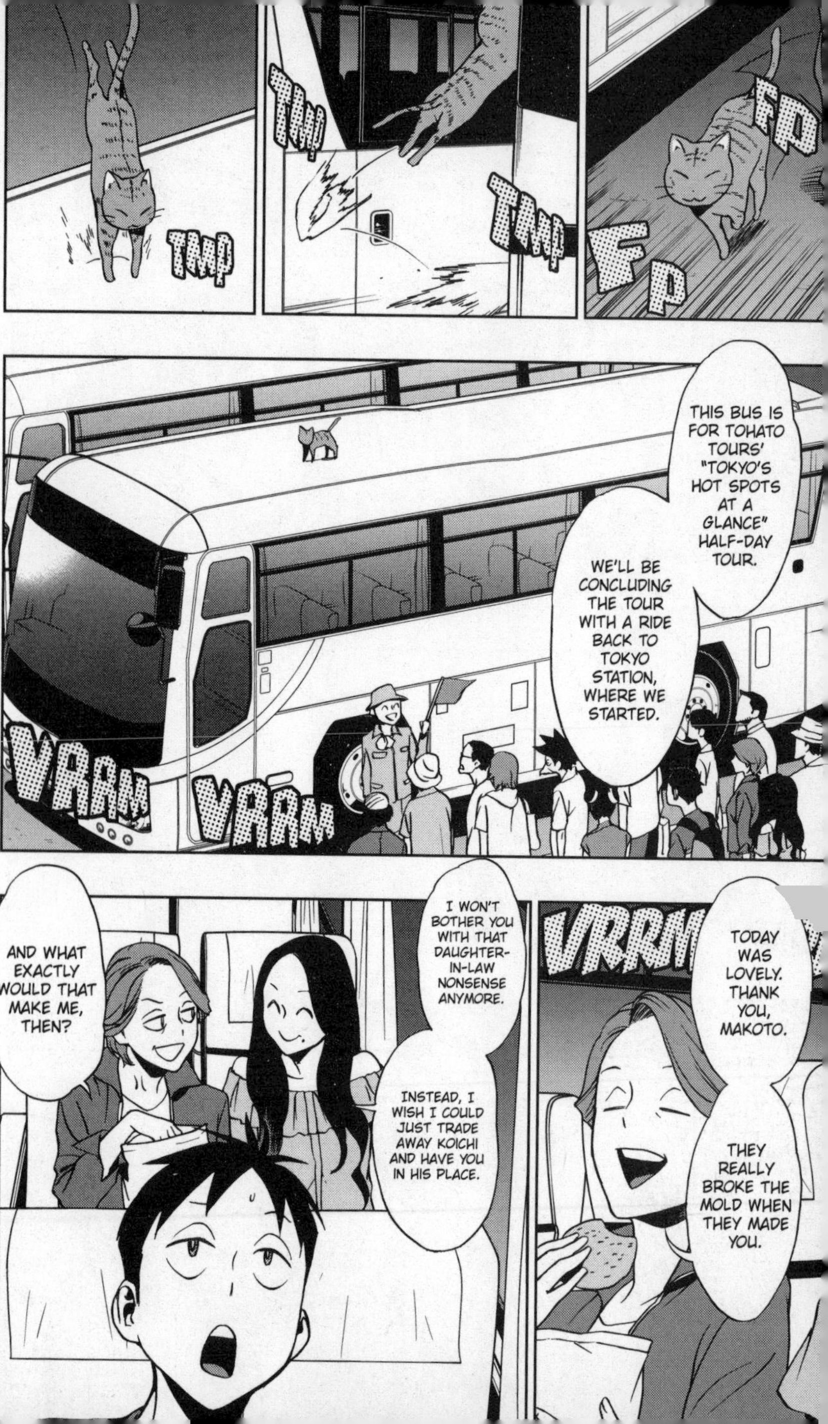
FP
Fp
TMP
TMP
TMP
THIS BUS IS FOR TOHATO TOURS' "TOKYO'S HOT SPOTS AT A GLANCE" HALF-DAY TOUR.
WE'LL BE CONCLUDING THE TOUR WITH A RIDE BACK TO TOKYO STATION, WHERE WE STARTED.
VRRM
VRRM
VRRM
TODAY WAS LOVELY. THANK YOU, MAKOTO.
THEY REALLY BROKE THE MOLD WHEN THEY MADE YOU.
I WON'T BOTHER YOU WITH THAT DAUGHTER-IN-LAW NONSENSE ANYMORE.
INSTEAD, I WISH I COULD JUST TRADE AWAY KOICHI AND HAVE YOU IN HIS PLACE.
AND WHAT EXACTLY WOULD THAT MAKE ME, THEN?

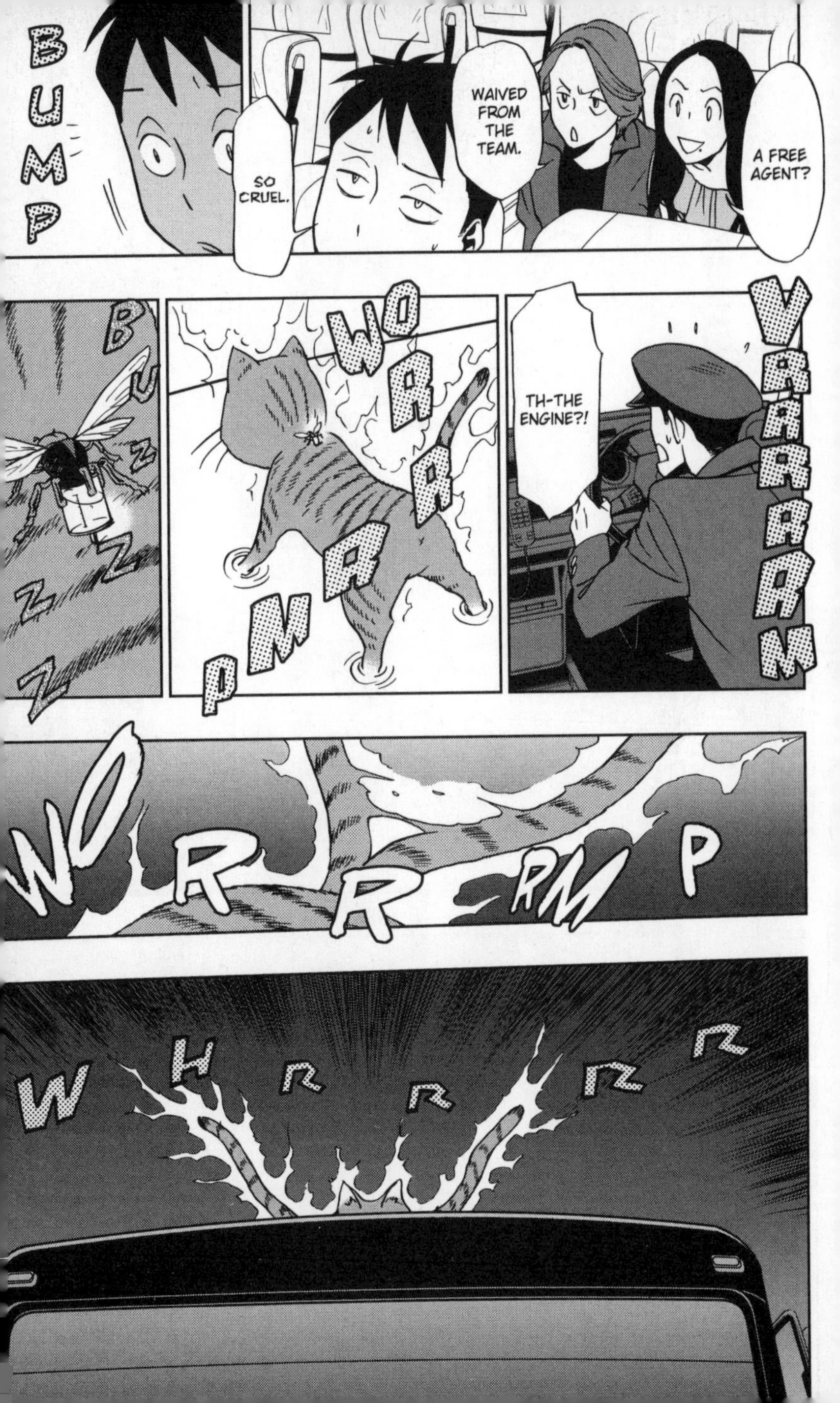
A FREE AGENT?
WAIVED FROM THE TEAM.
SO CRUEL.
BUMP
VRRRRRM
TH-THE ENGINE?!
WORRRMP
BUZZZZ
WORRRMP
WHRRRR

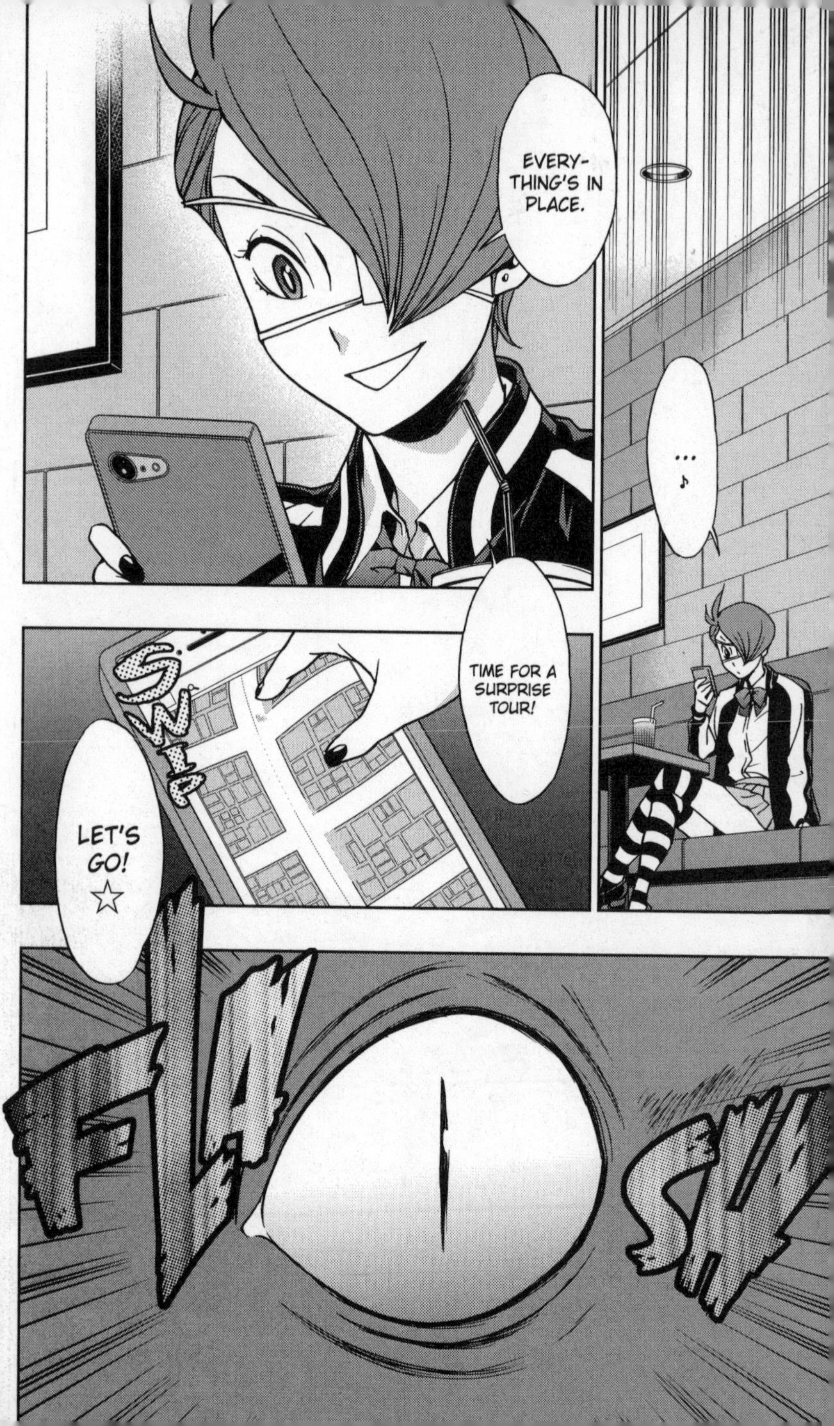

...♪
EVERY-THING'S IN PLACE.
TIME FOR A SURPRISE TOUR!
SWIP
LET'S GO! ☆
FLASH

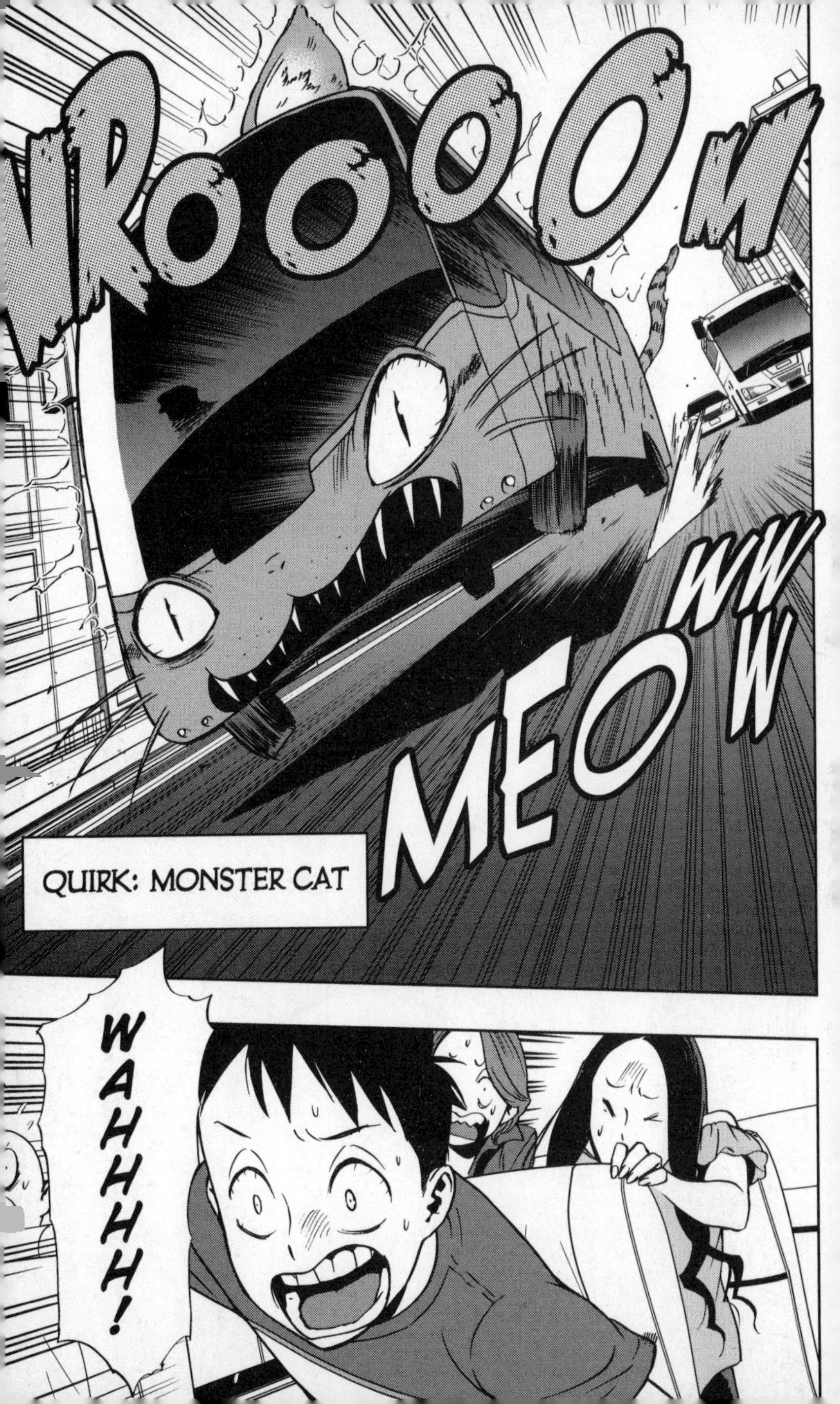
VROOOOM
MEOWWW
QUIRK: MONSTER CAT
WAHHHHH!

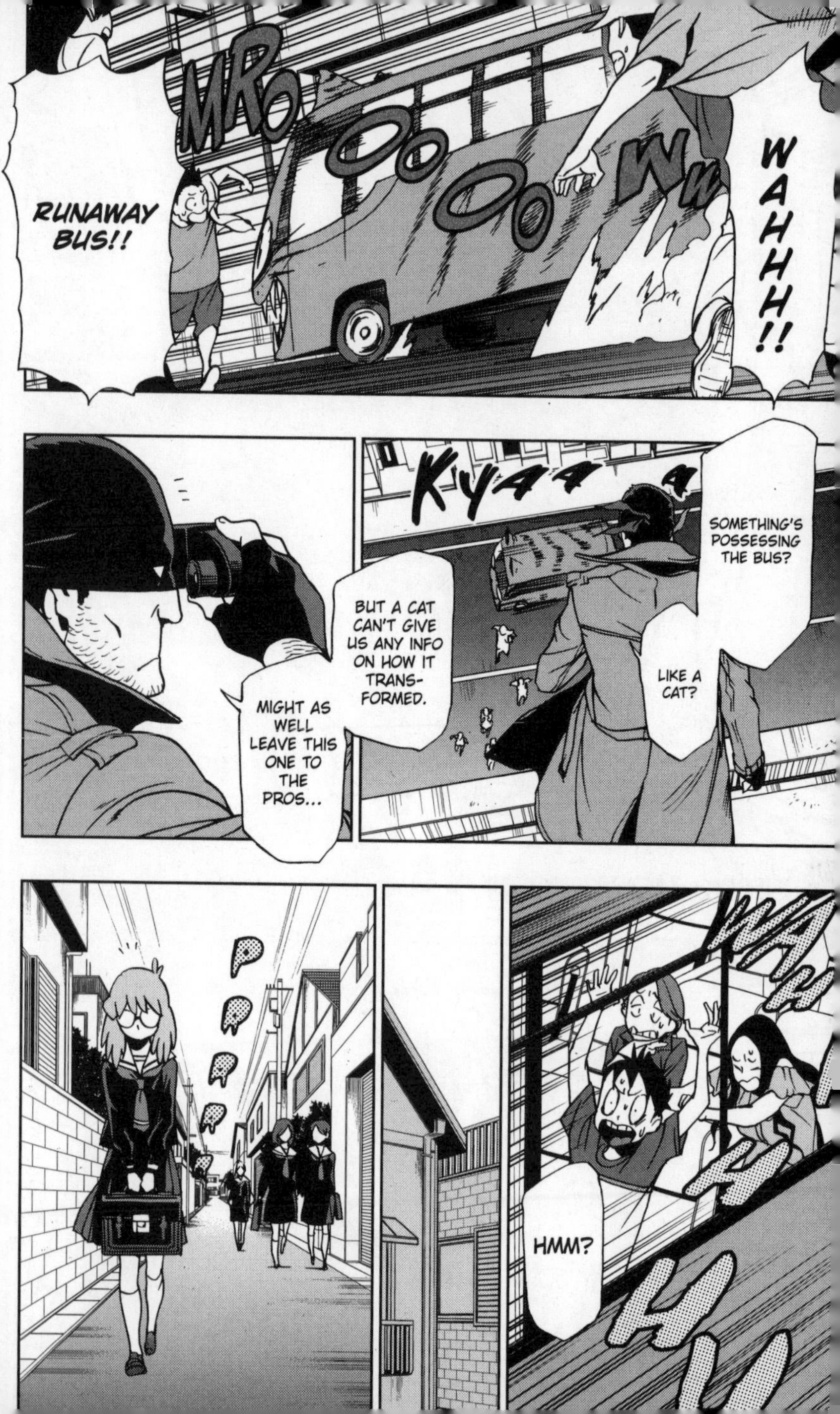

MROOOOOWW
WAHHHH!!
RUNAWAY BUS!!
KYAAA
SOMETHING'S POSSESSING THE BUS?
LIKE A CAT?
BUT A CAT CAN'T GIVE US ANY INFO ON HOW IT TRANS-FORMED.
MIGHT AS WELL LEAVE THIS ONE TO THE PROS...
HMM?
P P P P

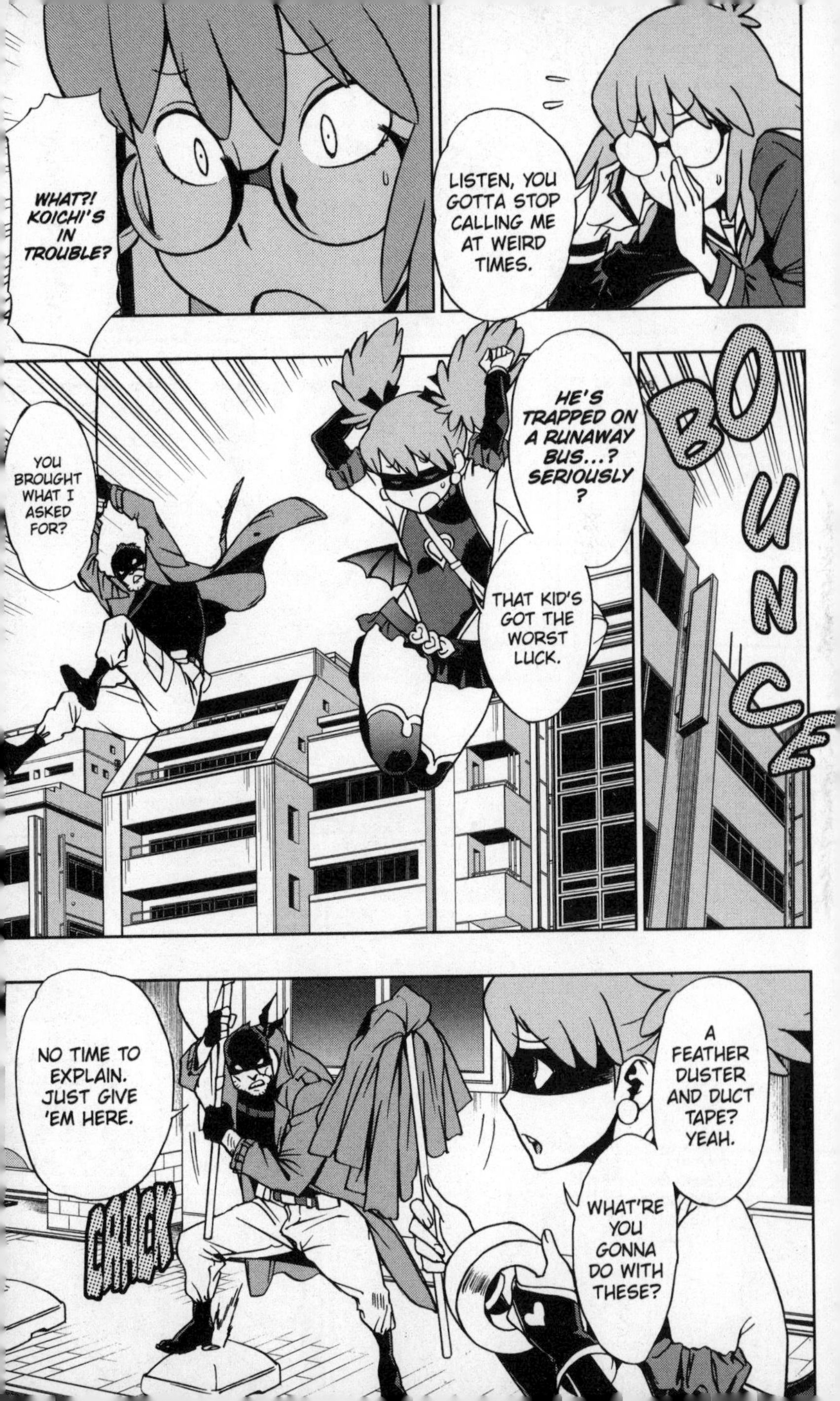
LISTEN, YOU GOTTA STOP CALLING ME AT WEIRD TIMES.
WHAT?! KOICHI'S IN TROUBLE?
BOUNCE
HE'S TRAPPED ON A RUNAWAY BUS...? SERIOUSLY?
THAT KID'S GOT THE WORST LUCK.
YOU BROUGHT WHAT I ASKED FOR?
A FEATHER DUSTER AND DUCT TAPE? YEAH.
WHAT'RE YOU GONNA DO WITH THESE?
NO TIME TO EXPLAIN. JUST GIVE 'EM HERE.
CRACK

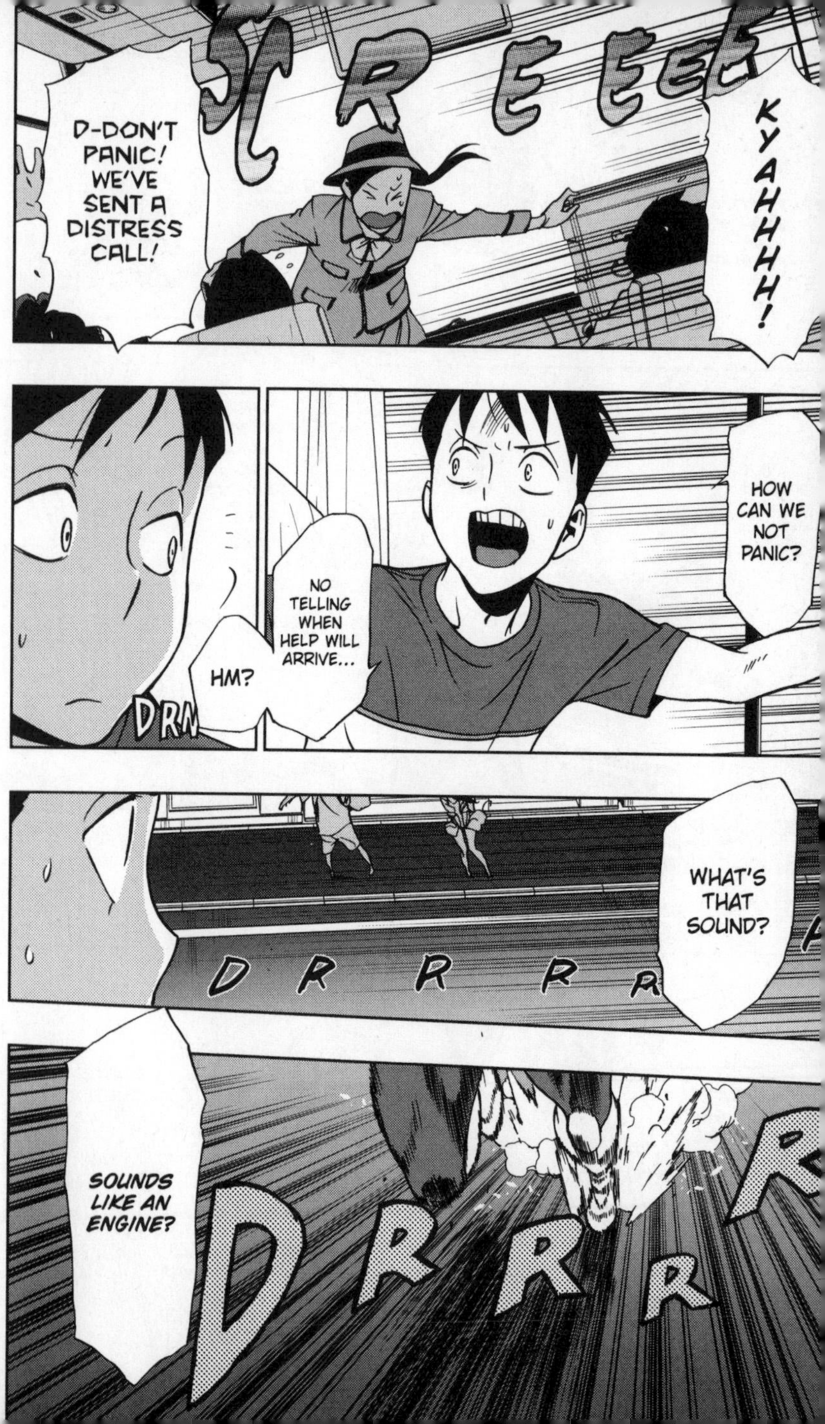
KYAHHHHH!
D-DON'T PANIC! WE'VE SENT A DISTRESS CALL!
HOW CAN WE NOT PANIC?
NO TELLING WHEN HELP WILL ARRIVE...
HM?
DRN
WHAT'S THAT SOUND?
DRRRR
SOUNDS LIKE AN ENGINE?
DRRRR

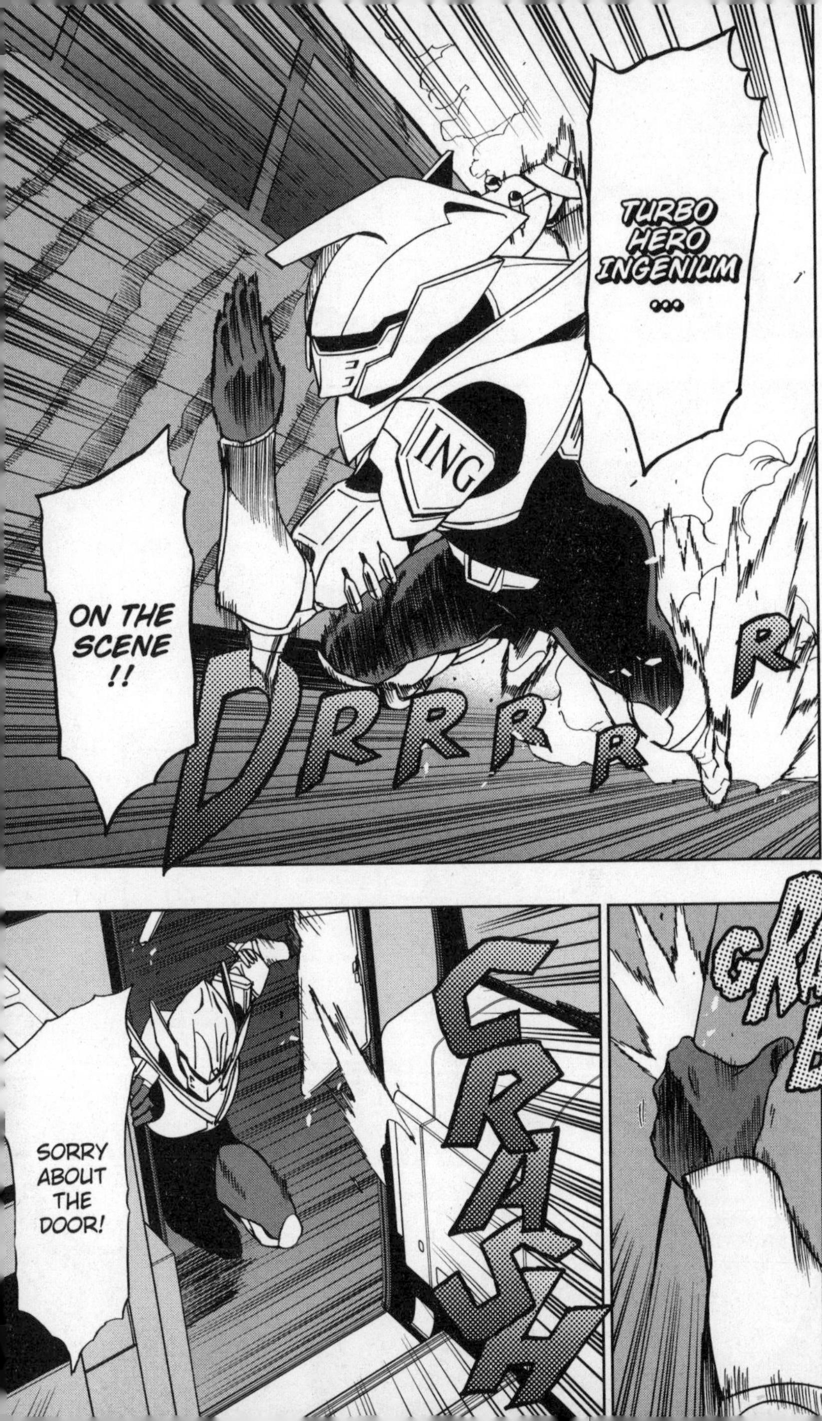
TURBO HERO INGENIUM ...
ON THE SCENE !!
DRRRRRR
GRAB
CRASH
SORRY ABOUT THE DOOR!

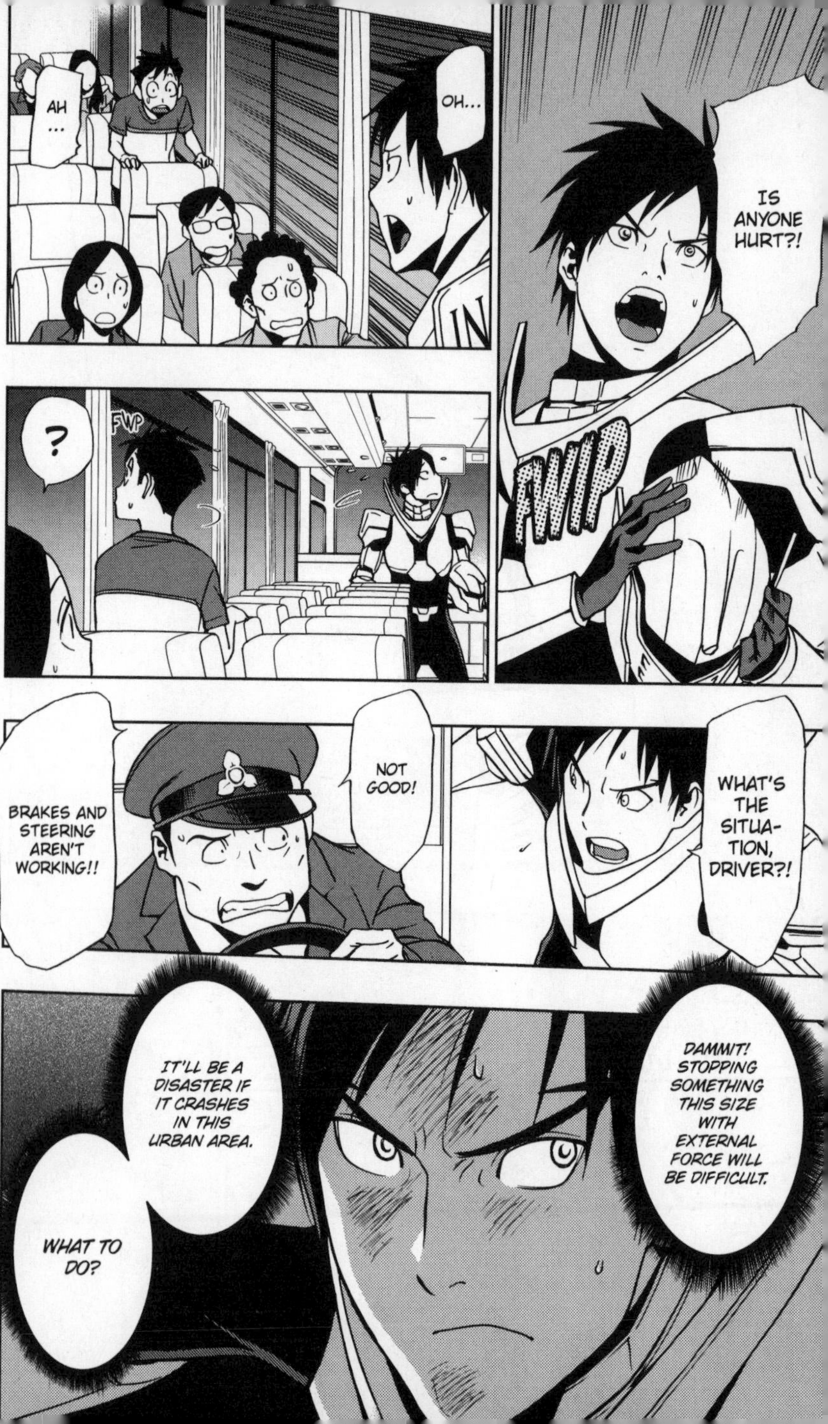
IS ANYONE HURT?!
FWIP
OH...
AH ...
FWP
?
WHAT'S THE SITUATION, DRIVER?!
NOT GOOD!
BRAKES AND STEERING AREN'T WORKING!!
DAMMIT! STOPPING SOMETHING THIS SIZE WITH EXTERNAL FORCE WILL BE DIFFICULT.
IT'LL BE A DISASTER IF IT CRASHES IN THIS URBAN AREA.
WHAT TO DO?

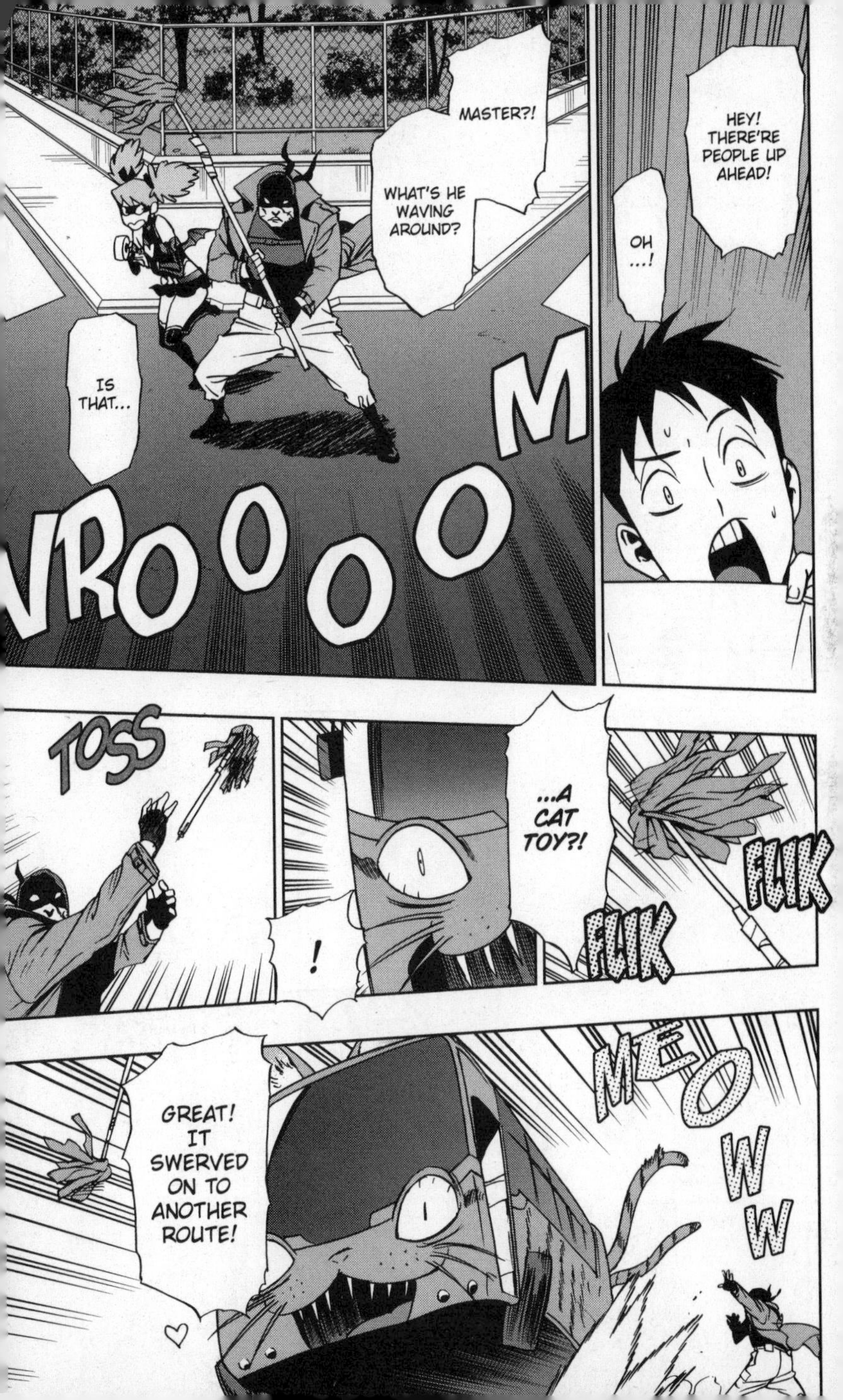
HEY! THERE'RE PEOPLE UP AHEAD!
OH ...!
MASTER?!
WHAT'S HE WAVING AROUND?
IS THAT...
VROOOOOM
FLIK
FLIK
...A CAT TOY?!
!
TOSS
MEOWWW
GREAT! IT SWERVED ON TO ANOTHER ROUTE!

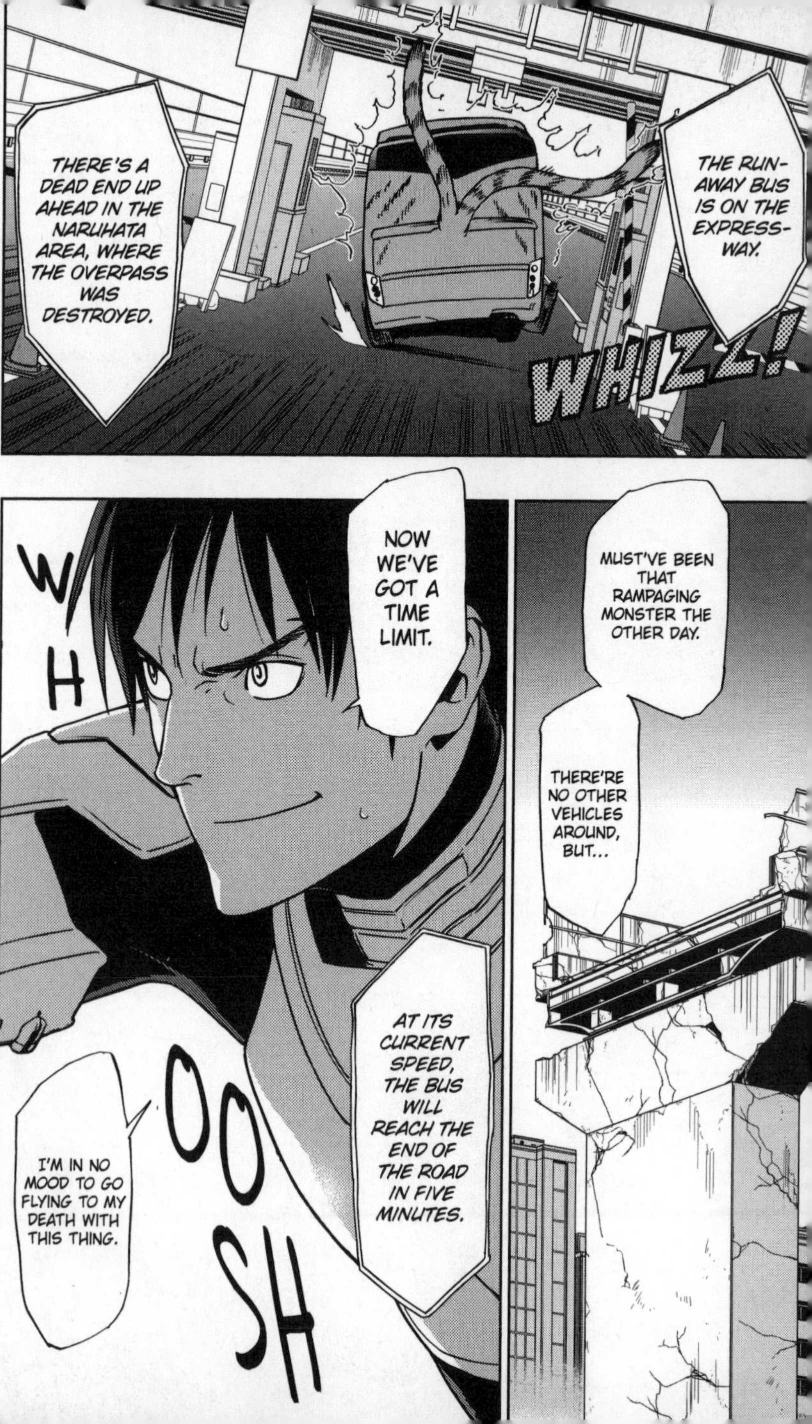
THE RUN-AWAY BUS IS ON THE EXPRESS-WAY.
THERE'S A DEAD END UP AHEAD IN THE NARUHATA AREA, WHERE THE OVERPASS WAS DESTROYED.
WHIZZ!
MUST'VE BEEN THAT RAMPAGING MONSTER THE OTHER DAY.
THERE'RE NO OTHER VEHICLES AROUND, BUT...
NOW WE'VE GOT A TIME LIMIT.
AT ITS CURRENT SPEED, THE BUS WILL REACH THE END OF THE ROAD IN FIVE MINUTES.
I'M IN NO MOOD TO GO FLYING TO MY DEATH WITH THIS THING.
WHOOSH

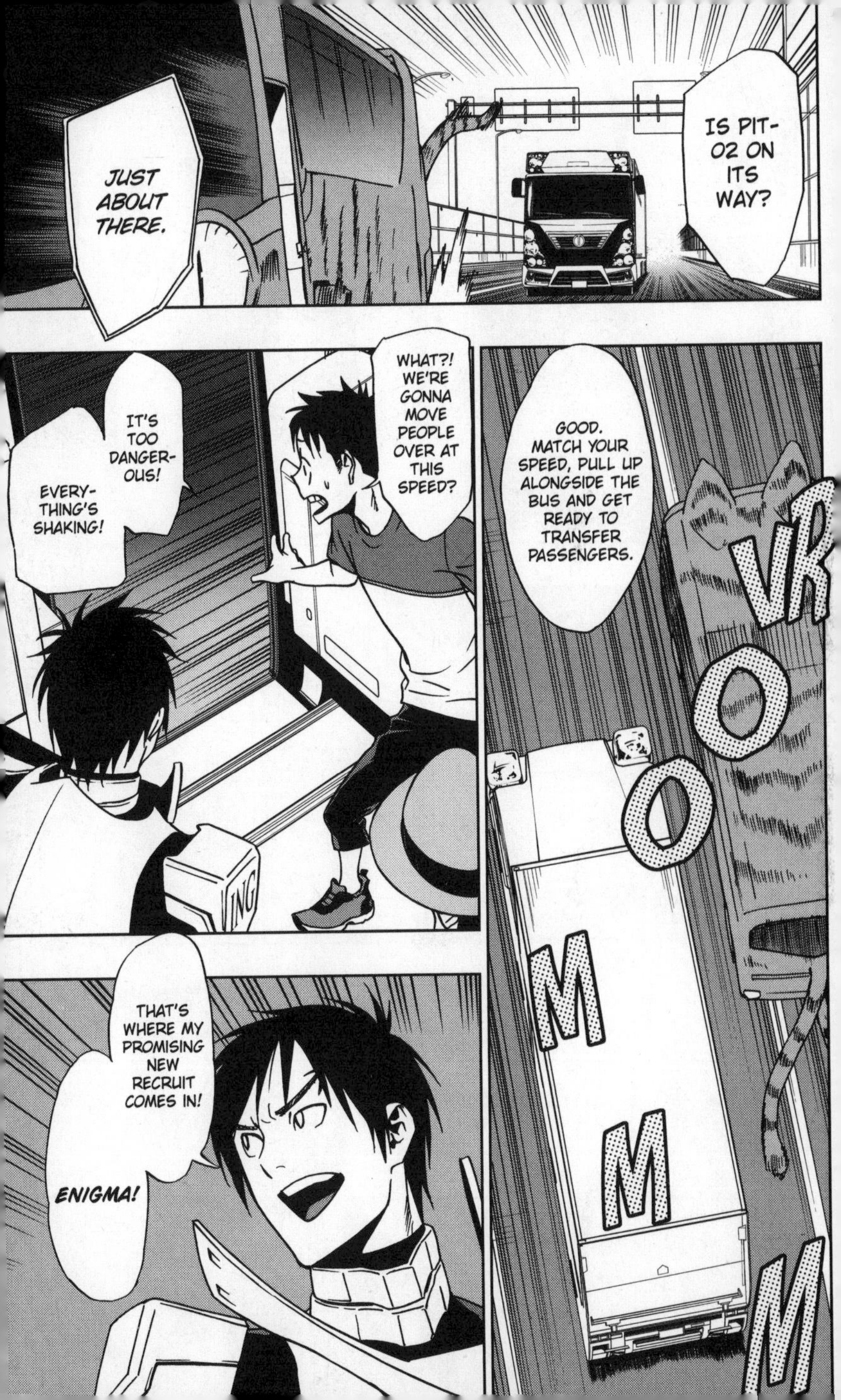
IS PIT-02 ON ITS WAY?
JUST ABOUT THERE.
GOOD. MATCH YOUR SPEED, PULL UP ALONGSIDE THE BUS AND GET READY TO TRANSFER PASSENGERS.
VROOMMM
WHAT?! WE'RE GONNA MOVE PEOPLE OVER AT THIS SPEED?
IT'S TOO DANGER-OUS!
EVERY-THING'S SHAKING!
THAT'S WHERE MY PROMISING NEW RECRUIT COMES IN!
ENIGMA!

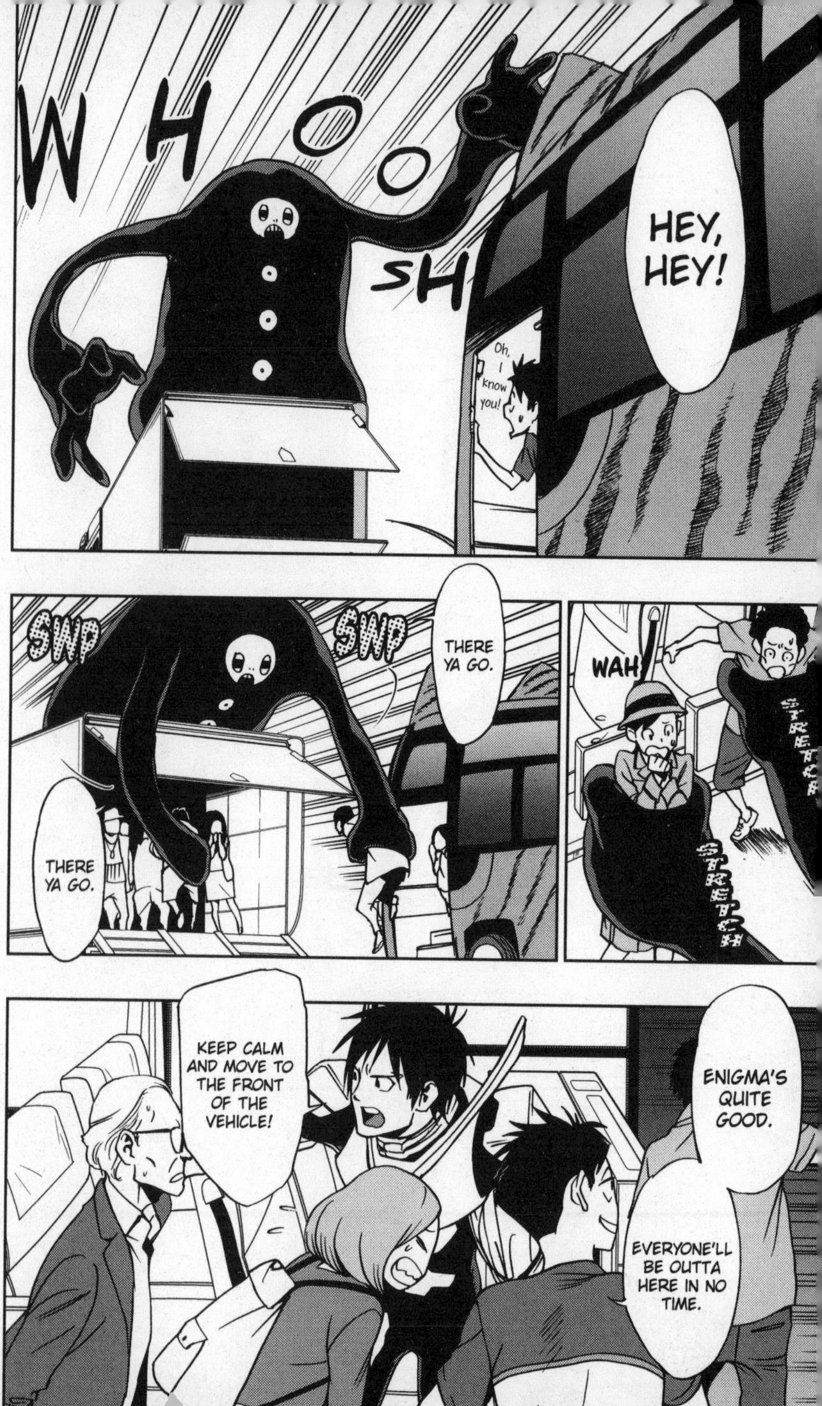
HEY, HEY!
Oh, I know you!
WHOOSH
WAH
STRETCH
STRETCH
THERE YA GO.
SWP
SWP
THERE YA GO.
ENIGMA'S QUITE GOOD.
EVERYONE'LL BE OUTTA HERE IN NO TIME.
KEEP CALM AND MOVE TO THE FRONT OF THE VEHICLE!

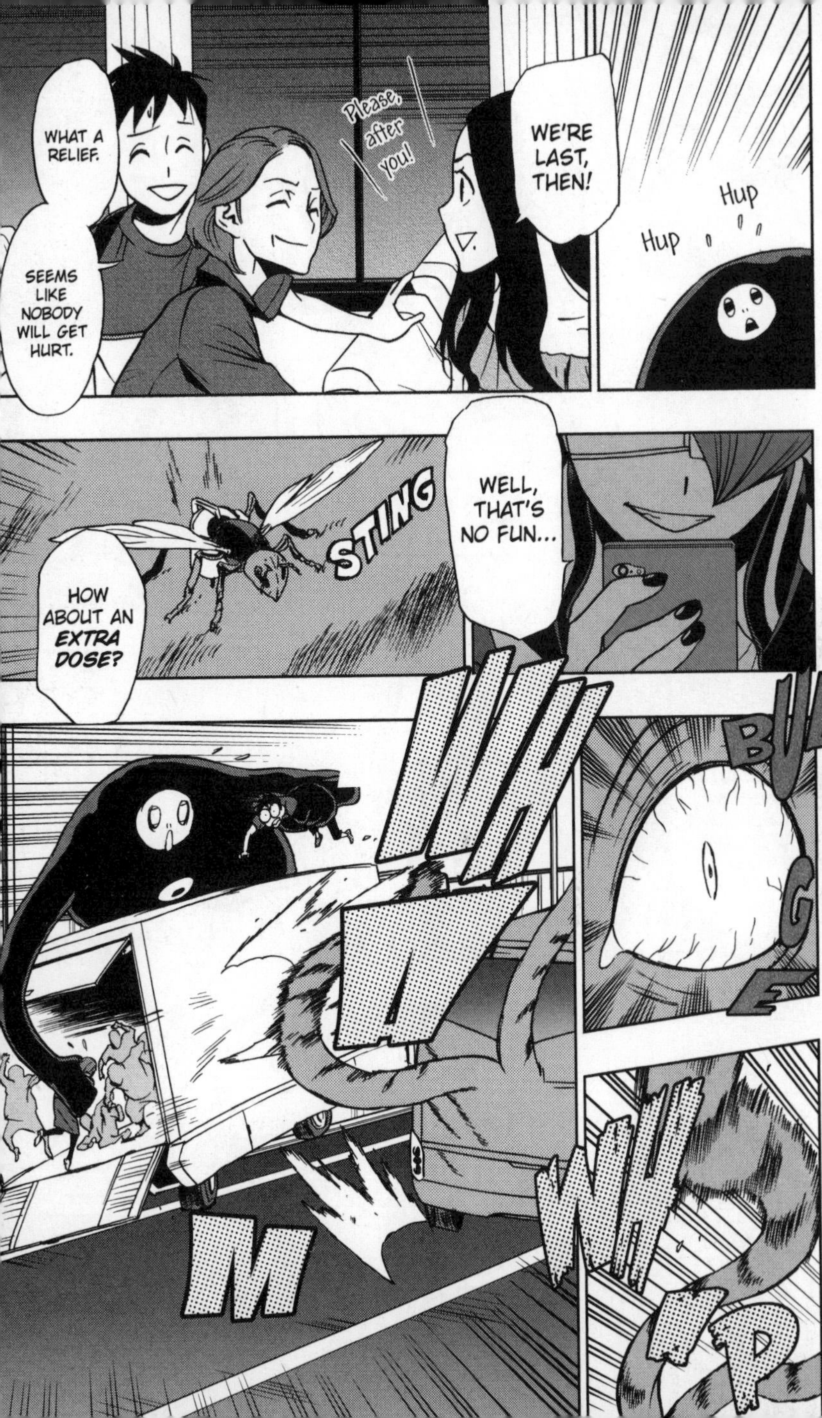
Hup
Hup
WE'RE LAST, THEN!
Please, after you!
WHAT A RELIEF.
SEEMS LIKE NOBODY WILL GET HURT.
WELL, THAT'S NO FUN...
STING
HOW ABOUT AN EXTRA DOSE?
BULGE
WHIP
WHAM

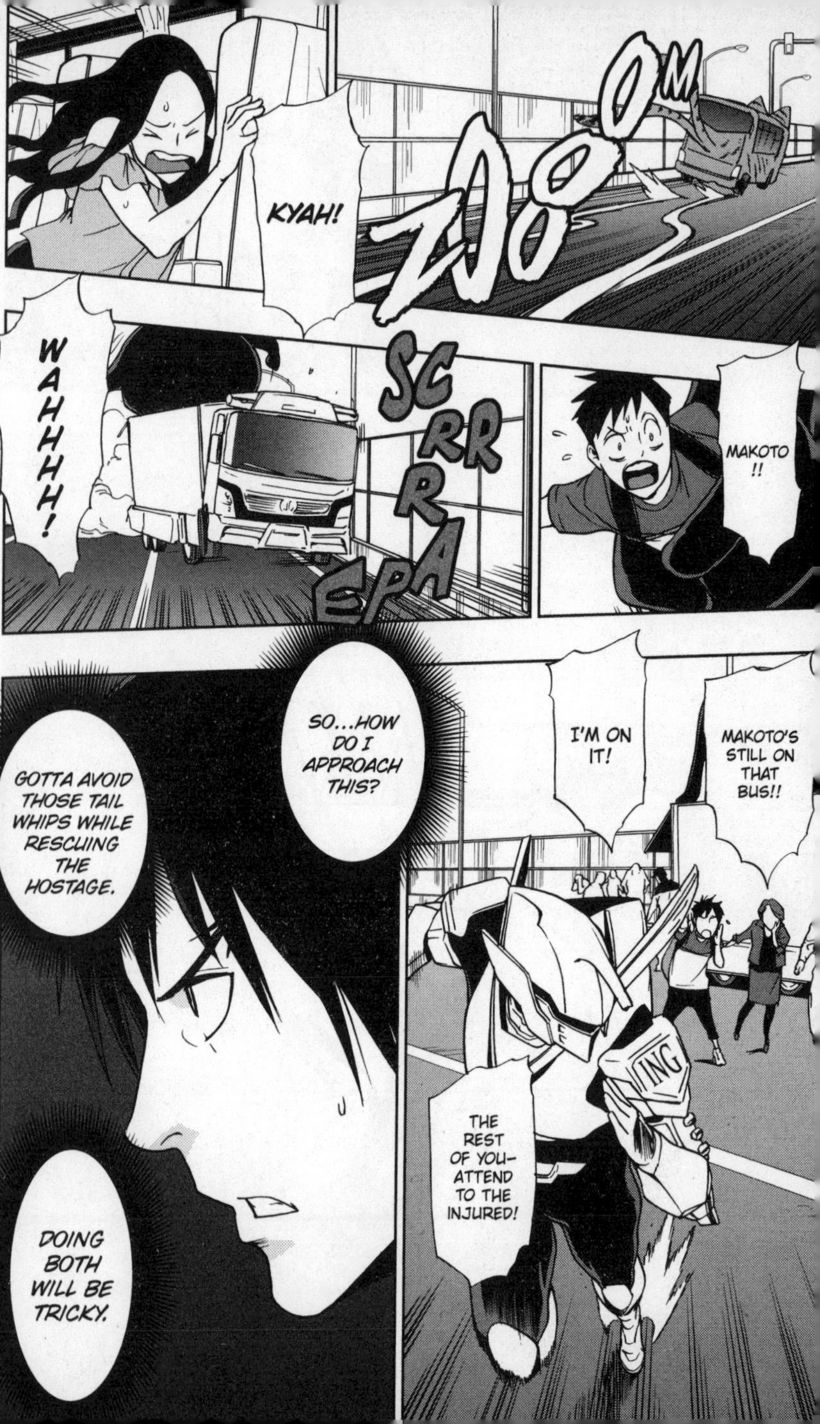
ZOOOOM
KYAH!
MAKOTO!!
SCRRRAPE
WAHHHHH!
MAKOTO'S STILL ON THAT BUS!!
I'M ON IT!
THE REST OF YOU—ATTEND TO THE INJURED!
SO...HOW DO I APPROACH THIS?
GOTTA AVOID THOSE TAIL WHIPS WHILE RESCUING THE HOSTAGE.
DOING BOTH WILL BE TRICKY.

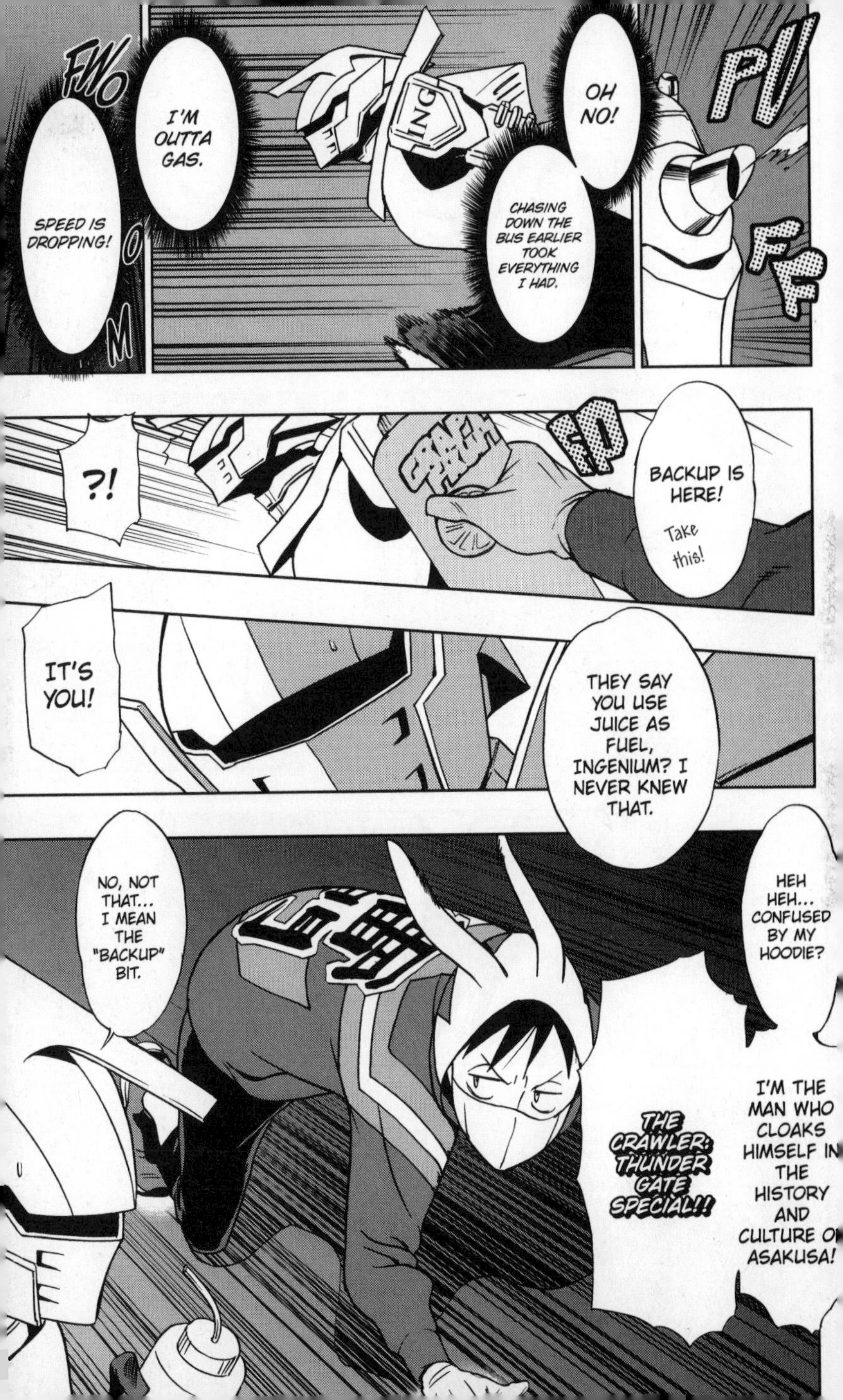
PFF
OH NO!
CHASING DOWN THE BUS EARLIER TOOK EVERYTHING I HAD.
I'M OUTTA GAS.
SPEED IS DROPPING!
FWOOM
BACKUP IS HERE!
Take this!
?!
THEY SAY YOU USE JUICE AS FUEL, INGENIUM? I NEVER KNEW THAT.
IT'S YOU!
HEH HEH... CONFUSED BY MY HOODIE?
NO, NOT THAT... I MEAN THE "BACKUP" BIT.
I'M THE MAN WHO CLOAKS HIMSELF IN THE HISTORY AND CULTURE OF ASAKUSA!
THE CRAWLER: THUNDER GATE SPECIAL!!

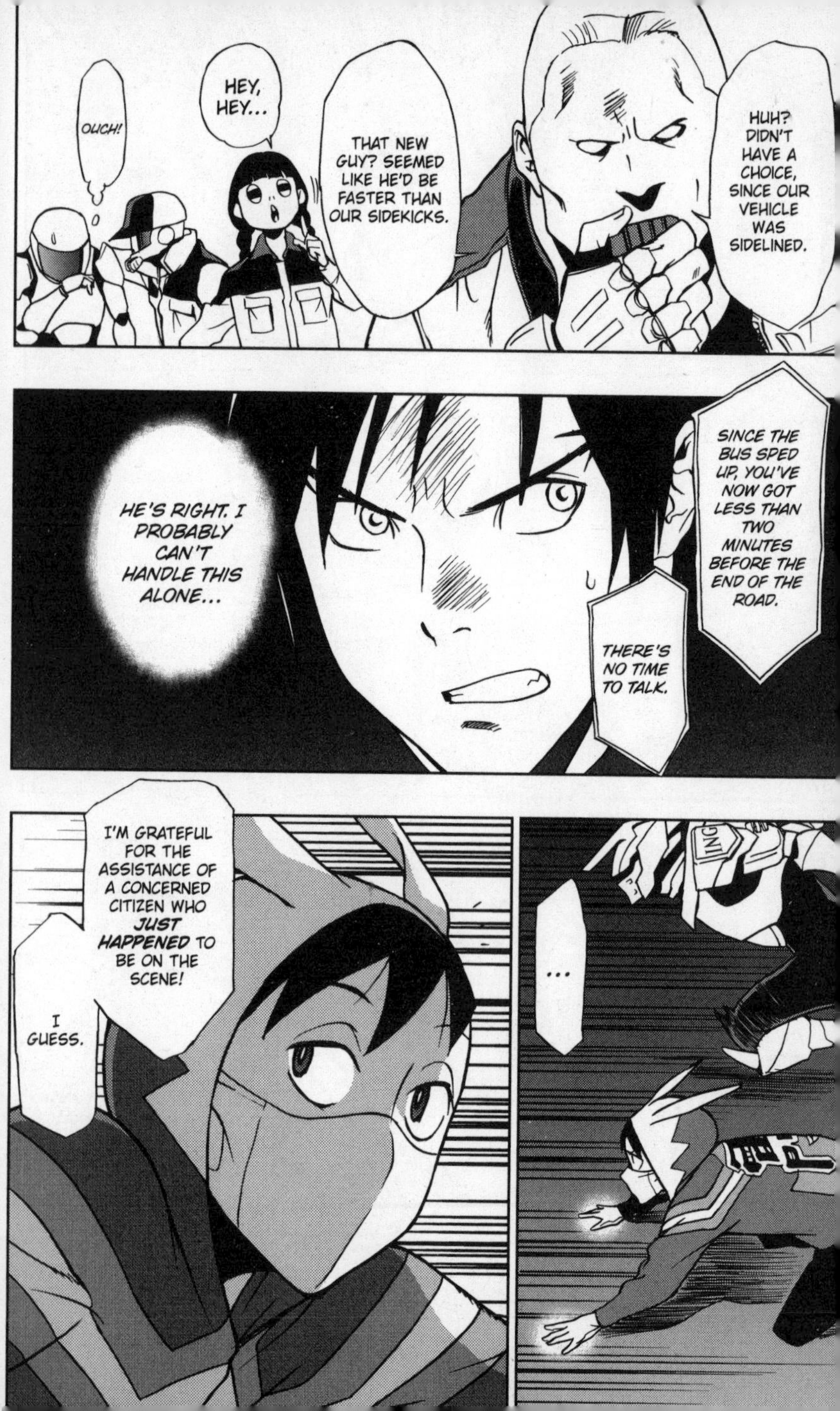
HUH? DIDN'T HAVE A CHOICE, SINCE OUR VEHICLE WAS SIDELINED.
THAT NEW GUY? SEEMED LIKE HE'D BE FASTER THAN OUR SIDEKICKS.
HEY, HEY...
OUCH!
SINCE THE BUS SPED UP, YOU'VE NOW GOT LESS THAN TWO MINUTES BEFORE THE END OF THE ROAD.
THERE'S NO TIME TO TALK.
HE'S RIGHT. I PROBABLY CAN'T HANDLE THIS ALONE...
...
I'M GRATEFUL FOR THE ASSISTANCE OF A CONCERNED CITIZEN WHO ***JUST HAPPENED*** TO BE ON THE SCENE!
I GUESS.

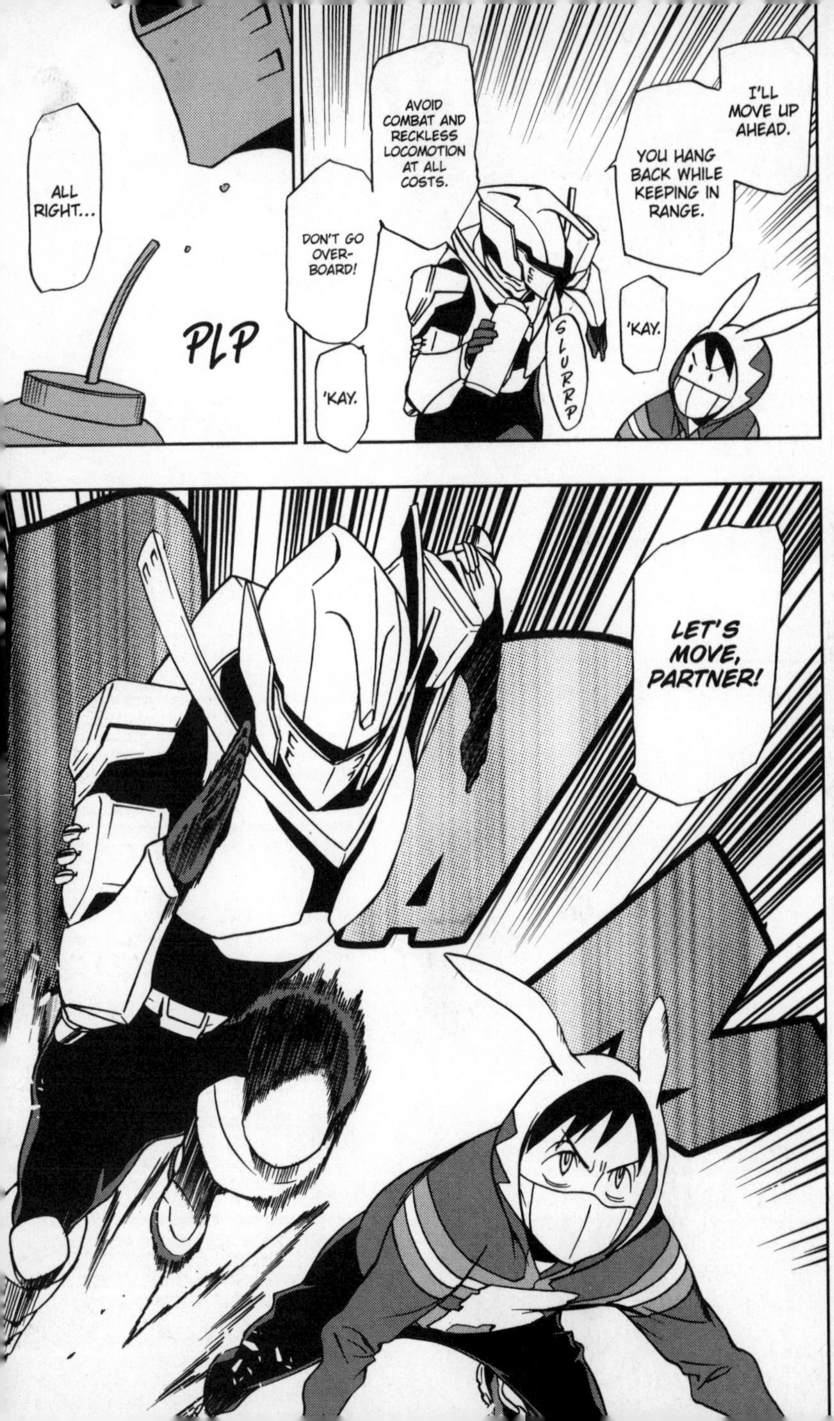
I'LL MOVE UP AHEAD.
YOU HANG BACK WHILE KEEPING IN RANGE.
'KAY.
AVOID COMBAT AND RECKLESS LOCOMOTION AT ALL COSTS.
SLURRP
DON'T GO OVER-BOARD!
'KAY.
ALL RIGHT...
PLP
LET'S MOVE, PARTNER!

KOICHI'S MOM

THE ROUGH DESIGN

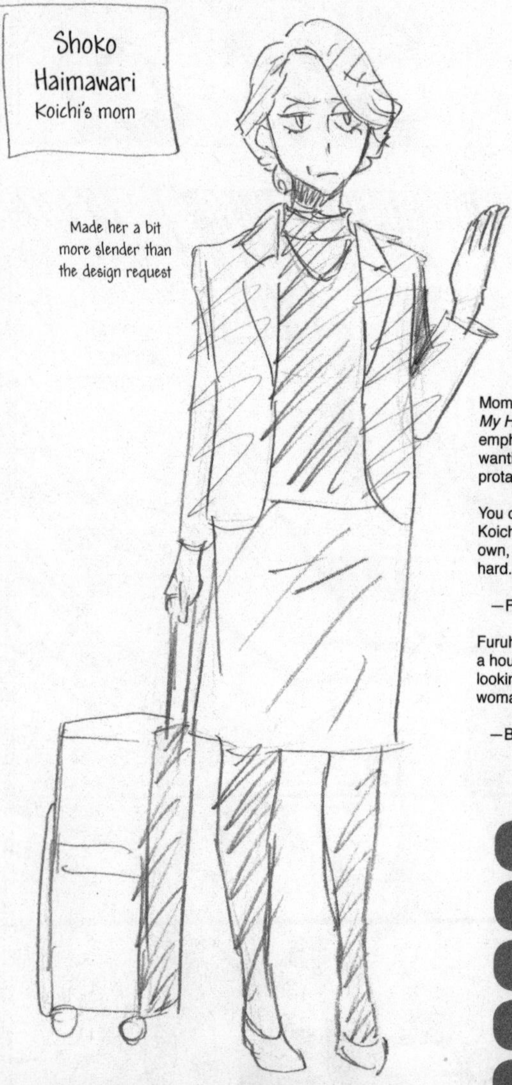

Shoko
Haimawari
Koichi's mom
Made her a bit more slender than the design request

BEHIND THE SCENES

Moms are also an important component of *My Hero Academia*, but in *Vigilantes*, the emphasis is more on growing up and not wanting to let one's child go, since the protagonist is a little older.

You can imagine what sorts of personalities Koichi's parents might have, based on his own, so making these decisions wasn't too hard.

—Furuhashi

Furuhashi-san's description painted her as a housewife by trade, but she ended up looking more like a dedicated career-woman. Whoops!

—Betten

REAL NAME: SHOKO HAIMAWARI

BIRTHDAY: 8/20

HEIGHT: 164 CM

FAVORITE THING: GYOZA

QUIRK: FLY SWATTER

EP. 18 - FORCE OF WILL ACCELERATION!

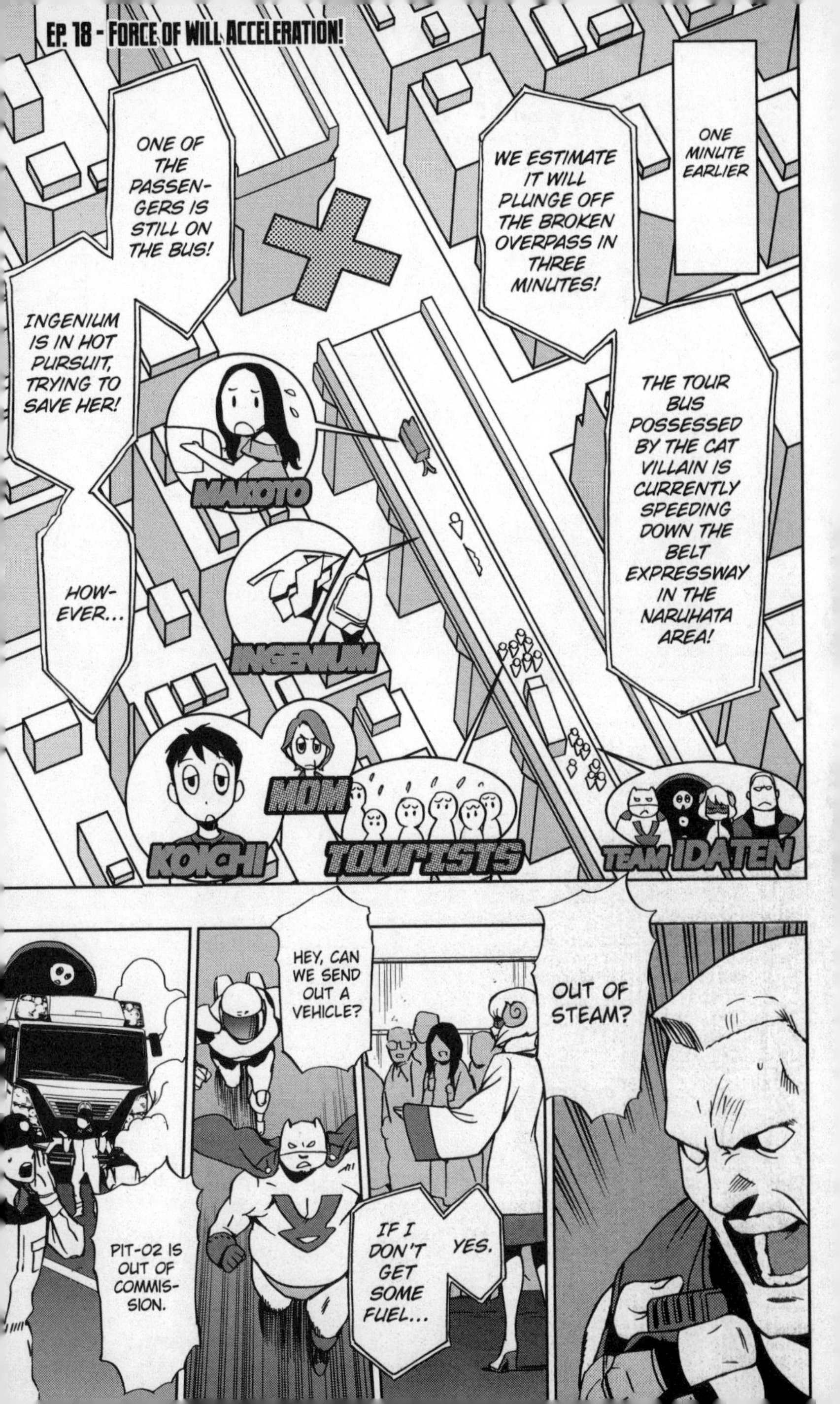
ONE MINUTE EARLIER
THE TOUR BUS POSSESSED BY THE CAT VILLAIN IS CURRENTLY SPEEDING DOWN THE BELT EXPRESSWAY IN THE NARUHATA AREA!
WE ESTIMATE IT WILL PLUNGE OFF THE BROKEN OVERPASS IN THREE MINUTES!
ONE OF THE PASSENGERS IS STILL ON THE BUS!
INGENIUM IS IN HOT PURSUIT, TRYING TO SAVE HER!
HOW-EVER...
MAKOTO
INGENIUM
TEAM IDATEN
TOURISTS
MOM
KOICHI
OUT OF STEAM?
HEY, CAN WE SEND OUT A VEHICLE?
YES.
IF I DON'T GET SOME FUEL...
PIT-02 IS OUT OF COMMISSION.

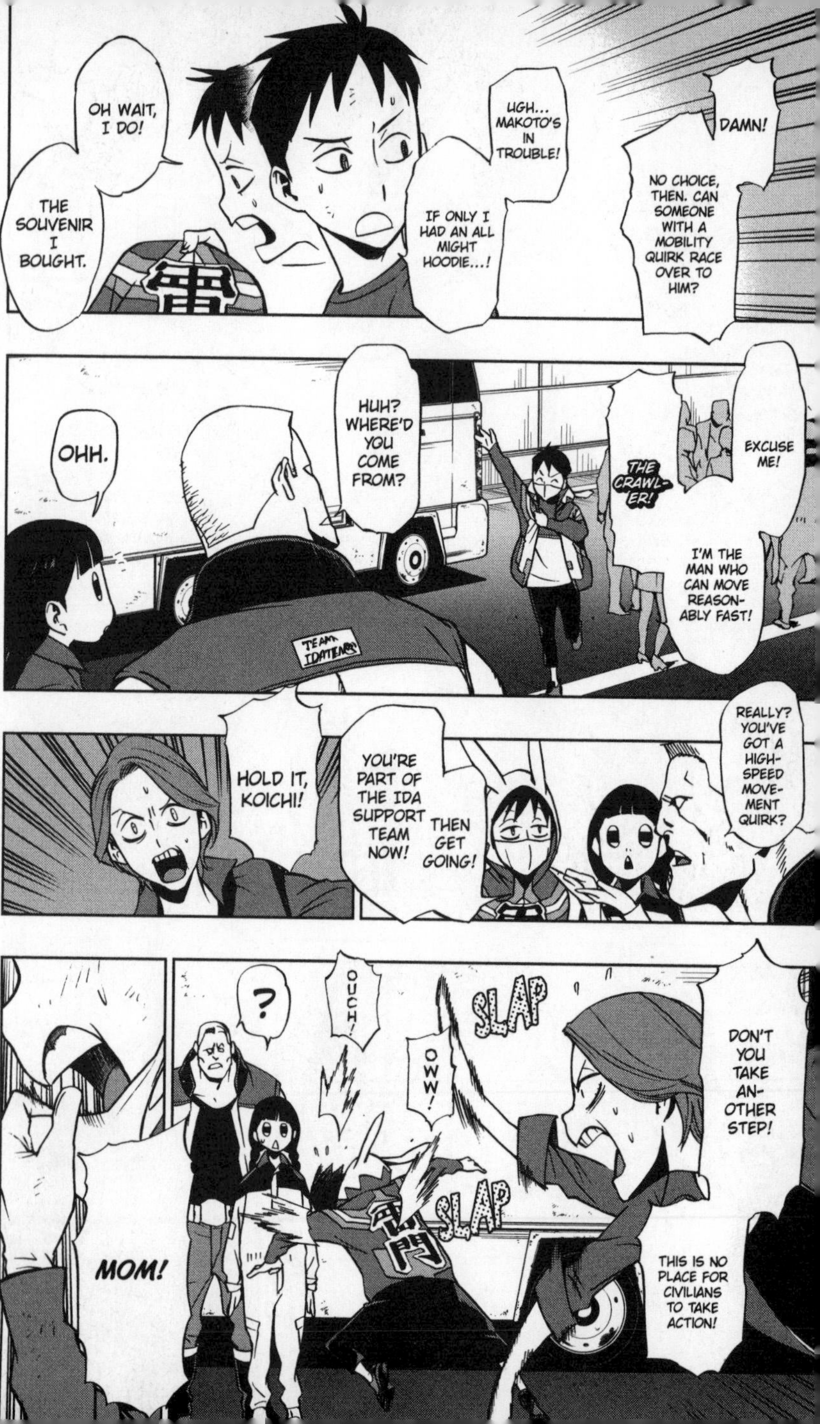
DAMN!
NO CHOICE, THEN. CAN SOMEONE WITH A MOBILITY QUIRK RACE OVER TO HIM?
UGH... MAKOTO'S IN TROUBLE!
IF ONLY I HAD AN ALL MIGHT HOODIE...!
OH WAIT, I DO!
THE SOUVENIR I BOUGHT.
EXCUSE ME!
THE CRAWLER!
I'M THE MAN WHO CAN MOVE REASONABLY FAST!
HUH? WHERE'D YOU COME FROM?
OHH.
TEAM IDATEN
REALLY? YOU'VE GOT A HIGH-SPEED MOVEMENT QUIRK?
THEN GET GOING!
YOU'RE PART OF THE IDA SUPPORT TEAM NOW!
HOLD IT, KOICHI!
DON'T YOU TAKE ANOTHER STEP!
SLAP
OUCH!
OWW!
?
SLAP
THIS IS NO PLACE FOR CIVILIANS TO TAKE ACTION!
MOM!

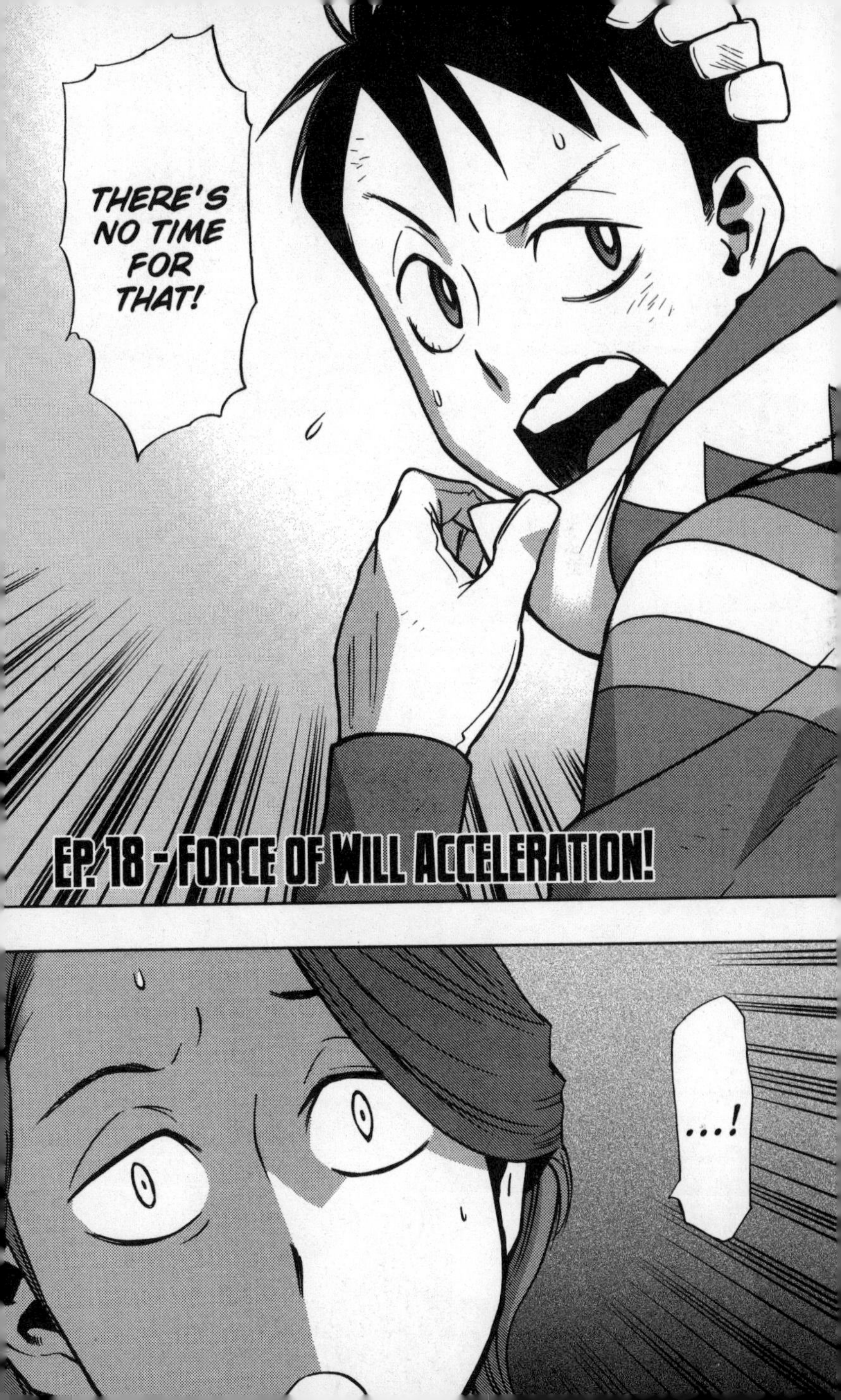
THERE'S NO TIME FOR THAT!
EP. 18 - FORCE OF WILL ACCELERATION!
...!

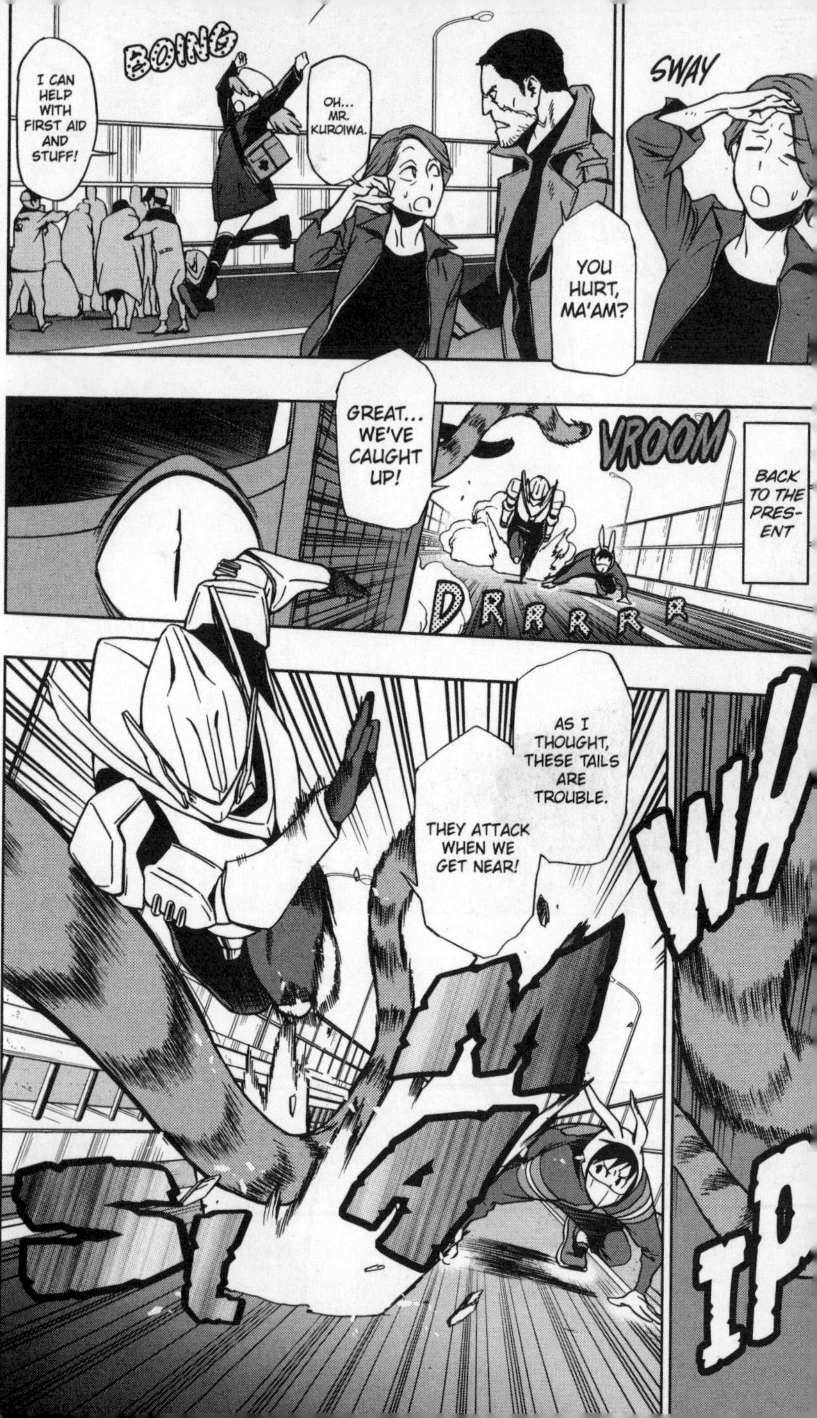
SWAY
YOU HURT, MA'AM?
OH... MR. KUROIWA.
BOING
I CAN HELP WITH FIRST AID AND STUFF!
BACK TO THE PRES-ENT
VROOM
GREAT... WE'VE CAUGHT UP!
DRRRRRR
WHIP
AS I THOUGHT, THESE TAILS ARE TROUBLE.
THEY ATTACK WHEN WE GET NEAR!
SLAM

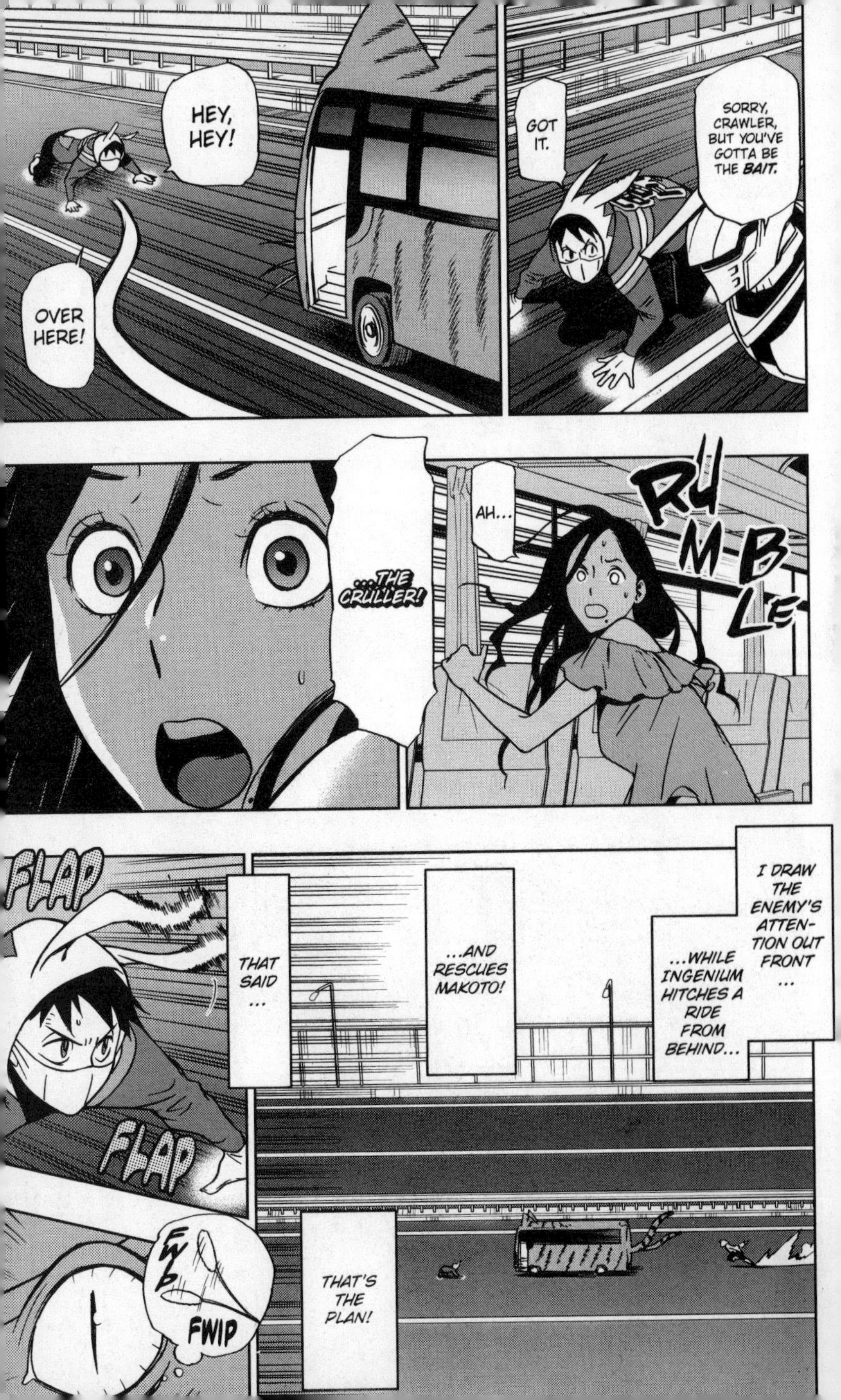
SORRY, CRAWLER, BUT YOU'VE GOTTA BE THE BAIT.
GOT IT.
HEY, HEY!
OVER HERE!
RUMBLE
AH...
...THE CRULLER!
I DRAW THE ENEMY'S ATTENTION OUT FRONT...
...WHILE INGENIUM HITCHES A RIDE FROM BEHIND...
...AND RESCUES MAKOTO!
THAT'S THE PLAN!
THAT SAID...
FLAP
FLAP
FWIP
FWIP

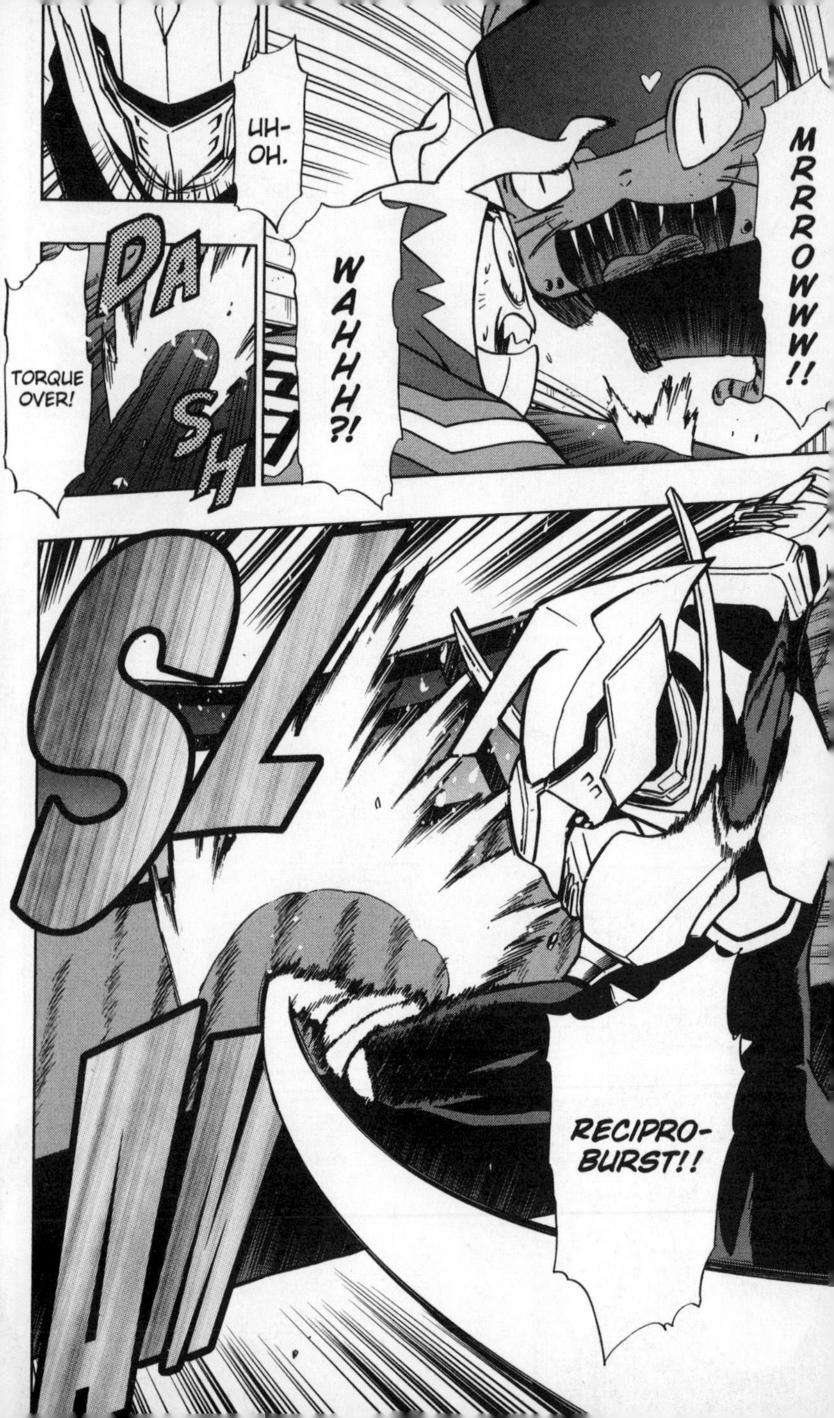
MRRROWWWW!!
WAHHHH?!
UH-OH.
DASH
TORQUE OVER!
RECIPRO-BURST!!

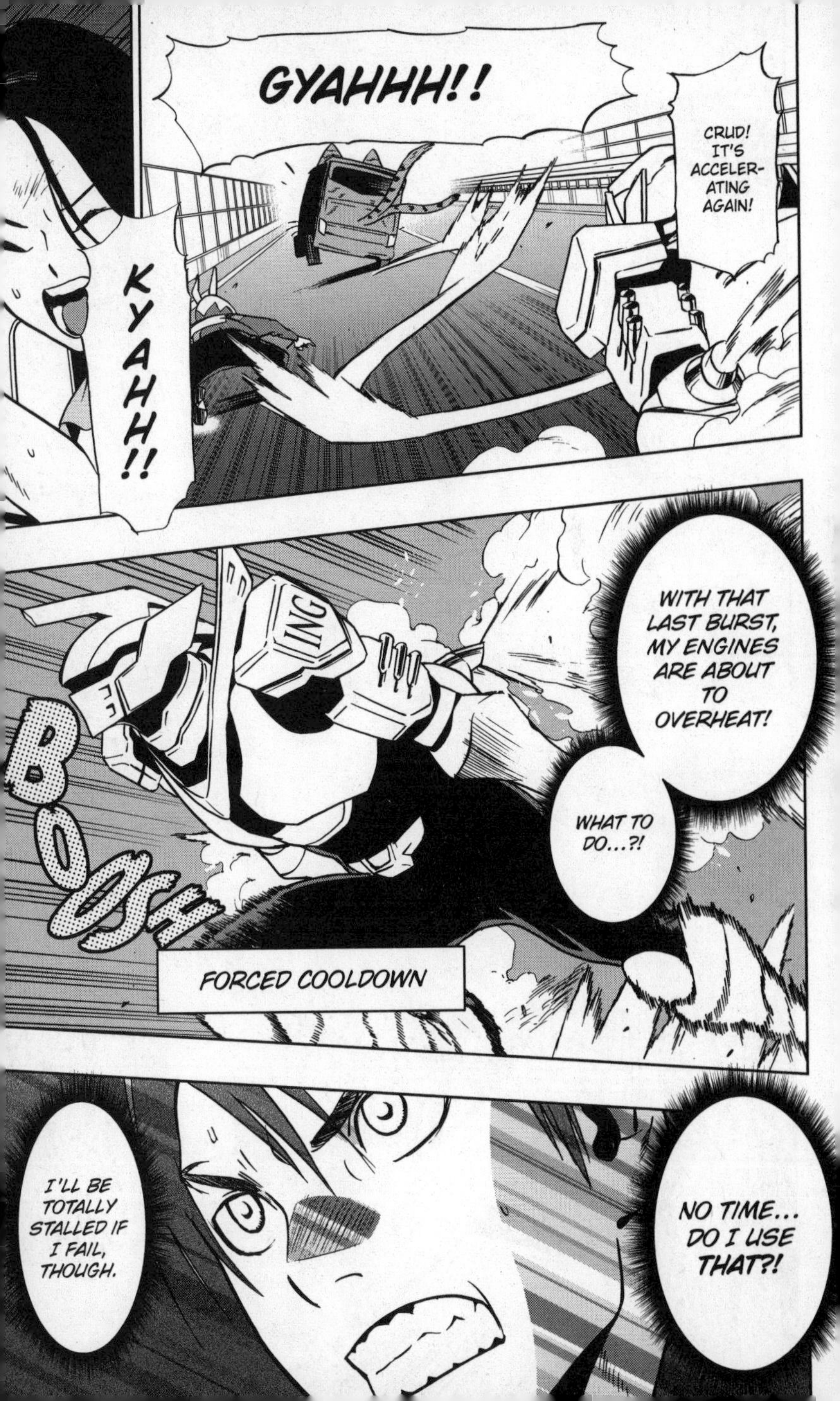
GYAHHH!!
CRUD! IT'S ACCELER-ATING AGAIN!
KYAHHH!!
WITH THAT LAST BURST, MY ENGINES ARE ABOUT TO OVERHEAT!
WHAT TO DO...?!
BOOSH
FORCED COOLDOWN
NO TIME... DO I USE THAT?!
I'LL BE TOTALLY STALLED IF I FAIL, THOUGH.

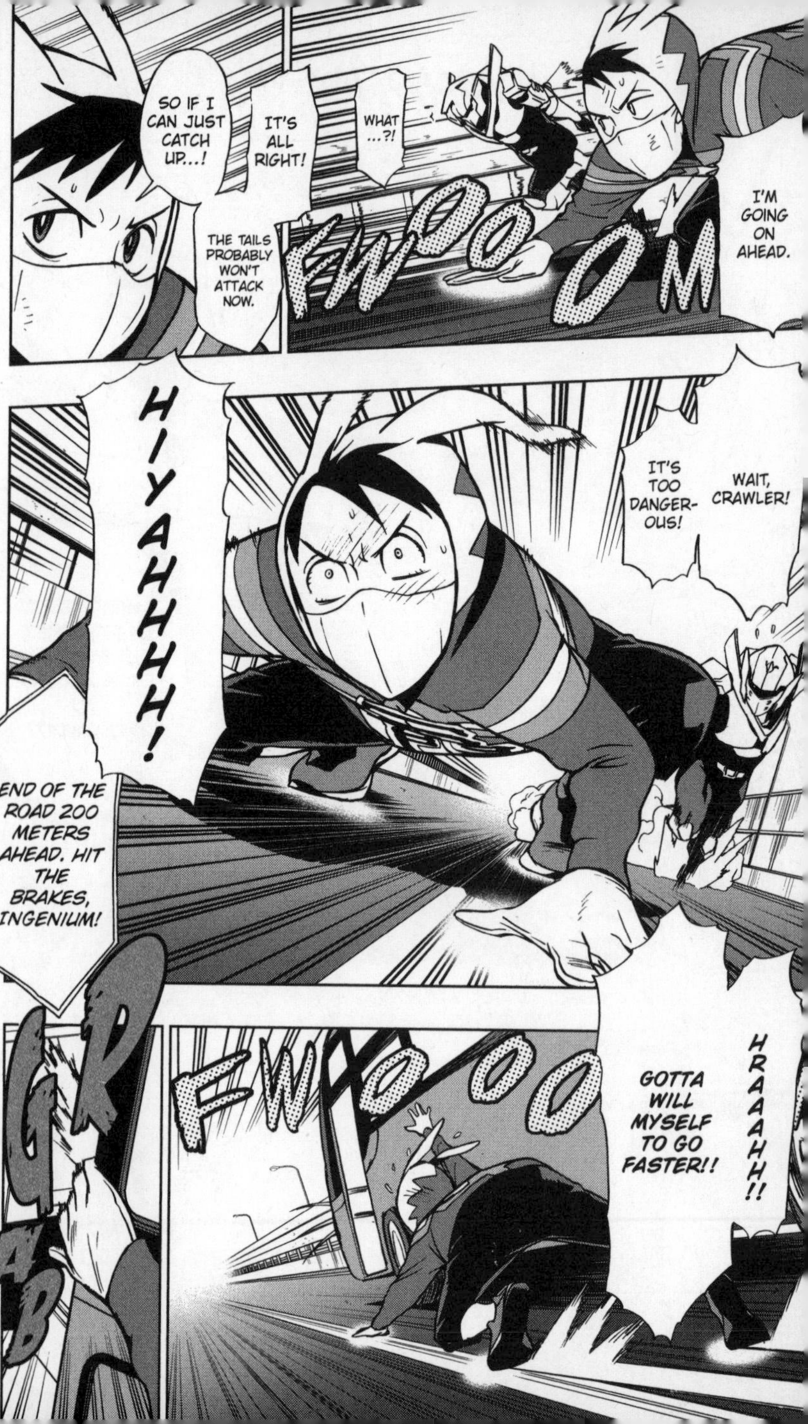
I'M GOING ON AHEAD.
FWOOOM
WHAT ...?!
IT'S ALL RIGHT!
SO IF I CAN JUST CATCH UP...!
THE TAILS PROBABLY WON'T ATTACK NOW.
WAIT, CRAWLER!
IT'S TOO DANGER-OUS!
HIYAHHHHH!
END OF THE ROAD 200 METERS AHEAD. HIT THE BRAKES, INGENIUM!
HRAAAAHH!!
GOTTA WILL MYSELF TO GO FASTER!!
FWOOOO
GRAB

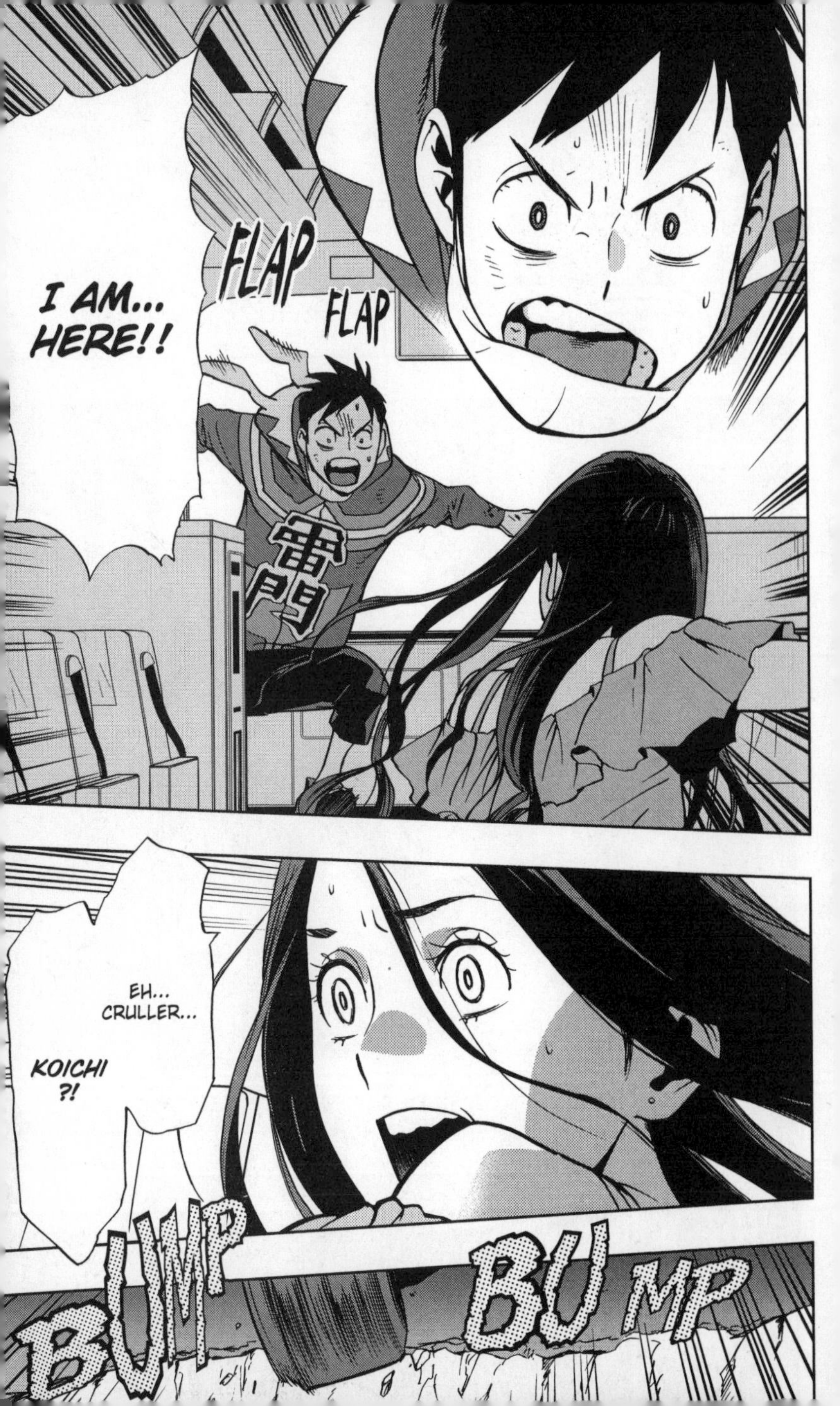

FLAP
FLAP
I AM... HERE!!
EH... CRULLER...
KOICHI ?!
BUMP
BUMP

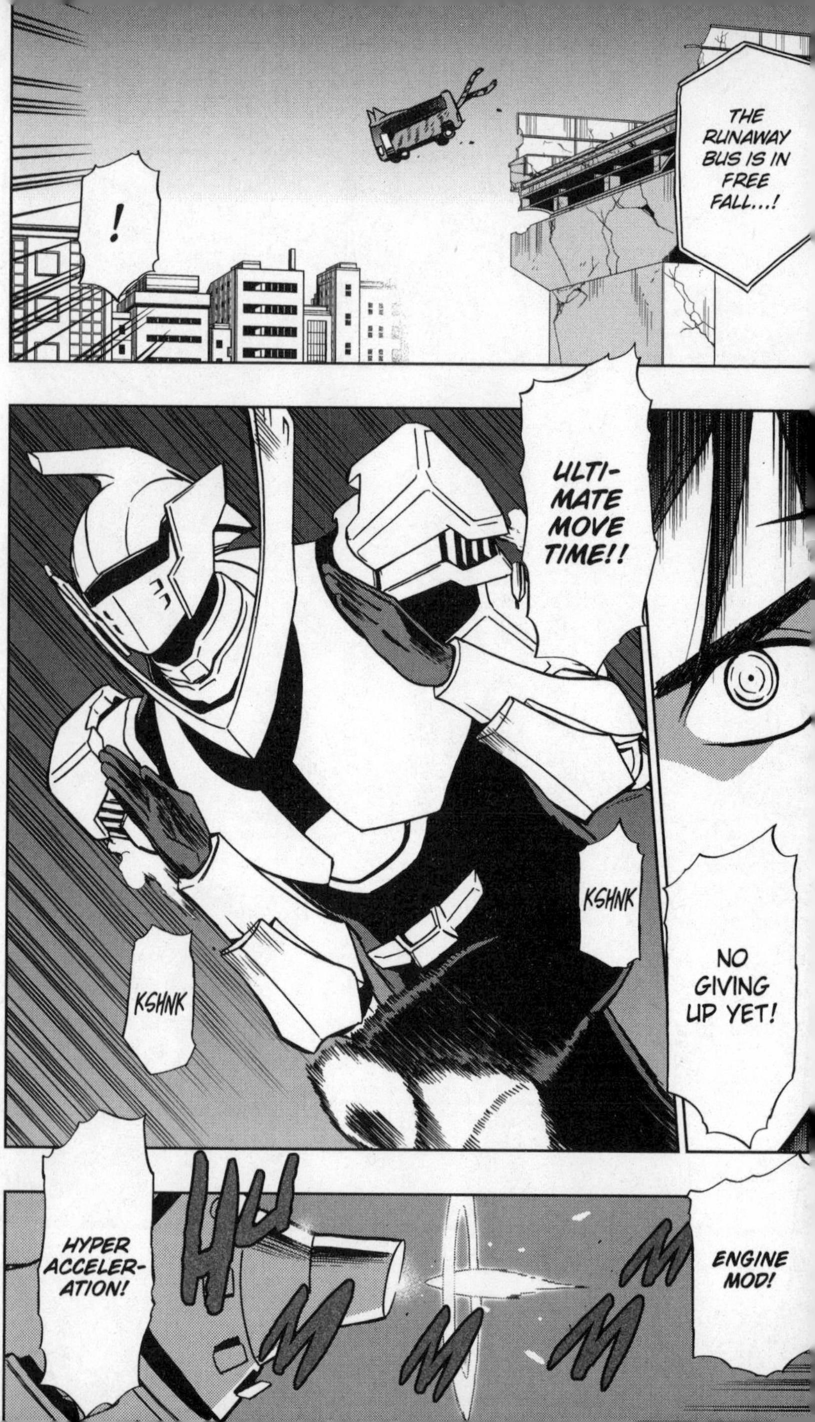
THE RUNAWAY BUS IS IN FREE FALL...!
!
ULTI-MATE MOVE TIME!!
NO GIVING UP YET!
KSHNK
KSHNK
ENGINE MOD!
HUMMMM
HYPER ACCELER-ATION!

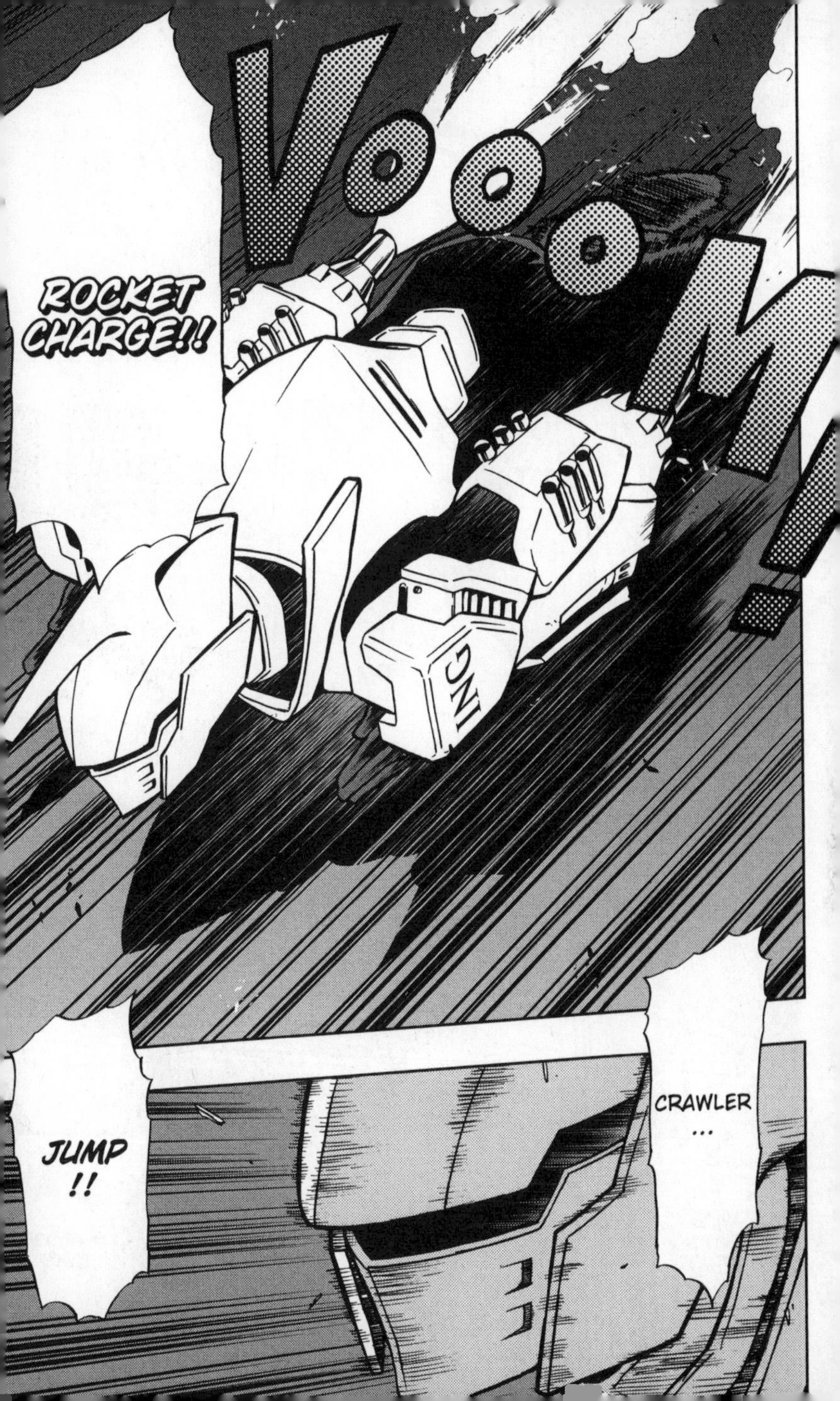
VOOOM!!
ROCKET CHARGE!!
CRAWLER ...
JUMP !!

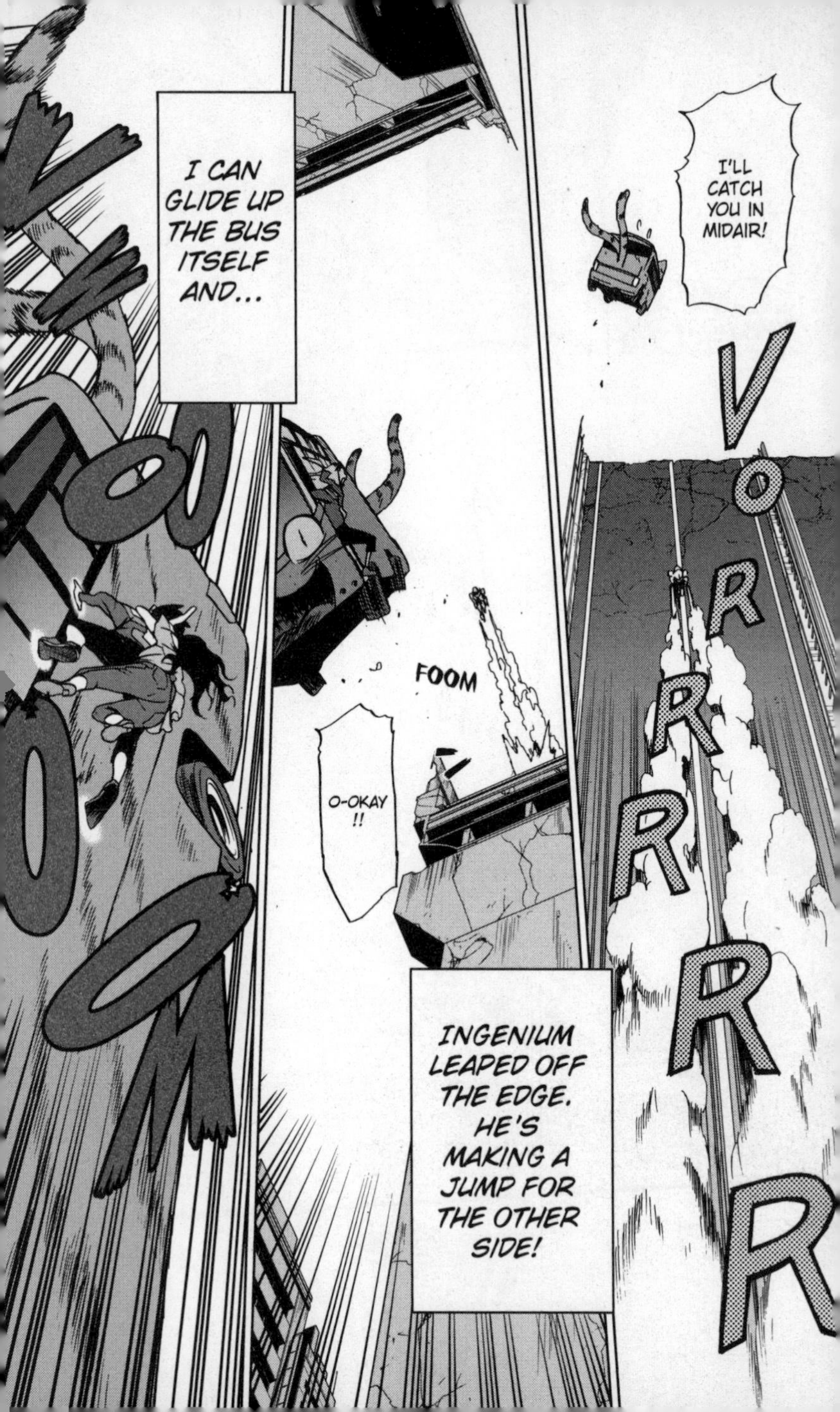
I'LL CATCH YOU IN MIDAIR!
VORRRRR
FOOM
O-OKAY!!
INGENIUM LEAPED OFF THE EDGE. HE'S MAKING A JUMP FOR THE OTHER SIDE!
I CAN GLIDE UP THE BUS ITSELF AND...
VWOOOM

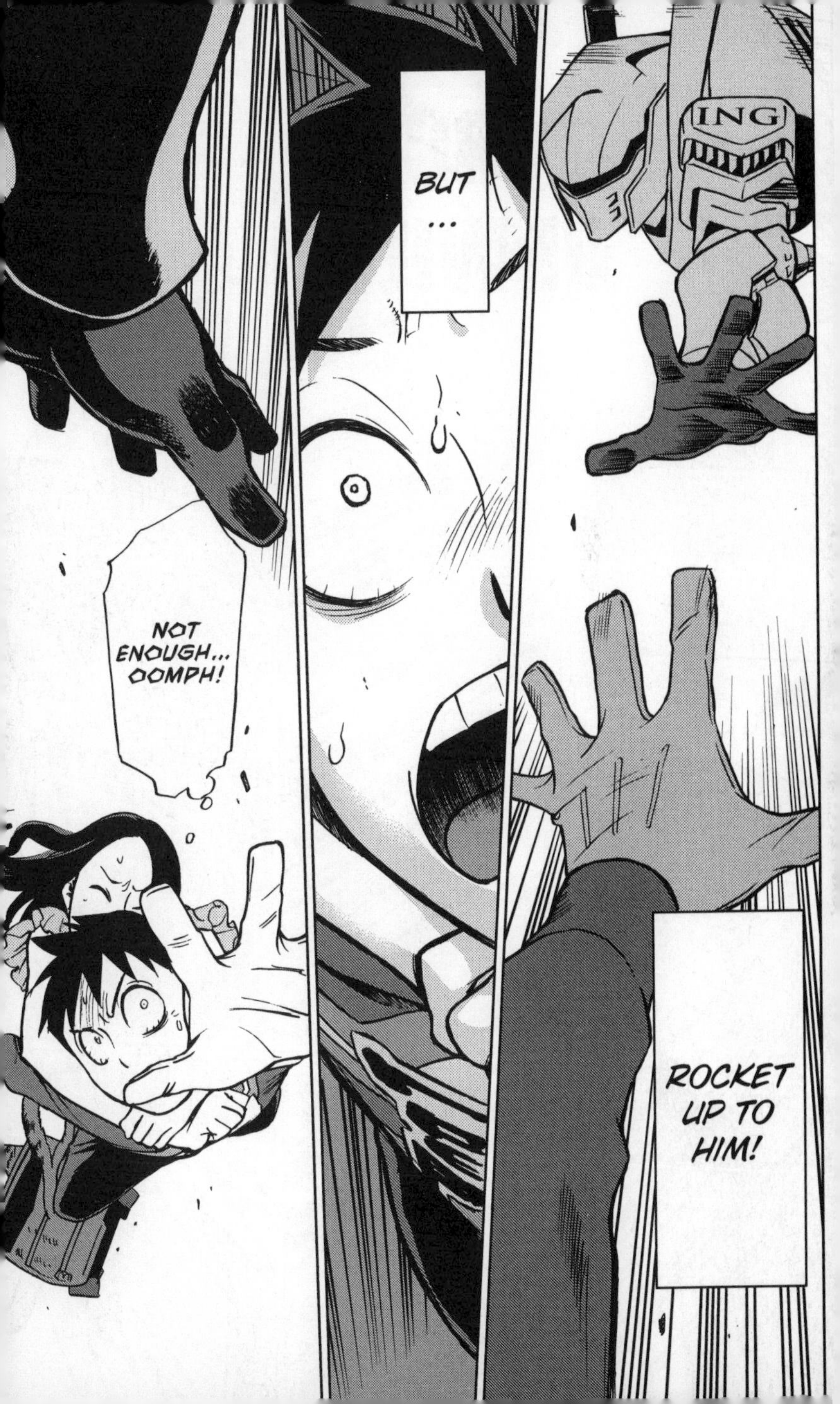
ING
ROCKET UP TO HIM!
BUT ...
NOT ENOUGH... OOMPH!

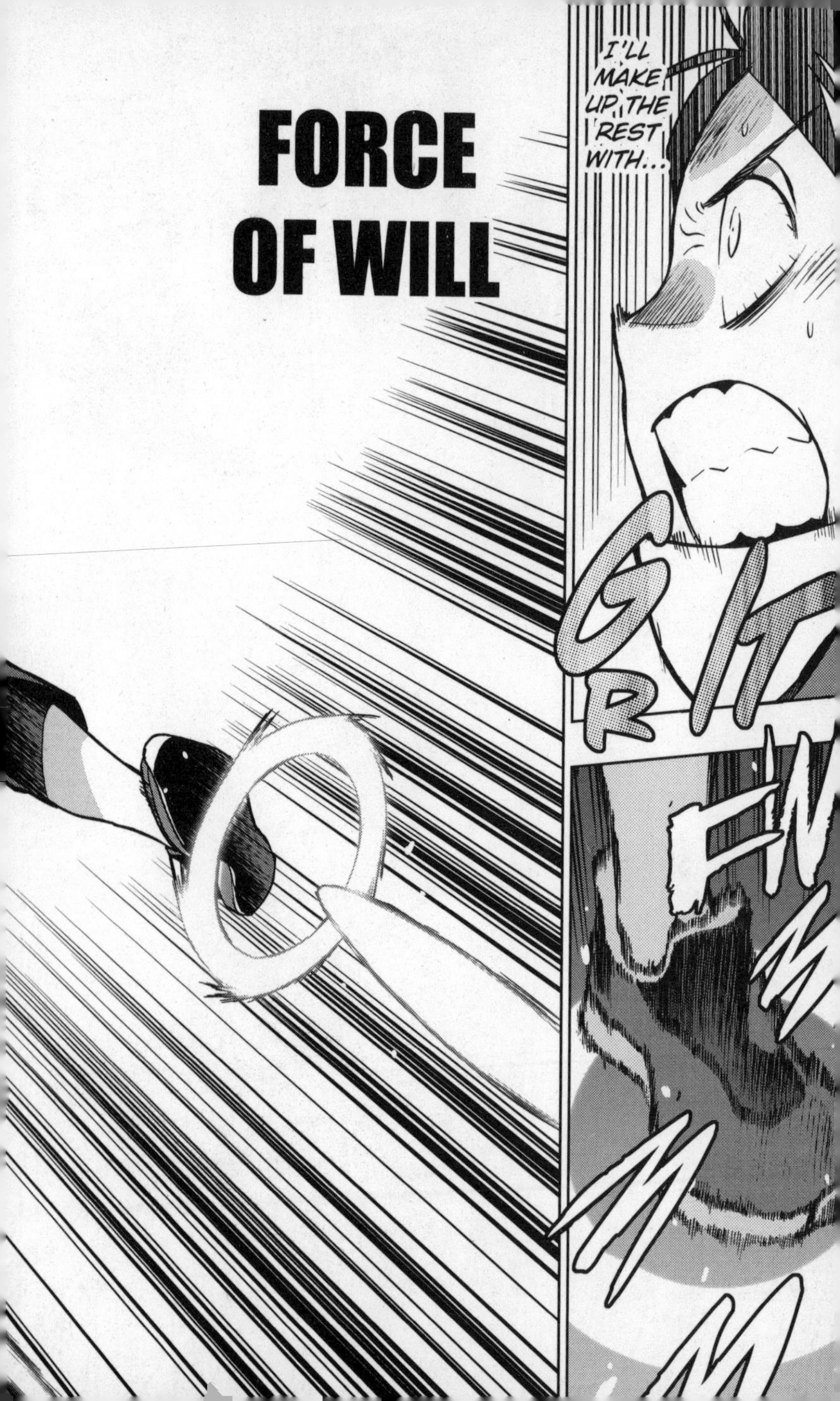
I'LL MAKE UP THE REST WITH...
GRIT
FORCE OF WILL

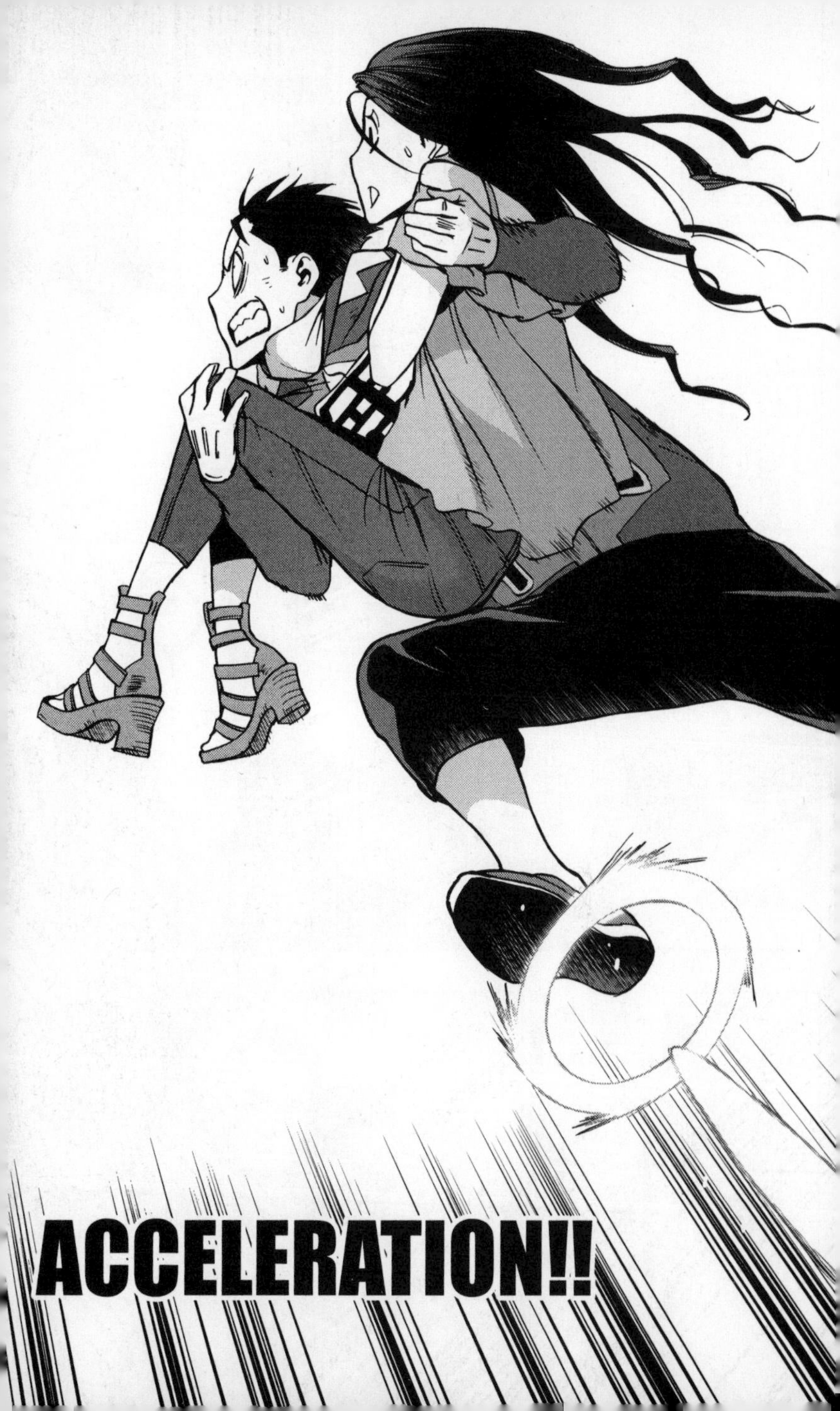
ACCELERATION!!

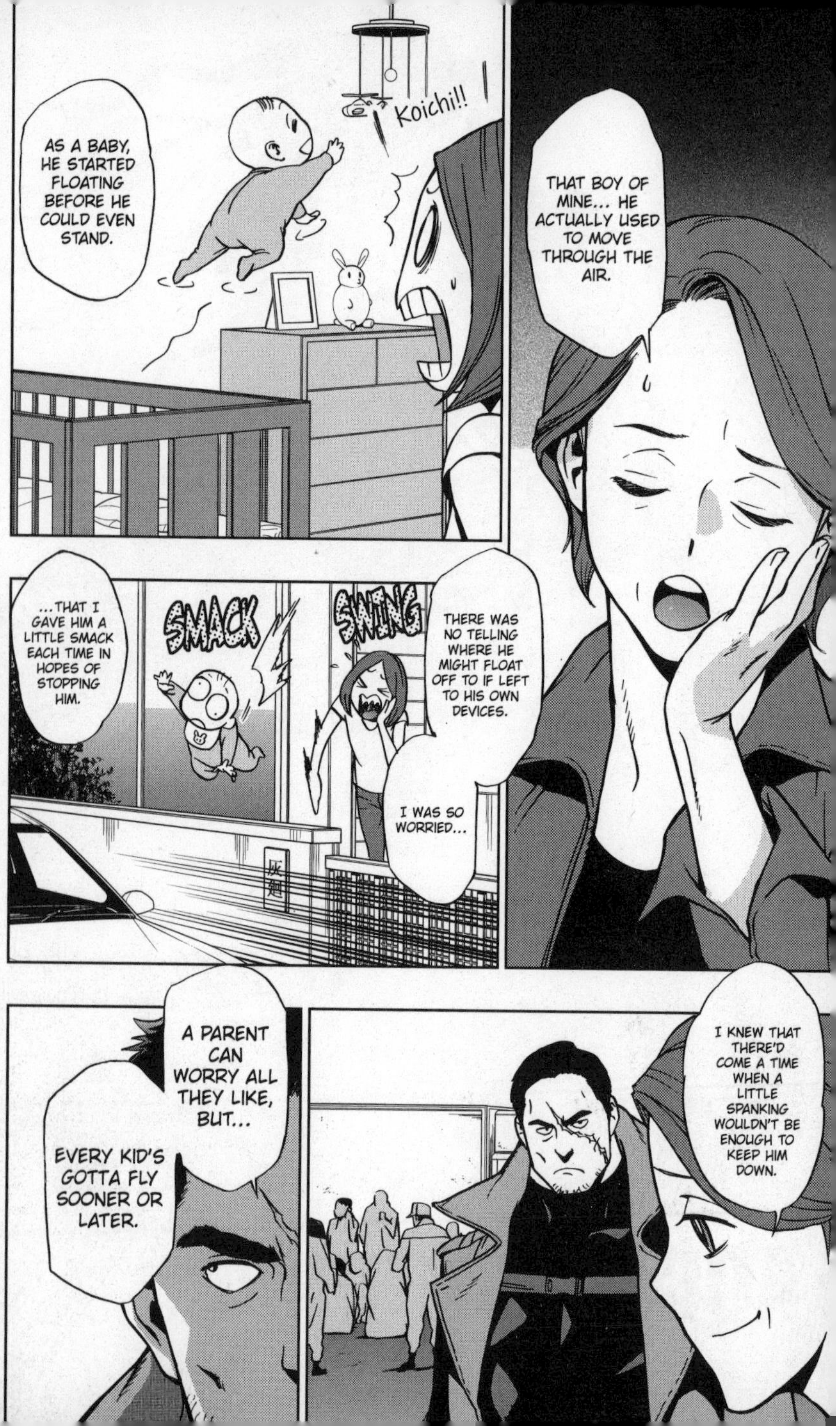
THAT BOY OF MINE... HE ACTUALLY USED TO MOVE THROUGH THE AIR.
Koichi!!
AS A BABY, HE STARTED FLOATING BEFORE HE COULD EVEN STAND.
THERE WAS NO TELLING WHERE HE MIGHT FLOAT OFF TO IF LEFT TO HIS OWN DEVICES.
I WAS SO WORRIED...
SWING
SMACK
...THAT I GAVE HIM A LITTLE SMACK EACH TIME IN HOPES OF STOPPING HIM.
I KNEW THAT THERE'D COME A TIME WHEN A LITTLE SPANKING WOULDN'T BE ENOUGH TO KEEP HIM DOWN.
A PARENT CAN WORRY ALL THEY LIKE, BUT...
EVERY KID'S GOTTA FLY SOONER OR LATER.

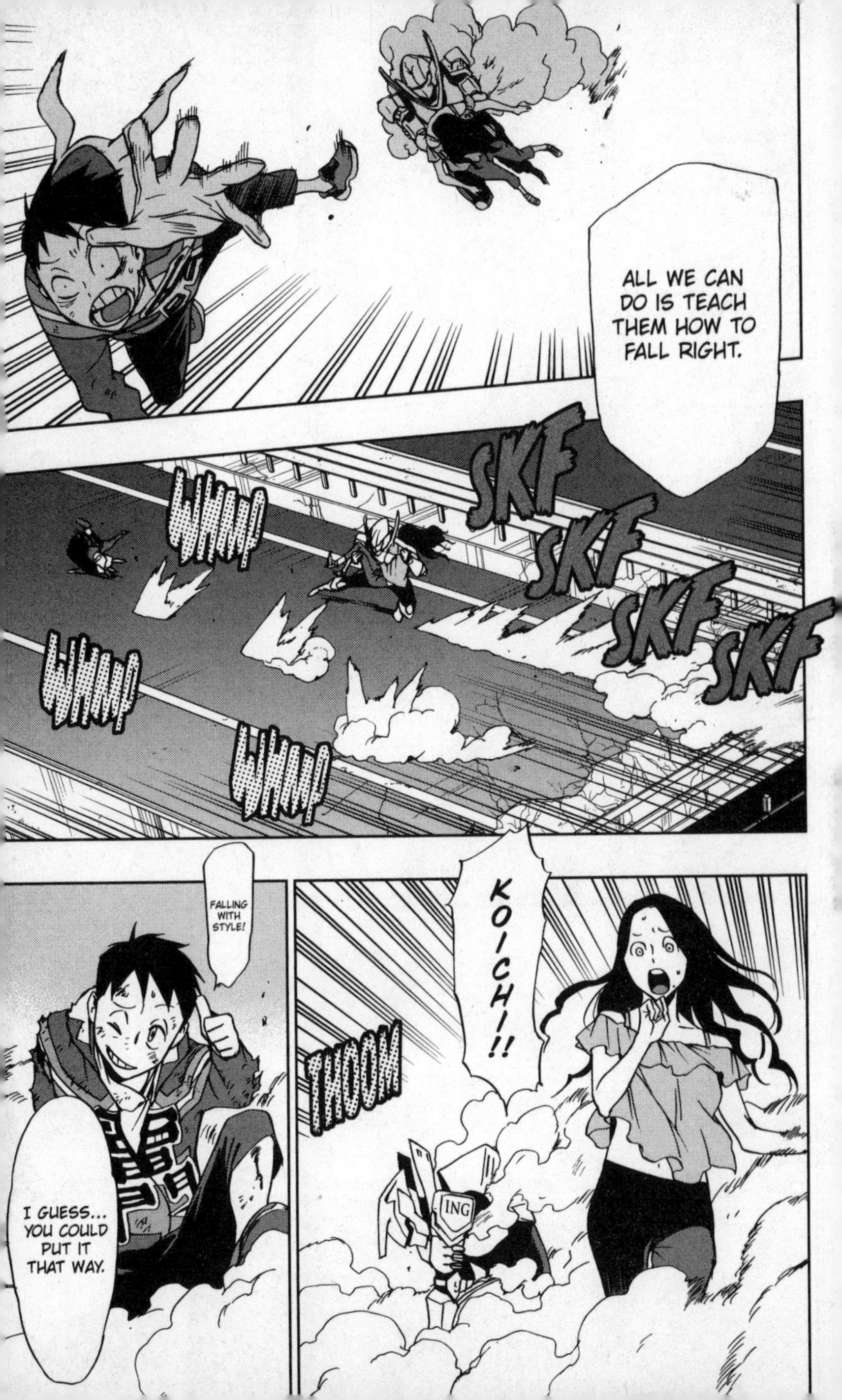
ALL WE CAN DO IS TEACH THEM HOW TO FALL RIGHT.
SKF
SKF
SKF
SKF
WHMP
WHMP
WHMP
KOICHI!!
THOOM
FALLING WITH STYLE!
I GUESS... YOU COULD PUT IT THAT WAY.

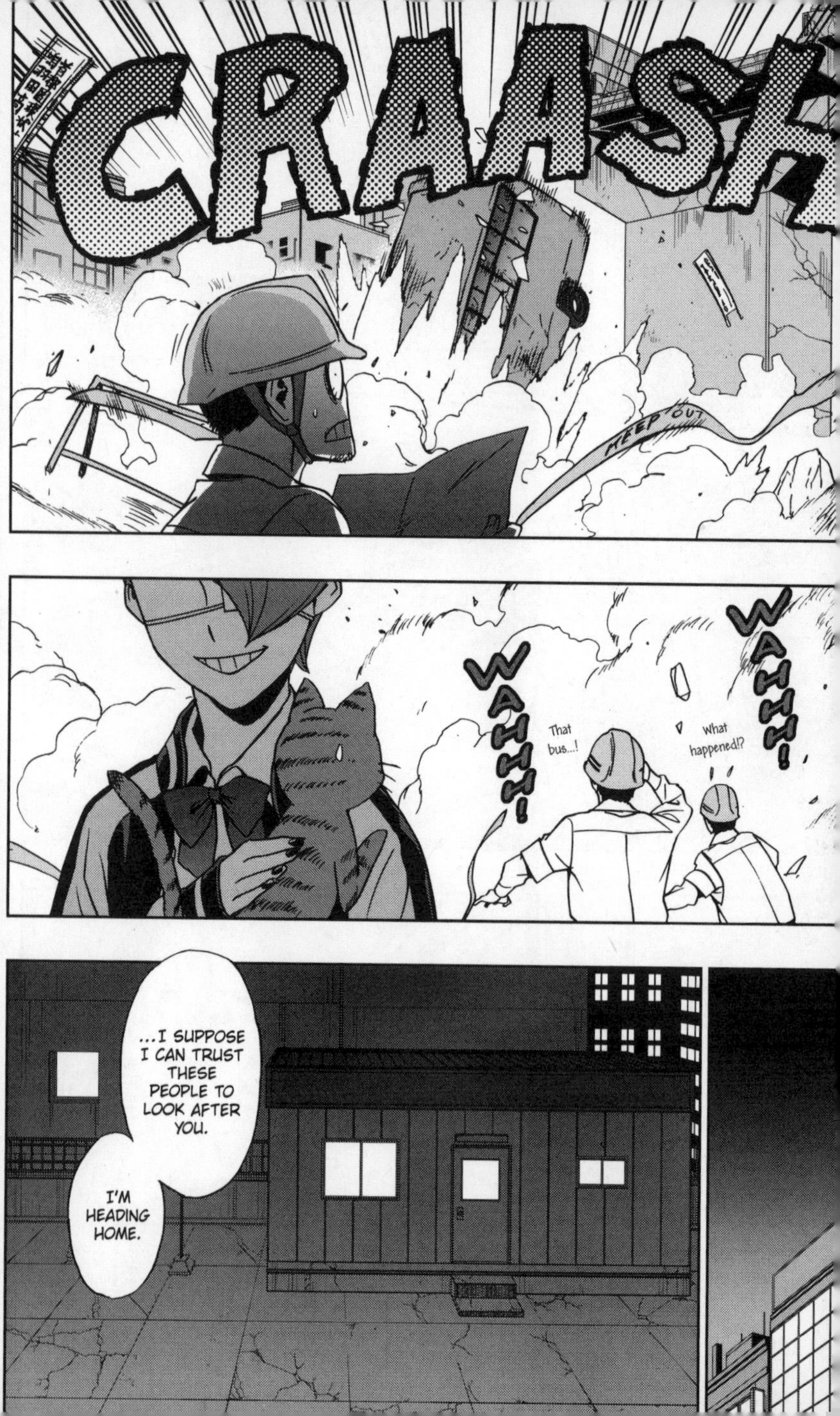
CRAASH
KEEP OUT
WAHHH!
What happened!?
That bus...!
WAHHH!
...I SUPPOSE I CAN TRUST THESE PEOPLE TO LOOK AFTER YOU.
I'M HEADING HOME.

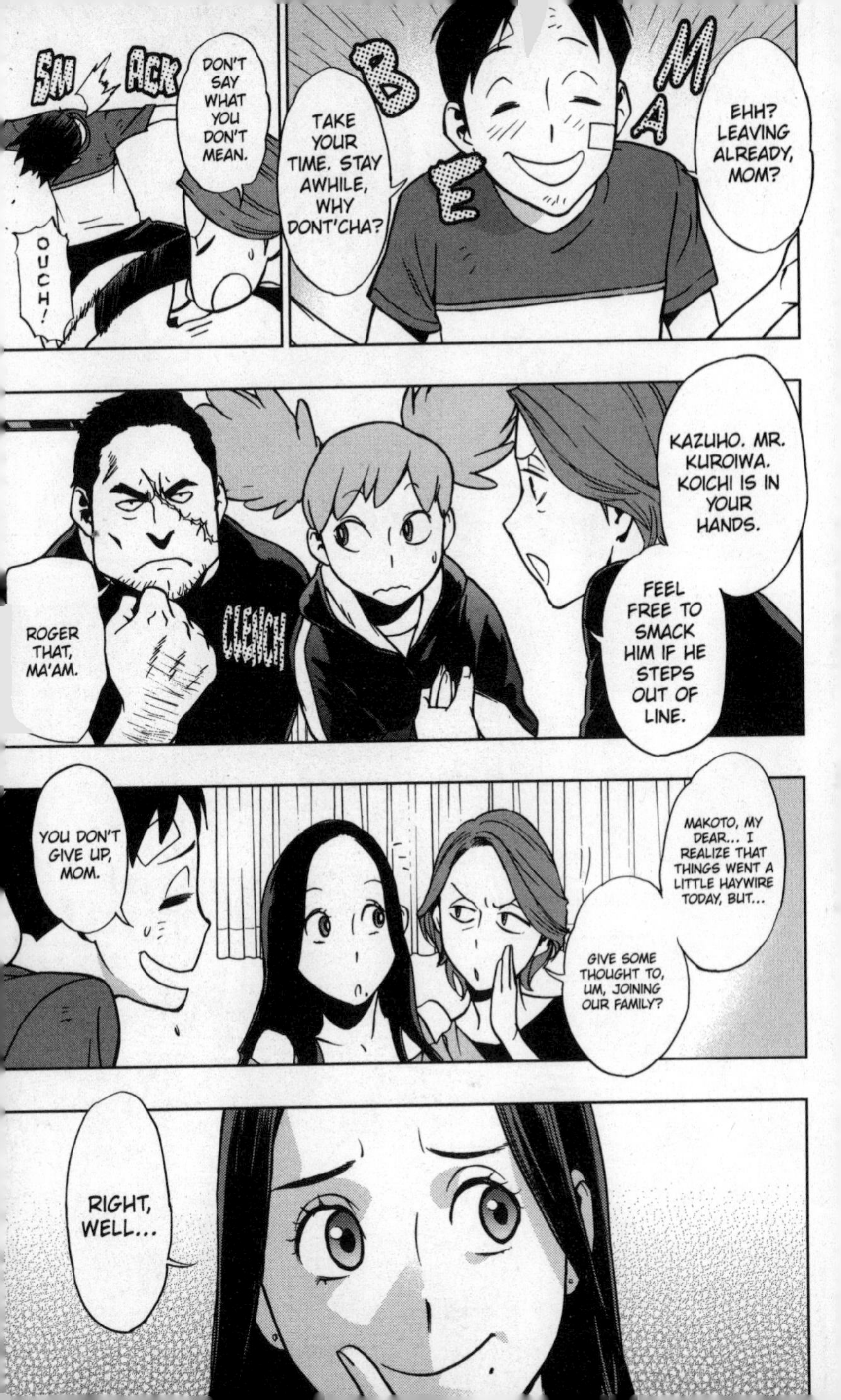
EHH? LEAVING ALREADY, MOM?
BEAM
TAKE YOUR TIME. STAY AWHILE, WHY DONT'CHA?
SMACK
DON'T SAY WHAT YOU DON'T MEAN.
OUCH!
KAZUHO. MR. KUROIWA. KOICHI IS IN YOUR HANDS.
FEEL FREE TO SMACK HIM IF HE STEPS OUT OF LINE.
CLENCH
ROGER THAT, MA'AM.
MAKOTO, MY DEAR... I REALIZE THAT THINGS WENT A LITTLE HAYWIRE TODAY, BUT...
GIVE SOME THOUGHT TO, UM, JOINING OUR FAMILY?
YOU DON'T GIVE UP, MOM.
RIGHT, WELL...

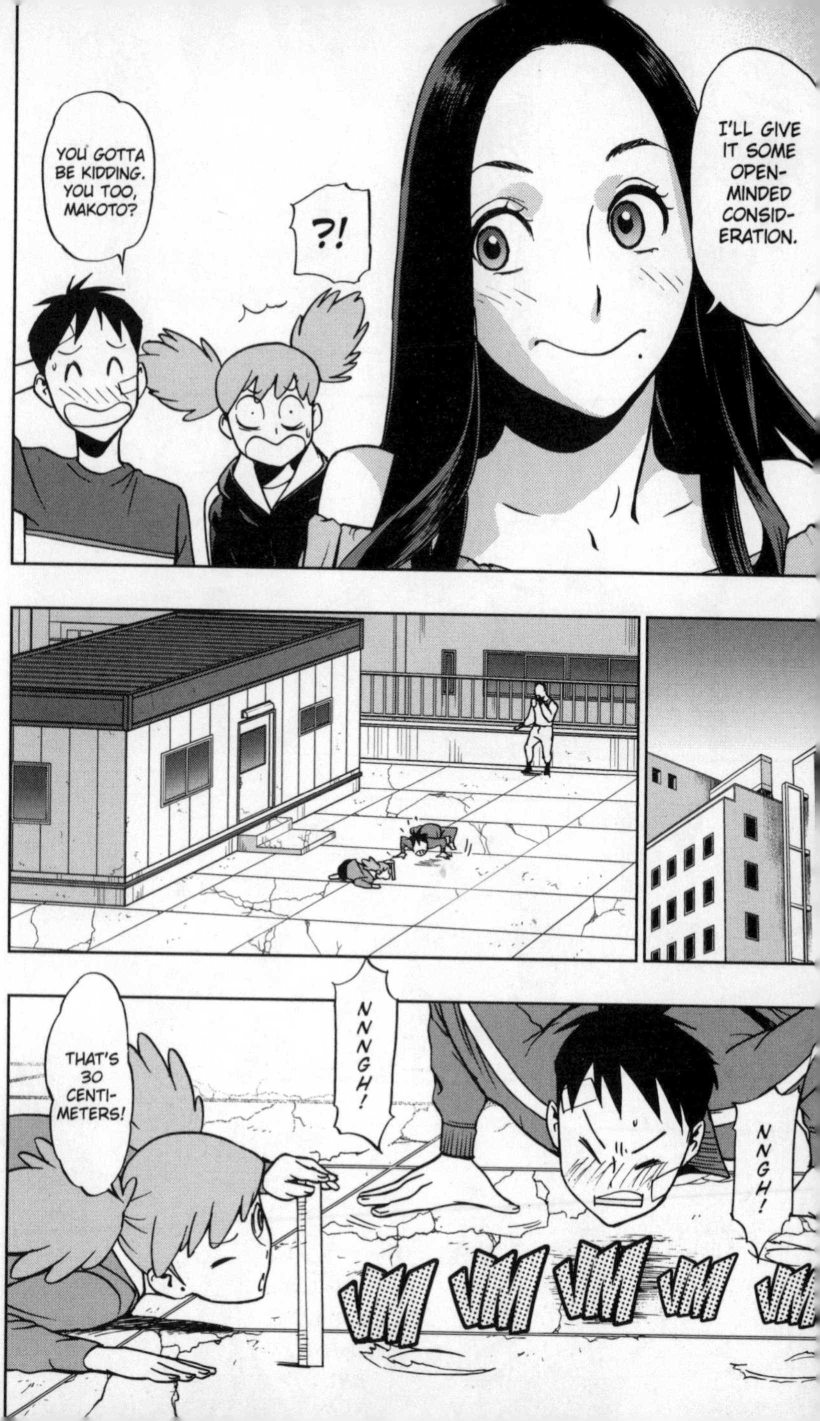
I'LL GIVE IT SOME OPEN-MINDED CONSID-ERATION.
?!
YOU GOTTA BE KIDDING. YOU TOO, MAKOTO?
NNGH!
NNNGH!
THAT'S 30 CENTI-METERS!
JM JM JM JM JM

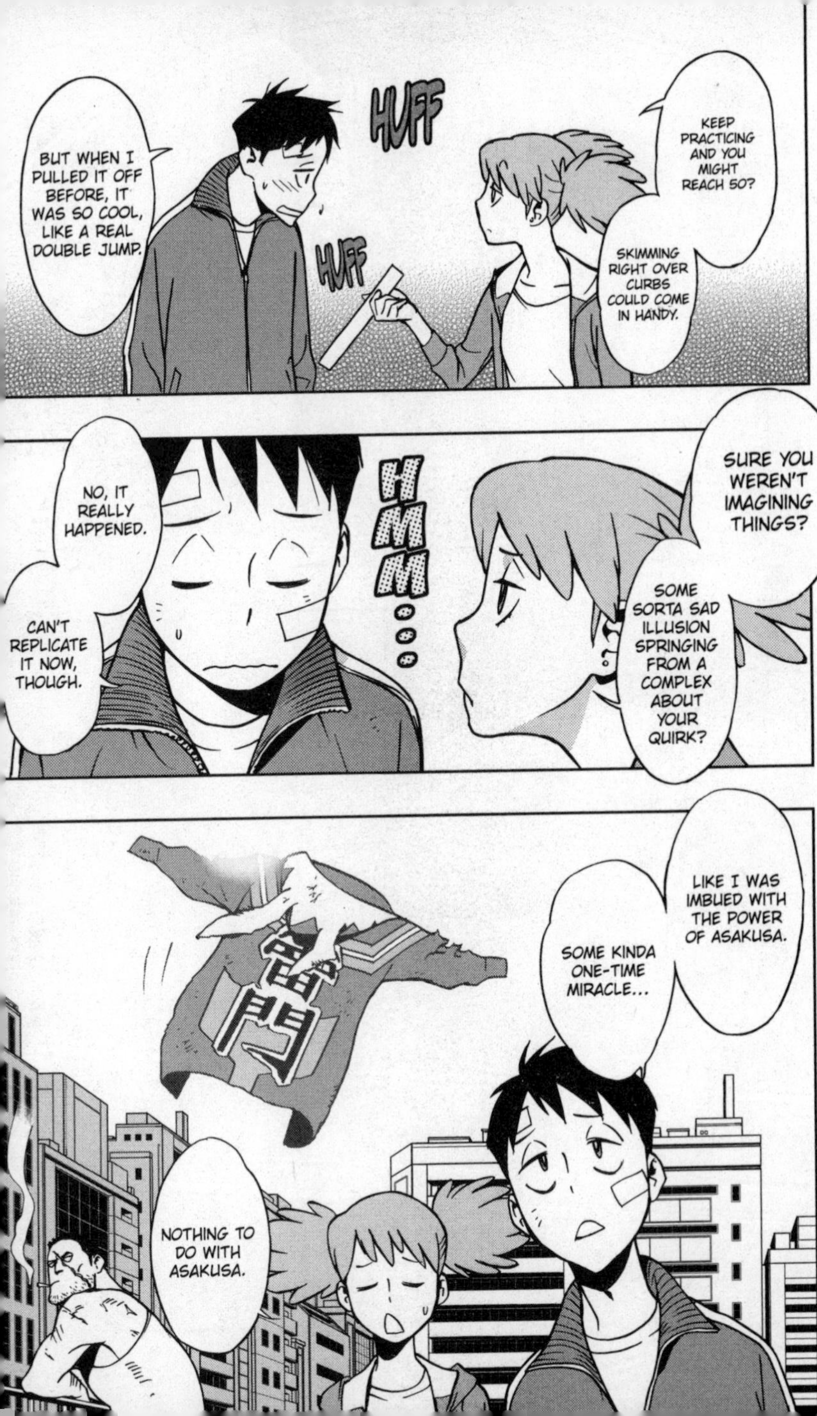
KEEP PRACTICING AND YOU MIGHT REACH 50?
SKIMMING RIGHT OVER CURBS COULD COME IN HANDY.
HUFF
HUFF
BUT WHEN I PULLED IT OFF BEFORE, IT WAS SO COOL, LIKE A REAL DOUBLE JUMP.
SURE YOU WEREN'T IMAGINING THINGS?
SOME SORTA SAD ILLUSION SPRINGING FROM A COMPLEX ABOUT YOUR QUIRK?
HMM...
NO, IT REALLY HAPPENED.
CAN'T REPLICATE IT NOW, THOUGH.
LIKE I WAS IMBUED WITH THE POWER OF ASAKUSA.
SOME KINDA ONE-TIME MIRACLE...
NOTHING TO DO WITH ASAKUSA.

EXPLANATION

The following chapters, "Hero Conference" and "Hero Visit," appeared in the *Shonen Jump* special *Jump Giga* and represent a serialized spin-off of the spin-off. Along with episode 7.5 "Appearance Matters," and episode 9.5 "Mask," (which were in *Vigilantes* volume 2), the four bonus chapters appeared throughout volumes 1 through 4 of the magazine in 2017.

Unlike the series in *Jump+*, these chapters would be encountered by more first-time readers, so they lean toward stand-alone stories with a slightly different flavor.

Our vigilante friends are notably absent from "Hero Conference" and "Hero Visit," as the focus is instead on the pro heroes.

In terms of the timeline, they take place around the same time as episode 6 "No Need To Hold Back," from the start of volume 2. The events at the end of volume 1 concern a surge of instant villains in the Naruhata neighborhood, and here we see how the police and pro heroes are dealing with all that.

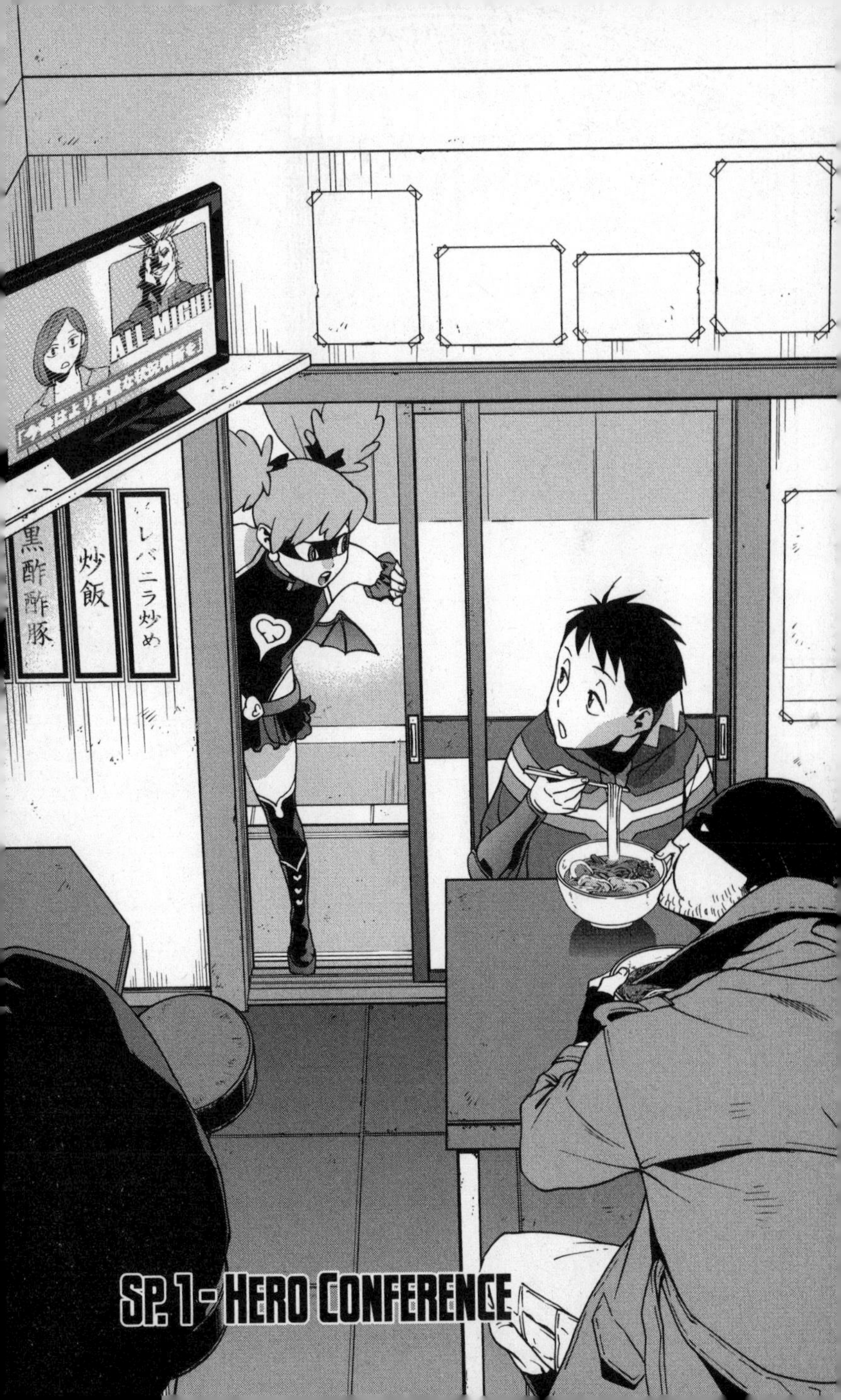
ALL MIGHT
黒酢酢豚
炒飯
レバニラ炒め
SP. 1 - HERO CONFERENCE

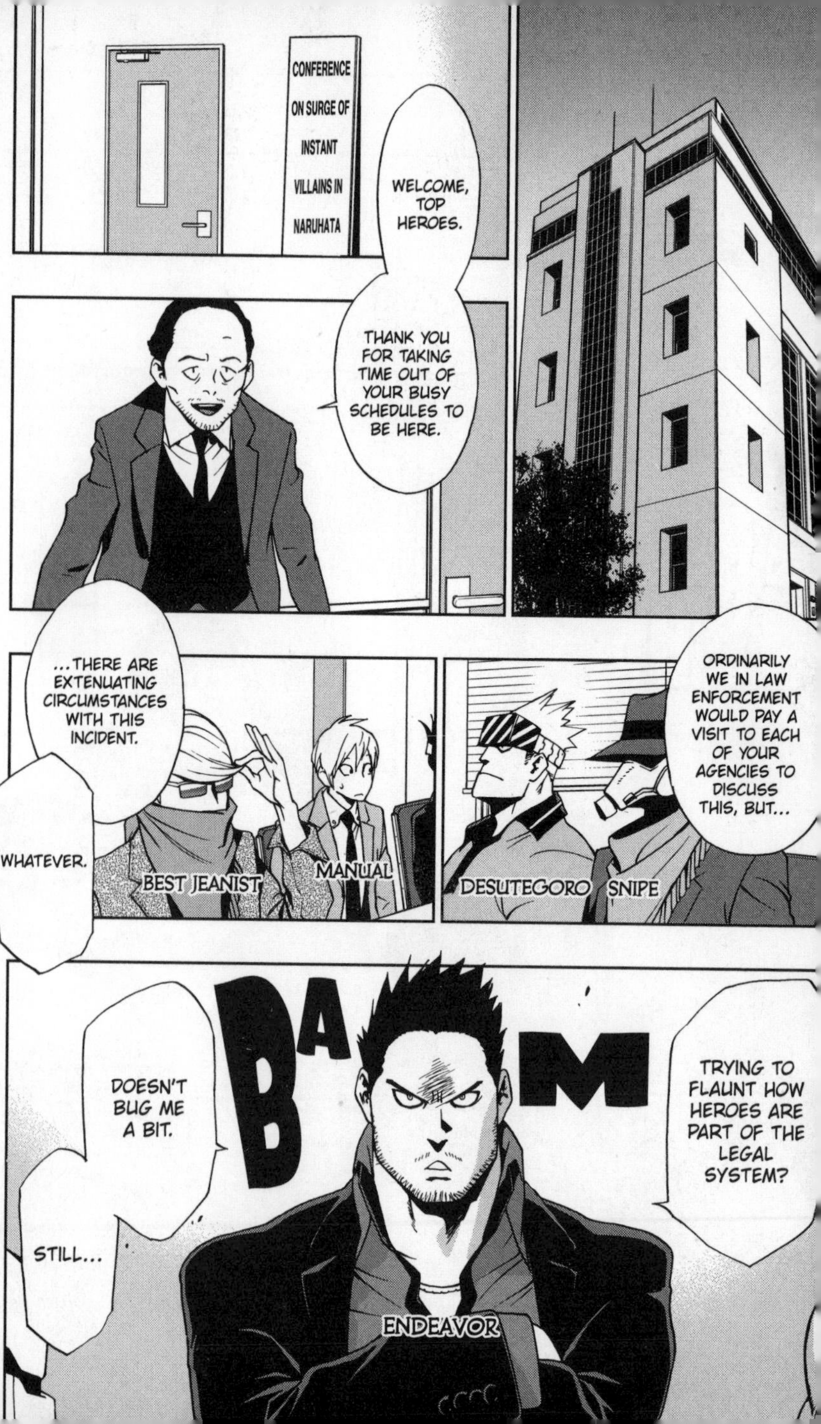
CONFERENCE ON SURGE OF INSTANT VILLAINS IN NARUHATA
WELCOME, TOP HEROES.
THANK YOU FOR TAKING TIME OUT OF YOUR BUSY SCHEDULES TO BE HERE.
ORDINARILY WE IN LAW ENFORCEMENT WOULD PAY A VISIT TO EACH OF YOUR AGENCIES TO DISCUSS THIS, BUT...
DESUTEGORO
SNIPE
...THERE ARE EXTENUATING CIRCUMSTANCES WITH THIS INCIDENT.
MANUAL
BEST JEANIST
WHATEVER.
TRYING TO FLAUNT HOW HEROES ARE PART OF THE LEGAL SYSTEM?
BAM
DOESN'T BUG ME A BIT.
STILL...
ENDEAVOR

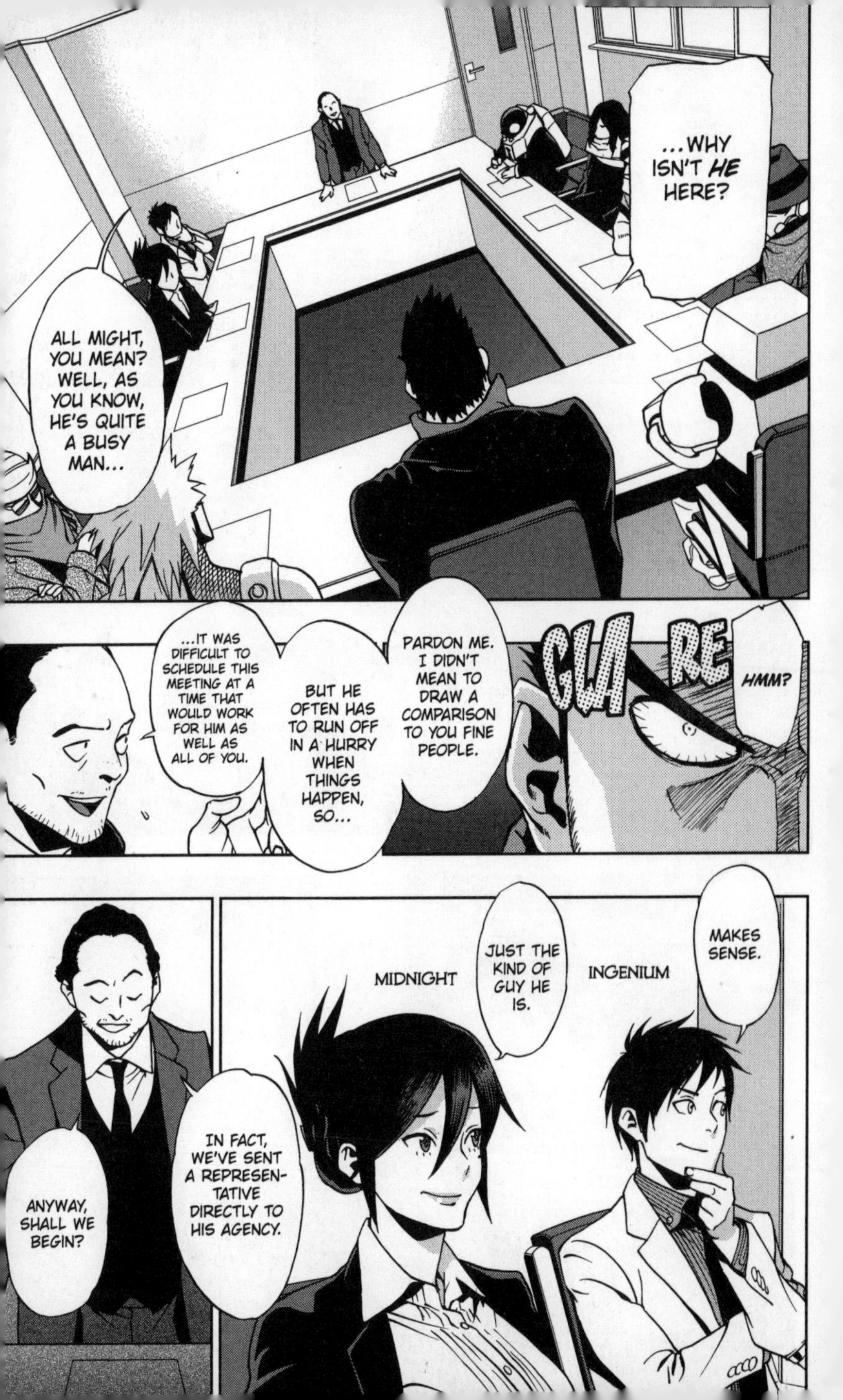
...WHY ISN'T HE HERE?
ALL MIGHT, YOU MEAN? WELL, AS YOU KNOW, HE'S QUITE A BUSY MAN...
BUT HE OFTEN HAS TO RUN OFF IN A HURRY WHEN THINGS HAPPEN, SO...
GLARE
HMM?
PARDON ME. I DIDN'T MEAN TO DRAW A COMPARISON TO YOU FINE PEOPLE.
...IT WAS DIFFICULT TO SCHEDULE THIS MEETING AT A TIME THAT WOULD WORK FOR HIM AS WELL AS ALL OF YOU.
MAKES SENSE.
INGENIUM
JUST THE KIND OF GUY HE IS.
MIDNIGHT
IN FACT, WE'VE SENT A REPRESENTATIVE DIRECTLY TO HIS AGENCY.
ANYWAY, SHALL WE BEGIN?

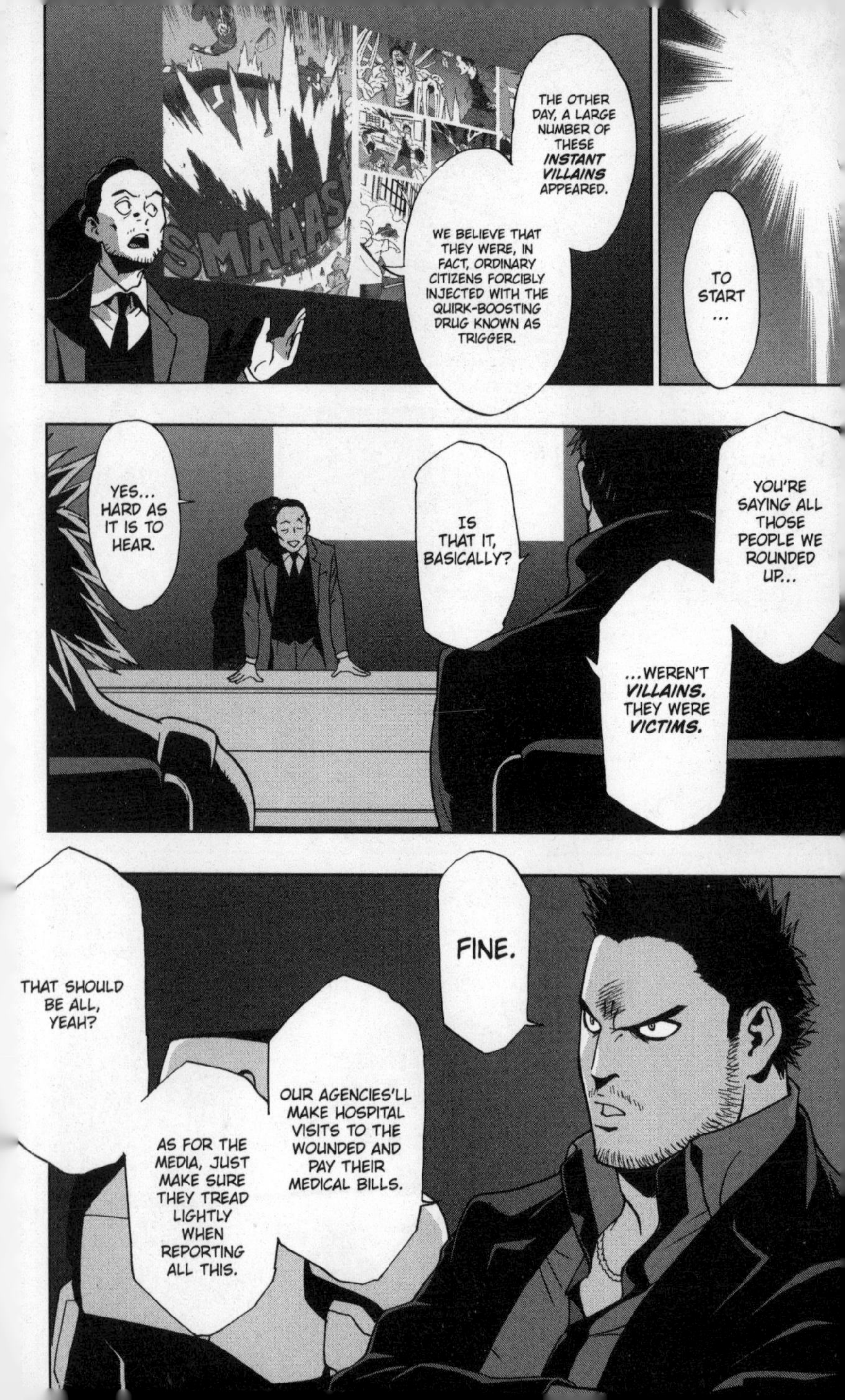
TO START...
THE OTHER DAY, A LARGE NUMBER OF THESE *INSTANT VILLAINS* APPEARED.
SMAAAS
WE BELIEVE THAT THEY WERE, IN FACT, ORDINARY CITIZENS FORCIBLY INJECTED WITH THE QUIRK-BOOSTING DRUG KNOWN AS TRIGGER.
YOU'RE SAYING ALL THOSE PEOPLE WE ROUNDED UP...
...WEREN'T *VILLAINS.* THEY WERE *VICTIMS.*
IS THAT IT, BASICALLY?
YES... HARD AS IT IS TO HEAR.
FINE.
OUR AGENCIES'LL MAKE HOSPITAL VISITS TO THE WOUNDED AND PAY THEIR MEDICAL BILLS.
AS FOR THE MEDIA, JUST MAKE SURE THEY TREAD LIGHTLY WHEN REPORTING ALL THIS.
THAT SHOULD BE ALL, YEAH?

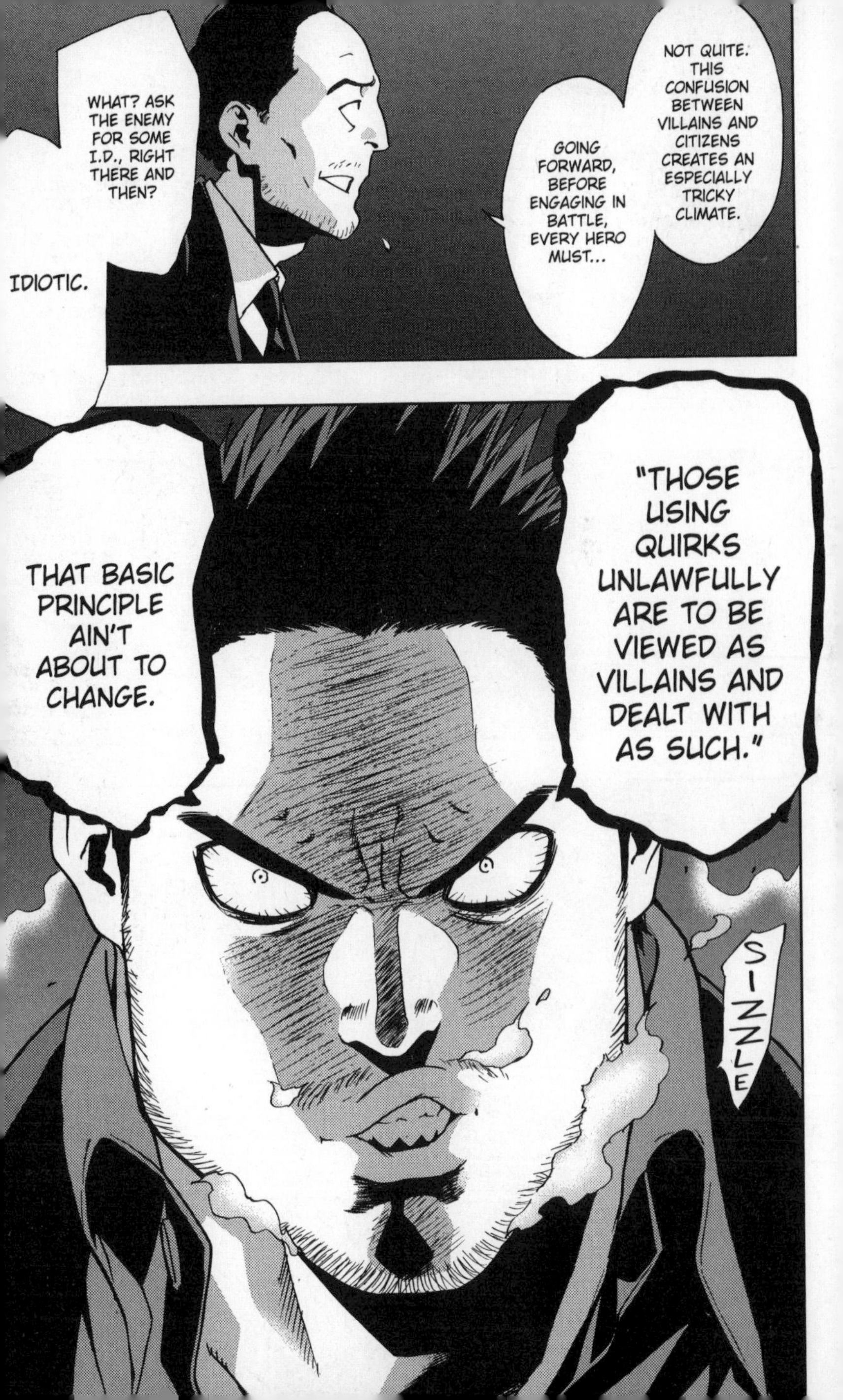
NOT QUITE. THIS CONFUSION BETWEEN VILLAINS AND CITIZENS CREATES AN ESPECIALLY TRICKY CLIMATE.
GOING FORWARD, BEFORE ENGAGING IN BATTLE, EVERY HERO MUST...
WHAT? ASK THE ENEMY FOR SOME I.D., RIGHT THERE AND THEN?
IDIOTIC.
"THOSE USING QUIRKS UNLAWFULLY ARE TO BE VIEWED AS VILLAINS AND DEALT WITH AS SUCH."
THAT BASIC PRINCIPLE AIN'T ABOUT TO CHANGE.
SIZZLE

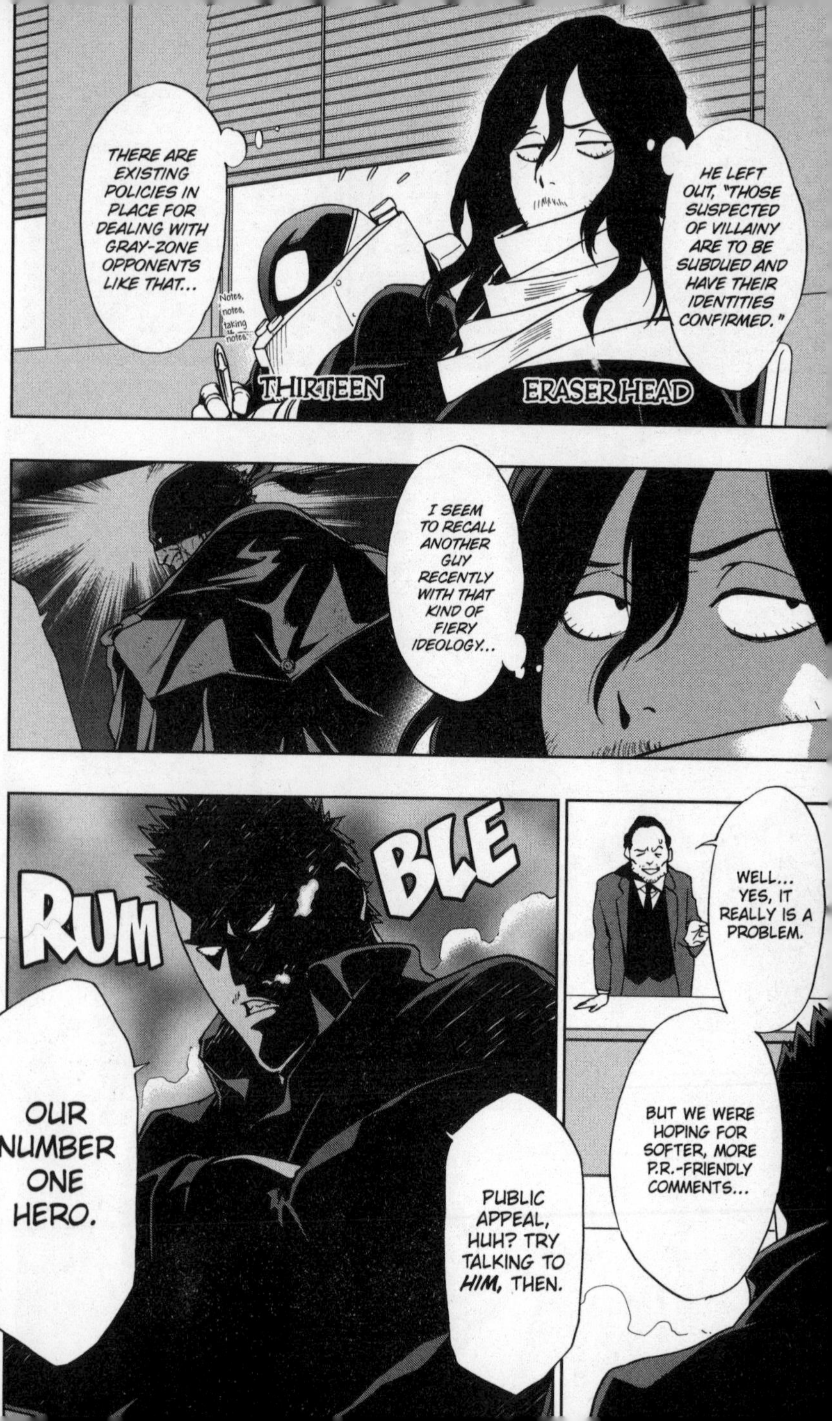
HE LEFT OUT, "THOSE SUSPECTED OF VILLAINY ARE TO BE SUBDUED AND HAVE THEIR IDENTITIES CONFIRMED."
THERE ARE EXISTING POLICIES IN PLACE FOR DEALING WITH GRAY-ZONE OPPONENTS LIKE THAT...
Notes, notes, taking notes.
ERASER HEAD
THIRTEEN
I SEEM TO RECALL ANOTHER GUY RECENTLY WITH THAT KIND OF FIERY IDEOLOGY...
WELL... YES, IT REALLY IS A PROBLEM.
BUT WE WERE HOPING FOR SOFTER, MORE P.R.-FRIENDLY COMMENTS...
PUBLIC APPEAL, HUH? TRY TALKING TO *HIM*, THEN.
RUMBLE
OUR NUMBER ONE HERO.

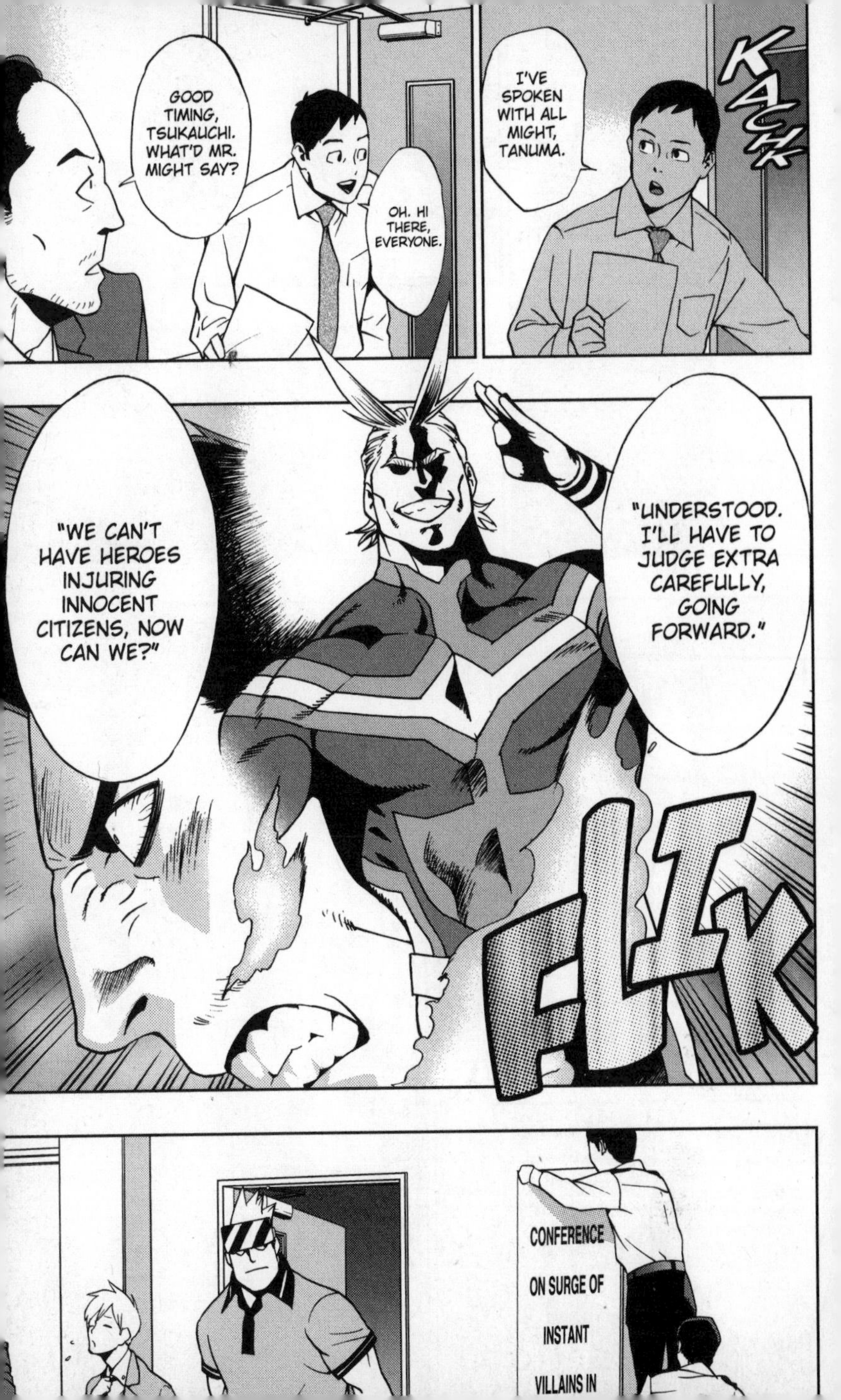
KACHK
I'VE SPOKEN WITH ALL MIGHT, TANUMA.
OH. HI THERE, EVERYONE.
GOOD TIMING, TSUKAUCHI. WHAT'D MR. MIGHT SAY?
"UNDERSTOOD. I'LL HAVE TO JUDGE EXTRA CAREFULLY, GOING FORWARD."
"WE CAN'T HAVE HEROES INJURING INNOCENT CITIZENS, NOW CAN WE?"
FLIK
CONFERENCE
ON SURGE OF
INSTANT
VILLAINS IN

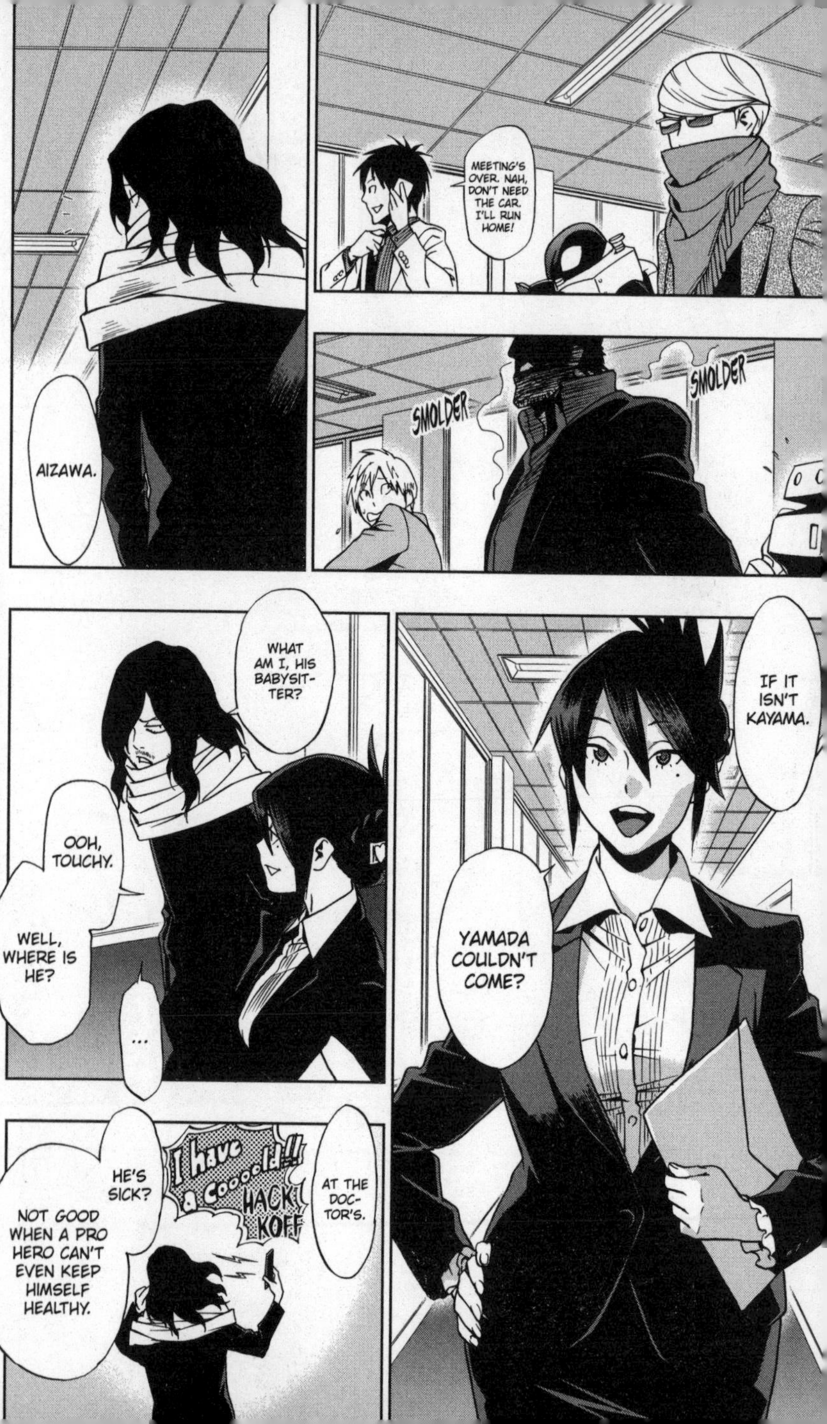
MEETING'S OVER. NAH, DON'T NEED THE CAR. I'LL RUN HOME!
SMOLDER
SMOLDER
AIZAWA.
IF IT ISN'T KAYAMA.
YAMADA COULDN'T COME?
WHAT AM I, HIS BABYSIT-TER?
OOH, TOUCHY.
WELL, WHERE IS HE?
...
AT THE DOC-TOR'S.
HE'S SICK?
I have a coooold!! HACK KOFF
NOT GOOD WHEN A PRO HERO CAN'T EVEN KEEP HIMSELF HEALTHY.

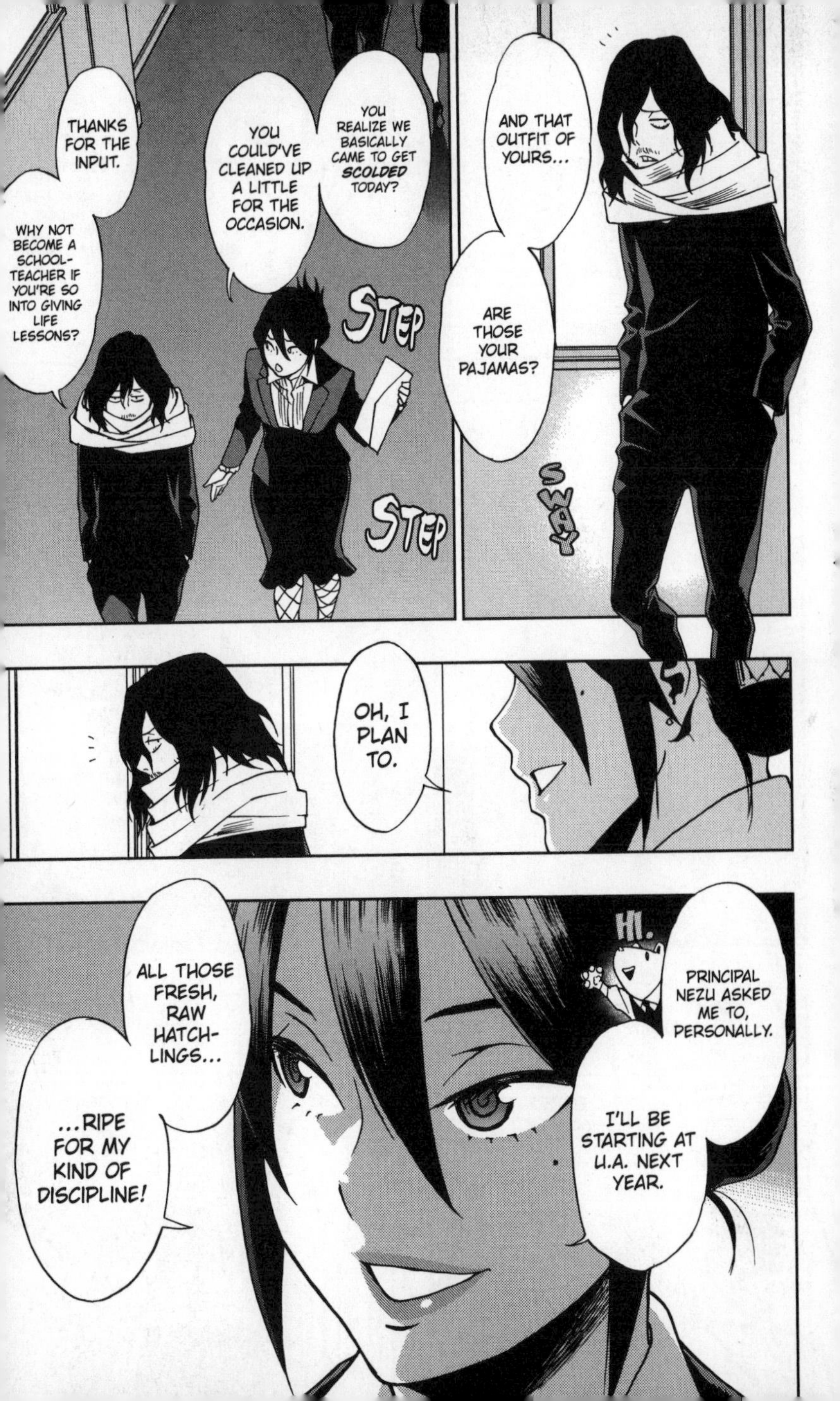
AND THAT OUTFIT OF YOURS...
ARE THOSE YOUR PAJAMAS?
SWAY
YOU REALIZE WE BASICALLY CAME TO GET SCOLDED TODAY?
YOU COULD'VE CLEANED UP A LITTLE FOR THE OCCASION.
THANKS FOR THE INPUT.
WHY NOT BECOME A SCHOOL-TEACHER IF YOU'RE SO INTO GIVING LIFE LESSONS?
STEP
STEP
OH, I PLAN TO.
HI.
PRINCIPAL NEZU ASKED ME TO, PERSONALLY.
I'LL BE STARTING AT U.A. NEXT YEAR.
ALL THOSE FRESH, RAW HATCH-LINGS...
...RIPE FOR MY KIND OF DISCIPLINE!

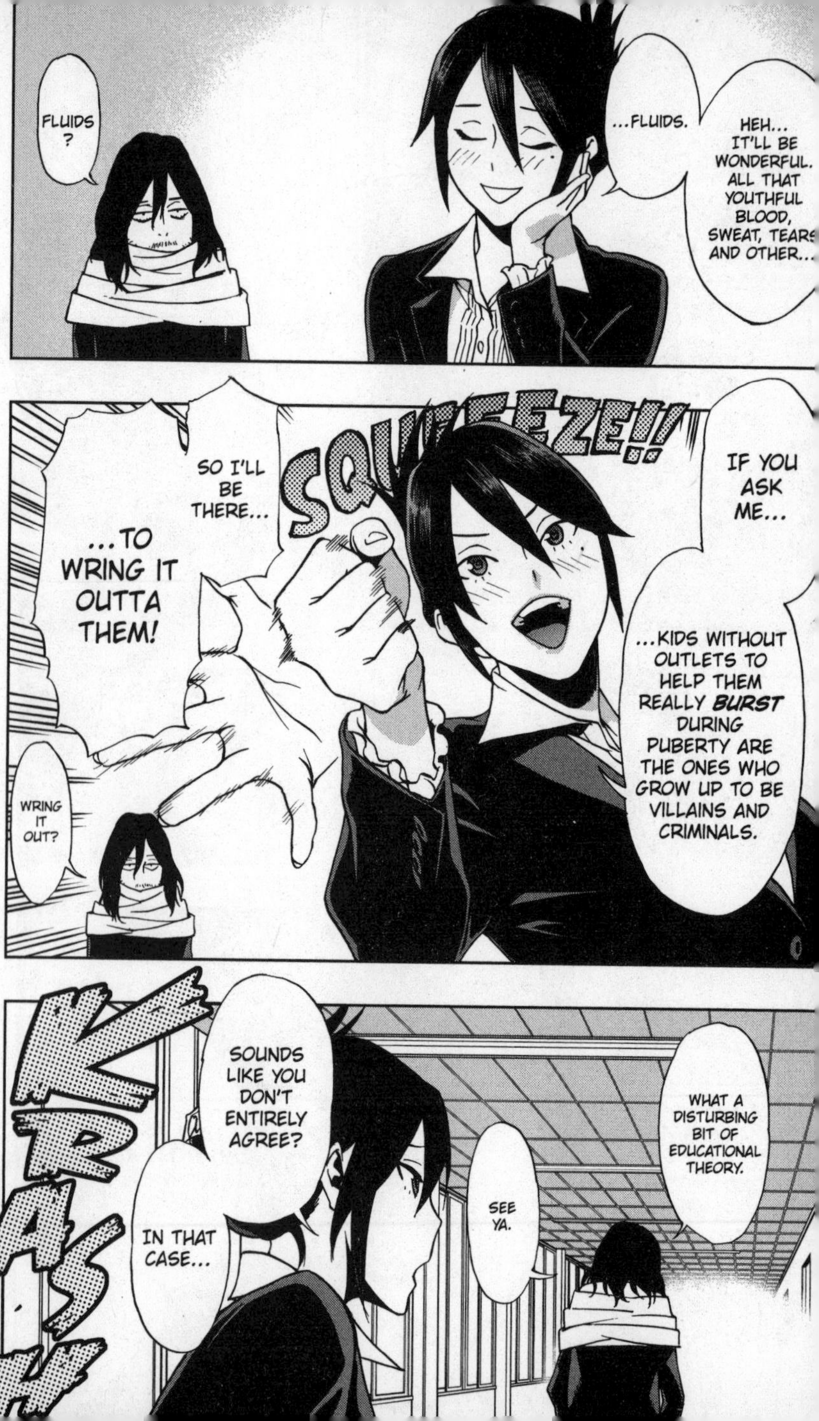

HEH... IT'LL BE WONDERFUL. ALL THAT YOUTHFUL BLOOD, SWEAT, TEARS AND OTHER...
...FLUIDS.
FLUIDS?
IF YOU ASK ME...
...KIDS WITHOUT OUTLETS TO HELP THEM REALLY **BURST** DURING PUBERTY ARE THE ONES WHO GROW UP TO BE VILLAINS AND CRIMINALS.
SQUEEZE!!
SO I'LL BE THERE...
...TO WRING IT OUTTA THEM!
WRING IT OUT?
WHAT A DISTURBING BIT OF EDUCATIONAL THEORY.
SEE YA.
SOUNDS LIKE YOU DON'T ENTIRELY AGREE?
IN THAT CASE...
KRASH

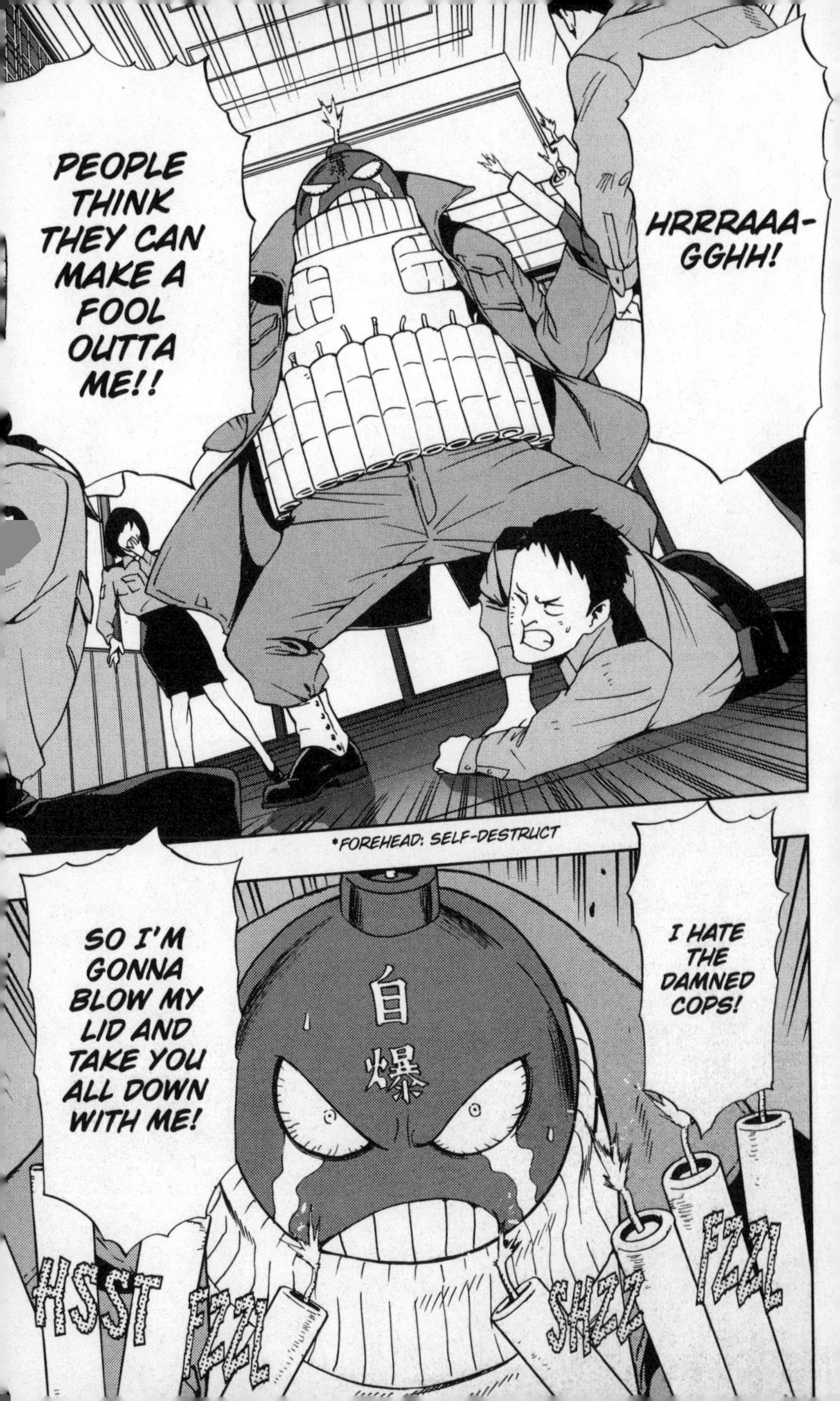
HRRRAAA-GGHH!
PEOPLE THINK THEY CAN MAKE A FOOL OUTTA ME!!
I HATE THE DAMNED COPS!
SO I'M GONNA BLOW MY LID AND TAKE YOU ALL DOWN WITH ME!
自爆
*FOREHEAD: SELF-DESTRUCT
FZZZ
SHZZ
FZZZ
HSST

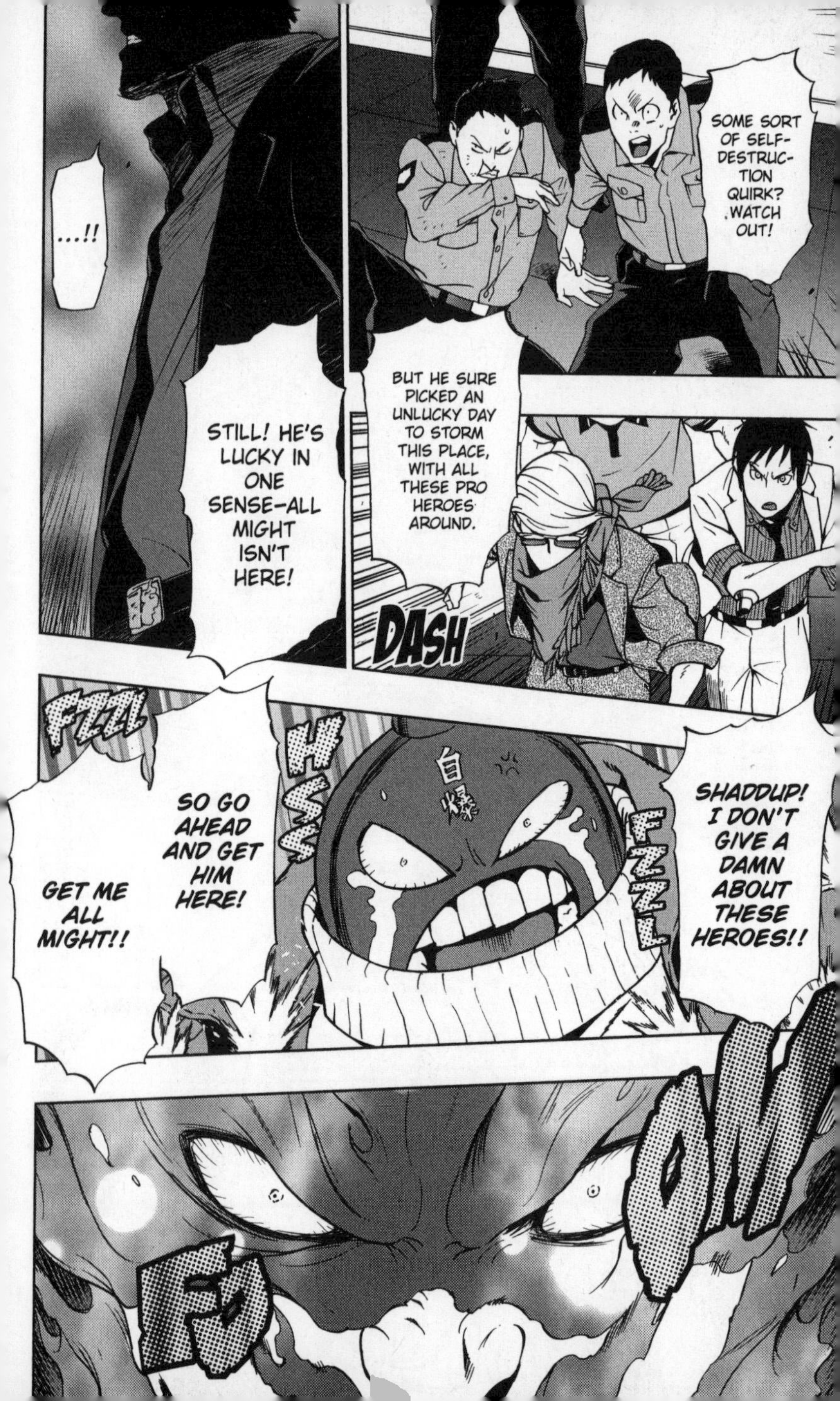
SOME SORT OF SELF-DESTRUCTION QUIRK? WATCH OUT!
BUT HE SURE PICKED AN UNLUCKY DAY TO STORM THIS PLACE, WITH ALL THESE PRO HEROES AROUND.
DASH
...!!
STILL! HE'S LUCKY IN ONE SENSE--ALL MIGHT ISN'T HERE!
SHADDUP! I DON'T GIVE A DAMN ABOUT THESE HEROES!!
SO GO AHEAD AND GET HIM HERE!
GET ME ALL MIGHT!!

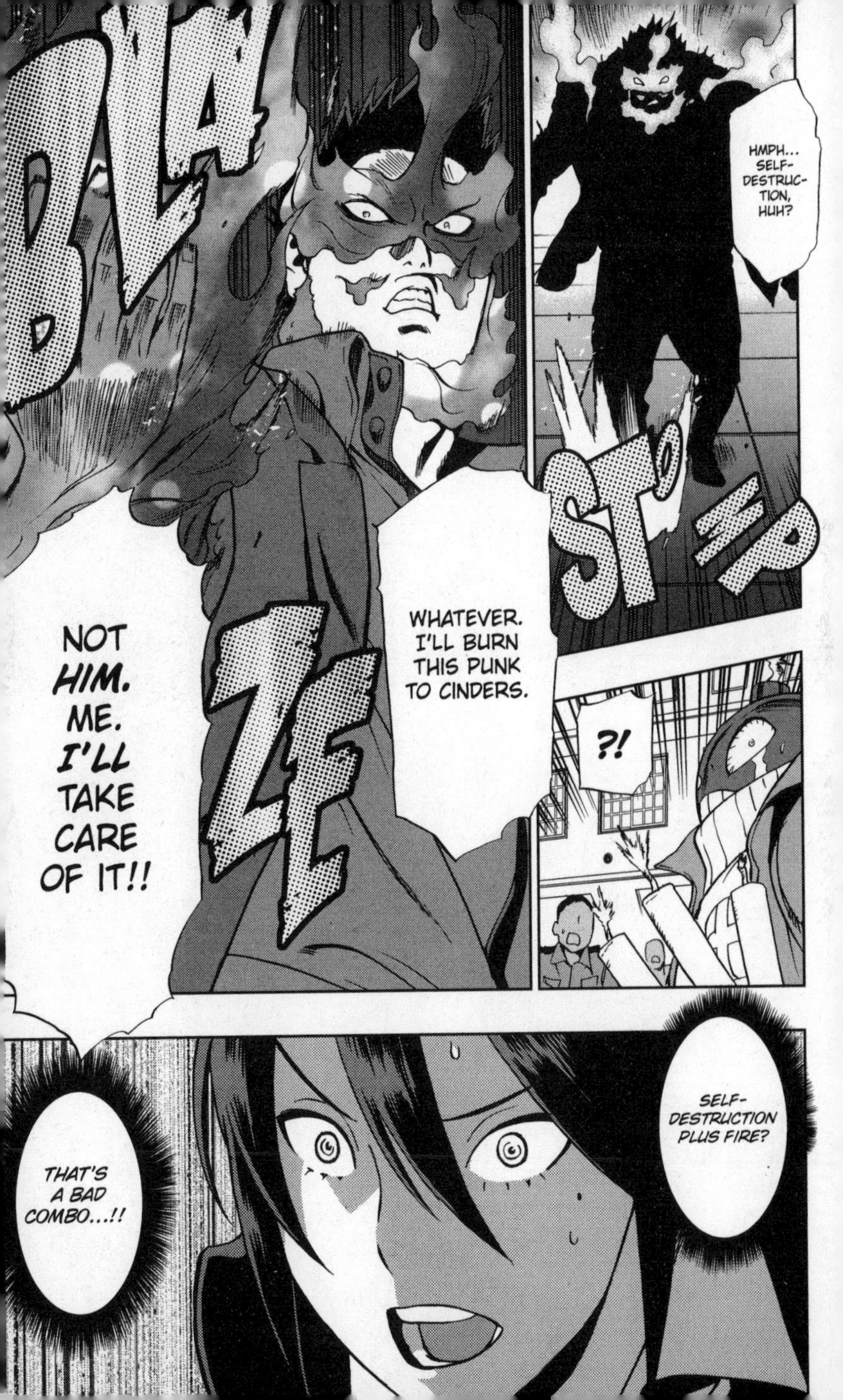
HMPH... SELF-DESTRUCTION, HUH?
STOMP
?!
WHATEVER. I'LL BURN THIS PUNK TO CINDERS.
NOT HIM. ME. I'LL TAKE CARE OF IT!!
SELF-DESTRUCTION PLUS FIRE?
THAT'S A BAD COMBO...!!

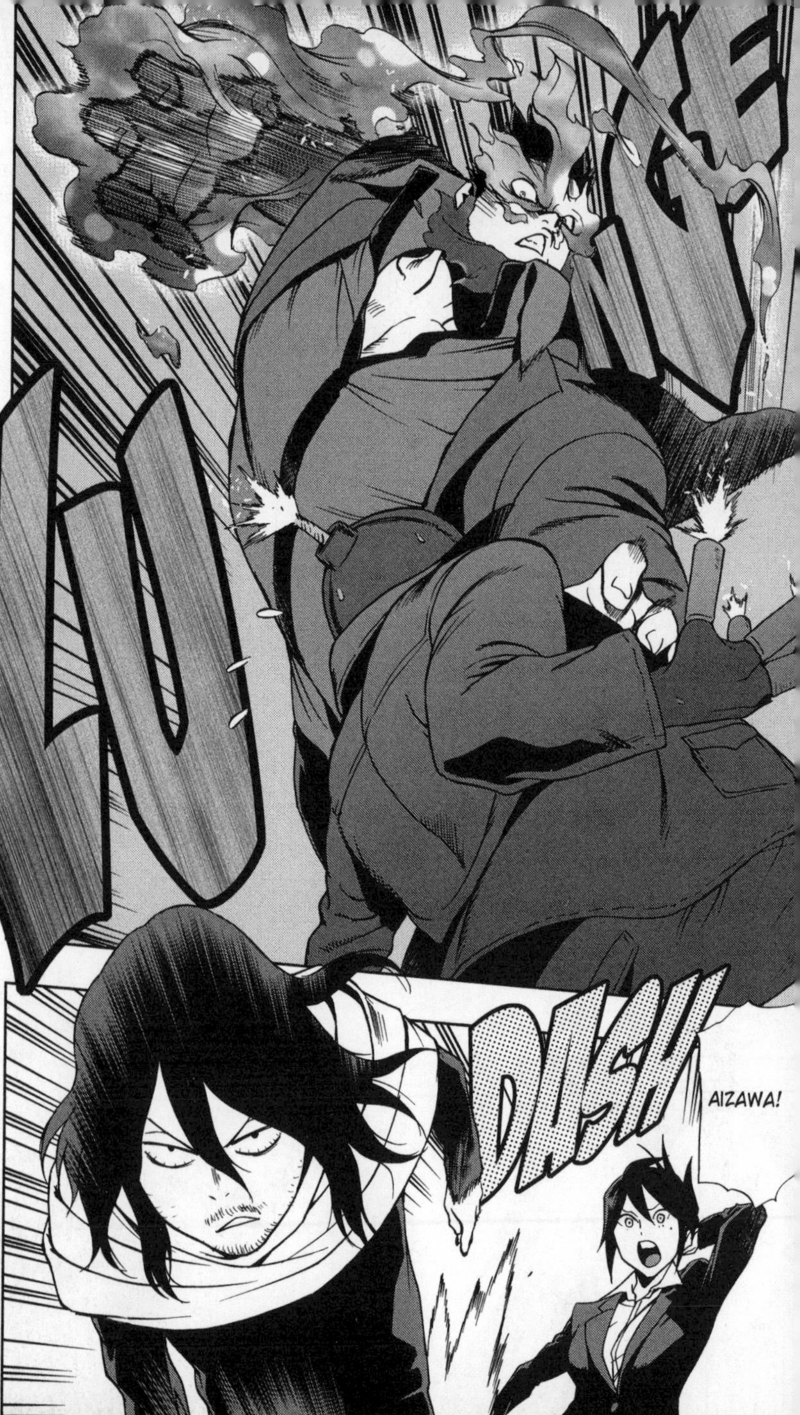
AIZAWA!
DASH

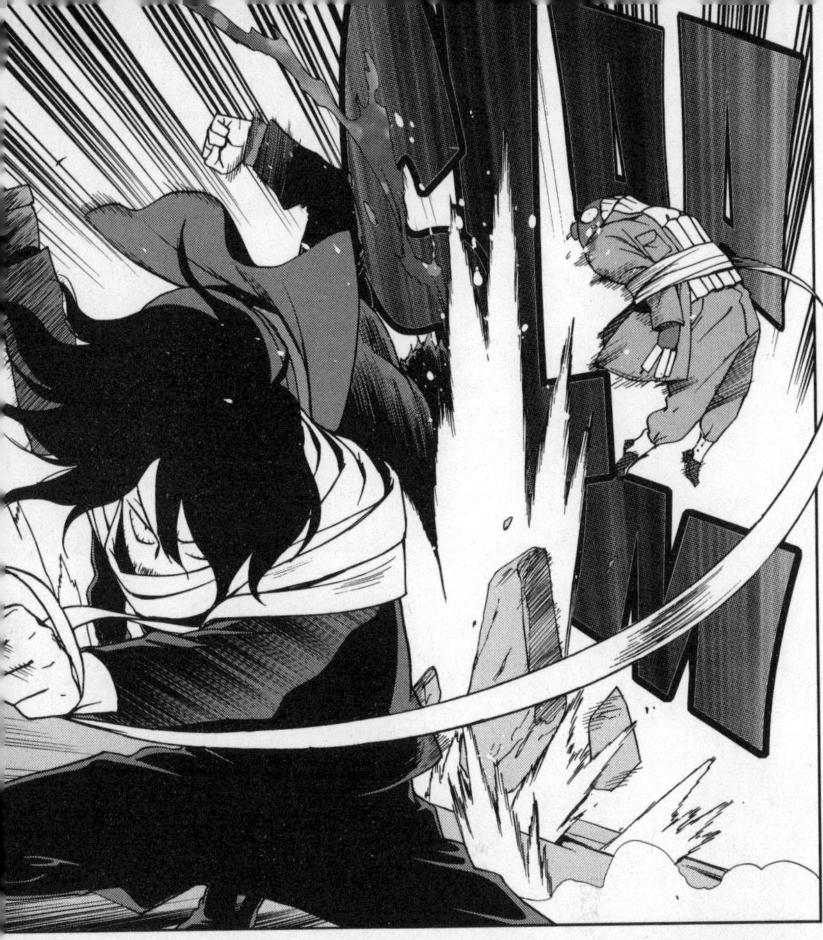

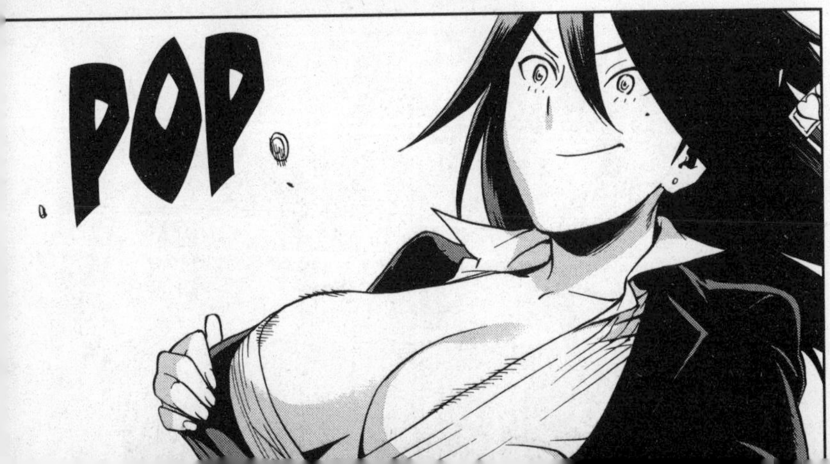
POP

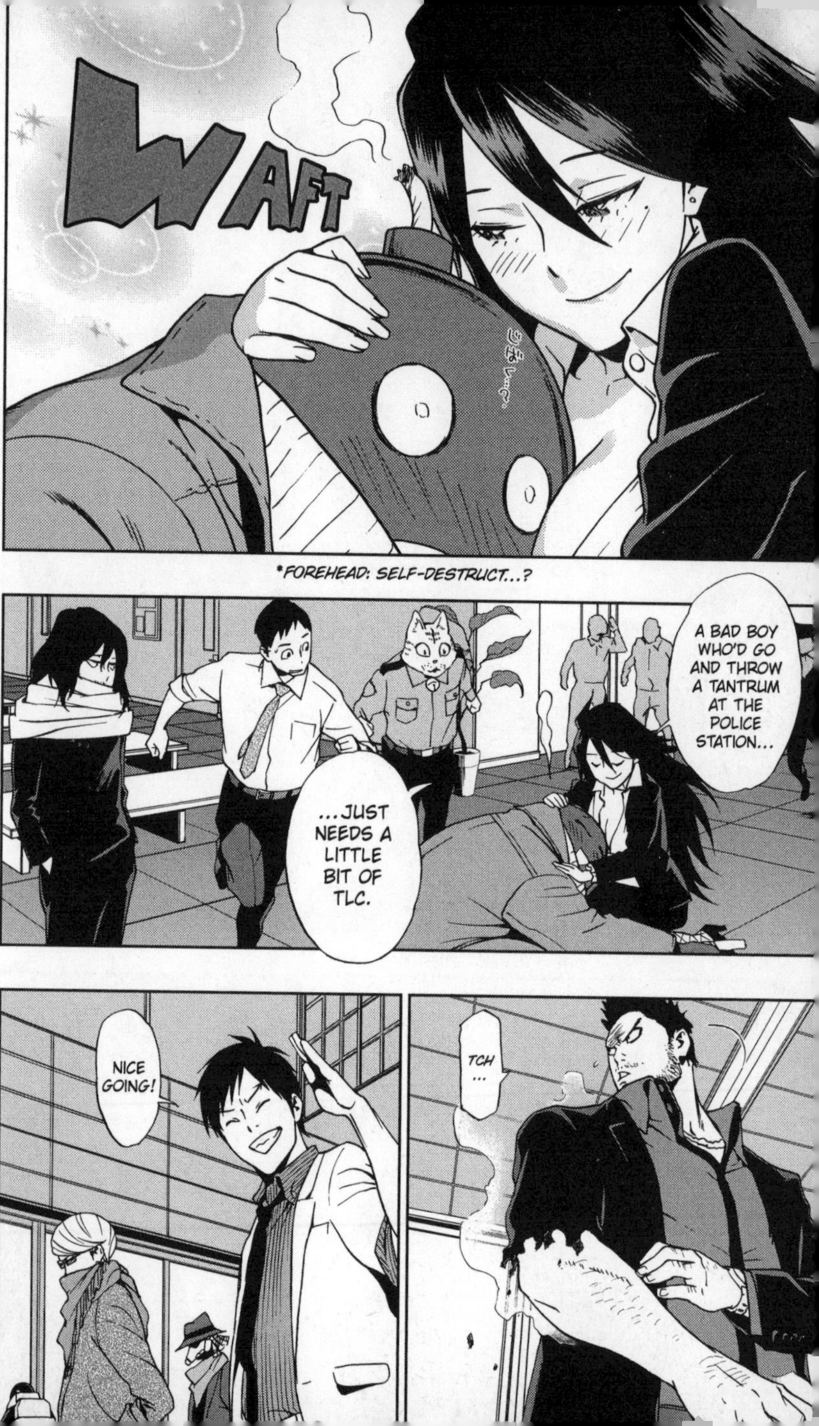
WAFT
*FOREHEAD: SELF-DESTRUCT...?
A BAD BOY WHO'D GO AND THROW A TANTRUM AT THE POLICE STATION...
...JUST NEEDS A LITTLE BIT OF TLC.
TCH ...
NICE GOING!

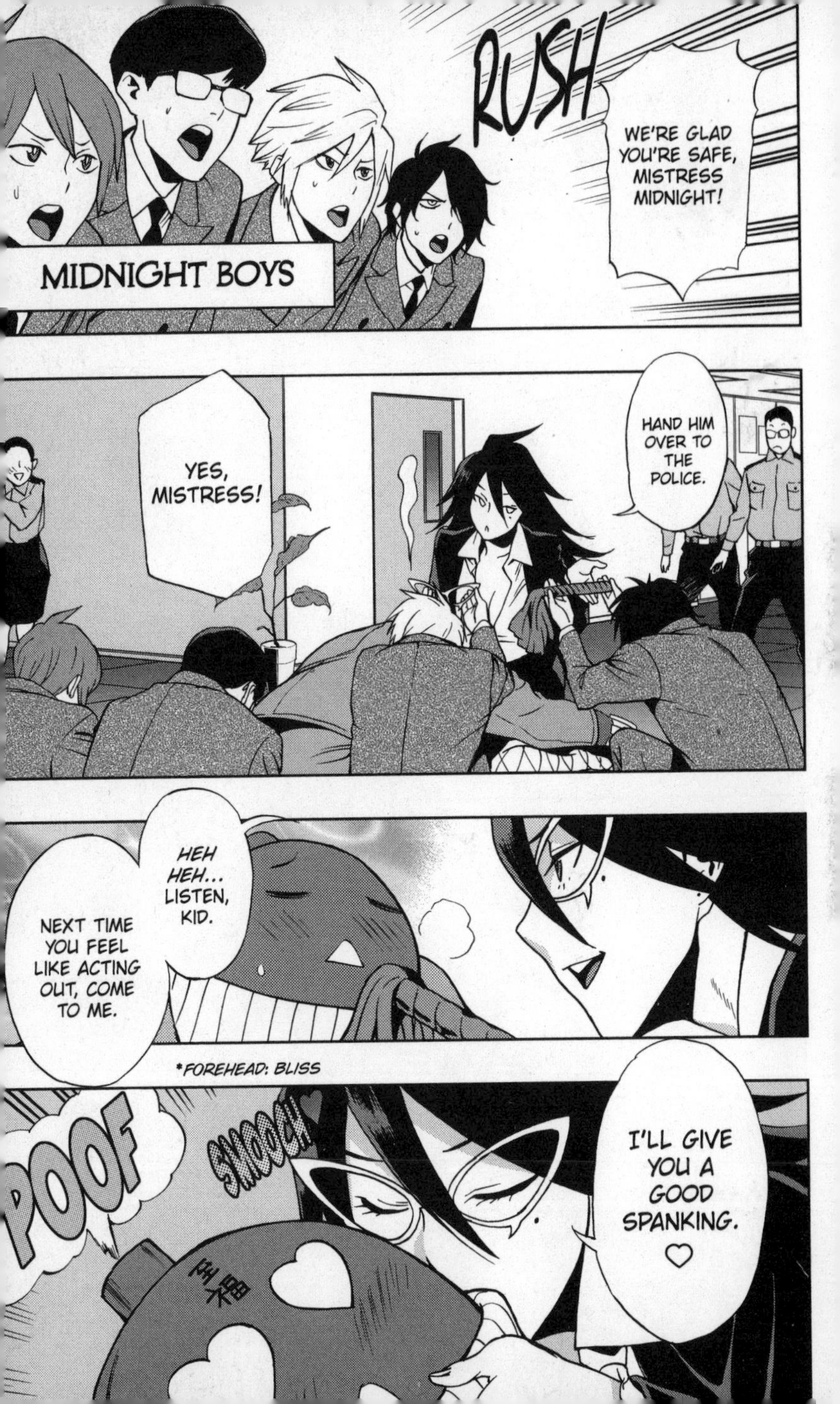
RUSH
WE'RE GLAD YOU'RE SAFE, MISTRESS MIDNIGHT!
MIDNIGHT BOYS
HAND HIM OVER TO THE POLICE.
YES, MISTRESS!
HEH HEH... LISTEN, KID.
NEXT TIME YOU FEEL LIKE ACTING OUT, COME TO ME.
*FOREHEAD: BLISS
I'LL GIVE YOU A GOOD SPANKING. ♡
SMOOCH
POOF

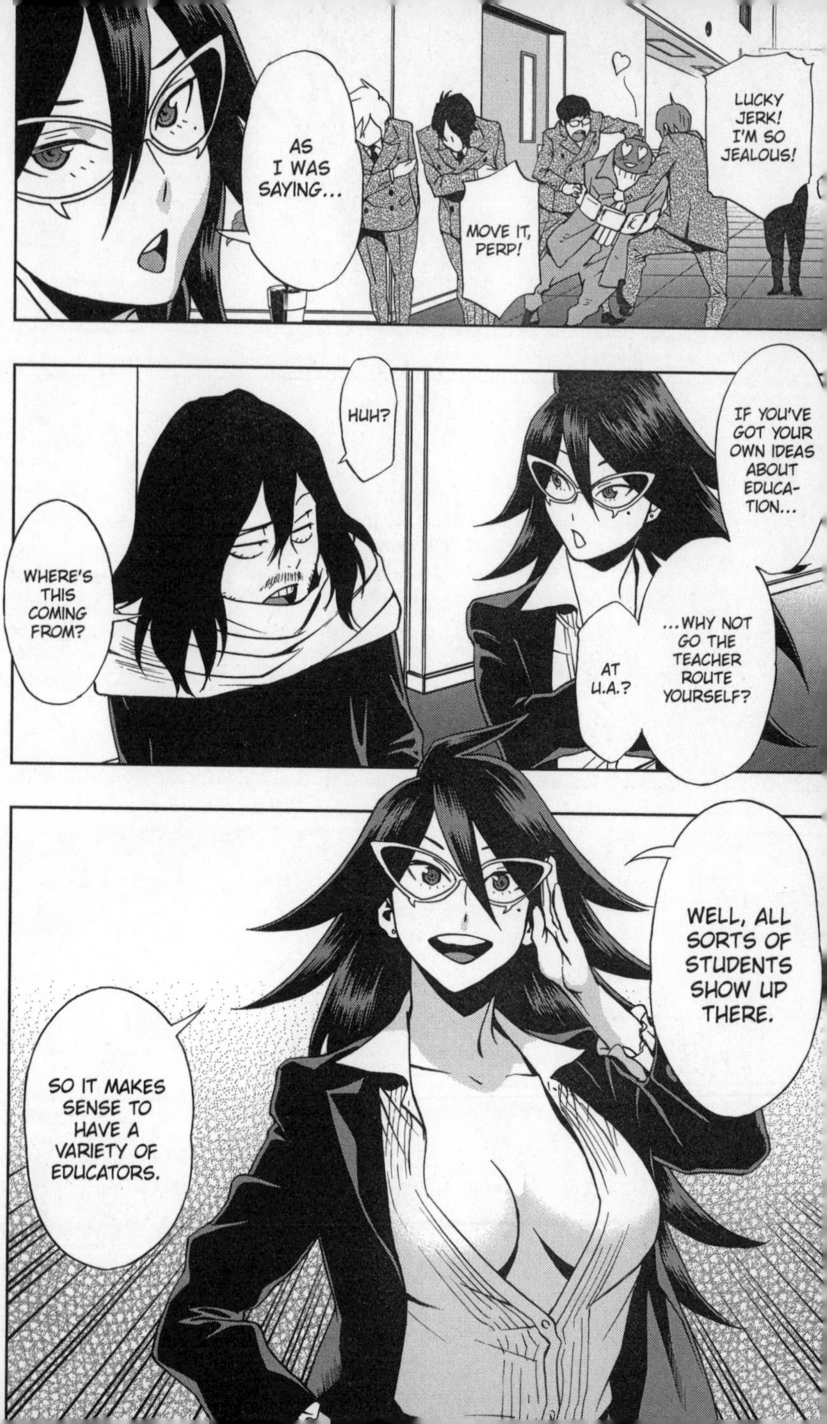
LUCKY JERK! I'M SO JEALOUS!
MOVE IT, PERP!
AS I WAS SAYING...
IF YOU'VE GOT YOUR OWN IDEAS ABOUT EDUCA-TION...
...WHY NOT GO THE TEACHER ROUTE YOURSELF?
AT U.A.?
HUH?
WHERE'S THIS COMING FROM?
WELL, ALL SORTS OF STUDENTS SHOW UP THERE.
SO IT MAKES SENSE TO HAVE A VARIETY OF EDUCATORS.

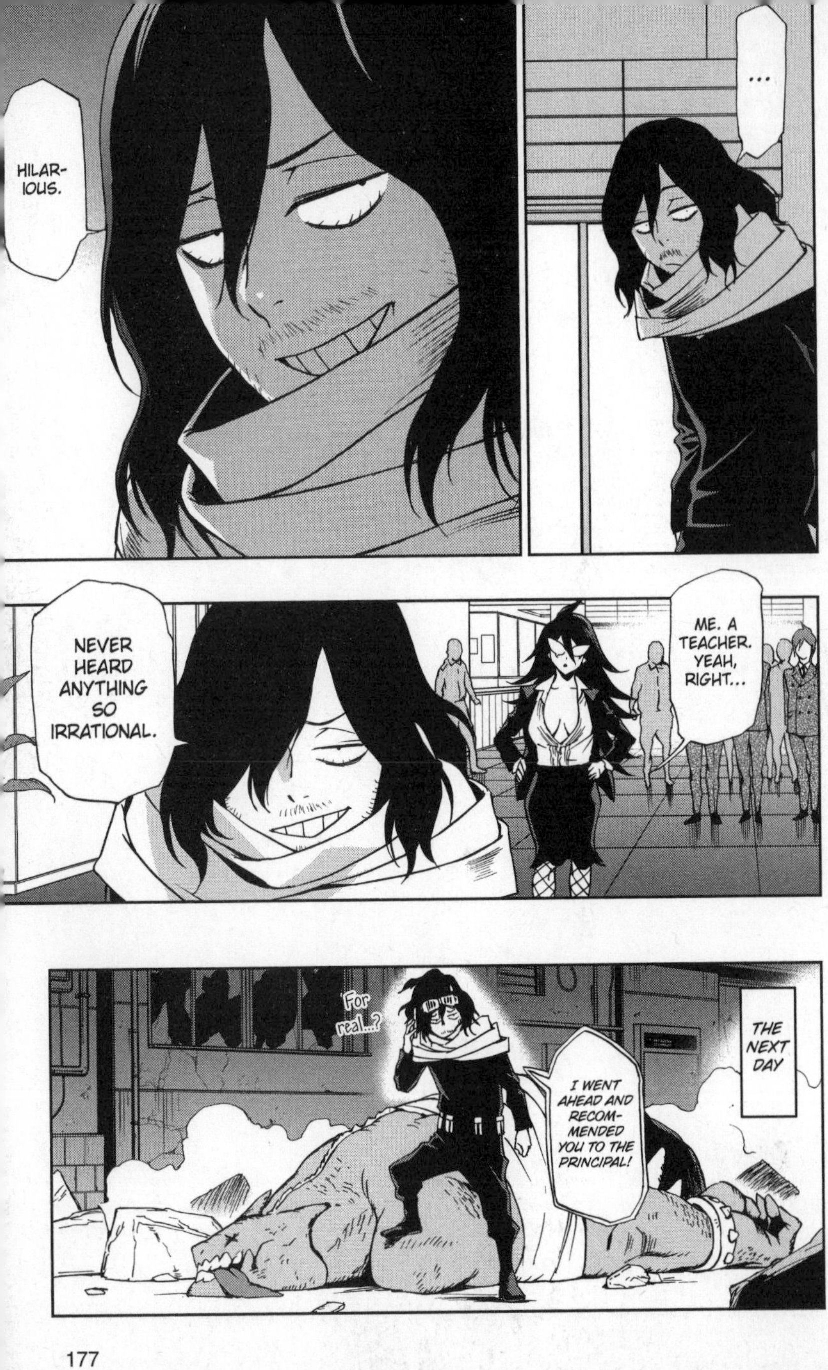
...
HILARIOUS.
ME. A TEACHER. YEAH, RIGHT...
NEVER HEARD ANYTHING SO IRRATIONAL.
THE NEXT DAY
I WENT AHEAD AND RECOMMENDED YOU TO THE PRINCIPAL!
For real...?

BOMB VILLAIN

THE ROUGH DESIGN

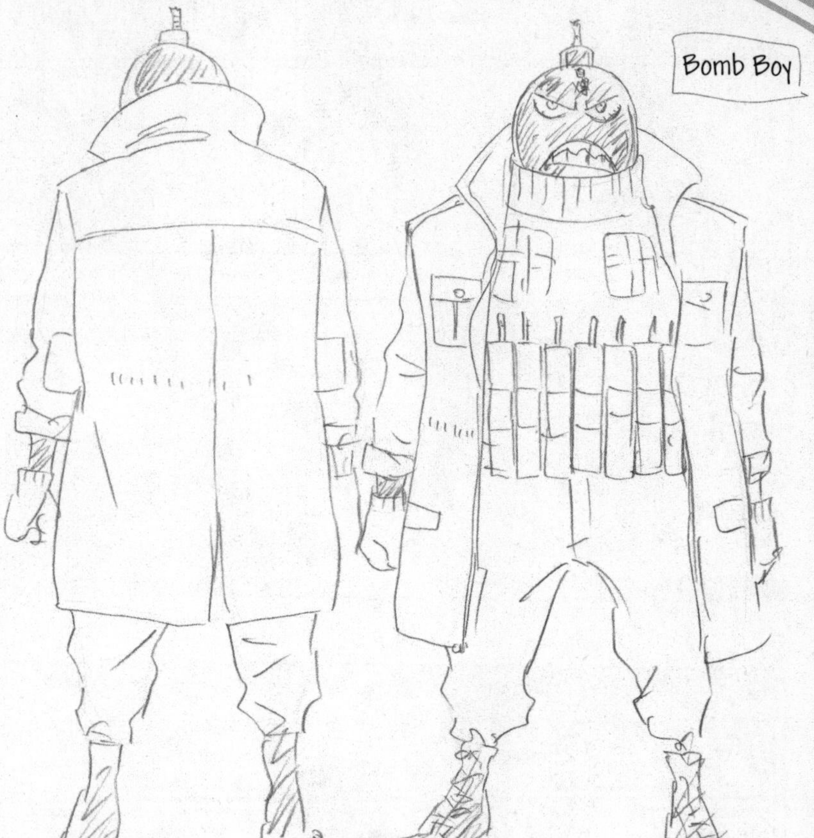
Bomb Boy

BEHIND THE SCENES

I wanted a villain who'd get saved by Midnight's motherly side, so I worked backwards from there. Almost seems like this guy was born to play the role of suicide bomber. No wonder he became a villain!

—Furuhashi

Given the whole bombing angle, I imagine he must've been a tunnel engineer or something, up until this point. Hence the blue-collar worker outfit.

—Betten

Sp. 2 - Hero Visit

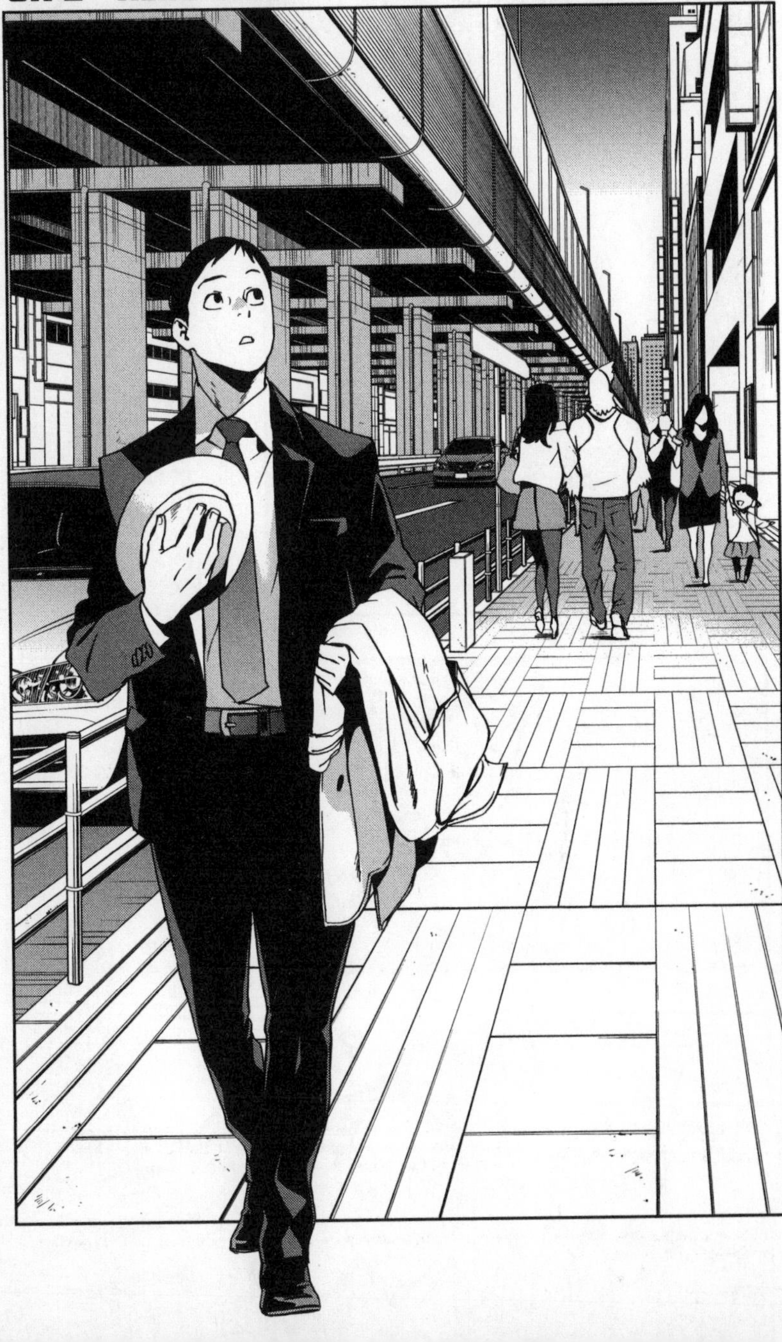

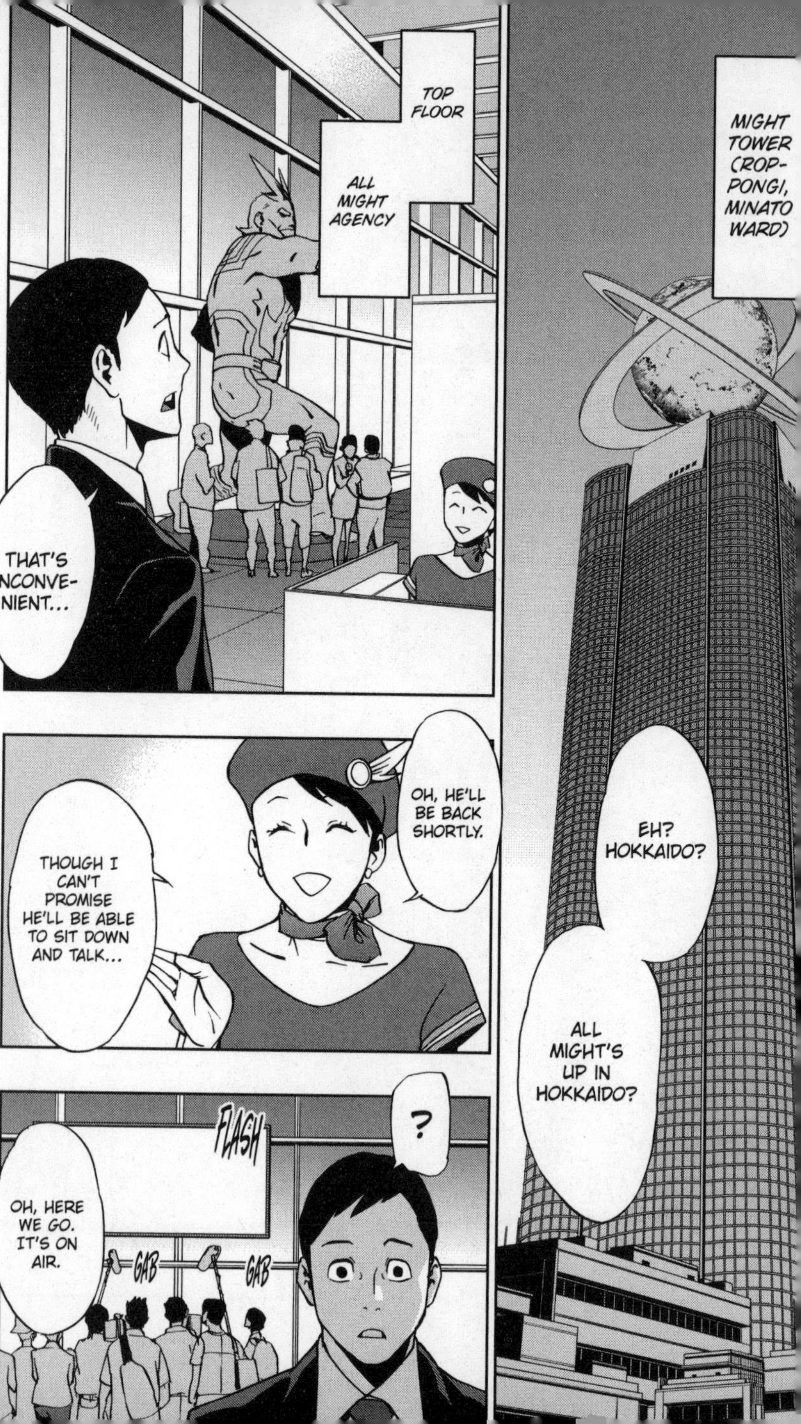
MIGHT TOWER (ROP-PONGI, MINATO WARD)
EH? HOKKAIDO?
ALL MIGHT'S UP IN HOKKAIDO?
TOP FLOOR
ALL MIGHT AGENCY
THAT'S INCONVE-NIENT...
OH, HE'LL BE BACK SHORTLY.
THOUGH I CAN'T PROMISE HE'LL BE ABLE TO SIT DOWN AND TALK...
?
FLASH
OH, HERE WE GO. IT'S ON AIR.
GAB
GAB

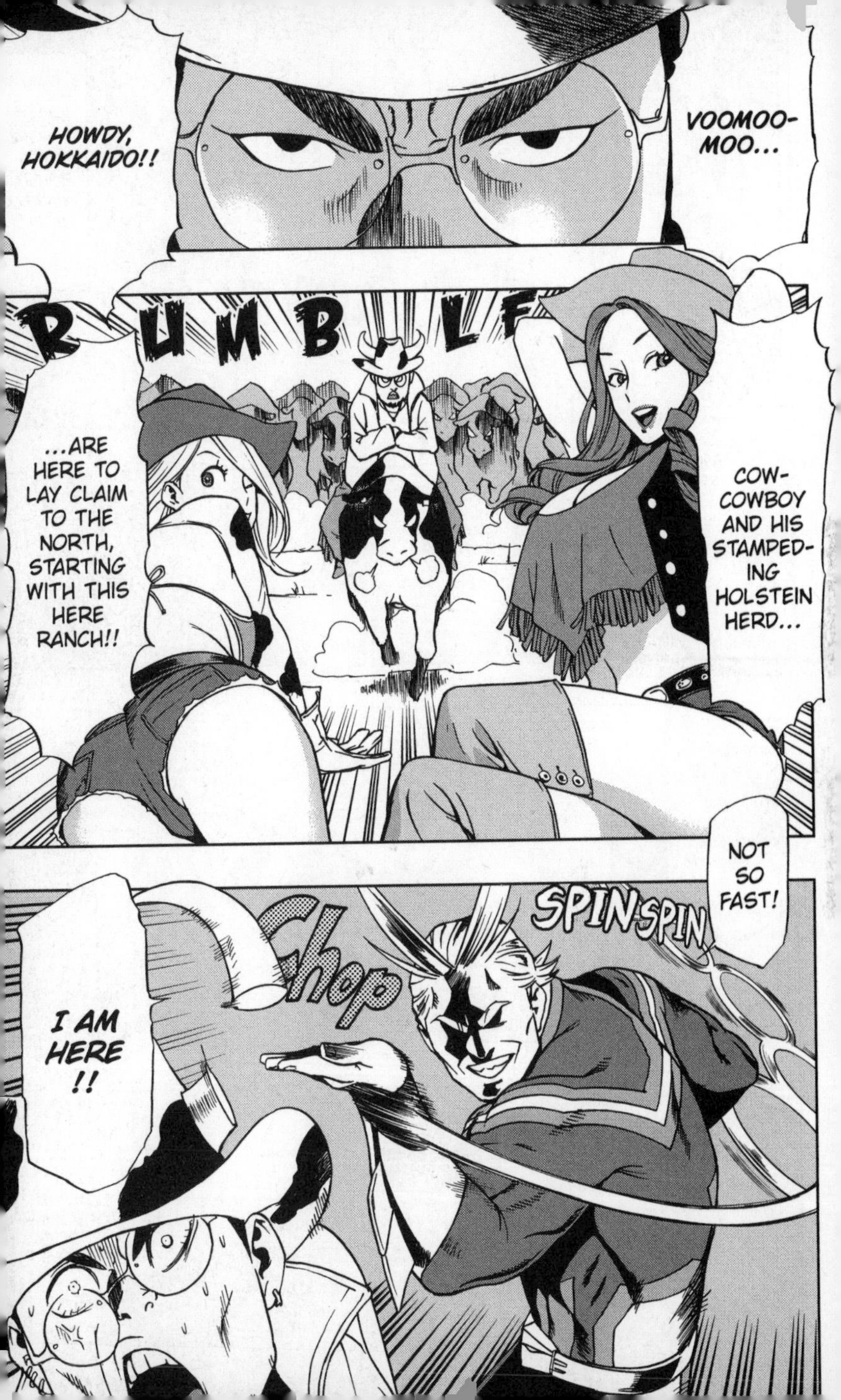
VOOMOO-MOO...
HOWDY, HOKKAIDO!!
RUMBLE
COW-COWBOY AND HIS STAMPEDING HOLSTEIN HERD...
...ARE HERE TO LAY CLAIM TO THE NORTH, STARTING WITH THIS HERE RANCH!!
NOT SO FAST!
SPIN SPIN
Chop
I AM HERE!!

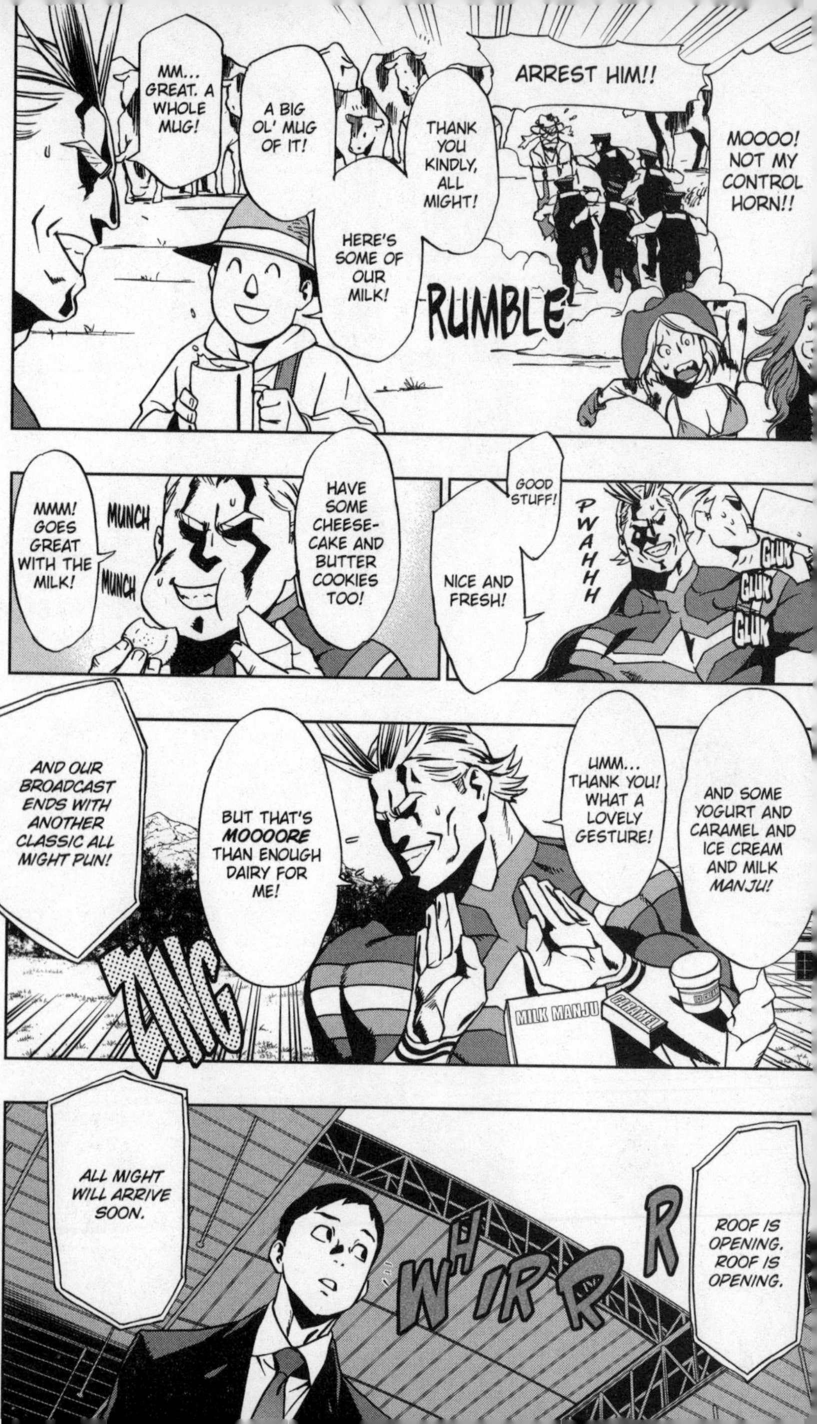
ARREST HIM!!
MOOOO! NOT MY CONTROL HORN!!
RUMBLE
THANK YOU KINDLY, ALL MIGHT!
HERE'S SOME OF OUR MILK!
A BIG OL' MUG OF IT!
MM... GREAT. A WHOLE MUG!
GOOD STUFF!
PWAHHH
GLUK GLUK GLUK
NICE AND FRESH!
HAVE SOME CHEESE-CAKE AND BUTTER COOKIES TOO!
MUNCH MUNCH
MMM! GOES GREAT WITH THE MILK!
AND SOME YOGURT AND CARAMEL AND ICE CREAM AND MILK MANJU!
UMM... THANK YOU! WHAT A LOVELY GESTURE!
ICE CREAM
CARAMEL
MILK MANJU
BUT THAT'S MOOOORE THAN ENOUGH DAIRY FOR ME!
ZING
AND OUR BROADCAST ENDS WITH ANOTHER CLASSIC ALL MIGHT PUN!
ROOF IS OPENING. ROOF IS OPENING.
WHIRRR
ALL MIGHT WILL ARRIVE SOON.

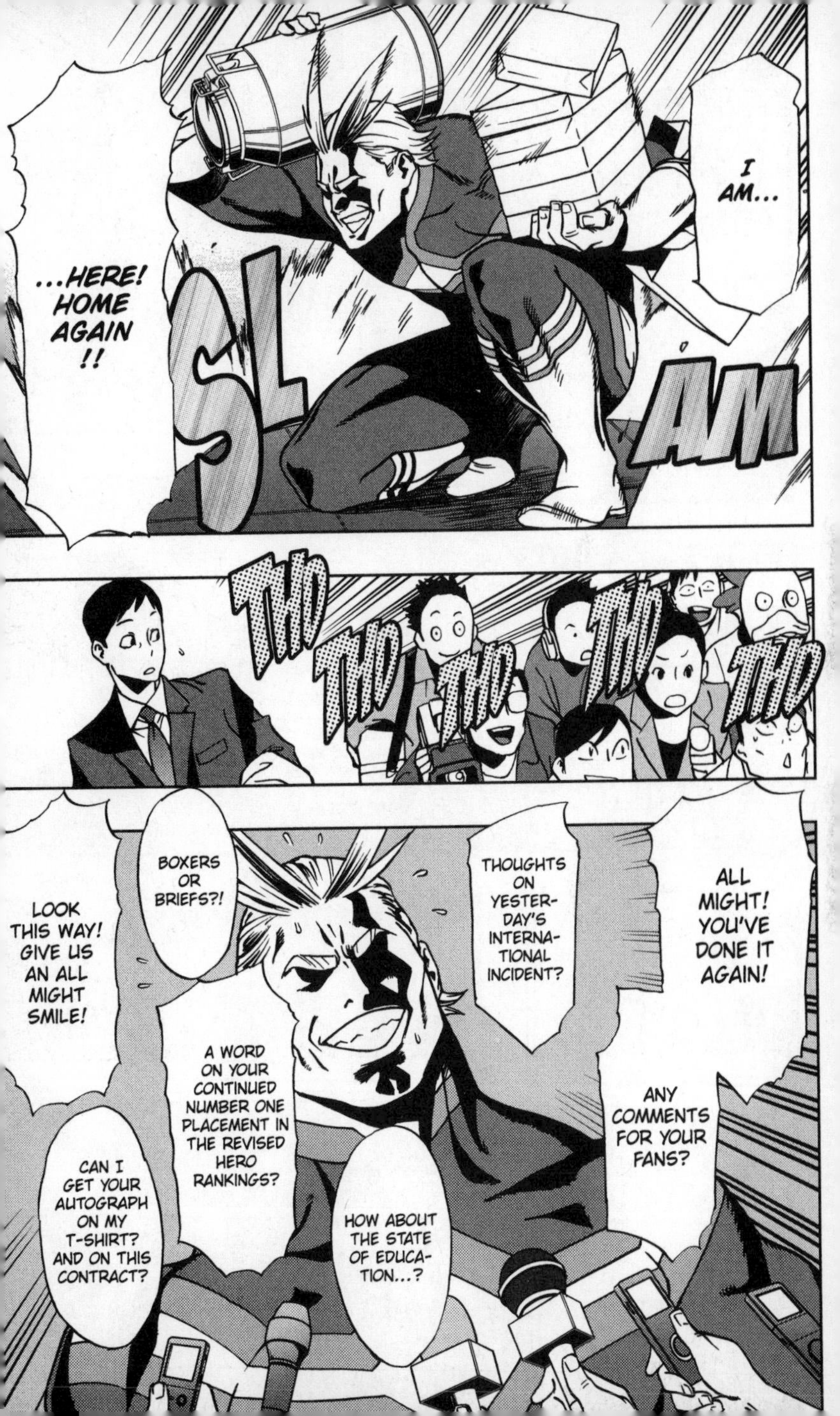
I AM...
...HERE! HOME AGAIN !!
SLAM
THD THD THD THD THD
ALL MIGHT! YOU'VE DONE IT AGAIN!
THOUGHTS ON YESTER-DAY'S INTERNA-TIONAL INCIDENT?
BOXERS OR BRIEFS?!
LOOK THIS WAY! GIVE US AN ALL MIGHT SMILE!
ANY COMMENTS FOR YOUR FANS?
A WORD ON YOUR CONTINUED NUMBER ONE PLACEMENT IN THE REVISED HERO RANKINGS?
HOW ABOUT THE STATE OF EDUCA-TION...?
CAN I GET YOUR AUTOGRAPH ON MY T-SHIRT? AND ON THIS CONTRACT?

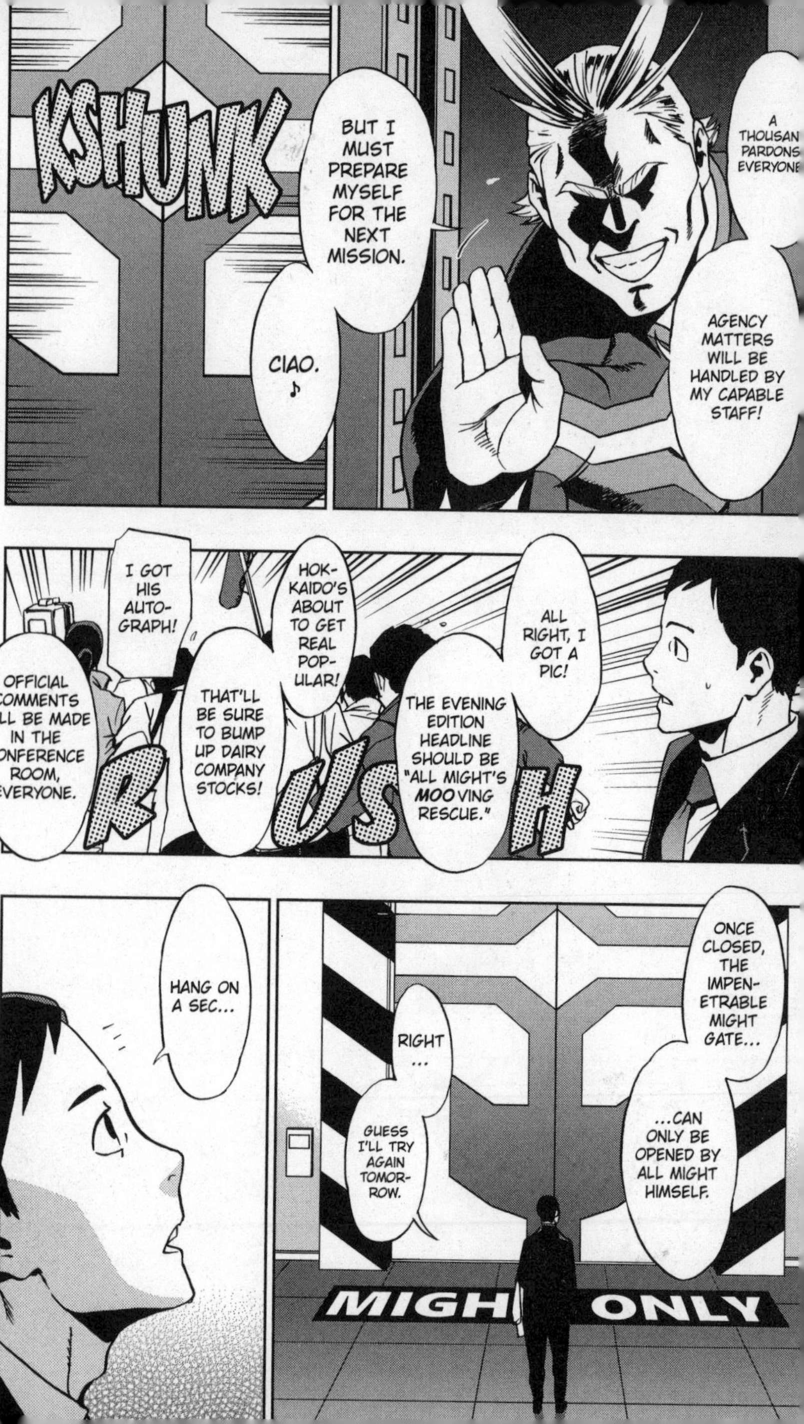
A THOUSAN PARDONS EVERYONE
AGENCY MATTERS WILL BE HANDLED BY MY CAPABLE STAFF!
BUT I MUST PREPARE MYSELF FOR THE NEXT MISSION.
CIAO. ♪
KSHUNK
ALL RIGHT, I GOT A PIC!
THE EVENING EDITION HEADLINE SHOULD BE "ALL MIGHT'S **MOO**VING RESCUE."
HOK-KAIDO'S ABOUT TO GET REAL POP-ULAR!
THAT'LL BE SURE TO BUMP UP DAIRY COMPANY STOCKS!
I GOT HIS AUTO-GRAPH!
OFFICIAL COMMENTS WILL BE MADE IN THE CONFERENCE ROOM, EVERYONE.
RUSH
ONCE CLOSED, THE IMPEN-ETRABLE MIGHT GATE...
...CAN ONLY BE OPENED BY ALL MIGHT HIMSELF.
RIGHT...
GUESS I'LL TRY AGAIN TOMOR-ROW.
MIGH ONLY
HANG ON A SEC...

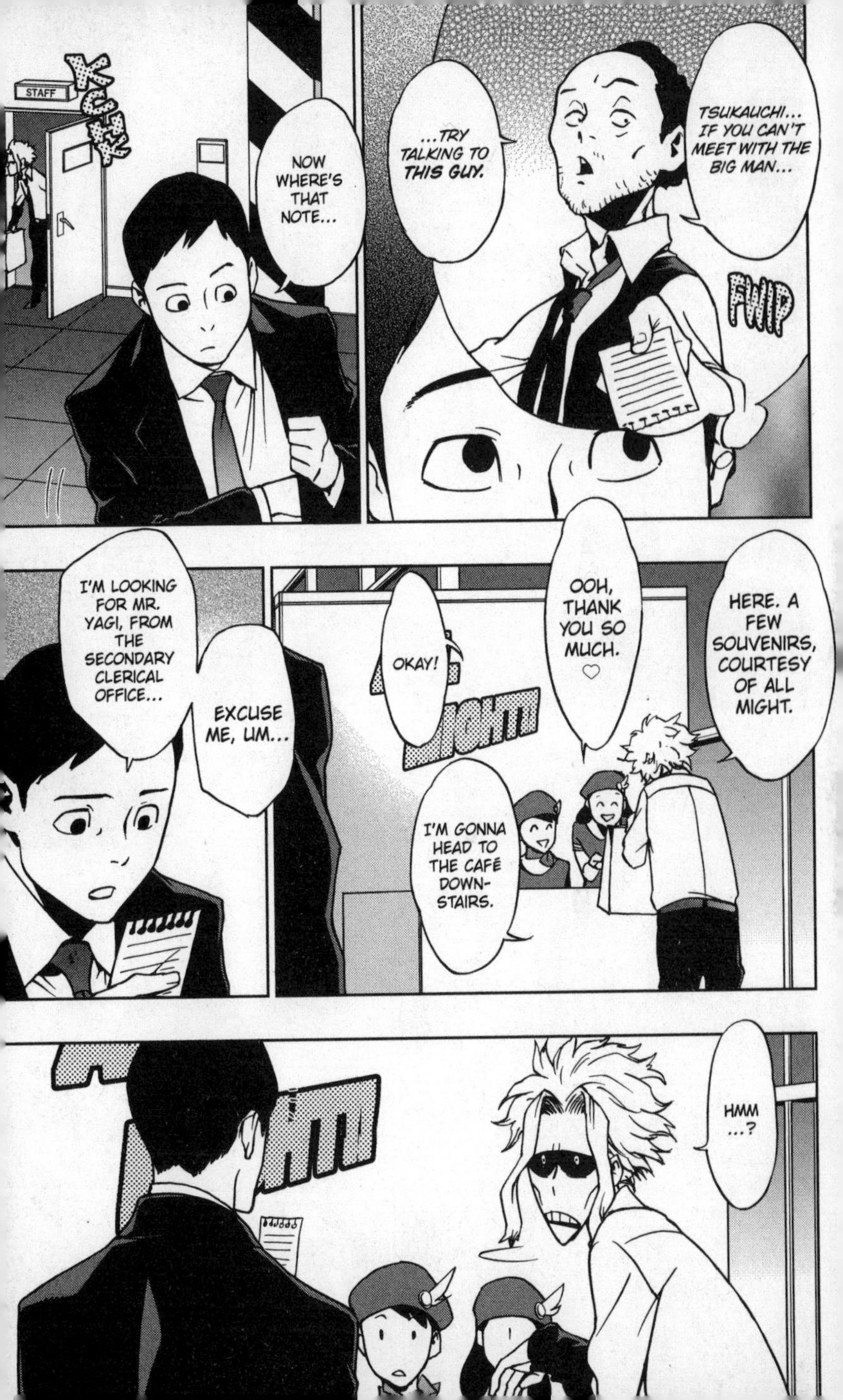
TSUKAUCHI... IF YOU CAN'T MEET WITH THE BIG MAN...
...TRY TALKING TO THIS GUY.
FWIP
STAFF
KCHK
NOW WHERE'S THAT NOTE...
HERE. A FEW SOUVENIRS, COURTESY OF ALL MIGHT.
OOH, THANK YOU SO MUCH. ♡
OKAY!
I'M GONNA HEAD TO THE CAFÉ DOWN-STAIRS.
EXCUSE ME, UM...
I'M LOOKING FOR MR. YAGI, FROM THE SECONDARY CLERICAL OFFICE...
HMM ...?

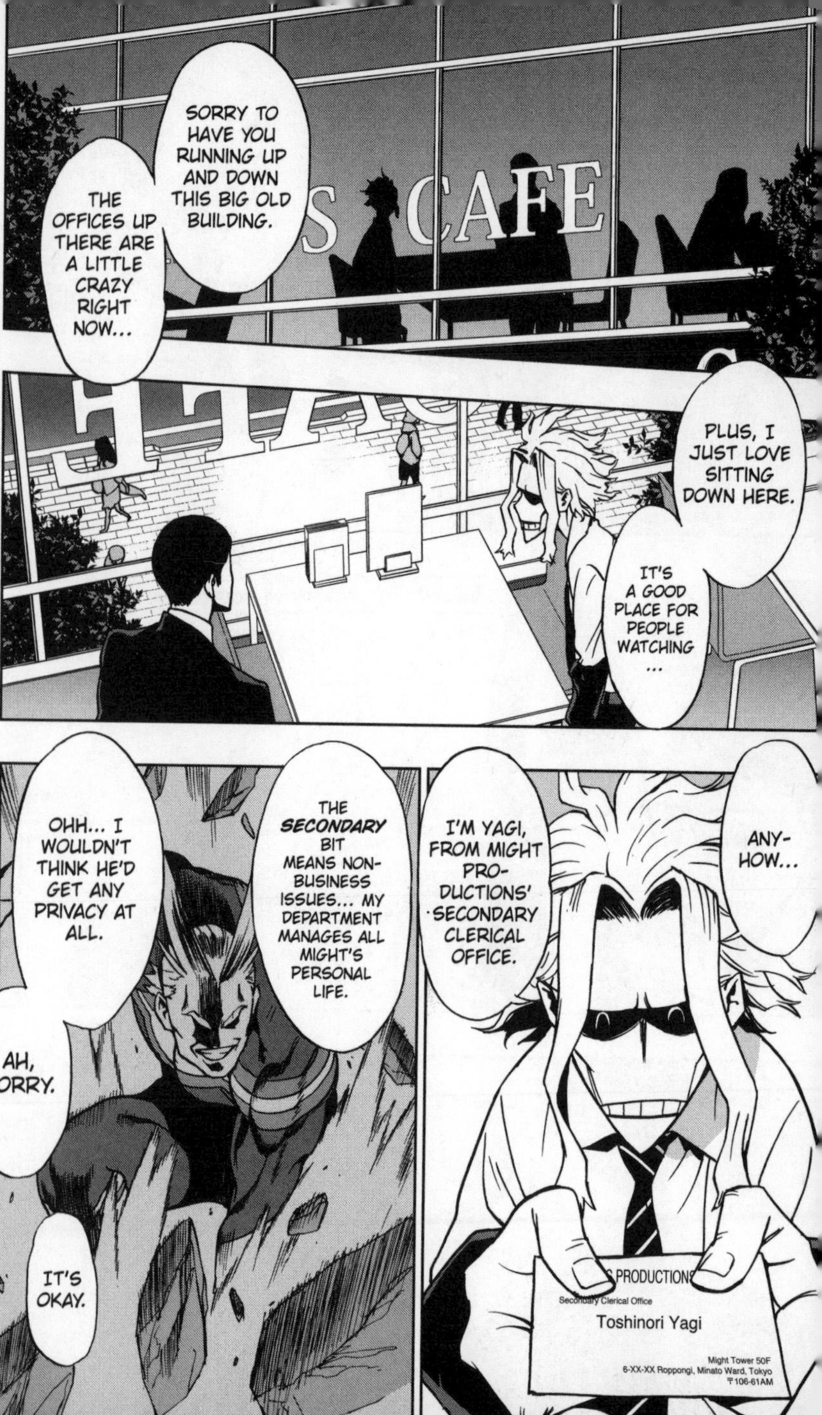
SORRY TO HAVE YOU RUNNING UP AND DOWN THIS BIG OLD BUILDING.
THE OFFICES UP THERE ARE A LITTLE CRAZY RIGHT NOW...
CAFE
PLUS, I JUST LOVE SITTING DOWN HERE.
IT'S A GOOD PLACE FOR PEOPLE WATCHING...
ANY-HOW...
I'M YAGI, FROM MIGHT PRO-DUCTIONS' SECONDARY CLERICAL OFFICE.
PRODUCTIONS
Secondary Clerical Office
Toshinori Yagi
Might Tower 50F
6-XX-XX Roppongi, Minato Ward, Tokyo
〒106-61AM
THE *SECONDARY* BIT MEANS NON-BUSINESS ISSUES... MY DEPARTMENT MANAGES ALL MIGHT'S PERSONAL LIFE.
OHH... I WOULDN'T THINK HE'D GET ANY PRIVACY AT ALL.
AH, SORRY.
IT'S OKAY.

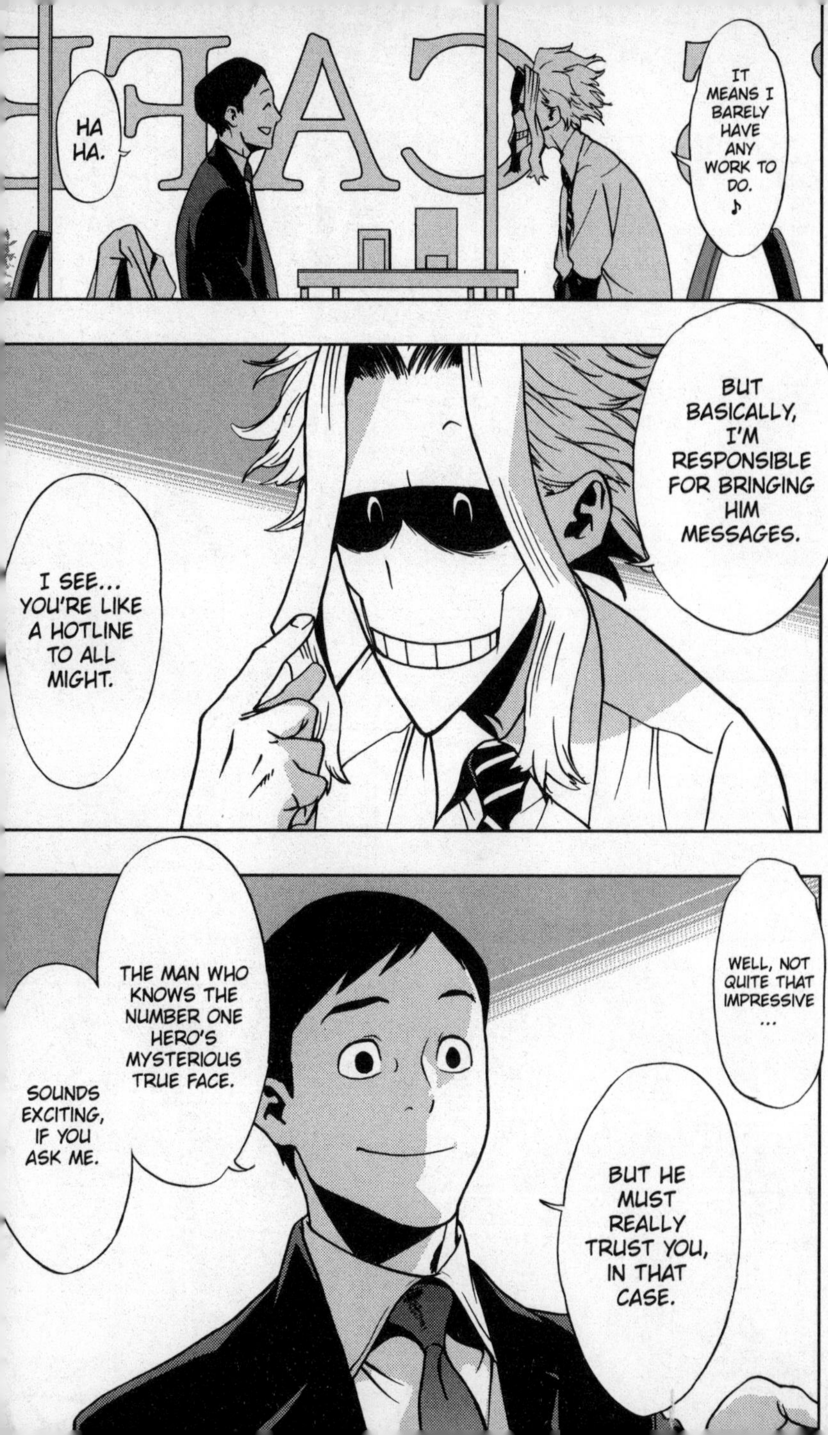
IT MEANS I BARELY HAVE ANY WORK TO DO. ♪
HA HA.
BUT BASICALLY, I'M RESPONSIBLE FOR BRINGING HIM MESSAGES.
I SEE... YOU'RE LIKE A HOTLINE TO ALL MIGHT.
WELL, NOT QUITE THAT IMPRESSIVE ...
BUT HE MUST REALLY TRUST YOU, IN THAT CASE.
THE MAN WHO KNOWS THE NUMBER ONE HERO'S MYSTERIOUS TRUE FACE.
SOUNDS EXCITING, IF YOU ASK ME.

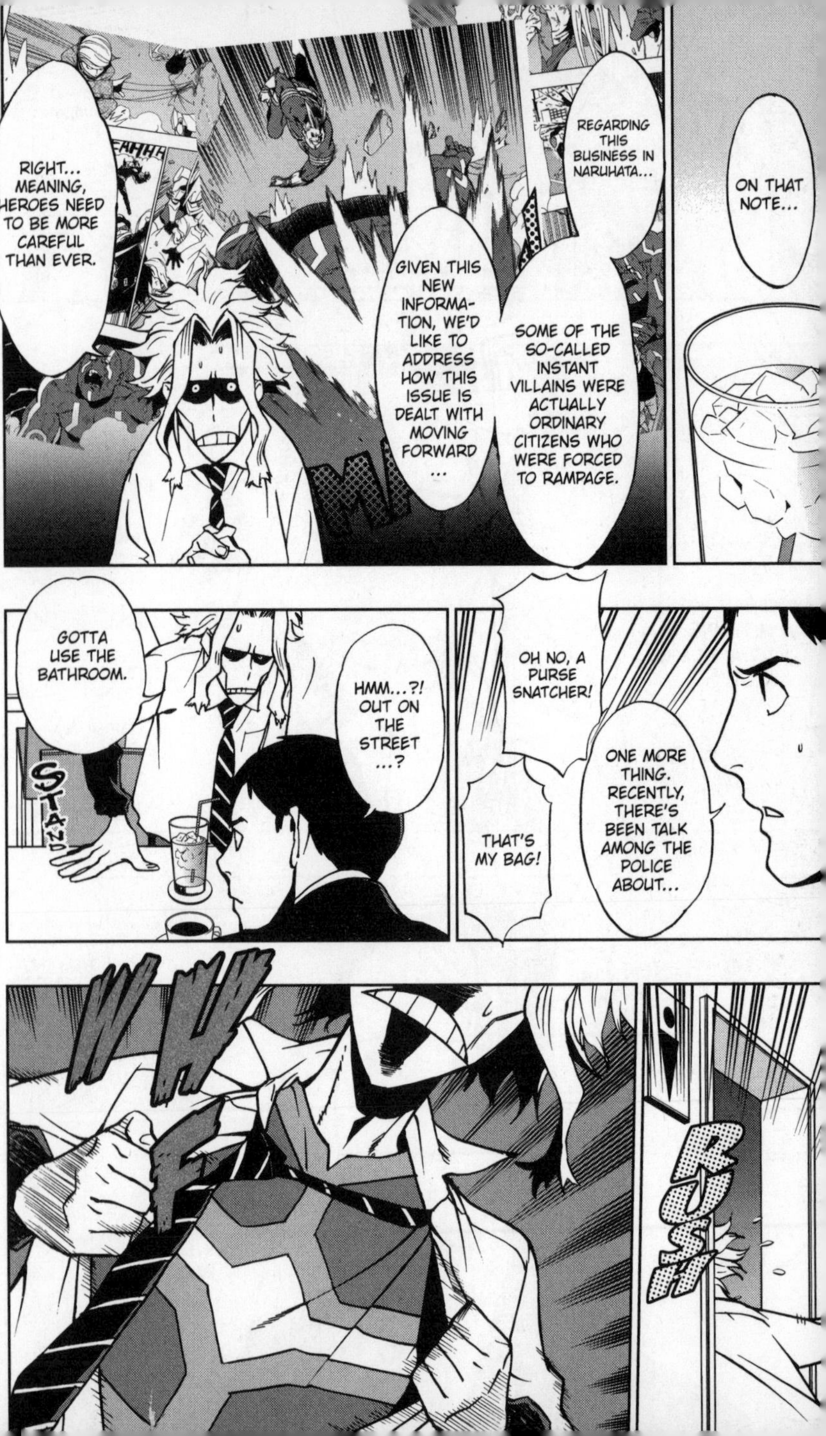
ON THAT NOTE...
REGARDING THIS BUSINESS IN NARUHATA...
SOME OF THE SO-CALLED INSTANT VILLAINS WERE ACTUALLY ORDINARY CITIZENS WHO WERE FORCED TO RAMPAGE.
GIVEN THIS NEW INFORMATION, WE'D LIKE TO ADDRESS HOW THIS ISSUE IS DEALT WITH MOVING FORWARD...
RIGHT... MEANING, HEROES NEED TO BE MORE CAREFUL THAN EVER.
OH NO, A PURSE SNATCHER!
ONE MORE THING. RECENTLY, THERE'S BEEN TALK AMONG THE POLICE ABOUT...
THAT'S MY BAG!
HMM...?! OUT ON THE STREET...?
GOTTA USE THE BATHROOM.
STAND
RUSH
WHF

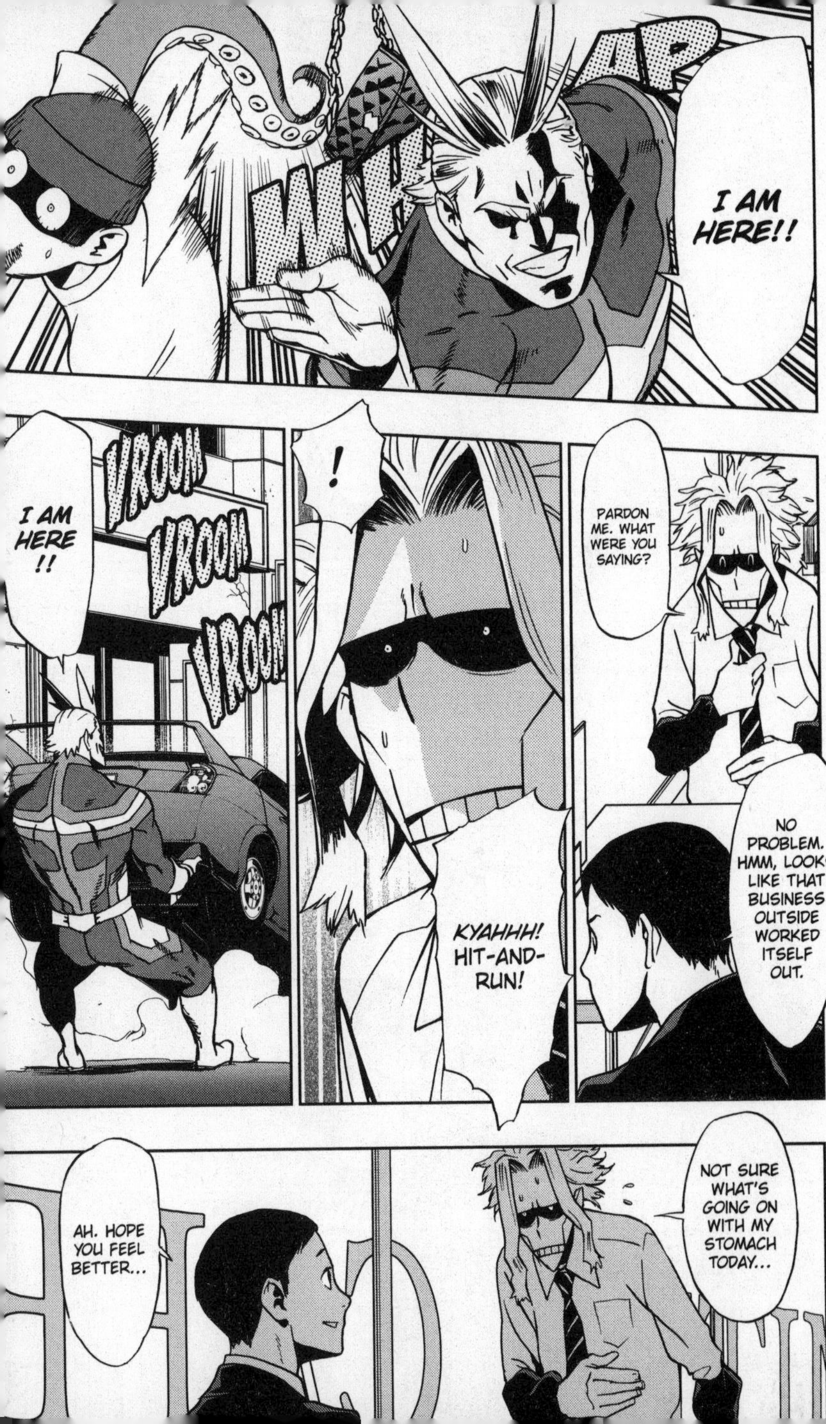
I AM HERE!!
PARDON ME. WHAT WERE YOU SAYING?
NO PROBLEM. HMM, LOOKS LIKE THAT BUSINESS OUTSIDE WORKED ITSELF OUT.
!
KYAHHH! HIT-AND-RUN!
I AM HERE !!
VROOM
VROOM
VROOM
NOT SURE WHAT'S GOING ON WITH MY STOMACH TODAY...
AH. HOPE YOU FEEL BETTER...

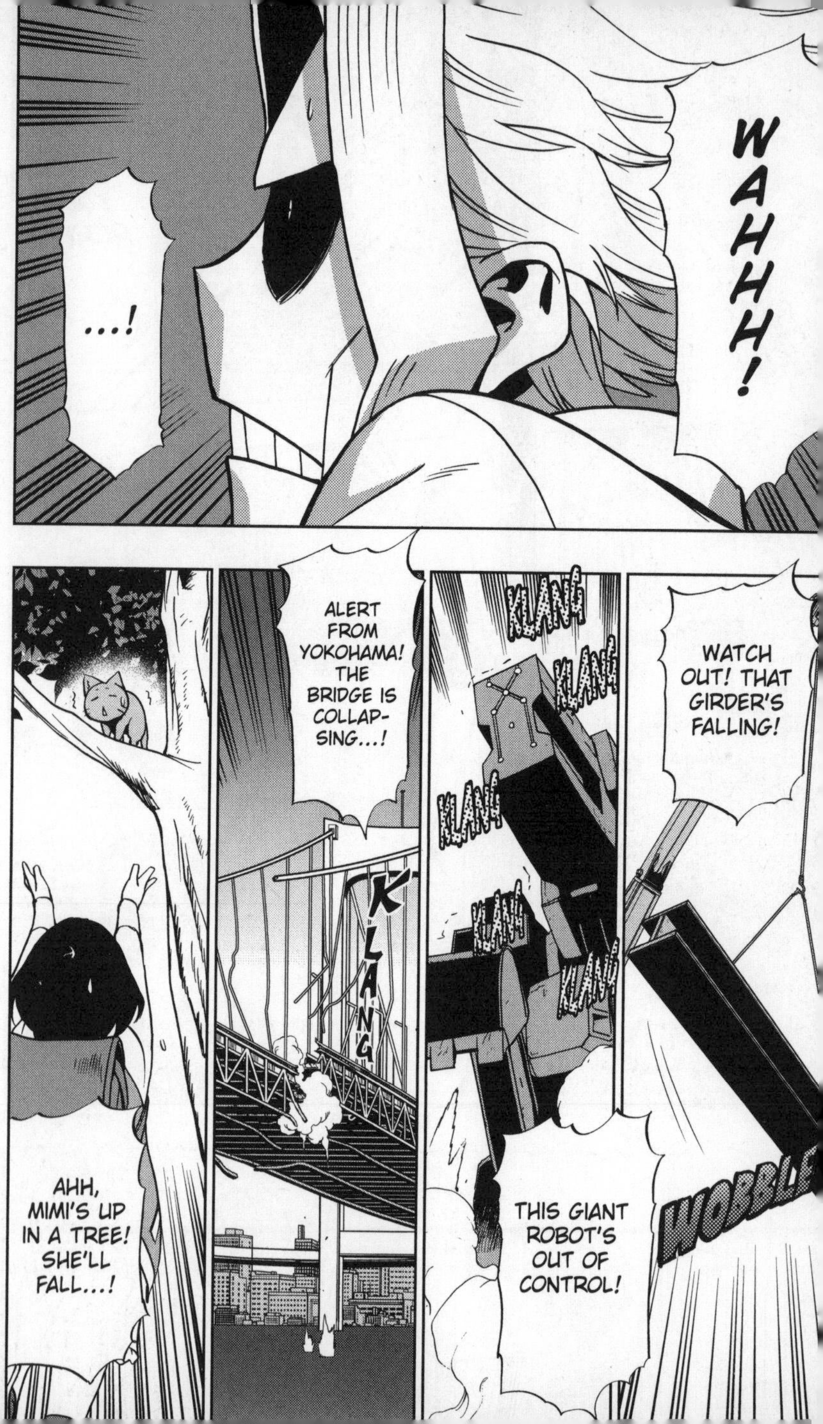
WAHHHH!
...!
WATCH OUT! THAT GIRDER'S FALLING!
WOBBLE
KLANG
KLANG
KLANG
KLANG
KLANG
THIS GIANT ROBOT'S OUT OF CONTROL!
ALERT FROM YOKOHAMA! THE BRIDGE IS COLLAP-SING...!
KLANG
AHH, MIMI'S UP IN A TREE! SHE'LL FALL...!

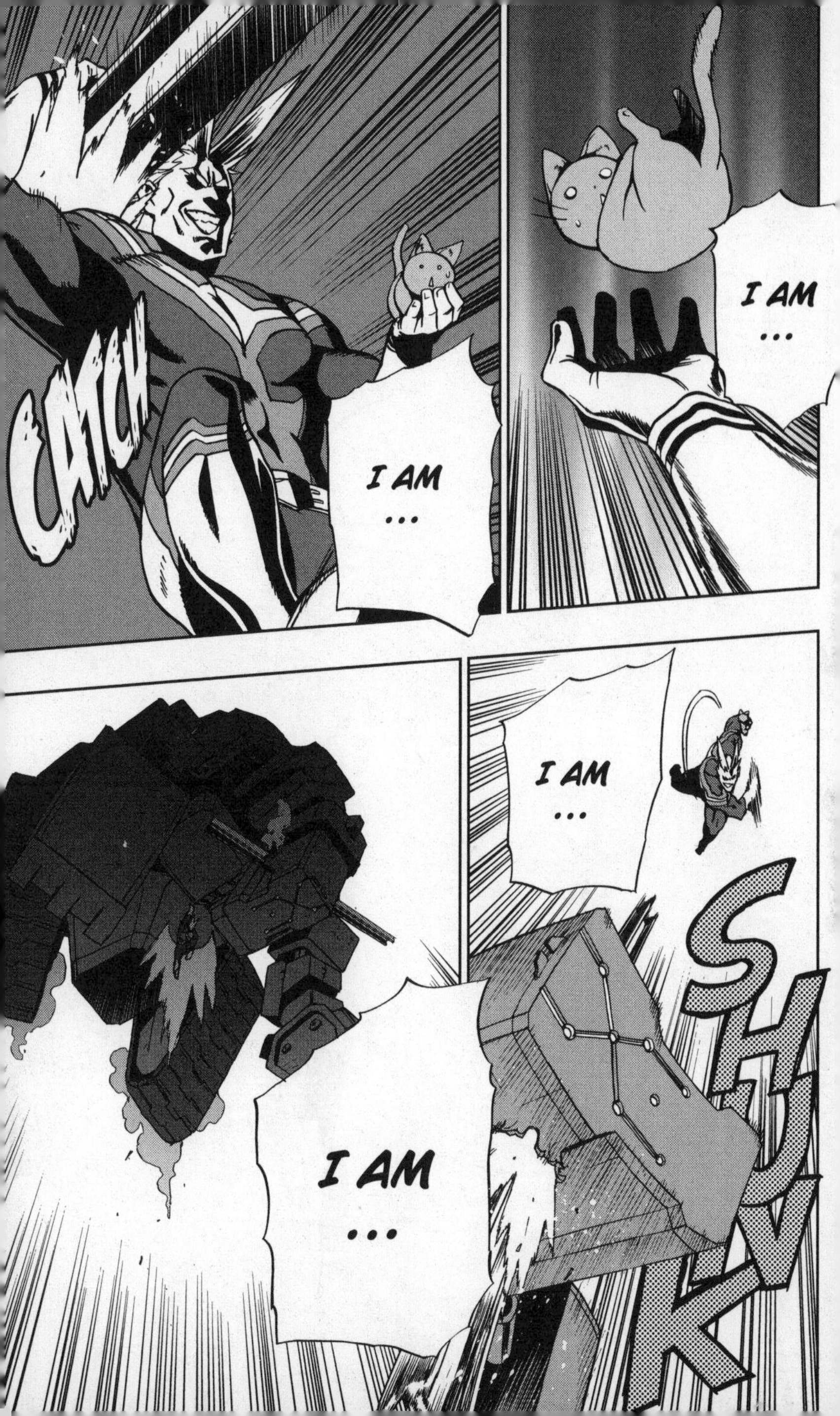
I AM ...
CATCH
I AM ...
I AM ...
SHUNK
I AM ...

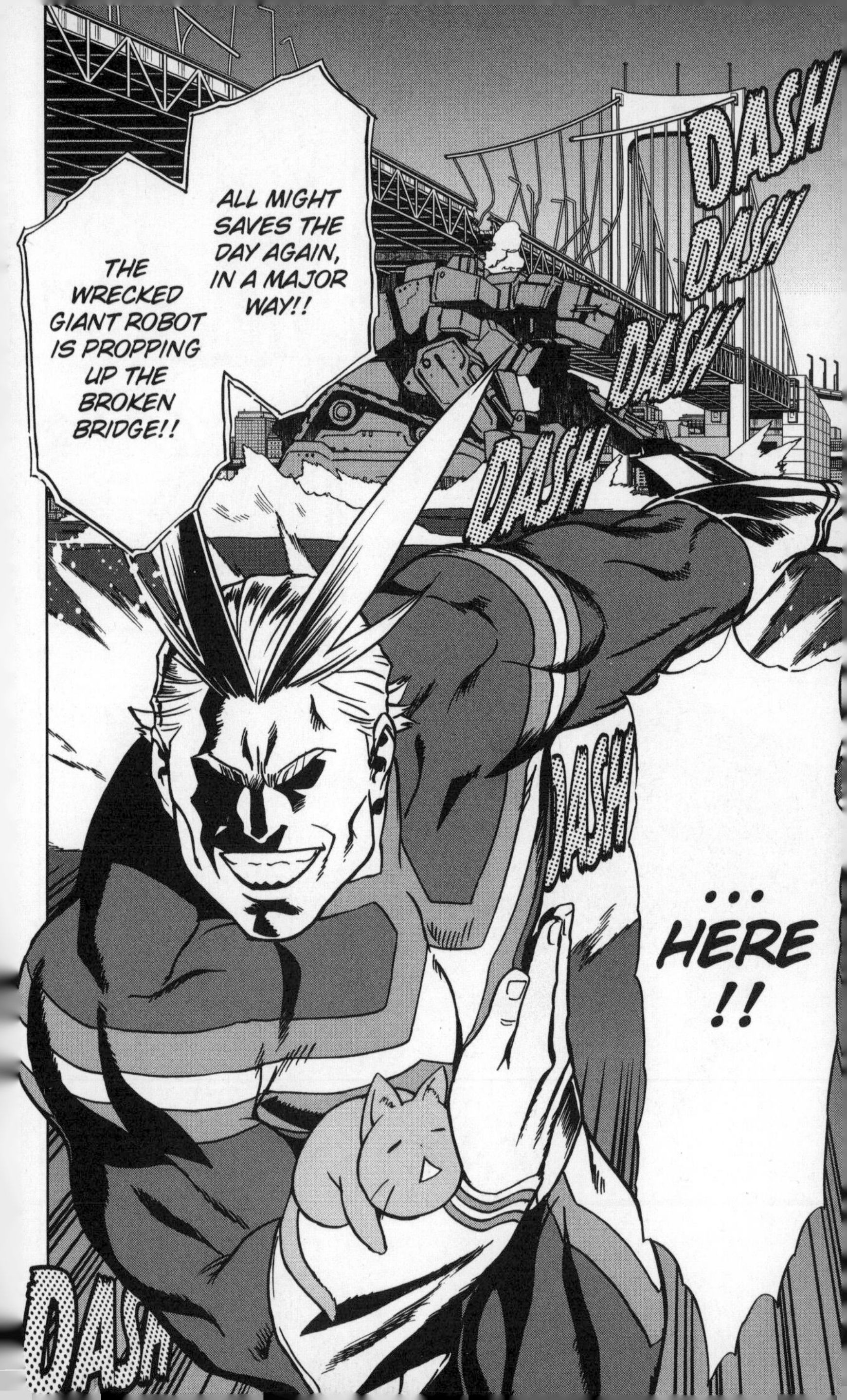
ALL MIGHT SAVES THE DAY AGAIN, IN A MAJOR WAY!!
THE WRECKED GIANT ROBOT IS PROPPING UP THE BROKEN BRIDGE!!
DASH DASH DASH DASH
DASH
... HERE !!
DASH

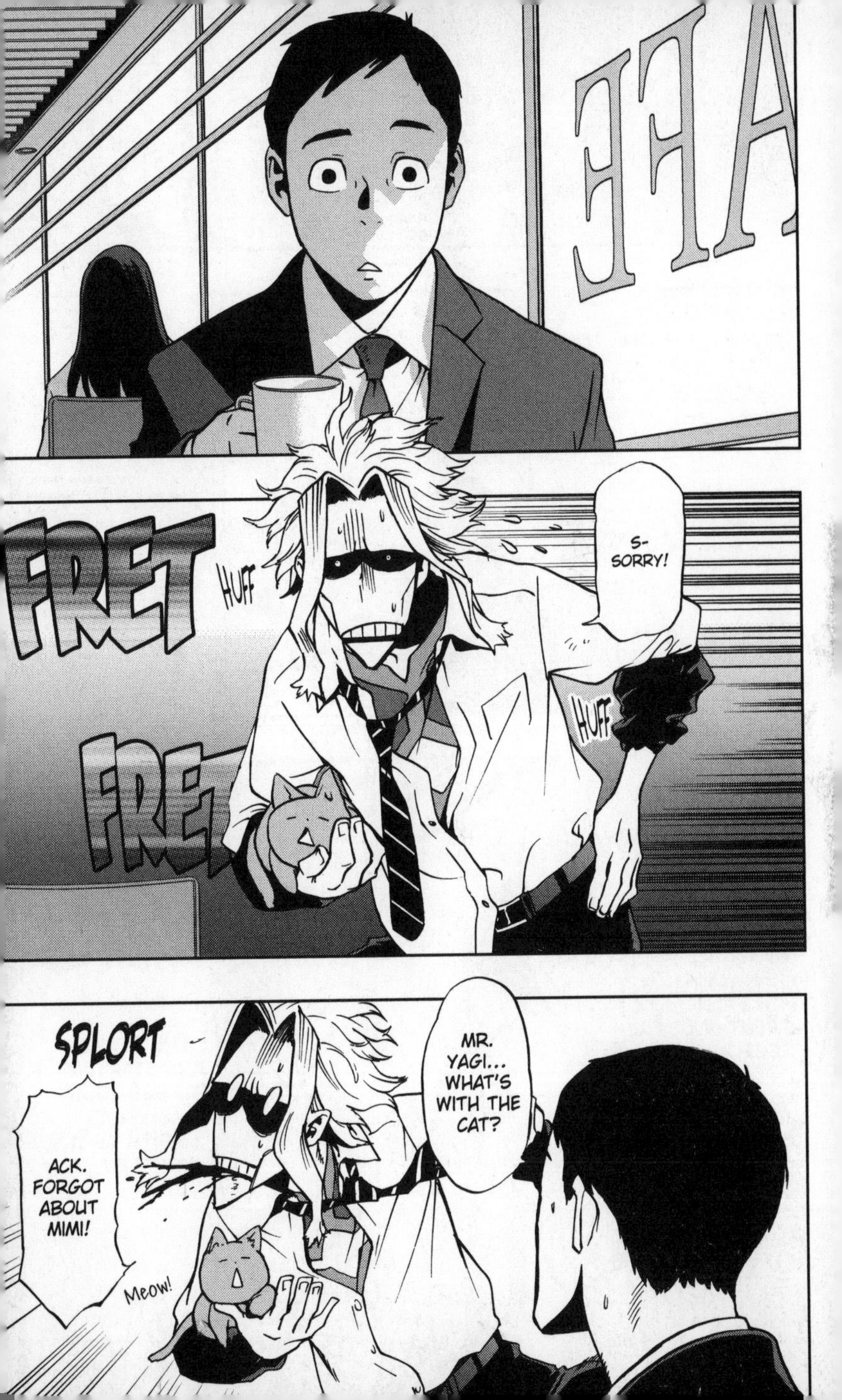
S-SORRY!
HUFF
HUFF
FRET
FRE
MR. YAGI... WHAT'S WITH THE CAT?
SPLORT
ACK. FORGOT ABOUT MIMI!
Meow!

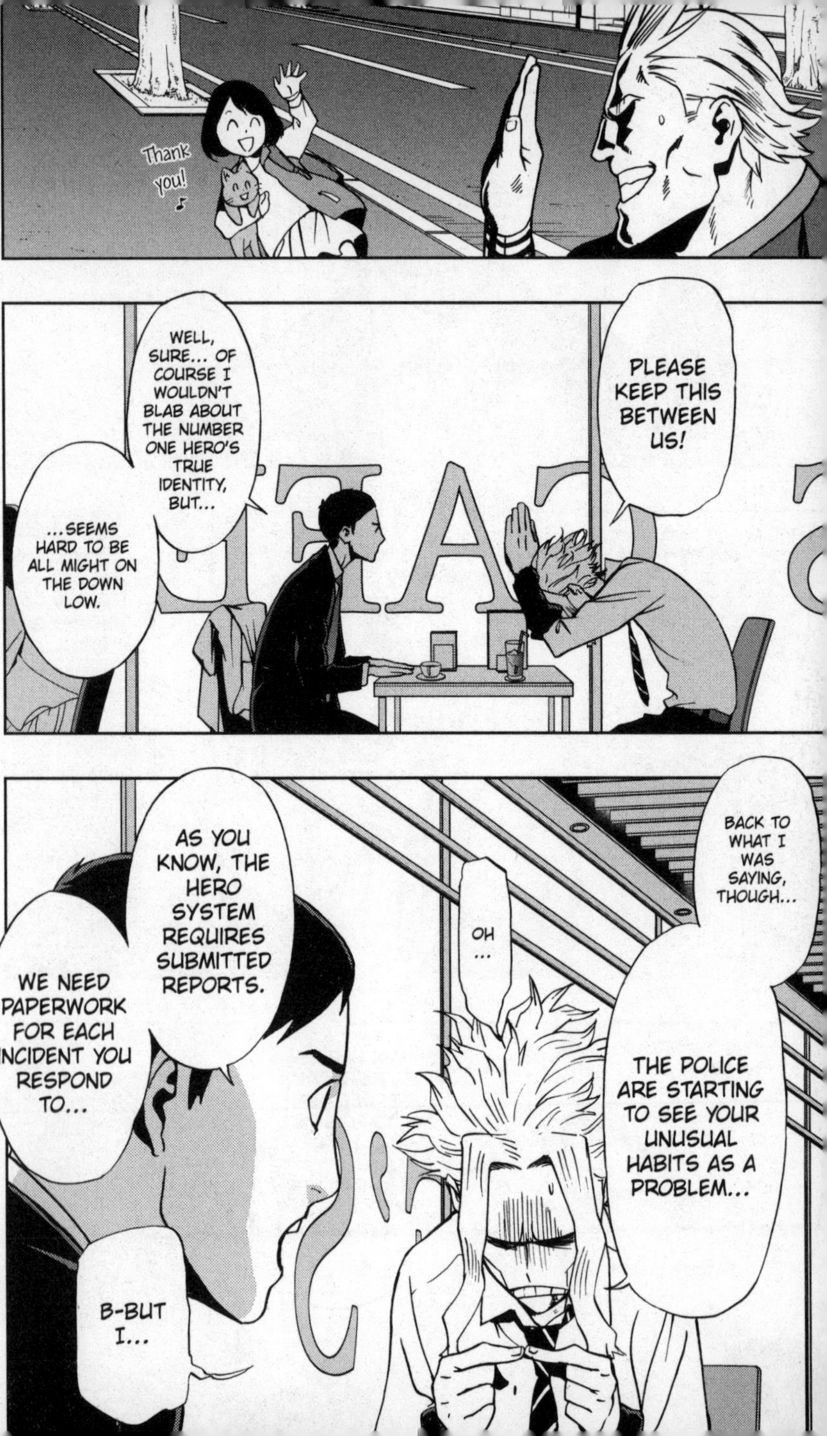
Thank you! ♪
PLEASE KEEP THIS BETWEEN US!
WELL, SURE... OF COURSE I WOULDN'T BLAB ABOUT THE NUMBER ONE HERO'S TRUE IDENTITY, BUT...
...SEEMS HARD TO BE ALL MIGHT ON THE DOWN LOW.
BACK TO WHAT I WAS SAYING, THOUGH...
THE POLICE ARE STARTING TO SEE YOUR UNUSUAL HABITS AS A PROBLEM...
OH ...
AS YOU KNOW, THE HERO SYSTEM REQUIRES SUBMITTED REPORTS.
WE NEED PAPERWORK FOR EACH INCIDENT YOU RESPOND TO...
B-BUT I...

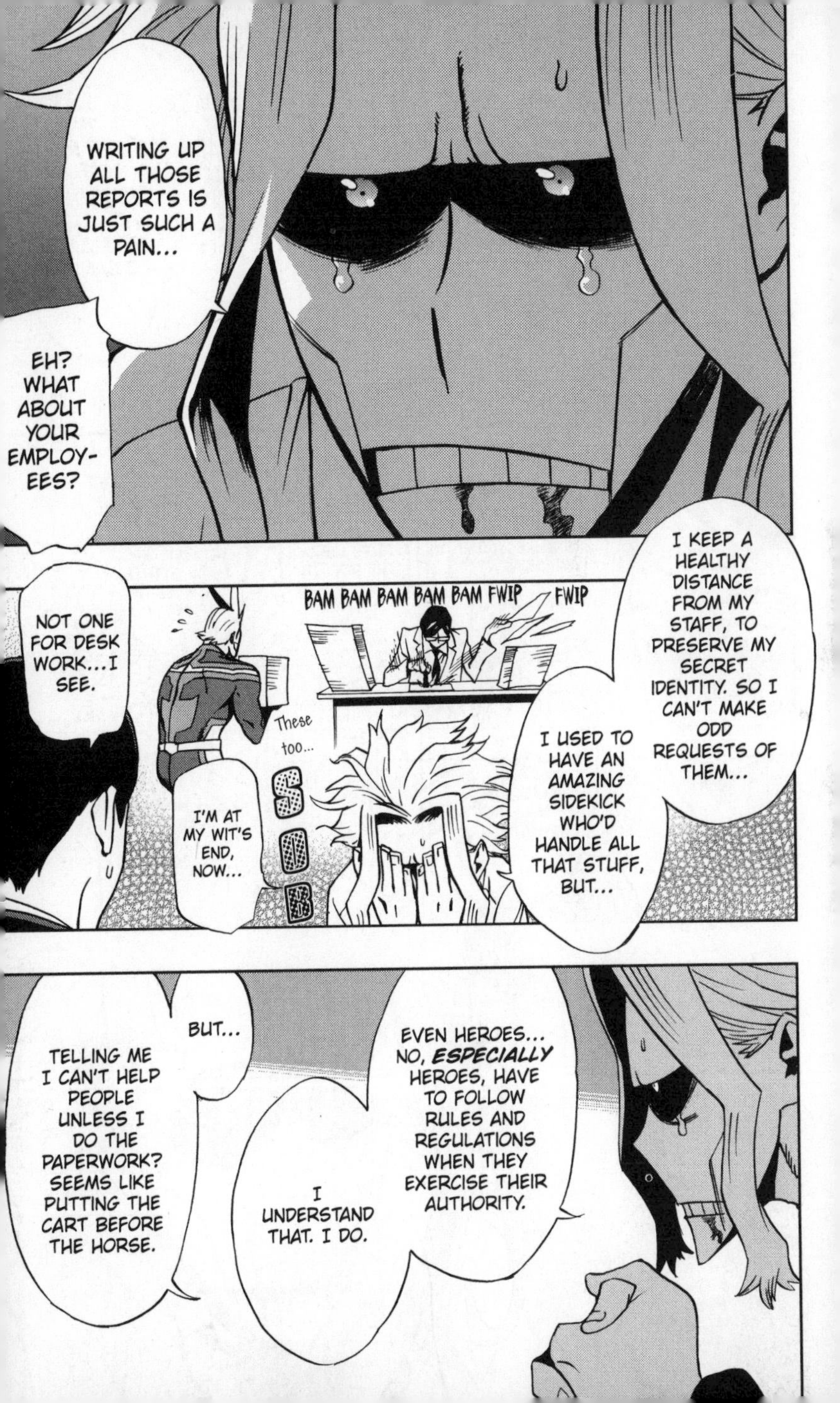
WRITING UP ALL THOSE REPORTS IS JUST SUCH A PAIN...
EH? WHAT ABOUT YOUR EMPLOY-EES?
I KEEP A HEALTHY DISTANCE FROM MY STAFF, TO PRESERVE MY SECRET IDENTITY. SO I CAN'T MAKE ODD REQUESTS OF THEM...
I USED TO HAVE AN AMAZING SIDEKICK WHO'D HANDLE ALL THAT STUFF, BUT...
BAM BAM BAM BAM BAM FWIP FWIP
These too...
SOB
I'M AT MY WIT'S END, NOW...
NOT ONE FOR DESK WORK...I SEE.
EVEN HEROES... NO, *ESPECIALLY* HEROES, HAVE TO FOLLOW RULES AND REGULATIONS WHEN THEY EXERCISE THEIR AUTHORITY.
I UNDERSTAND THAT. I DO.
BUT...
TELLING ME I CAN'T HELP PEOPLE UNLESS I DO THE PAPERWORK? SEEMS LIKE PUTTING THE CART BEFORE THE HORSE.

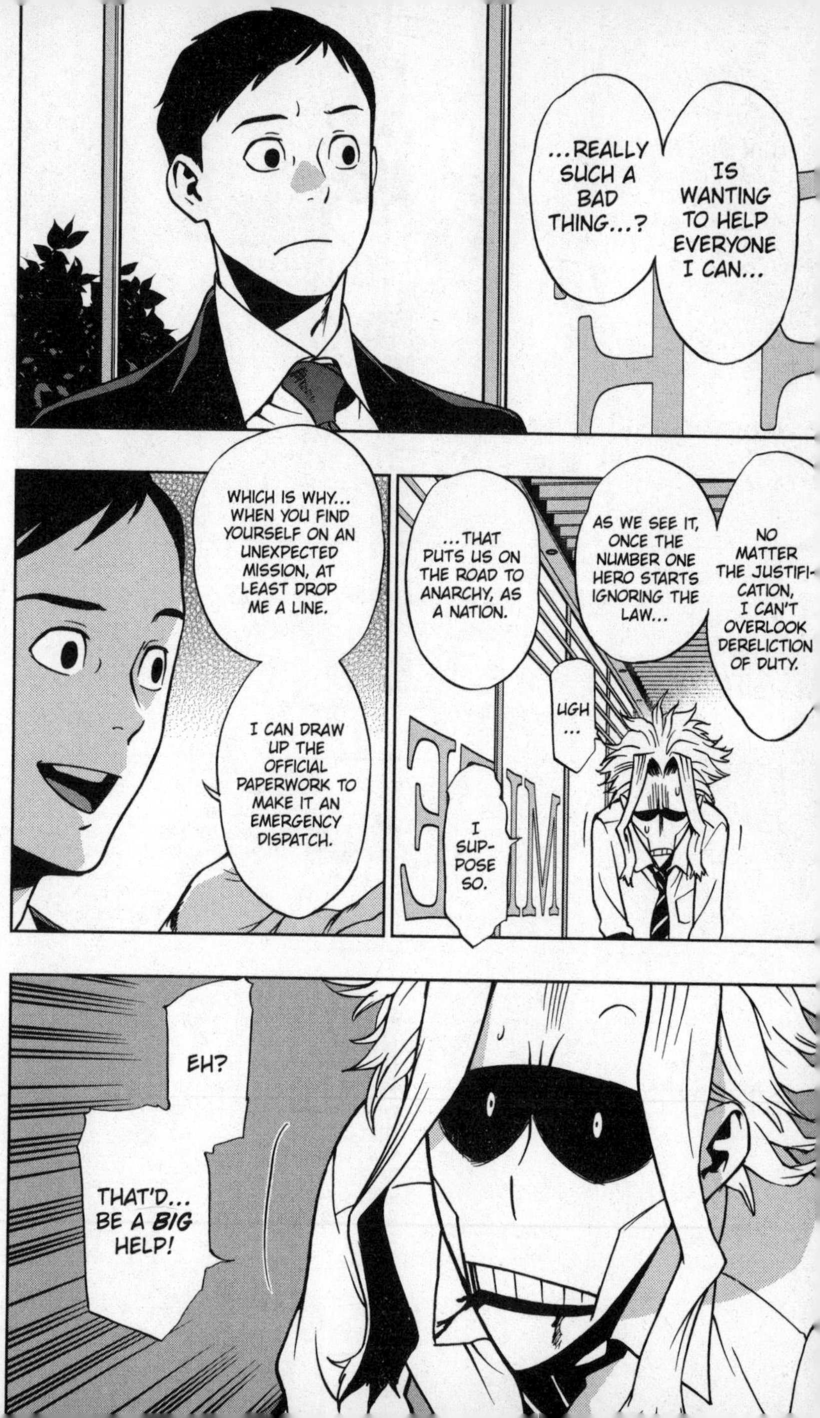
IS WANTING TO HELP EVERYONE I CAN...
...REALLY SUCH A BAD THING...?
NO MATTER THE JUSTIFI-CATION, I CAN'T OVERLOOK DERELICTION OF DUTY.
AS WE SEE IT, ONCE THE NUMBER ONE HERO STARTS IGNORING THE LAW...
...THAT PUTS US ON THE ROAD TO ANARCHY, AS A NATION.
UGH...
I SUP-POSE SO.
WHICH IS WHY... WHEN YOU FIND YOURSELF ON AN UNEXPECTED MISSION, AT LEAST DROP ME A LINE.
I CAN DRAW UP THE OFFICIAL PAPERWORK TO MAKE IT AN EMERGENCY DISPATCH.
EH?
THAT'D... BE A *BIG* HELP!

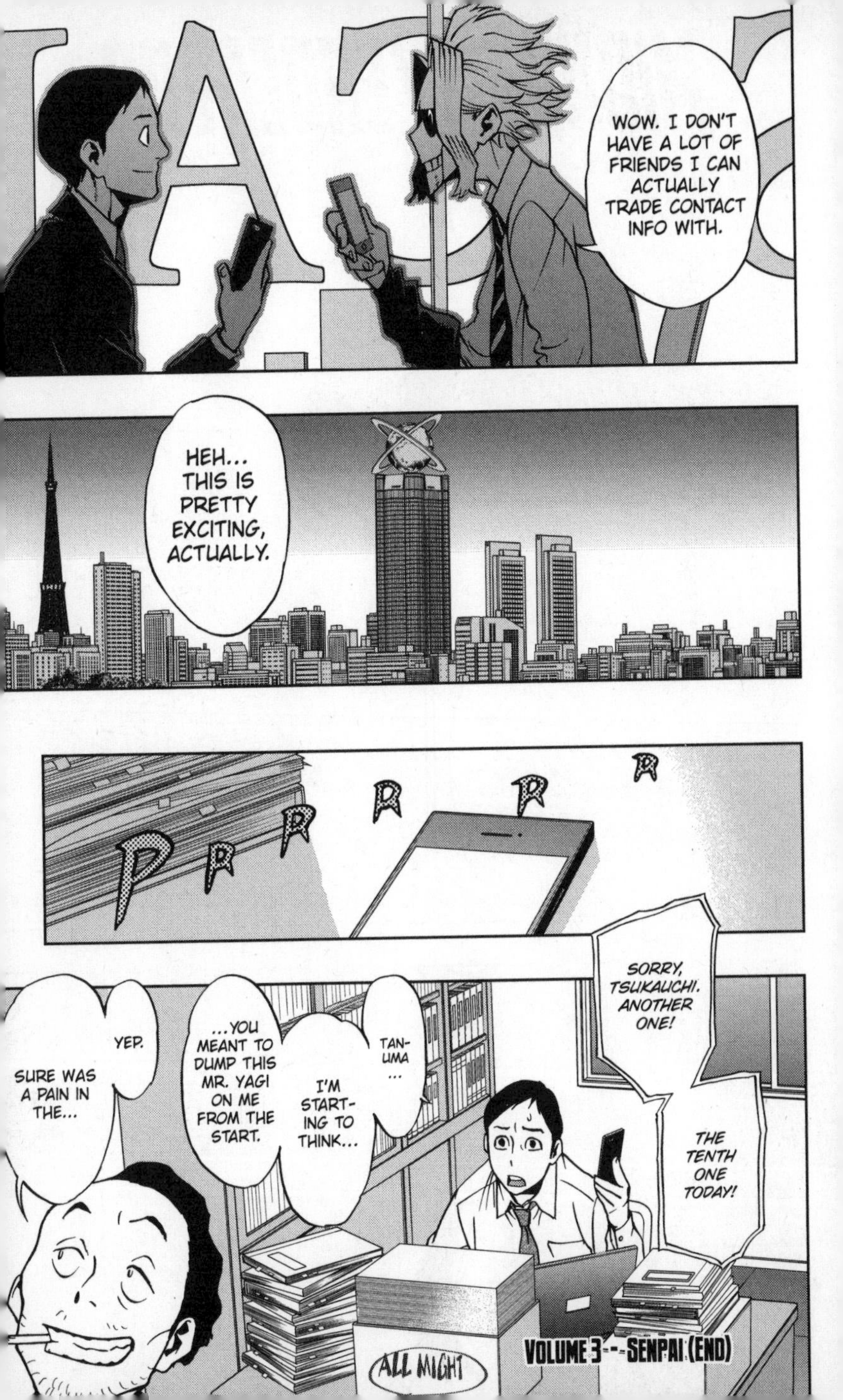
WOW. I DON'T HAVE A LOT OF FRIENDS I CAN ACTUALLY TRADE CONTACT INFO WITH.
HEH... THIS IS PRETTY EXCITING, ACTUALLY.
PRRRRR
SORRY, TSUKAUCHI. ANOTHER ONE!
THE TENTH ONE TODAY!
TAN-UMA...
I'M STARTING TO THINK...
...YOU MEANT TO DUMP THIS MR. YAGI ON ME FROM THE START.
YEP.
SURE WAS A PAIN IN THE...
ALL MIGHT
VOLUME 3 -- SENPAI (END)

MIDNIGHT/ENDEAVOR

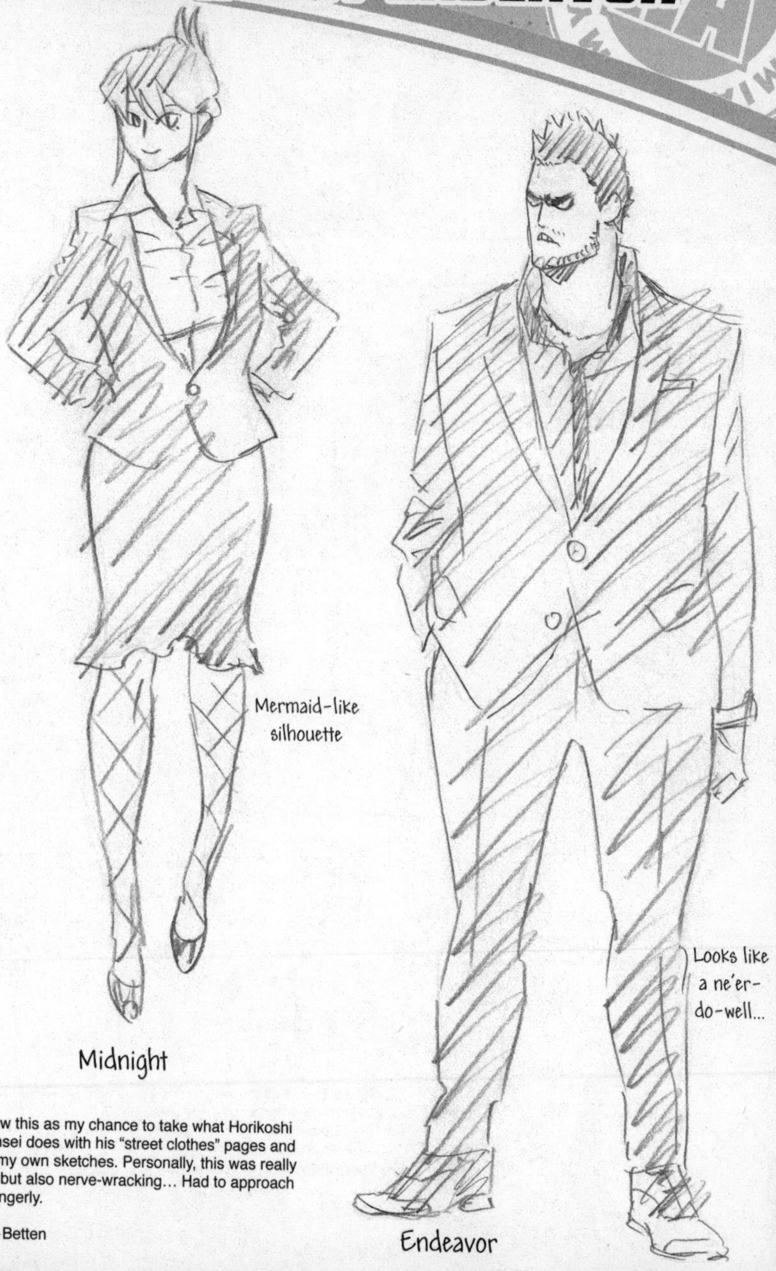
Mermaid-like silhouette
Looks like a ne'er-do-well...
Midnight
Endeavor

I saw this as my chance to take what Horikoshi Sensei does with his "street clothes" pages and do my own sketches. Personally, this was really fun but also nerve-wracking… Had to approach it gingerly.

—Betten

INGENIUM/JEANIST

THE ROUGH DESIGN

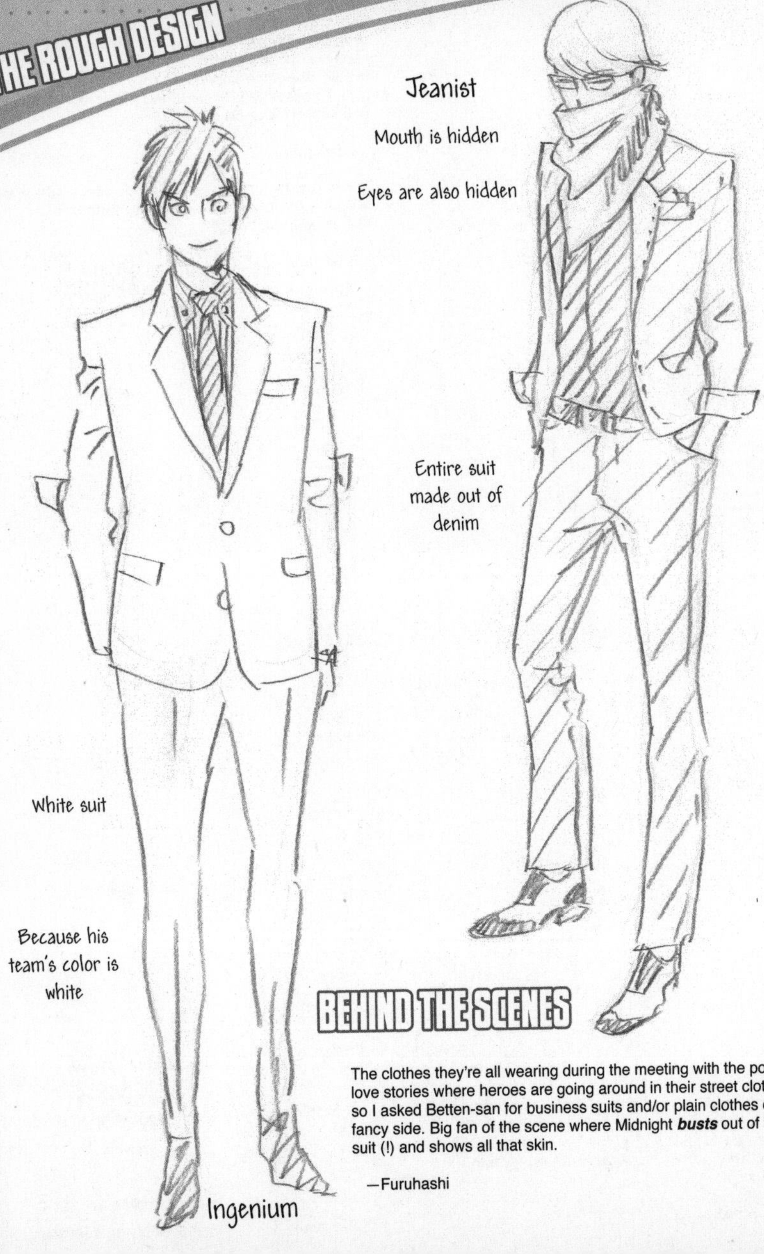

Jeanist
Mouth is hidden
Eyes are also hidden
Entire suit made out of denim
White suit
Because his team's color is white
Ingenium

BEHIND THE SCENES

The clothes they're all wearing during the meeting with the police. I love stories where heroes are going around in their street clothes, so I asked Betten-san for business suits and/or plain clothes on the fancy side. Big fan of the scene where Midnight ***busts*** out of her suit (!) and shows all that skin.

—Furuhashi

MANUAL/THIRTEEN

For the relatively minor characters (ones who haven't been unmasked in the main story yet), readers wouldn't even know them by their faces, so I asked Betten-san to preserve certain elements of their hero costumes. Manual (the guy who oversees Ida's internship) makes a gimmick out of his plainness. He's barely recognizable without that frill on his head!

—Furuhashi

There wasn't a lot to go on with these fellows, which left me pretty desperate. (LOL) I can say that drawing Manual was fun, though!

—Betten

BEHIND THE SCENES

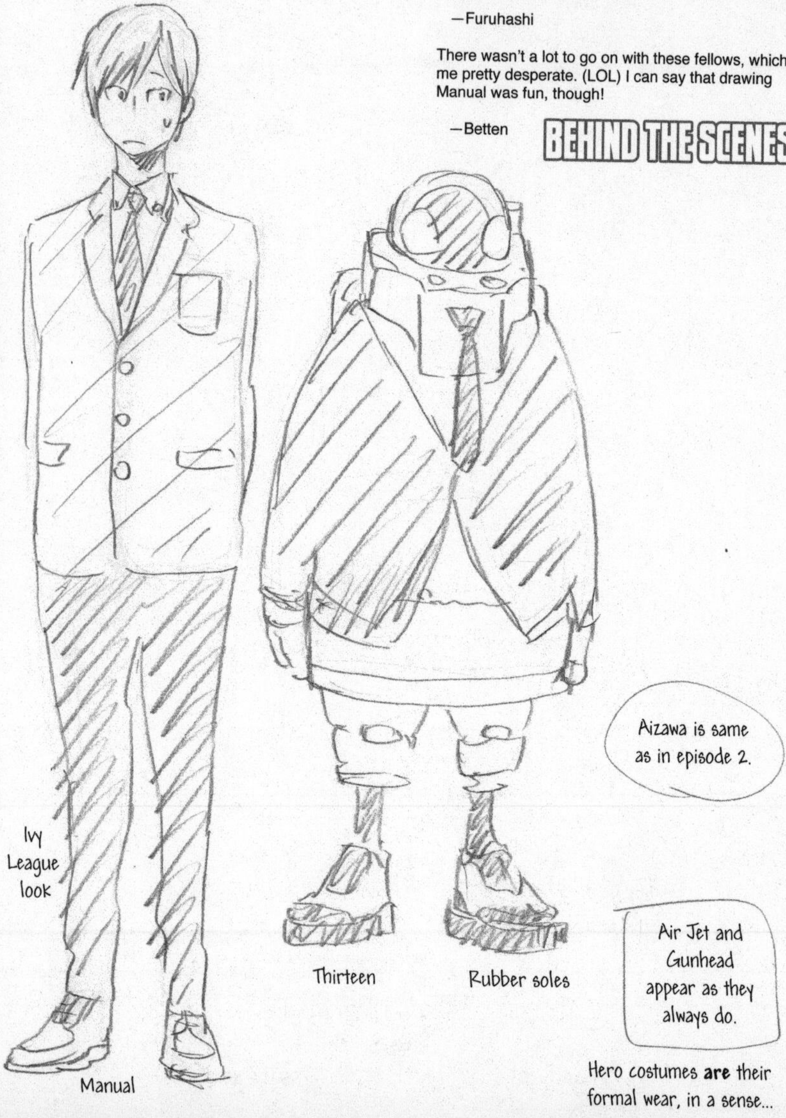

Aizawa is same as in episode 2.
Ivy League look
Thirteen
Rubber soles
Air Jet and Gunhead appear as they always do.
Manual
Hero costumes **are** their formal wear, in a sense...

SNIPE/DESUTEGORO

THE ROUGH DESIGN

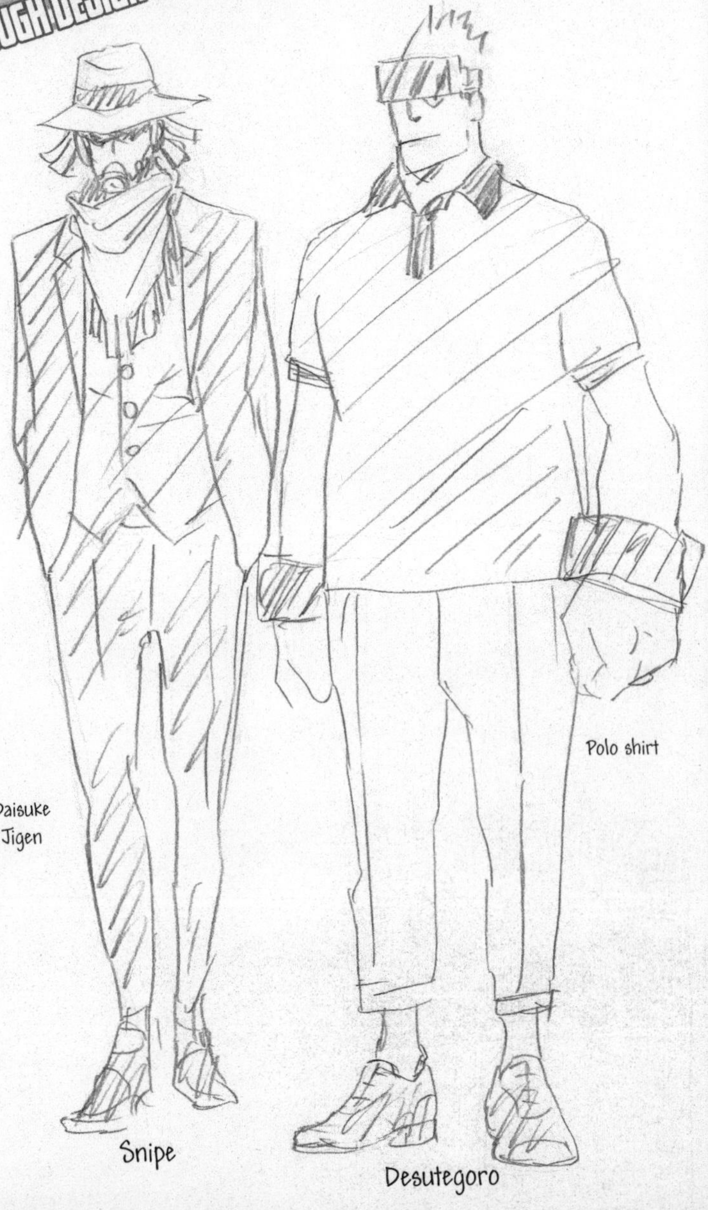

Daisuke Jigen
Polo shirt
Snipe
Desutegoro

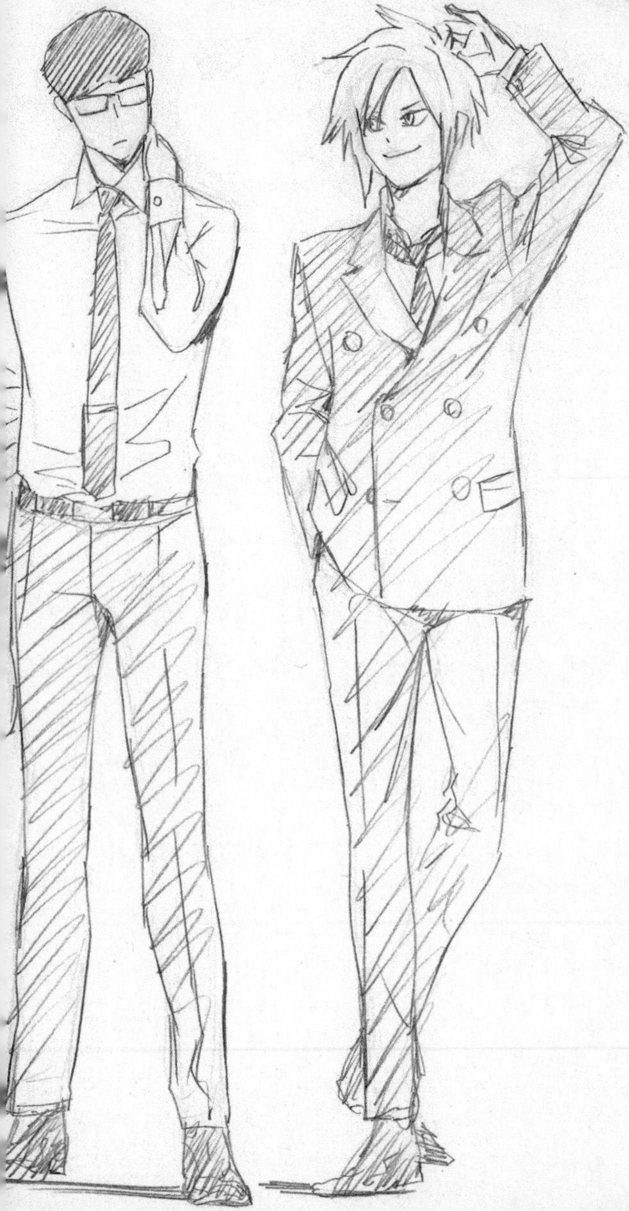

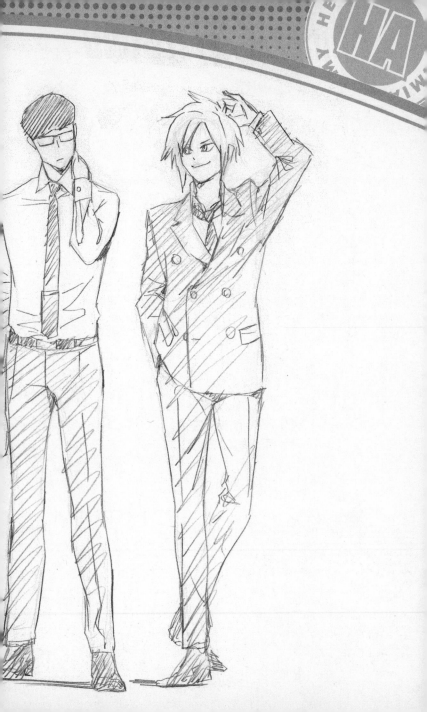

MIDNIGHT BOYS

THE ROUGH DESIGN

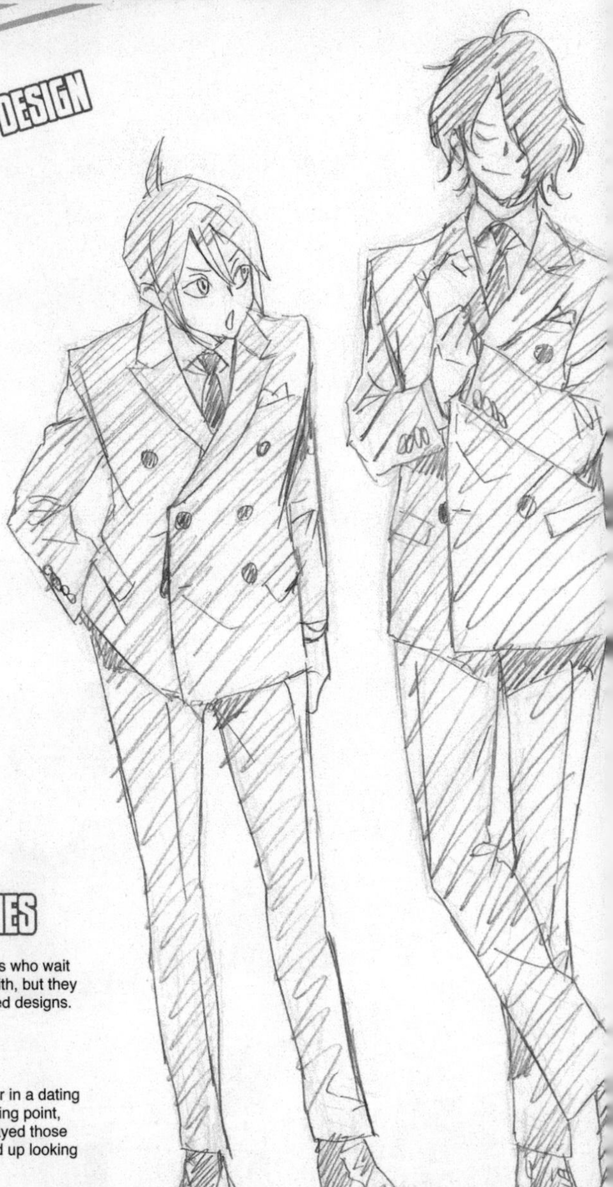

BEHIND THE SCENES

The band of pretty-boy sidekicks who wait on Midnight…is all I came up with, but they emerged with these very detailed designs. Weird.

—Furuhashi

What kind of guys would appear in a dating sim for girls? That was my starting point, here. But I've never actually played those games, so they probably wound up looking a little different. (LOL)

—Betten

Afterword

I'm the artist, Betten!
We've somehow made it all the way to volume 3!

Springing off from Horikoshi-san's impressive MHA-verse, Furuhashi-san and his talent have taken the helm while I'm propelling the ship from behind with my doggy-paddling.

Look forward to volume 4 and beyond!!

January 2018

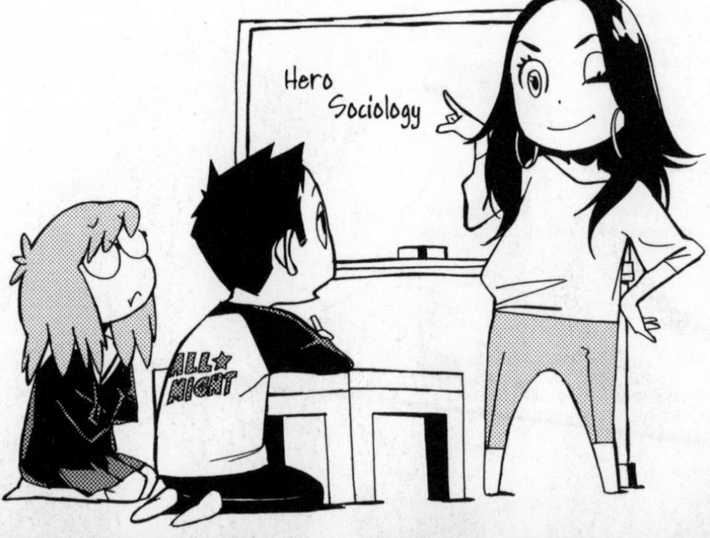
Hero
Sociology
ALL☆
MIGHT

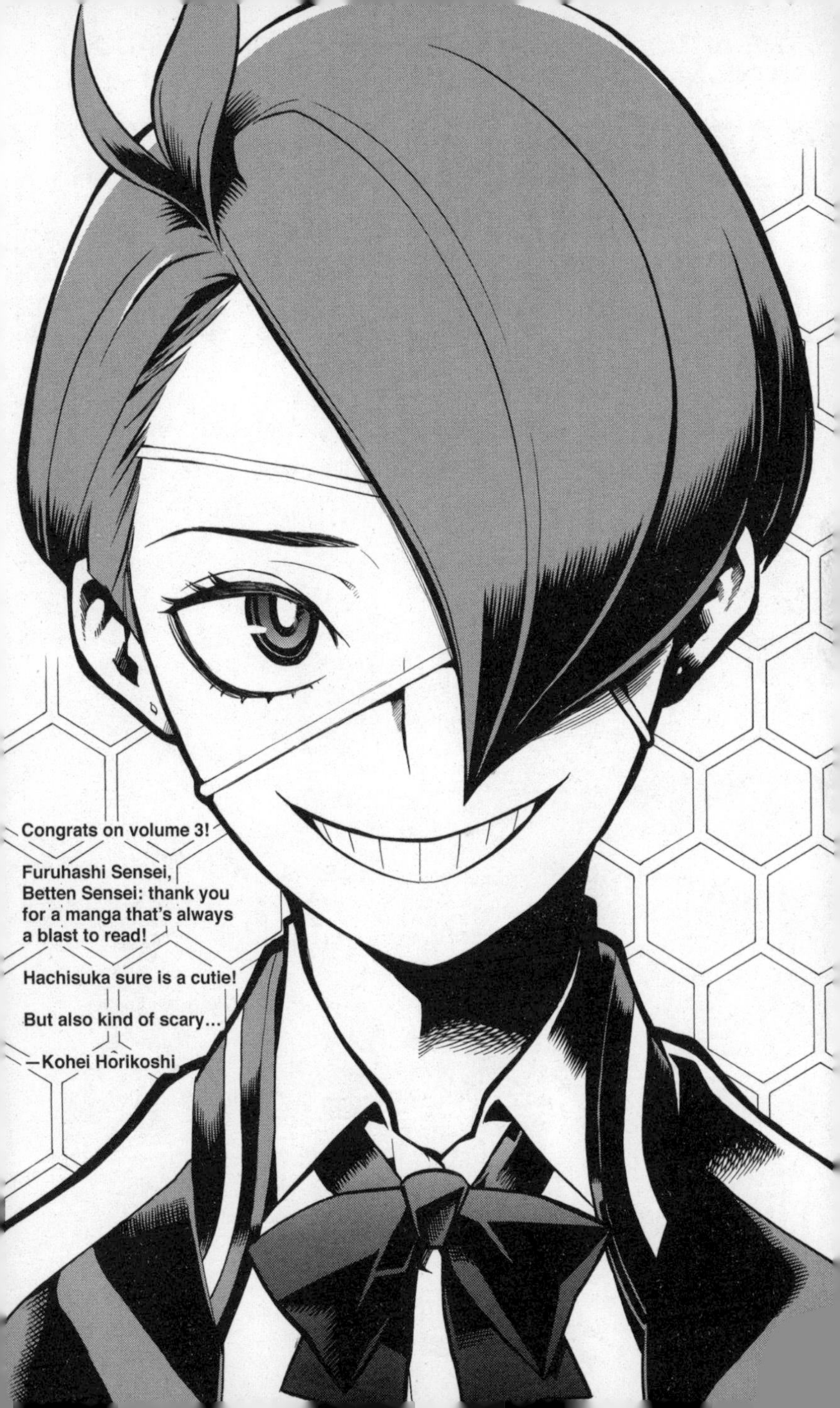
Congrats on volume 3!
Furuhashi Sensei, Betten Sensei: thank you for a manga that's always a blast to read!
Hachisuka sure is a cutie!
But also kind of scary...
—Kohei Horikoshi

THE ACTION-PACKED SUPERHERO COMEDY ABOUT ONE MAN'S AMBITION TO BE A HERO FOR FUN!

ONE-PUNCH MAN

STORY BY
ONE

ART BY
YUSUKE MURATA

Nothing about Saitama passes the eyeball test when it comes to superheroes, from his lifeless expression to his bald head to his unimpressive physique. However, this average-looking guy has a not-so-average problem—he just can't seem to find an opponent strong enough to take on!

Can he finally find an opponent who can go toe-to-toe with him and give his life some meaning? Or is he doomed to a life of superpowered boredom?

www.viz.com

ONE-PUNCH MAN © 2012 by ONE, Yusuke Murata/SHUEISHA Inc.

ASTRA
LOST IN SPACE

CAN EIGHT TEENAGERS FIND THEIR WAY HOME FROM 5,000 LIGHT-YEARS AWAY?

It's the year 2063, and interstellar space travel has become the norm. Eight students from Caird High School and one child set out on a routine planet camp excursion. While there, the students are mysteriously transported 5,000 light-years away to the middle of nowhere! Will they ever make it back home?!

ASTRA
LOST IN SPACE

Story and Art by KENTA SHINOHARA

viz.com

RATED TEEN

KANATA NO ASTRA © 2016 by Kenta Shinohara/SHUEISHA

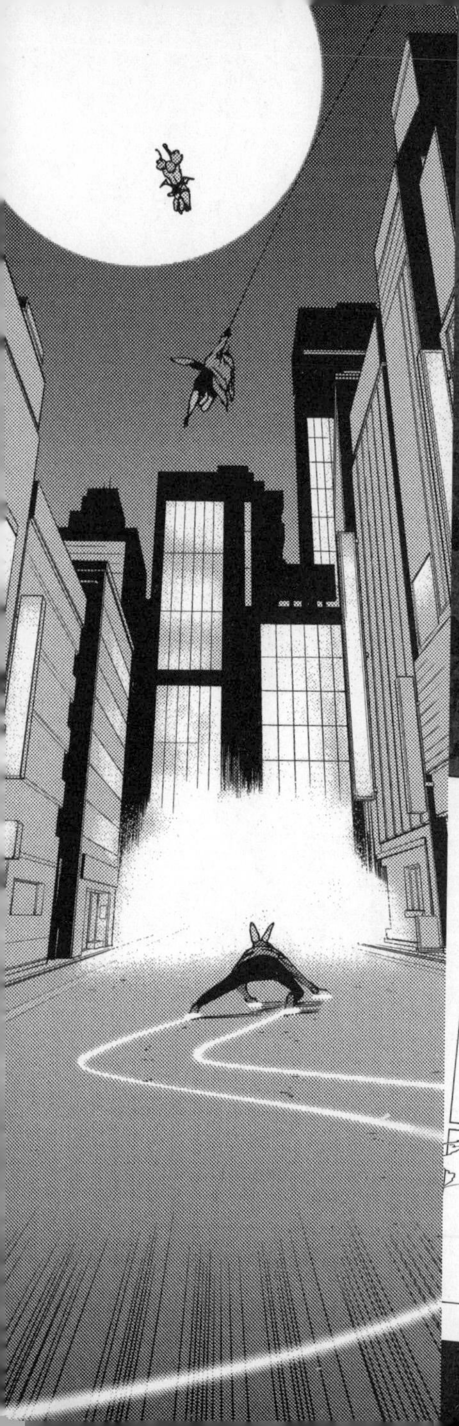

YOU'RE READING THE WRONG WAY!!

MY HERO ACADEMIA VIGILANTES

reads from right to left, starting in the upper-right corner. Japanese is read from right to left, meaning that action, sound effects and word-balloon order are completely reversed from English order.

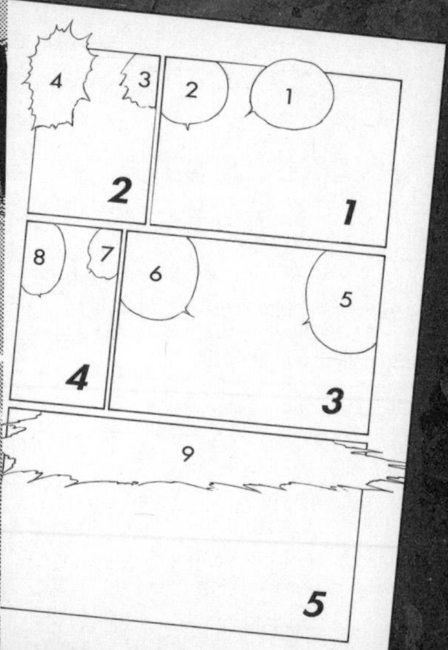
1
2
3
4
1
2
5
6
7
8
3
4
9
5
142